DISRUPT AND DENY

DISRUPT AND DENY

SPIES, SPECIAL FORCES, AND THE SECRET PURSUIT OF BRITISH FOREIGN POLICY

RORY CORMAC

UNIVERSITY PRESS

OXFORD
UNIVERSITY PRESS

Great Clarendon Street, Oxford, OX2 6DP,
United Kingdom

Oxford University Press is a department of the University of Oxford.
It furthers the University's objective of excellence in research, scholarship,
and education by publishing worldwide. Oxford is a registered trade mark of
Oxford University Press in the UK and in certain other countries

Published in the United States of America by Oxford University Press
198 Madison Avenue, New York, NY 10016, United States of America

British Library Cataloguing in Publication Data
Data available

Library of Congress Control Number: 2017954183

ISBN 978-0-19-878459-3

Printed in Great Britain by
Clays Ltd, St Ives plc

For Joanne

Acknowledgements

I began this book in 2011 as a postdoctoral researcher at King's College London and finished it in 2018 as an associate professor at the University of Nottingham. It has been an ever-present, a reliable old friend, as my career and family have grown. The research has taken me to places I am privileged to have visited and people I am fortunate to have met.

I am very grateful to the Arts and Humanities Research Council for funding the research through my early career fellowship. The money, and more importantly the time, created the space which allowed me to realize the potential of such a vast undertaking. Tracing British covert action, which does not officially exist and for which the files are indefinitely closed, has required years of archival research around the UK and the US. I am also grateful for the Institute of Historical Research's Scouloudi Subsidy which allowed me to first visit archives in Washington DC.

There is no way I could have completed this project without regular support, advice, and tip-offs from friends and colleagues. I'd like to thank Christopher Andrew, Gordon Corera, Philip Davies, Andrew Defty, Rob Dover, Huw Dylan, Paul Elston, David Gill, David Gioe, Anthony Glees, Peter Hennessy, Michael Herman, Claudia Hillebrand, Davinia Hoggarth, Gerry Hughes, Loch Johnson, Clive Jones, Matthew Jones, Paul Maddrell, Tom Maguire, Steve Marrin, Peter Martland, Paul McGarr, Chris Moran, Philip Murphy, David Omand, Mark Phythian, David Porter, Mike Poznansky, Dina Rezk, Julian Richards, Len Scott, Zakia Shiraz, Mark Stout, Phil Tinline, Chris Tuck, Damien van Puyvelde, Calder Walton, Cees Weibes, Simon Willmetts, and John W. Young. I am also particularly grateful to all those who have spoken to me off the record. Special mention goes to Huw Bennett, Steve Long, and Andrew Mumford for reading various chapters and offering valuable feedback.

I would like to offer particular thanks to three colleagues who are sadly no longer with us. Alex Danchev provided intellectual guidance and great company when I first started at Nottingham. Keith Jeffery was always so generous with his time and support for early career researchers, myself included. Chikara Hashimoto generously shared archival files and FOI requests with me. He was a great scholar whose potential will tragically be unfulfilled.

I have been fortunate to visit numerous archives over the last few years, where the staff have been unfailingly courteous and helpful. I have always particularly enjoyed working at Churchill College Cambridge and I had a fabulous time at the Eisenhower Presidential Library and Archive in Kansas. I would like to thank Churchill College for permission to cite the Amery papers. Most of my research was conducted at the National Archives at Kew and I am grateful to the staff there for bringing me thousands of files, many of which I promptly returned and then asked for yet more. King's College London, the University of Warwick, and the University of Nottingham all also provided wonderful environments for research. Digital copies of some of the key documents used in this book as well as those secured using the Freedom of Information Act are available at https://www.nottingham. ac.uk/cst/research/most-unusual-measures/index.aspx.

There are a few individuals to whom I owe a particular debt. My literary agent Andrew Lownie managed to secure me the perfect publisher for this book. Matthew Cotton, Luciana O'Flaherty, and the team at Oxford University Press put their faith in it and helped it become a reality. My research assistant, Annabelle de Heus, kept me on the straight and narrow. I would not be where I am today without two great scholars who have shaped this project and my career more broadly. They have helped the book reach its potential, always had my back, and, most importantly, kept academia fun. Michael Goodman has read not only the entire manuscript but also tens of thousands of words left on the cutting-room floor. And Richard Aldrich is simply Richard Aldrich.

This is a history of things that did not officially happen using primary sources that few realize exist. I am very proud of the story I've been able to tell but mistakes are mine alone. Please do write with corrections and clarifications to rory.cormac@nottingham.ac.uk.

Finally, my wife Joanne has, as ever, listened to my witterings and encouraged my endeavours. And I'd like to add an anti-acknowledgement to my son, Finlay: he was born two months before the book was due and did his very best to stop me completing it. For that I will always be grateful.

Contents

Abbreviations and Acronyms

9/11	Universal shorthand for the terrorist attacks on America, 11 September 2001
AC(M)	Ministerial Committee on Communism
AC(O)	Official Committee on Communism (Overseas)
C	Chief of the British Secret Intelligence Service
CIA	Central Intelligence Agency (US)
CSC	Counter-Subversion Committee
FRU	Force Research Unit
GCHQ	Government Communications Headquarters
IRA	Irish Republican Army
IRD	Information Research Department
ISC	Intelligence and Security Committee
JAC	Joint Action Committee
JIC	Joint Intelligence Committee
KGB	Committee for State Security (Soviet intelligence)
MI5	Security Service
MI6	Secret Intelligence Service, or SIS
MRF	Military Reaction Force
NATO	North Atlantic Treaty Organization
NCFA	National Committee for a Free Albania
NSA	National Security Agency (US)
NSC	National Security Council
OID	Overseas Information Department
OPC	Office of Policy Coordination (US)
PKI	Indonesian Communist Party
PSIS	Committee of Permanent Secretaries on the Intelligence Services
PUSD	Permanent Under-Secretary's Department
PWE	Political Warfare Executive
RICU	Research, Information and Communications Unit
RUC	Royal Ulster Constabulary

SAF	Sultan's Armed Forces (Oman)
SAS	Special Air Service
SBS	Special Boat Service
SF	Special Forces
SIS	Secret Intelligence Service, also MI6
SOE	Special Operations Executive
SPA	Special Political Action
UDA	Ulster Defence Association
UDR	Ulster Defence Regiment
UN	United Nations
UVF	Ulster Volunteer Force

Introduction

Covert Action

It is no doubt a national characteristic of the British to dislike and distrust secret organisations working in peacetime. Despite this, national interest sometimes overrides such caution and inherent reluctance. British covert policy is therefore defensive and not aggressive. Special operations are an instrument of policy and in no means a rogue elephant.

Lord Selborne, 1945[1]

The United Kingdom (UK) has long enjoyed a loud voice in global affairs. Successive governments have intervened around the world militarily, diplomatically, and economically, either as a colonial or post-colonial power. This ability to project a broad spectrum of power, together with an independent nuclear deterrent, has helped to bolster Britain's diplomatic position at the top table and its place as a permanent member of the United Nations Security Council. Much of this activity is conducted audibly in the form of everyday diplomatic negotiations, trade deals, overseas aid, peacekeeping operations, and ultimately the cacophony of war. But simultaneously Britain relies on a quieter timbre to pursue its interests more covertly. Sometimes a conventional military response is not possible because enemy strength is overwhelming. Sometimes political intervention invites charges of neo-imperialist meddling, of negotiating with terrorists, or even risks escalating to war. Sometimes pursuing the global role is simply too expensive economically. When unable to act transparently, British leaders have consistently resorted to intervening in the affairs of others deniably.

The existence of covert action is an open secret and seasoned observers understand that it represents the shadowy side of international relations.

Professionals often refer to it as the dark arts of foreign policy: a key asset, but rarely acknowledged and one which requires experience and a complex skill set. Covert action is inherently controversial, much mythologized, a magnet for conspiracy theorists. And it is often misunderstood. Covert action is interference in the affairs of another state or non-state actor in an unacknowledged or plausibly deniable manner. The outcomes are visible, and may include the death of a leader, a coup, or an insurrection; but they—theoretically at least—cannot be traced back to the sponsor. Most commonly, covert action is associated with the Americans, the Central Intelligence Agency (CIA), and paramilitary activities during the Cold War. That is part of the story, but few appreciate that for the UK, a country seemingly in perennial decline from its great power status, covert action has been even more important. The British are just better at keeping it covert.

In reality, London's deniable interventions stretch back hundreds of years to before the United States (US)—and the UK for that matter—even existed. As long ago as the sixteenth century, Queen Elizabeth I used 'covert meanes' to influence the Dutch Protestant revolt against Spain. Threatened by Spanish activity in the Low Countries but militarily and economically unable to wage open warfare, she sent aid to rebels in the form of money, supplies, and mercenary volunteers—on the condition that it could not be traced back to England.[2] British covert action waxed and waned over the following centuries. It spanned the political intrigues and proxy wars of the nineteenth-century Great Game, special operations and sponsorship of revolts during the First World War, and mass bribery to control the Arab world in the early twentieth century. Recruiting agents of influence to manipulate governments became almost a trademark of British policy in the Middle East, with examples ranging from efforts to discreetly buy elections in Lebanon and Syria to manoeuvres which ensured the crowning of Faisal I as king of Iraq in 1921.[3] Fluid connections between intelligence officers, policymakers, and political fixers enhanced British influence across the Middle East.[4]

The Second World War forced Britain to professionalize its approach to covert action, and create new shadowy organizations. With war on the immediate horizon, one, known as Electra House, used propaganda to influence German opinion, whilst another, run out of the Secret Intelligence Service (SIS or MI6), focused on the potential for sabotage.[5] Most famously, and once war had broken out, the Special Operations Executive (SOE) supported underground resistance movements and engaged in irregular warfare, sabotage, and special operations deep behind enemy lines. Created in 1940 following the fall of France and tasked to 'set Europe ablaze', SOE encompassed some 5,000 agents operating in tight secrecy not only across Europe but in Southeast Asia as well.[6] Meanwhile, from 1941 its sister organization, the Political Warfare Executive (PWE), used propaganda to damage enemy morale and keep the spirit of resistance alive.[7] Economic warfare also developed increasingly devious methods, including mass forgery to undermine enemy currencies.

Neither organization formally outlived the war, but the promise of peace did not herald the end of covert action. Far from it. Politicians in Westminster and their senior officials in Whitehall still saw Britain as a global power with ambition and responsibility to match. Yet the country was in visible decline, a fate from which its leaders could not hide indefinitely. The era after the Second World War imposed myriad challenges on Whitehall's impecunious elite. Cold War soon emerged, characterized by Soviet subversion and intrigue; nationalist uprisings, unable to be quashed by military force alone, swept across the empire; a new generation of charismatic leaders threatened Britain's trade routes, defence commitments, and economic resources in places such as Iran, Egypt, and Indonesia; more and more colonies became independent, providing openings for hostile regimes to replace longstanding British influence; and terrorist groups attacked targets from Latin America to Northern Ireland to Iraq.

At the same time, non-interventionism and anti-imperialism became more powerful forces, not least because swathes of newly independent countries were joining the United Nations (UN). This made it more difficult for Britain to keep up its long tradition of interfering in the affairs of others. Politically constrained and armed with dwindling capabilities, successive governments have struggled to meet these challenges and maintain their complex overseas commitments. Many have turned to covert action as a force multiplier, a silver bullet, a means of closing—or at least concealing—the growing gap between responsibilities and resources. Covert action has provided successive governments with the smoke and mirrors needed to navigate the realities of decline. Like intelligence more broadly, it is a form of state power.[8] Leaders obviously do not take public credit for covert action, but it creates a space in which their interests can be more overtly pursued.

Since 1945, Britain has spread misinformation designed to divide and discredit targets around the world: from the Middle East to Eastern Europe, from Southeast Asia to Latin America to the streets of Northern Ireland. It has instigated whispering campaigns and planted false evidence on officials working behind the Iron Curtain. Using agents trained in sabotage and insurrection, Britain has tried to stimulate revolution in Albania. It has disabled ships to prevent the passage of refugees to Israel. It has secretly funnelled aid to insurgents in Afghanistan and dissidents in Poland. Britain has launched cultural and economic warfare against Iceland and go-slow campaigns against Czechoslovakian industry. It has tried to instigate coups in Congo, Egypt, Syria, Saudi Arabia, Iran, Abu Dhabi, and elsewhere. Through bribery and blackmail, Britain has rigged elections as colonies moved to independence. It has fought secret wars in Yemen, Indonesia, and Oman—and discreetly used special forces to eliminate enemies from Malaya to Libya. On more than one occasion, Britain has—at the very least—seriously considered assassination.

This remains the case today. Policymakers, hamstrung by austerity and public weariness of warfare, use intelligence resources and special forces to disrupt a range of targets from terrorists to people traffickers. From Syria to Libya, Pakistan to the UK itself, policymakers rely on tried and tested techniques developed over decades of deniable interventions. Those direct-ing these deeds have done so with the full knowledge of the most senior policymakers in the land: prime ministers, foreign secretaries, and cabinet secretaries. Covert action is a vital tool of statecraft. If used judiciously, it can play an important—if facilitative—role in pursuing national interests in a dangerous world. If used insouciantly, it can bring political scandal and diplomatic embarrassment. Worse still, it can result in needless deaths, or foment chaos and instability. Covert action is a provocative and risky business and one which requires careful consideration.

British understandings of covert action

The expression may seem an Americanism, but British officials have fre-quently referred to 'covert action'. They specifically discussed 'covert action' in relation to debates about the future of the Special Operations Executive in 1945; early Cold War activity in Indonesia; the remits of Whitehall's secretive counter-subversion bodies; and when supporting Afghan resistance against Soviet occupation in the 1980s. More recently, the Intelligence and Security Committee (ISC), Britain's principal oversight body, has recognized both the importance of 'covert action' against terrorism and the need for SIS to strengthen its 'covert action capability'.[9] And SIS is not alone: Government Communications Headquarters, or GCHQ, Britain's signals intelligence agency, now talks of 'online covert action'.[10]

Nonetheless, covert action is perhaps the most secret of all state activities and no official cross-departmental definition exists. Leaked military doctrine defines it as operations which 'are so planned and executed as to conceal the identity of, or permit plausible denial by, the sponsor'.[11] Elsewhere, it is deliberately kept vague, with SIS interpreting covert action simply as intelligence 'doing stuff'.[12] The 1994 Intelligence Services Act, which placed SIS and GCHQ on a statutory footing, permitted SIS to engage in 'other tasks' on top of spying. But those drafting it ensured the language was suitably woolly to allow flexibility and prevent operations from being held up by bureaucracy and inter-departmental competition.[13] By 2015, SIS admitted that its role included 'using covert contacts overseas to shape developments and exploit opportunities in the UK's interest'.[14] Perhaps this talk was too loose, as by the following year SIS amended its mission statement to simply 'shaping developments'.[15]

Beyond this, Britain deliberately lacks a clear framework. This forms a stark contrast to the US, where covert action is publicly defined as 'activities conducted in support of national foreign policy objectives abroad which are planned and executed' to ensure that the role of the government 'is not apparent or acknowledged publicly'.[16] In America, the written constitution, separation of powers between the White House and Congress, and numerous intelligence scandals over the years have forced a more visible and tangible position. Covert action is delineated from intelligence and from military special operations. Britain, by contrast, is more informal. Spy chiefs are free to act nimbly in grey zones, with policymakers confident they need never confirm nor deny operations. Any public definition would undermine this long-held practice.

Since the Second World War, Whitehall's terminology has variously included special operations, special military operations, special political action, counter-subversion, deniable action, and disruptive action. All of these, as we shall see, were slightly different, reflect the broad spectrum of covert action, and complicate not only the historian's endeavours, but also the business of secret statecraft itself. Excessive secrecy and lack of a clear foundation can lead to misuse or neglect of covert action, and risk undermining the legitimacy of those who carry it out.[17]

There are many means of conducting covert action. In a legacy of the roles of the PWE and SOE, British officials have generally divided it into two categories: unattributable propaganda and operations. The former, and associated influence activity, formed the backbone of UK covert action. In Britain, as in America, the vast majority of deniable intervention involves intangible attempts to influence. It may gather more headlines when uncovered, but covert action involving guns and bombs takes up a tiny proportion in comparison. The bulk of unattributable propaganda was known as 'grey' material. The information was often true, albeit selectively edited, but crucially the sponsor stayed hidden. In its 1950s heyday, grey propaganda exposed what Britain saw as Soviet, nationalist, and terrorist lies in an attempt to win hearts and minds around the globe. So-called 'black' propaganda was far more devious—and dangerous. It could contain disinformation and was either unattributable or falsely purported to come from a different author, often to discredit the target. Examples included forged material linking Communist Party officials to illegal slush funds and subversive activity against the Kremlin or material incriminating Irish republican leaders in embezzlement. Both grey and black propaganda, at least in the British mind, constitutes covert action. The sponsors tried to influence events in a deniable manner. Importantly, grey and black material supplemented broader attributable information or public relations work sometimes known as 'white' propaganda.

Like many liberal democracies using propaganda techniques, Britain sought to raise doubts about individuals rather than whole groups. Attacking swathes of society was more reminiscent of campaigns waged by authoritarian regimes such as Nazi Germany. Instead, British propagandists tried to challenge the competence and sincerity of particular leaders such as the Egyptian President Gamal Abdel Nasser, Congolese Prime Minister Patrice Lumumba, certain Communist Party officials, and named terrorist leaders.[18] Occasionally though, Britain crossed the line, especially during colonial counter-insurgency campaigns, attacking entire groups such as the Mau Mau in Kenya.

Operational covert action encompassed political, economic, and special operations. The first includes bribery, encouraging resistance, funding political parties, and rigging elections. Economic operations involve forging currencies, manipulating trade prices, or denying competitors access to goods. Special operations are more militaristic and might comprise sabotage, training rebel groups, and even assassination. In the British tradition, they tend to take place during some form of conflict such as in Libya and

Syria recently. Unsurprisingly, the definition of conflict is also deliberately left vague, thereby allowing SIS and special forces to be active in grey zones, including in Somalia or Yemen after 2010. As one SIS officer put it: definitions get in the way of doing the right thing.[19] As we shall see, these categories overlap. For example, Britain considered sabotaging Czechoslovakian factories in the early Cold War—a special operation to hit the economy. Planners have traditionally favoured an informal and fluid understanding of operational covert action. The key point here is that for Britain, covert action is as ill-defined as it is broad. Recently serving intelligence officers have pointed to such acts as detaining terrorists, seizing ships carrying weapons, and releasing hostages as other examples of operational covert action. Covert action is not just about arranging coups. It can be small, tactical, and quotidian.

Propaganda and operations work together. Propaganda is not an end in itself, but often forms the cornerstone of covert action. It was a background constant, seeking to divide, discredit, and exploit. In doing so, it created a more amenable environment for political, economic, and special operations. In the late 1940s, propaganda, whilst providing its own attack on communism, was used in conjunction with economic operations disrupting Czechoslovakian industry.[20] Around the same time, diplomats hoped to use it alongside sabotage to target Italian elections and alongside both sabotage and deception to prevent illegal immigration to Israel. In Iran, propaganda from as early as 1951 worked in conjunction with bribery to play an important role in the eventual coup two years later.[21] Similarly, plans for covert action in Syria in the 1950s saw propaganda, bribery, and sabotage working side by side, whilst propaganda provided the backbone of Britain's anti-Nasser operations too. It formed a constant during longer campaigns in South Arabia and Indonesia in the following decade, as well as in 1970s Northern Ireland, providing the backdrop for disruptive and special military operations in all three theatres. Britain continued to draw on propaganda to frustrate Soviet expansionism in the 1980s, and it remained an important part of the so-called War on Terror long after the Cold War had ended, again working in conjunction with special operations to disrupt terrorist networks.

Although practitioners prefer to keep them separate, a fine line can exist between intelligence and action.[22] British understandings of intelligence revolve around gathering secret information and the process of analysing it.[23] Covert action, by contrast, is a policy tool.[24] Officials traditionally therefore saw covert action as separate: something which relied on intelligence. The line between the two, however, began to blur during the Second World War when SIS ruefully accepted that SOE had far out-paced it in the business of intelligence-gathering, especially in Asia. Likewise, the PWE, also supposedly a user of intelligence, had quickly begun to gather material on the enemy-occupied territories to be used in covert propaganda activities.[25] The divide was further challenged during the Cold War. Stewart Menzies, chief of SIS between 1939 and 1952, saw it as an intelligence war and realized that intelligence needed an active dimension.[26] Although, like many spymasters, he worried about covert action compromising intelligence-gathering efforts, which of course was and remains SIS's primary task,[27] he believed that covert action could stimulate the flow of intelligence from Soviet-controlled countries.[28] As the cabinet secretary, Norman Brook, informed Prime Minister Clement Attlee in 1951: 'S.O. [Special Operations] work in peace-time is not to be regarded as an unprofitable diversion of effort from S.I. [Secret Intelligence] work, but rather as an essential com-plement to it.'[29] Covert action was not part of intelligence, but the two were mutually reinforcing.[30]

Operations in Albania offer an instructive example. The agents infiltrated into the country from 1949 doubled up as spies and covert partisans. They sought to determine whether conditions were favourable for liberation operations and this involved both gathering intelligence and testing the population.[31] When diplomats requested intelligence first and action second, Menzies pointed out that SIS had to conduct small covert operations to test resistance rather than passively gather intelligence. More broadly, SIS viewed its agents simultaneously as both intelligence and political assets. It seemed only logical that any agent well enough placed to provide high-grade infor-mation would also be able to exert a high degree of influence and vice versa.[32] Likewise, as one Whitehall deception planner pointed out, the development of secret channels into the Soviet machine could be used for deception, subversion, and intelligence-gathering.[33] This ran in stark contrast to America, where a strict line separated agents of influence from intelligence. The CIA feared that it was impractical to use the same person for both, as the intelligence would likely become compromised. Yet unlike larger CIA stations, SIS lacked the personnel to be able to divide intelligence and influence operations so distinctively.

Covert arms deals offer another important facet that is rarely discussed. Arming a government, if done deniably, is a significant form of covert action; it can simultaneously generate vital intelligence on that country's arms requirements and, by extension, war readiness.[34] The latter is often the overriding priority, leaving action more a means of gathering intelligence than shaping events. For example, covert British involvement in arms deals with Iran and Iraq in the 1980s primarily sought to acquire intelligence on both countries' arsenals. Deniably intervening in the Iran–Iraq War was a covert action by-product. The same can be said of apparent liberation operations in Eastern Europe in the early Cold War. Many of these were actually intelligence-gathering operations, cynically couched in the language of liberation to secure the support of agents unwilling to risk their lives for anything less. More recently, British foreknowledge of—and apparent complicity in—mercenary activity in Africa in the 1990s was more a means of gathering intelligence than sponsoring coups. This also forms a classic dilemma in counter-terrorism, regularly faced during the Troubles in Northern Ireland, of allowing something to happen to protect or develop an intelligence source. This does not necessarily constitute covert action, unless the individual deliberately interferes to shape events in an unacknowledged or plausibly deniable manner.

British covert action is flexible, decentralized, and draws on all relevant personnel able to intervene deniably, affect change, and quietly execute government policy. SIS does not have the capability or resources to do everything itself. Unlike American or French secret services, it does not have its own paramilitary wing and so works closely with special forces. In the late 1940s, it plucked former SOE personnel out of retirement to conduct top-secret missions from Iran to Albania. By the War on Terror, SIS had a special forces team embedded within its headquarters ready to initiate action. Special forces currently work with SIS to train friendly countries in interrogation techniques; provide protection for SIS officers, as happened during a botched operation in Libya in 2011 when such a unit found themselves detained by rebel fighters; and act swiftly on current intelligence to target terrorists, thereby creating a virtuous circle between intelligence and action as first articulated by Menzies back in the late 1940s. These days, though, a clearer division of expertise exists between the intelligence gathered by SIS and the action executed by special forces. Unlike their American counterparts which are fundamentally a military asset, Britain's special forces are a national instrument, paid for by the Ministry of Defence, but working closely with SIS, GCHQ, and the Foreign Office.[35]

In addition to SIS and special forces, covert action has included propaganda units such as the Information Research Department (IRD), military deception planners, as well as GCHQ, for which the rise of cyberspace created possibilities for online manipulation. Even MI5 can be considered as having engaged in defensive covert action through its training of friendly Middle Eastern security services in the 1950s.[36] This was, after all, a deniable intervention in the region. Whitehall has long understood covert action as a function rather than in terms of a specific agency. Each element was—and still is—brought in where it could make a difference.

Above all, covert action is a means of executing policy. It is not the policy itself. Overthrowing a government can be done both overtly and covertly. It is therefore the means of execution which relies on plausible deniability.[37]

From war to peace

This book unravels the narrative of British covert action from 1945 to beyond the War on Terror. It is a history of secret scheming against enemies— as well as against friends; of intrigue and manoeuvring within the darkest corridors of Whitehall where officials fought to maintain control of this most seductive aspect of their work; and, above all, of Britain's attempt to use smoke and mirrors to mask decline. It takes a chronological approach, revealing hitherto secret operations, the slush funds that paid for them, and the recurring battles deep inside Whitehall that shaped them.

Intelligence is, by nature, a secretive business. Covert action goes further still and is possibly *the most* sensitive activity a government can undertake. SIS files are closed; so too are those relating to special forces and the various Whitehall bodies trying to coordinate such activity. The government cites security reasons and a danger to Britain's international relationships for extending the closure of these files. But the questions posed here are significant, relating to a controversial—and little understood—aspect of British contemporary history and foreign policy.[38]

The overwhelming majority of pages devoted to covert action consider the American context, and it is misleading to view British operations through this prism given Washington's more rigid approach.[39] Far less is written on British activity, where serious historians have tended to emphasize the collection or analysis of intelligence over attempts to shape developments actively.[40] Many of those who do acknowledge British covert action wrongly assume that special operations or special political action are simply translations of an American phrase,[41] exaggerate or sensationalize operations, downplay political oversight, or offer empirically sound but very narrow case studies.[42] None have attempted to distil British approaches to covert action. Yet revealing a British 'way' not only unlocks further historical revelations but also helps understand contemporary policy.

This is an ambitious book: the first account of UK covert action based on primary documents. It contends that Britain has long used covert action flexibly and pragmatically as a means of bypassing or masking constraints heralded by decline. Covert action can be traced back to senior policymakers in Whitehall and Westminster and was not the domain of so-called 'rogue elephants' acting of their own volition. Covert action can be preventative, defensive, or offensive,[43] yet Britain internally portrayed even the most offensive operations as necessary self-defence. Above all, covert action was often reactive and indicative of Britain's propensity to muddle through.[44]

To overcome government secrecy, this book draws on original material from multiple archives across the UK and US. Much of this has only very recently been released: some through the Freedom of Information Act, some via public inquiries. Other files have lain hidden for years, unwittingly slipping through the weeders' net. Some are buried amongst seemingly unrelated or innocuous files, and found only after years of rifling through dusty yellowing documents. Some require careful reading to unpick euphemisms such as 'influencing', 'preventing', 'shaping', and 'discrediting' to determine cases of covert action. This archival material has been corroborated with other government files and myriad private papers, and then triangulated with interviews and secondary sources to provide the confidence needed in this murkiest of areas.

★　★　★

Who should control covert action? Tension between the diplomats and the military over this important question existed during the Second World War, exacerbated by the creation of SOE. Despite support from the prime minister, SOE was never a particularly popular organization and ruffled feathers throughout its brief existence. SIS and the Foreign Office, in particular, grew exasperated by some of its more extravagant operations. As the war wound down, senior diplomats wasted little time in pointing out that the decision to create SOE was a mistake. They claimed that its existence as an organization separate to SIS had led to confusion, friction, unnecessary expense, and a waste of personnel.[45]

Unsurprisingly, SOE strongly resisted. Lord Selborne, minister of economic warfare overseeing SOE, made constant appeals to his friend Winston

Churchill and, as one former colleague remembered, fought 'against every conceivable obstacle and attack'.[46] No sooner had the guns fallen quiet in Europe than Selborne reminded Churchill of SOE's wartime achievements: running resistance movements in enemy-occupied countries; sabotage; subversive propaganda; and clandestine financial operations. Playing on fears of the future, he argued that such activity would remain necessary in an uncertain world. Accordingly, a small nucleus should be kept—even if only as an insurance measure.[47]

Pushing for a continued post-war existence, Selborne emphasized how special operations would prove a 'valuable instrument' in implementing British peacetime policy.[48] This was one point on which some Whitehall consensus existed. Anthony Eden, the wartime foreign secretary, had been thinking along similar lines and noted the potential utility of a 'covert organisation' to further British policy after the war.[49] The core difference between him and Selborne, unsurprisingly, was who should run these operations. Selborne indignantly wrote that diplomatic control would be 'like inviting an abbess to supervise a brothel'.[50] The diplomats, although unable to match the simile, felt equally strongly: 'we are firmly of the opinion that the present system of separate S.O.E. and S.I.S. organisations should be terminated immediately after the cessation of organised resistance in Germany and should never be revived'. The idea of a secret organization operating in foreign countries but not responsible to the foreign secretary horrified them.[51]

Meanwhile, senior military figures contested Foreign Office control. They feared that the diplomats would wilfully neglect covert action, allowing skills and expertise to be lost forever. Field Marshal Bernard Montgomery, soon to become chief of the imperial general staff, hoped that SOE—and even SIS—would be transferred to military control on a long-term basis.[52] Despite this, Ernest Bevin, the new Labour foreign secretary, echoed his predecessor and recommended SOE be dissolved with remnants falling inside SIS, which in turn was responsible to him. Clement Attlee, who had taken over power from Churchill in July 1945, concurred. This happened in January 1946, when SOE's agent network merged into that of SIS and dispersed around the world, its capabilities for coordinating stay-behind operations and wartime sabotage became an SIS Directorate of War Planning, and its training and technical expertise amalgamated into the SIS Directorate of Training and Development.[53] The cabinet secretary, Norman Brook, summed up the outcome for Attlee after the dust had settled: SIS is 'responsible for the conduct of Special Operations so far as they may be authorised in peace, and for planning and preparing for the conduct of Special Operations work on a much larger scale in time of war'.[54]

Special forces were largely absent from these discussions of peacetime operations. Founded in 1941, the Special Air Service (SAS) had fought behind enemy lines in North Africa, whilst the Special Boat Service (SBS), created a year before, was particularly active in the Mediterranean. The SAS only featured in relation to future conflicts, insofar as they would implement the sabotage and resistance operations coordinated by the SIS Directorate of War Planning.[55] This was because they were strictly part of the military's chain of command, had failed to capture the political imagination, and senior War Office figures remained deeply sceptical of irregular units. By April 1945, much SAS fighting had petered out and, although Churchill granted permission to begin a new irregular offensive against the Japanese, the American nuclear strike on Hiroshima made it unnecessary.[56] Consequently, the SAS disbanded in October 1945, with the SBS following suit shortly afterwards.[57] Special forces did not feature prominently in top-level discussions about covert action, outside of war planning and counter-insurgency contexts, until the early 1960s. The government had little call for paramilitary skills in the early post-war years and, when it did, turned instead to former SOE members who had worked more closely with SIS during the war.

In November 1945, the Foreign Office gained a veto over special operations.[58] Rumblings of discontent reverberated from the War Office, where the chiefs of staff feared this would be used drastically. In an attempt to stamp out the inevitable future squabbling, the diplomats decided to lay out some ground rules. Harold Caccia, chairman of the Joint Intelligence Committee (JIC), was sent on the short walk to set the chiefs straight. He bluntly informed them that the Foreign Office had little predisposition towards an active programme of 'politically dangerous' special operations.[59] Although diplomats singled out the Middle East as the one area where covert action might be useful, it was neither necessary nor appropriate elsewhere, especially in Europe.[60]

In the pre-Cold War world, this was not an unreasonable assumption. Indeed, SOE's own post-war planning intended to reduce activity to a minimum.[61] Similarly, Field Marshal Sir Alan Brooke, a less hot-headed chief of the imperial general staff than his successor Montgomery, agreed that subversive operations were not necessary.[62] This consensus was short-lived.

As the diplomats held firm on their aversion to the hidden hand whilst the Soviet Union trampled over the neat distinction between war and peace, the military swiftly called for a revival of offensive covert activity.

Aside from residual wartime operations, predominantly in troubled countries such as Greece and Indonesia, covert activity significantly decreased in the immediate aftermath of the war.[63] The main explanation of Foreign Office reluctance was that war was over. Britain no longer faced the very real threat of invasion. As Alec Cadogan, the permanent under-secretary at the Foreign Office, reminded the chiefs of staff, 'the requirements of war or of an "amber" light period were totally different from what would be reasonable in peacetime'.[64] Covert action may today be seen as a means to manage risk by achieving objectives without recourse to conventional warfare, but this idea was not shared in 1945 at the end of a long and bloody war which seriously threatened British independence. After six years, Britain had finally secured peace. The Foreign Office was adamant that this was not to be jeopardized by risky manoeuvres with potentially serious political and military consequences.[65] At the same time, many diplomats remained unconvinced that Russia was a menace to British strategic interests. And it was they who possessed the veto over special operations.[66] On this occasion, the military read the developing threat environment more astutely, storing up a great deal of frustration for the future.

Peacetime also complicated covert action practically and administratively. In war, SIS (or SOE) merely had to conceal its activities to the extent necessary to protect agents. Peacetime was a quite different proposition. SIS now had to conceal the very fact that it was operating at all; that it even existed. Agents could no longer be easily dropped in by the navy or the air force. As Brook lamented, a great deal of administration was therefore required for even the simplest of tasks.[67] Likewise, planning deniable operations for a future peace was much more difficult than for a future war. SIS acknowledged that it was relatively simple to construct stay-behind networks in friendly countries ready for a future war. They found it 'immensely more difficult to plan in advance for operations which must be conducted <u>deniably</u> under political conditions which cannot be foreseen'.[68]

The Foreign Office's victory in gaining control of peacetime covert action in 1945 had long-lasting ramifications which are still felt today. It ensured that covert action was tied to a policymaking department, thereby shaping the evolving concept of special political action which was to characterize SIS activity in the 1950s. It also went some way towards ensuring

a more controlled or cautious approach in which operations were embedded
in clearly defined policy. Not all covert action was successful. Far from it.
Planners made numerous errors and, as we shall see, many operations had
serious negative consequences in both the short and long term. Likewise,
much Whitehall thinking about covert action was ad hoc, reactive, and
merely muddled through. That said, decisions taken at the end of the Second
World War were wise. An independent special operations unit could have
led to rogue elephant activity competing with strategic policy. Similarly, one
can only speculate on how the British culture of covert action may have
developed had the military gained control—not least because from the late
1940s, the chiefs of staff, led by ebullient figures such as Montgomery, put
SIS under strong and consistent pressure to engage in special operations.
With the Cold War on the horizon, much was at stake.

PART 1

COLD war

1

FaLSE STaRTS

From Counter–Attack to Liberation

. . . to return blow for blow and to embark on open political warfare against communism.

Sir Maurice Peterson, ambassador in Moscow, June 1947[1]

Ominous international developments, alongside ongoing Whitehall squabbling, gradually transformed attitudes towards covert action in peacetime. As Stalin pre-empted American dominance after the Second World War, Soviet designs became more apparent. He tried to press home his own post-war advantage by oppressing the countries of Eastern Europe, placing threateningly large military forces in Eastern Germany, and supporting communist parties in Western Europe, notably in France and Italy.[2] The intensification of the Soviet threat, the ideologies underpinning its apparent expansionism, and Moscow's use of what Whitehall called 'all methods short of war' pushed Britain towards a covert Cold War. If the UK sought to maintain a global role—policymakers believed the economic and political predicaments in which they found themselves to be a temporary aberration—then covert action would be unavoidable, if not always desirable.[3] By September 1946, the Joint Intelligence Committee, usually so reticent about offering policy advice, recommended that 'some immediate counter-action should be taken against this danger'.[4]

Rising tensions abroad soon translated into rising tensions at home with disagreement over who owned nascent Cold War policy. The resulting lack of cross-Whitehall planning and the cautious approach to covert action exhibited by the first post-war foreign secretary, Ernest Bevin, left the

British response confused. Whitehall's early Cold War strategy developed gradually. It included the positive projection of Britain as a 'third force' operating independently of the emerging American and Soviet blocs.[5] At the same time, the UK began a piecemeal counter-attack as policymakers took their first steps towards, as they saw it, playing the Soviets at their own game. Yet unlike broader strategies, covert action developed as a sporadic reaction to events. Bevin initially authorized only a cautious case-by-case covert Cold War. Given the huge uncertainties engulfing international politics at the time, this was no bad thing.

A reactive defensive-offensive

At the heart of Whitehall disagreements lay a fundamental difference between military and Foreign Office approaches. The chiefs of staff saw covert action as a proactive tool: something which could soften the enemy in preparation for conventional warfare. By contrast, for the Foreign Office, covert action was a reactive tool, to be used only when necessary to defend interests and maintain the status quo. This was the accusation levelled against the diplomats time and time again: that they lacked initiative and refused to plan ahead. The insults did contain some truth though and struck a nerve with senior diplomats.[6]

Partly in response, the Foreign Office created a small planning section of just three people inside its Services Liaison Department, which worked closely with intelligence and the military, to consider Russia policy.[7] More importantly, and accepting the need for a holistic approach as the Soviet threat became more apparent, the Foreign Office established a new body in April 1946: the Russia Committee. But fearing the inevitable attempts by the chiefs of staff to muscle in, they kept it a secret for over two years.[8] It proved a sensible decision. As soon as the chiefs discovered its existence, they began to complain, perhaps reasonably, along all too familiar lines. Chief of the Imperial General Staff, William Slim, lamented that it was too defensive and reactive, only considering counter-action after the Russians had struck.[9]

The Russia Committee brought together senior officials from across the Foreign Office to ensure a unified interpretation of Soviet policy and a coherent response.[10] Its chairman, Christopher Warner, head of the Northern Department, proposed a 'defensive-offensive' approach. Warner had championed cooperation with the Soviets throughout the war but, by 1946, his faith had finally been broken and he became a key advocate of Cold War within the Foreign Office, deliberately comparing the Soviet Union to Nazi Germany.[11] His plan involved 'resisting Communism with all the means open to us everywhere', whilst supporting democratic opponents of communism in foreign countries.[12] It was a counter-attacking strategy. The emerging cold warriors had to fight fire with fire or, as another senior diplomat put it, 'to remember that one is dealing with a tiger not arguing with a professor of epistemology'. Britain had to have 'recourse to most unusual methods: but then we are dealing with most unusual people'.[13] After all, the Soviets were now using a dangerous combination of intelligence, subversion, and intimidation to shore up their position in the East and undermine Anglo-American interests, often through mobilizing communist parties, in the West.[14]

Although Clement Attlee approved the broader theme,[15] Warner and his colleagues spent the first couple of years merely trying to convince an intransigent Bevin to actually implement their methods. They lobbied for a propaganda counter-attack, as a less controversial means of covert action,[16] but had to make do with a limited struggle with the Soviets for control of international cultural organizations.[17] Rotund, stubborn, and domineering, the foreign secretary proved a key player in the development—or lack thereof—of British covert action. Holding Attlee's full confidence, he initially viewed diplomats in the Foreign Office as affected aristocrats, although this soon gave way to mutual respect and loyalty. Reluctant to escalate the Cold War, Bevin imposed strict constraints, banning the use of propaganda to incite subversion in countries already under communist control and limiting his support to material portraying the positive achievements of the UK.[18]

Accordingly, this defensive-offensive approach began in haphazard fashion.[19] Despite Bevin's reservations, the Russia Committee did consider propaganda and, aside from debating how it could influence the 1946 French elections to prevent a communist victory,[20] the primary focus was the Middle East. With severe restrictions in place on operations in Eastern Europe, the region formed an ideal testing ground for peacetime covert activity and here even Bevin showed some leeway, not least because he saw it as a defensive action to protect British interests.[21]

In the Middle East, Foreign Office propaganda attacked the imperialism of Soviet Russia rather than communism. Diplomats argued that communism as an idea held too much appeal amongst the lower classes in the region for attacks against it to be successful.[22] Small, dapper, and decisive, Ivone Kirkpatrick was the driving force. Having been appointed assistant under-secretary responsible for information work in 1945, he was at the forefront of the Foreign Office's nascent Cold War propaganda activity. It was a position he relished, having engaged in similar work during both world wars, developing a loathing of totalitarian regimes in the process.[23]

Kirkpatrick's first testing ground for clandestine propaganda was in Iran, then called Persia, in 1946. During the Second World War, Britain and Russia had occupied Persia, ostensibly to keep the Germans away from the valuable oil reserves. The Russians did not want to leave. Shortly after the war, the Tudeh Party, a radical pro-Soviet group, seized power in its Northern Province and set up an autonomous government. As strikes broke out in the oil fields in the south, the British ambassador warned that leftist influence stretched across the country.[24] Given the weakness of the government in Tehran, the British grew deeply concerned that Persia, economically and strategically vital, was on the brink of allowing a large province to break away and join the Soviet Union.[25]

The situation seemed ripe for covert intervention. On the one hand obligation, commitments, and status necessitated action, but on the other hand Soviet strength prevented conventional military manoeuvres. This, combined with an opportunity for counter-attack, persuaded Britain to resort to covert action to protect its interests and allow negotiations from a position of strength. Covert propaganda was the primary method selected but, not for the last time, planners integrated it with other forms of secret activity. Planned outside of the Russia Committee, the military was involved from the outset and the chiefs of staff instructed the Joint Intelligence Committee (JIC) to 'examine the possibility of taking some positive action to counter Russian subversive propaganda'.[26] Aided by Kirkpatrick, the JIC advocated 'both overt and covert propaganda campaigns'.[27] For the former, officials in London and on the ground used the BBC, British companies in the Middle East, and the Trades Union Congress to highlight the benevolent impact of British interests in the region.[28]

The Foreign Office and SIS directed the covert propaganda campaign. This was supplemented by plans for SOE-style special operations to be used if the Russians took control of the region. Intriguingly, the JIC moved beyond its traditional assessments role and organized the special operations planning.[29] Meanwhile, Orme Sargent, the permanent under-secretary at the Foreign Office and a quiet enthusiast for covert action, advocated supporting local demands for provincial autonomy. As a result, an SOE

veteran on the ground in Tehran and a range of covert propaganda instigated a short-lived rebellion by pro-British tribes in south-west Persia. It
showed that, if necessary, the region could also break away—taking its valuable oil reserves with it—and forced the government to take a stronger line
against the Tudeh. The Persia crisis formed the first exploratory response to
communist pressure and propaganda.[30]

Palestine served as another testing ground.[31] Drawing on existing machinery and personnel, covert action formed a bridge between wartime and
peacetime operations, demonstrating that such activity could still be successful. Here, both Attlee and Bevin strongly supported moves to stem illegal
immigration from Europe which threatened the delicate balance of peoples
in the region but also appeared to be feeding a troublesome Zionist insurgency against British rule. Attlee wanted action. Unfortunately for Britain,
however, global opinion was hostile to any attempts to prevent the Jewish
people, who had suffered such persecution in Nazi Germany, from reaching
their homeland. British intervention therefore had to be covert. Attlee took
the lead, urging 'all possible steps to stop this traffic at source'.[32]

Between 1947 and 1948, SIS conducted a daring operation called Operation
Embarrass. This was a top-secret, three-pronged attack involving black
propaganda, deception, and sabotage. The operation drew heavily on wartime experience and drew former SOE men from retirement to engage in
direct action against potential refugee ships. One such SOE veteran was
David Smiley. Stocky, tough, and with a thirst for adventure, Smiley had
served with distinction behind enemy lines in Albania and Siam. He had
no intention of giving it all up once the war had ended. Under the cover
of a yachting trip, Smiley and his colleagues began motoring around the
Mediterranean.[33] They placed limpet bombs on ships in Italian ports, badly
damaging three. This was not an assassination mission, however; they only
targeted empty ships.

A simultaneous propaganda and deception offensive complemented the
sabotage. This aimed to divert suspicion away from the British by creating
a notional organization called the Defenders of Arab Palestine to claim
responsibility for the attacks. Propaganda also attempted to implicate Soviet
Russia in the illegal immigration. Deemed a success, Operation Embarrass
showed observers in Whitehall what peacetime covert action could achieve.[34]
Attlee and Bevin knew, however, that it was far less risky to conduct such
operations in Palestine than Eastern Europe. There was little chance of
escalation and SIS could, and did, simply use channels and personnel already
in place from the war.

Heating up

Meanwhile, Cold War tensions intensified as Soviet propaganda and policies became increasingly aggressive. Moscow broke a welter of post-war agreements with the West, interfered in the Bulgarian elections to install a pro-Soviet prime minister, and supported communist forces in Greece and Turkey. Stalin also used his intelligence organizations to undermine the Marshall Plan for European economic recovery, accepted by Western Europe in 1947, by mobilizing national communist parties against it.[35] To help achieve this, the Soviets launched the Cominform, designed to coordinate international action between communist parties under Soviet control, in the autumn of 1947. This strongly emphasized the idea of two competing blocs—the communists versus the capitalists—and demonstrated increased Soviet control over its satellites.[36] Gladwyn Jebb, an influential diplomat who had previously been SOE's chief executive and now enjoyed Bevin's ear, warned of a growing sense of inevitable conflict.[37]

Bevin was far less alarmist in his appraisal,[38] and it took a series of personal setbacks to harden his resolve. At the United Nations in October 1947, for example, senior Soviets belaboured him with a torrent of well-researched information which was clearly the product of a large machine designed to influence opinion. Likewise, the collapse of the Council of Foreign Ministers in London two months later frustrated him personally.[39] The Czechoslovakian coup at the end of February 1948 also hardened attitudes, especially after the Russians assassinated the only non-communist minister in the Czech government, Jan Masaryk, a man well known to the Labour Party.[40] Shortly afterwards, Herbert Morrison, deputy prime minister, joined calls for a black propaganda drive.[41]

Inside Whitehall, military pressure continued unabated. John Slessor, assistant chief of the air staff, was particularly virulent and advocated 'every weapon from bribery to kidnapping—anything short of assassination'.[42] The chiefs of staff, who saw this as a form of conflict even though there was no shooting, wanted a global political warfare plan, with sabotage in the Balkans and false rumour-mongering in Germany and Austria.[43] They demanded action. Slessor's belligerent persistence frustrated Bevin, who grew increasingly sensitive about what he saw as military encroachment on his turf. Although the chiefs might well have been right to fear Soviet expansionism and KGB operations, Bevin later moaned to Attlee that

Slessor's zeal had 'rather outrun both his knowledge and his judgement'.[44] That said, Bevin did hold off-the-record conversations with people such as Douglas Dodds-Parker, an SOE planner turned Conservative MP, who told him how best to destabilize authoritarian states. Bevin took notes and sent them to his officials, but never admitted his source.[45]

With much at stake and emotions naturally running high, some ministers now requested a more inter-departmental approach to the covert Cold War, including potential revival of the Political Warfare Executive in some form or another. Although Attlee saw some merit in this, Bevin was horrified and, after a lengthy debate, managed to survive with sole Foreign Office control intact.[46] Nonetheless, Attlee fired a warning shot reminding his colleagues that the 'machinery and organisation required will be considered by me'.[47] He went on to chair various committees on anti-communist propaganda himself. For now, Attlee backed Bevin, but the prime minister was growing frustrated by his foreign secretary's intransigence.

Under pressure from both Soviet expansionism and domestic opponents, Bevin launched a new propaganda strategy in early 1948. Relaxing some of his earlier restraint, which had exasperated the more pugnacious information warriors in the Foreign Office, he agreed 'to oppose the inroads of Communism by taking the offensive against it'.[48] Although much of this took place via open channels, Bevin created an Information Research Department (IRD) in the Foreign Office to run Britain's unattributable propaganda. It got to work straight away, anonymously briefing journalists about the harsh realities of life under Soviet rule.[49] Stung by the personal attacks, Bevin visited the new IRD office early and urged: 'we need useful and usable material because we are under very strong pressure. See what your boys can find'.[50]

The IRD was not in the business of spreading lies and its staff believed 'anything but the truth is too hot to handle'.[51] Nonetheless, Soviet oppression gave them an embarrassment of riches and the propagandists refused to use some true stories on the grounds that they were too awful to be credible.[52] It engaged in grey anti-communist propaganda, much of which was true but selectively edited to portray a certain message. The IRD quickly grew adept at exploiting secret information for publicity purposes and, despite being small beer compared to Soviet propaganda, formed an important part of the UK's burgeoning covert Cold War.[53]

The IRD expanded quickly to serve a range of clients, from friendly governments to trade union leaders.[54] Denis Healey, who ran the Labour

Party's International Department liaising with foreign socialists, was a secret partner, and about a third of the material it sent out in fact originated with IRD.[55] It started out as a fairly small organization with initial requirements for only ten members including four clerical staff, but by 1952 employed 126 members of staff at home and overseas.[56] The IRD's existence was avowable, but its size, funding, and function remained secret—including from the wider Foreign Office. Such secrecy, according to its first head, Ralph Murray, allowed the IRD to avoid parliamentary scrutiny, bypass ordinary hiring and expenses procedures, and pay its propagandists above civil service rates.[57] Drawing on key elements from the earlier defensive-offensive strategy, the new propaganda directive indicated a more unified strategy to countering communism.[58]

There still remained a long way to go before Whitehall's thinking became sufficiently coherent. Unsurprisingly, the IRD did not satisfy the military's appetite for action.[59] Under pressure, Sargent asked Stewart Menzies, chief of SIS, to examine possible covert actions which his service could provide.[60] Menzies responded with a veritable menu of capabilities ranging from black propaganda and stink bombs (to disrupt communist meetings) to sabotage, kidnapping, arson, and, as he put it, 'liquidation'.[61] It is highly likely that the dramatic list was written as a means to appease military voices: for the diplomats not to be seen as ostriches burying their heads in the sand, as the wartime chairman of the Joint Intelligence Committee had once put it.[62] In truth, Menzies feared that subversive operations behind the Iron Curtain would compromise attempts to gather intelligence.[63] But his menu backfired as the military got more and more excited, leaving the Foreign Office panicking about dangerous plans to prevent the Soviets from consolidating their position in Eastern Europe.[64] Ralph Murray, head of the IRD, was forced to defend the entire defensive-offensive approach to the impatient military chiefs.[65]

If anything was to be done, Bevin's position had to be reversed. He still thought it wrong to incite subversion behind the Iron Curtain as, unlike during the war, resistance could not be supported by military force.[66] Sargent appreciated the benefits of limited covert operations and, condemning the Russians for not playing fair, thought the time was right to broach the issue with the foreign secretary. Bevin had, after all, just authorized a revised directive on propaganda. Sargent went surprisingly far and recommended that SIS 'be given a free hand to carry out such special operations as are possible in the Soviet Union itself and in the Soviet Zones of Germany and Austria'. The aim would be to disrupt the economy and 'keep the Russian authorities on tenterhooks'. He even suggested that SIS be allowed to create small organizations for subversive activities in the satellite states.[67] Bevin was furious and expressed his 'grave objection' in a hastily scribbled note. Nothing, Bevin decreed, should be done along these lines.[68] Any covert activity had to be limited to countries not yet under communist control.[69]

Meanwhile, officials in Washington were going further and increasingly targeting propaganda at communist-controlled countries.[70] President Truman, who later criticized the CIA during the Eisenhower years, had begun America's covert Cold War. Seeking to contain the spread of communism, he endorsed covert subversive political activities to support groups opposing Moscow. It was a global approach and soon became integral to American foreign policy.[71]

This alarmed Bevin and his most senior advisers. In April 1948, Hector McNeil, who held ministerial responsibility for intelligence matters and propaganda on a day-to-day basis, warned him that the Americans were acting dangerously. He feared they would work with 'the wrong people', such as bitter ex-politicians, and that American operations would give populations behind the Iron Curtain false hope, inciting them 'to ill-designed and useless subversive activities'. His underlying point was that if the Americans worked alone they would 'make a mess of it'. After all, America, he argued, was too far away and too inexperienced in such activity to succeed.[72] William Hayter, overseeing intelligence and security in the Foreign Office, agreed, fearing the American plans were 'wild and ill-advised'. He therefore recommended the UK should conceal that it had ruled out subversive propaganda behind the Iron Curtain so as to be taken into American confidence. Once inside, the Foreign Office could influence their plans.[73] Not only were the Foreign Office seeking to play the military, they now also attempted to mislead the Americans.

The Americans had created the CIA in March 1947. But covert action was conducted by a semi-detached organization called the Office of Policy Coordination. The name was ironic since this dispersal of roles resulted in disorder. George Kennan, of the State Department, confided in a British friend that American ideas for subversive operations behind the Iron Curtain had 'made his hair stand on end'. He added, as a sop to the British, that SIS was far more experienced than anything in America and that Washington would proceed with caution.[74] But Kennan was in fact rather keen on covert warfare and was not being entirely honest with the British about his views.[75] In a world of smoke and mirrors, it would not be the last time that the US and UK misled each other on covert action.

Back in Whitehall, fears grew that Moscow could subvert or take over European governments closer to home.[76] Prevented from targeting Eastern Europe, Britain's propaganda therefore focused on Germany, Austria, Italy, and France.[77] As early as 1947, McNeil had acknowledged that the only forms of counter-measure open to the UK in France and Italy was propaganda and 'covert assistance, where possible to the Social Democrat movements'.[78] This would act as a counter-attack against discreet Soviet support for communist parties there. With a forthcoming election and a strong communist party, the diplomats feared Italy was a prime candidate for another Soviet coup. As a result, Christopher Warner, who had become assistant under-secretary responsible for information activities, called for measures to influence the Italian elections and prevent the communists from obtaining control. The initial discussions saw propaganda intertwined with operational action. Warner dramatically wanted to bring 'the Italian machine to a standstill' through sabotage.[79] True to form though, Britain's nascent cold warriors opted for the less controversial option of propaganda and the IRD distributed unattributable papers to key contacts in Italy.[80] A committee formed in the Rome embassy, chaired by the ambassador, to coordinate the campaign.[81] At around this time, Bevin admitted that, although he overwhelmingly preferred white propaganda, Britain was using some covert methods and that more could be done to insert favourable articles in foreign newspapers. He suggested doing so through bribery rather than buying the newspapers outright.[82]

It transpired that the Americans too were discreetly sending similar anti-communist information into Italy designed, like the British material, to influence the elections. It was on a far grander scale: they laundered some $10 million supporting favoured political parties.[83] This was backed by propaganda, highlighting the violence of the Red Army in Eastern Europe, to ensure a 'democratic' government was elected.[84] It proved a humbling experience for Britain's diplomats, who soon realized that any action had to be coordinated with Washington.[85] Unsurprisingly, the American campaign, both overt and covert, made all the difference in Italy.[86] That said, SIS psychological warfare activity, notably including the creation of the Don Camillo stories about a priest at odds with his town's communist mayor, did prove influential.[87] Viewing the problem from a regional rather than national perspective, the Americans also ran a similar—albeit far smaller—operation in France during 1947. Both operations, in Italy and France, formed classic examples of American defensive covert action: of using political warfare to contain the spread of communism. More importantly, they convinced Washington policymakers of the value of covert action when allied with broader policy.[88] The power in the Anglo-American relationship was changing. Senior American intelligence officials found themselves sick of relying 'blindly and trustingly on the superior intelligence system of the British', as they had done in the Second World War. They vowed to close the gap on Britain's lead in special operations expertise which some felt had been developing since the days of Queen Elizabeth I.[89]

By the summer of 1948, the Foreign Office had ruled out further covert propaganda in Italy and France, perhaps as a result of American success, and discussions turned to Germany and Austria.[90] Although Bevin's ban against inciting subversive action in the Soviet satellites remained in place, Germany and Austria were grey areas: regarded as 'occupied', rather than technically behind the Iron Curtain.[91] Sensing an opportunity, plans involved using bribery and blackmail to insert material into local newspapers.[92] However, Bevin had not yet given approval and even the most senior diplomats seemed afraid to send the plans up to him for fear of a brusque refusal.[93] But pressure was building inside the Foreign Office, this time from the upper echelons of SIS. Menzies grew increasingly frustrated and embarrassed about continued delays in Germany and Austria.[94] He had several SIS officers, whose services were much needed elsewhere, standing by.[95] Warner and Sargent echoed Menzies,[96] whilst the British legation in Austria was also keen. In March 1948, they moaned that plans had not been implemented early enough to give them a 'chance of softening up the Russians before the present treaty talks in London'.[97] It was another false start caused by Bevin's heel-dragging.

In Bevin's defence, secret operations in Germany were temporarily under a cloud. A few weeks earlier, SIS had contemplated recruiting a Russian officer in Germany as a defector. Without proper discussion or authorization, he was swiftly flown to London. Things did not go to plan. The Foreign Office, MI5, and the JIC all complained at not having been consulted. Russia, meanwhile, accused SIS of outright kidnap. To make matters worse, the defector had a change of heart and tried to escape from his police cell and return to Russia to face the charges of treason. Menzies had stubbornly attempted to defend SIS's role in the saga, but Hayter was distinctly unimpressed.

Accordingly, Patrick Dean, then head of the Foreign Office's German Political Department, warned against covert propaganda in the Soviet zones of Germany and Austria: the moment was not a propitious one for SIS to be 'given liberty to fish in such dangerous waters'.[98]

The temperature—and possibility of 'Hot War'—was rising. The Berlin Blockade began that summer as Moscow prevented all traffic in and out of the city, denying its residents food and dramatically forcing the West to airlift supplies to besieged residents. Reviewing the situation on 7 July, the British chiefs of staff thought that the only way to remain in Berlin was 'to start a shooting war'.[99] Coming only months after the Czechoslovakian coup in February, the Berlin Blockade starkly demonstrated the dangers of the Soviet threat and the steps the Kremlin would take to get its own way.

This was the first major crisis of the Cold War and altered the mood inside the Foreign Office. Reluctant to take no for an answer, eager covert action planners continued to plot operations on a case-by-case basis, but tried to limit them so as to appeal to Bevin.[100] Over the summer of 1948, Menzies and Sargent decided to lift the ban on intelligence-gathering, as opposed to subversive, operations inside the Soviet Union.[101] On hearing the news, Hayter politely reminded them that they should probably run this by Bevin. Hayter was right and the foreign secretary, who could be prickly about these things, was not best pleased. In October, he scrawled, 'No I cannot have it'.[102] Bevin had still not shifted on subversive operations either.

The job of informing the chiefs of staff, who were still pressing strongly for an aggressive covert action campaign, fell to Ivone Kirkpatrick. The fiery diplomat was certainly up to the task—not only did he have a reputation for being combative and perfunctory, but he had more sympathies with the military than many of his colleagues did. By this time, Kirkpatrick had been promoted to deputy under-secretary overseeing Western Europe. He informed the disappointed chiefs that whilst a great deal of thought had been given to covert activities in support of the Cold War, 'things had gone wrong on two or three occasions' and so Bevin did not think they would pay a dividend.[103] Nonetheless, and with or without Bevin's knowledge, certain operations did take place from the British Zone of Germany where, a year later, officials reported that 'some success has been achieved in sowing distrust and dissension amongst the Communist Party'.[104]

Intelligence officers also seem to have enjoyed surprising freedom of action in the Middle East, where small-scale covert action was part of everyday

British practice. Several SOE officers stayed on after 1945 to undertake what Lord Killearn, the British ambassador in Cairo, casually called 'the payment of baksheesh'. Meanwhile, the ambassador in Tehran told London that he only wished to retain one SOE officer after the war, Dr Zaehner, whose chief function was bribing the Persian press. Zaehner stayed in Tehran to do this work until 1947, before becoming involved in other covert operations, as we shall see.[105] Perhaps because this was a time-honoured business and because he thought it unlikely to provoke the Russians, in May 1948 Bevin 'accepted without difficulty' the expansion of 'covert propaganda in the Middle East'.[106]

One scheme involved subsidizing advertisements in Middle Eastern newspapers. Here SIS used what they described as a 'covert organisation' to buy advertising space to influence local opinion.[107] Plans were also afoot for Egypt, where Whitehall hoped to secretly build up a liberal party to challenge the authority of both the Communist Party and the nationalist prime minister. These twin threats were to become familiar foes over the next decade or so. Although the British embassy in Cairo took the lead, guidance from the Foreign Office and SIS in London was never far away. There was much debate about how best to achieve this, with diplomats ruling the idea of covertly running Egyptian newspapers impractical. Anything which was obvious or overstepped the mark would have been swiftly closed down by the regime; propaganda had to be subtle. One suggestion involved creating a small organization to distribute pamphlets and spread whispering campaigns. Another involved discrediting individual Egyptian leaders again through rumours, forged letters, and planted evidence. A third option saw Britain liaising with the Americans—on the assumption that Washington was not already covertly running newspapers in Egypt.[108]

It is not clear exactly which of these plans came to fruition. We do know that by the spring of 1948, 'certain black propaganda operations' had been carried out in the Middle East for over a year. SIS operated a wireless station and ran news agencies but disguised British control. This was most likely aimed at Iran or Egypt—or both. We also know that from 1946 SIS secretly bribed friendly tribal groups and charities in Iraq to enhance Britain's prestige in the country. This cannot have been too successful, however, as it was scaled back to a meagre £120 per annum in 1949 as part of a cost-saving drive.[109] These Middle Eastern testing grounds proved instructive. Britain was developing a peacetime *modus operandi* which involved using propaganda as a cornerstone but combining it with other forms of political action and bribery when necessary. And, as we shall see, Menzies had a top-secret slush fund to pay for it.

Whether Bevin enjoyed close control over covert political action elsewhere in the Middle East, especially in the Levant, is open to doubt. As a region in which the Colonial Office, the military, and major British corporations were active, several parallel policies soon developed. Diplomats pursued cooperation with the French over the first steps towards decolonization, yet officers and agents in the field used covert political action to bolster control over Syria, create a pro-British Greater Syria (incorporating Lebanon, Transjordan, and Palestine), and fashion some sort of Iraqi–Syrian union. Tactics, used regularly during the interwar years, involved bribery, extortion, and agents of influence.[110] These local attempts failed miserably, angering both the French and the Foreign Office, and left the Americans to take the initiative in covertly orchestrating a coup in Syria in 1949.[111] As we shall see, reining in the more ambitious plans developed at a local level would become a regular challenge for Whitehall's diplomats throughout the 1950s and 1960s.

Liberation

When Kirkpatrick met the chiefs of staff in September 1948, he did not merely pass on the message that Bevin still opposed covert action. He also tried to alleviate the military's frustration at Whitehall's perceived lack of planning. Desperate to stamp their authority on covert action, the chiefs had persistently asked for an equivalent of the Joint Planning Staff to fight the Cold War. Under growing pressure, the Foreign Office was now forced to play its hand. To fend off the military, Kirkpatrick finally informed a surprised audience about the Russia Committee. He disingenuously described the top-secret body as, in effect, Whitehall's Cold War planning staff and invited them to send a representative. As the chiefs eagerly accepted, he warned them not to get their hopes up in terms of ambitious new operations.[112]

The Foreign Office's concession had immediate and dramatic implications. The most senior members of the military had now wedged their collective foot in the door, in the form of Arthur Tedder, chief of the air staff and advocate of aggressive covert action against the Soviets. He believed that containment was not enough and, as soon as he pulled up a chair, the parameters of the debate changed. Liberation operations were on the agenda for the first time. The chiefs were excited. They had high hopes that the Russia Committee would be able to wage Cold War and treat it like a military operation. It did not last and Tedder eventually gave up his seat in dismay. As Patrick Reilly, who went on to oversee the Foreign Office's intelligence and security apparatus, recalls, 'it didn't fulfil his idea that you could plan Cold War operations in the way that you move divisions here and move divisions there and so on'.[113] Initially, though, the chiefs believed they could finally shape British Cold War planning—including covert action. Their first thoughts were of launching guerrilla warfare in places like Poland.

Gladwyn Jebb now chaired the Russia Committee. He was sharp, commanding, and sometimes arrogant, laughing derisorily at ideas he deemed foolish.[114] Assistant under-secretary and one of Bevin's most trusted lieutenants, he had seen SOE activity up close during the war and subtly endorsed a more offensive approach against the Soviets. Discussing covert options, Jebb, Tedder, and their colleagues wisely concurred that targeting Russia itself was not worthwhile.[115] Instead, they secretly pondered the merits of proactively starting a civil war elsewhere behind the Iron Curtain. Whitehall's cold warriors now agreed that their aim 'should certainly be to liberate the countries within the Soviet Orbit by any means short of war'.[116] This formed a sizeable step forward from using stink bombs. It was not, however, wholly out of line with broader Foreign Office thinking during the uncertain winter of 1948 and 1949. In a continuation of defensive-offensive thinking, the diplomats expressed two objectives: 'the defensive one of protecting the rest of the world from Communist domination, and the offensive one of successfully detaching those countries which have already been subjugated'. Achieving this required a holistic approach encompassing diplomatic manoeuvrings, public relations, economic action, and special operations. The latter, according to the Foreign Office, included covert propaganda and subversion. In this, SIS would prove vital. Demonstrating its ongoing two-dimensional role, SIS would be charged both with executing the special operations and providing the intelligence which underpinned all British activities.[117]

With liberation now on the agenda, Tedder and the rest of the committee looked for a target country to detach from the Soviet bloc. Their minds swiftly turned to ongoing events in the Balkans where, back in June, the Soviets had expelled Yugoslavia from the Cominform, raising question marks over the cohesion of the Soviet bloc.[118] Some saw opportunities for exploitation, but Bevin urged his staff not to read too much into the split. He was, however, happy to exacerbate it by giving discreet encouragement to the Yugoslav leader, Josip Tito.[119] Crucially, the split did mean that Albania was now physically detached from the Soviets, and suddenly offered a seemingly isolated, vulnerable, and exposed target for liberation.[120]

Plans for Albania did not exist in isolation. Senior officials met in top secret to flesh out a proposed liberation strategy. In December 1948, they outlined four key objectives. First, to make the Soviet orbit so disaffected that in the event of war it would become a dangerous area requiring large armies of occupation. This reflected the military perception of covert action as an offensive weapon to soften up an enemy rather than a defensive means to protect the status quo. Second, they hoped to loosen the Soviet hold on the orbit countries and ultimately enable them to regain their independence. Exploitable cracks had appeared in the Soviet monolith. This led to the third objective: seizing every opportunity of discrediting the Soviet regime or weakening its position in the satellite states. Fourth, Britain should frustrate Soviet efforts to build up its economic war potential. All four objectives were to be attained by 'all available means short of war'.[121]

By late 1948, SIS had already begun to make serious efforts to exploit resistance movements from Ukraine and Poland.[122] The former primarily involved supplying them with technical means for maintaining communications with Ukraine, as well as training small groups in the UK before infiltrating them back into their homeland. SIS and the CIA backed rival factions, with the British supporting that led by Stepan Bandera, a man they described as 'a professional underground worker with a terrorist background and ruthless notions about the rules of the game'. SIS spent much energy encouraging Bandera to cooperate with the other faction but eventually grew frustrated with his arrogance and factionalism, breaking links in early 1954.[123] In Poland, British and American intelligence supplied the Freedom and Independence Movement with money, ammunition, and communications equipment before Polish radio revealed that the organization was bogus in late 1951. Russian military intelligence had duped the West into thinking that resistance fighters had survived the aftermath of the war.[124]

Meanwhile, senior SIS officers quietly embarked on a programme of support for Latvian partisans. Britain's occupied zone of Germany included the

Baltic coast, putting SIS in a strong position to use naval patrols as cover to infiltrate agents ashore. With SIS short of funds, the Americans provided finance in a resource-for-expertise deal which characterized the relationship in the immediate post-war years.[125] Unfortunately, the real rebels had been captured and SIS fell into a Soviet deception trap.[126] The same applied to Estonia where, after the war, SIS had sent agents to establish a base for nationalist resistance. Once more, the Soviets turned it into a deception ploy.[127] Two years later, Operation Climber saw émigrés infiltrated back into Georgia through the mountainous border with Turkey. The first operation, in 1948, ended when two died mysteriously.[128] Kim Philby, as SIS station chief in Turkey, betrayed many of these agents—as well as their families and contacts inside the Soviet Union.[129]

For SIS and the Foreign Office at least, these operations did not form part of a broader liberation strategy. Despite their being couched in the language of liberation, the primary aim was actually intelligence-gathering, followed by propaganda purposes and creating stay-behind networks for use in a future war. They were preparatory and must be understood in the context of what was a one-sided spying game with the Soviets. Whereas Moscow had some impressive assets inside the West, SIS had none. Playing catch-up, they targeted the frontiers of the Soviet Union.[130] In Ukraine, SIS informed the resistance that the main purpose of collaboration was to collect intelligence and one SIS officer even threatened that covert British support would stop if the intelligence dried up.[131] There was some confusion, though, not least because wartime special operations had worked their way into SIS training programmes carried out at Fort Monckton, near Gosport. As a result of incorporating leftovers from the SOE, intelligence officers now had to be proficient in a range of skills from classic agent handling to using explosives and blowing up trains.[132] In some areas, therefore, SOE experience lingered, yet the main aim in Eastern Europe was to harness this for war planning rather than peacetime special operations.

Discussion even extended to liberating parts of China under communist control during its civil war. Seeing Mao's China as a 'potentially major satellite' of the Soviet Union,[133] the Foreign Office and SIS considered liberation operations. Transposing the same thinking from Albania to Asia, the Russia Committee advocated using resistance movements inside communist-controlled Chinese towns. These movements, they hoped, would disseminate covert propaganda and instigate anti-communist resistance, especially amongst students.[134] Meanwhile, Orme Sargent asked the British ambassador in China whether covert measures could be taken to create internal security problems for the Chinese communist administration. This, Sargent hoped, would deter them from further expansion.[135]

Ralph Stevenson, the ambassador, was sceptical, fearing that, if uncovered, covert action would provoke Chinese repercussions.[136] On a practical level, SIS found potential Chinese agents deeply unwilling to take part in any stay-behind schemes and had little intelligence on China in the first place.[137] Plans were therefore put on hold, with Stevenson preferring unobtrusive counter-propaganda instead.[138]

China was no ordinary Russian satellite, all the more so during the civil war. Liberation, even merely of occupied areas, proved overly ambitious. British intelligence had overplayed the monolithic nature of international communism, and officials reluctantly agreed that apart from protecting Britain's trade position there was nothing they could do overtly or covertly to combat the advance of communism in China itself and focused on intelligence-gathering by recruiting junior members of the Communist Party instead.[139] Only the Americans believed that they had the clout to halt Chinese communism through covert action, a theme which would become increasingly prominent in the post-war years.[140] Even after the end of the civil war, covert action would have been strategically incoherent alongside Britain's broader China policy, which stressed the need to keep a foot in the Chinese communist door, culminating in recognition of Mao's regime at the start of 1950. When the vice-chief of nationalist forces, General Cheng Chish-min, in talks with guerrilla leaders, sought British help to recover South China from the communists, officials in Hong Kong politely declined. Likewise, the British ambassador in Burma expressed concern to his American counterpart about CIA covert support for nationalist troops on the Chinese–Burmese border.[141] Despite this, Chinese nationalists in Hong Kong maintained a secret agreement with SIS to pass information to them in exchange for permission to remain active in the colony.[142]

Unable to counter communism at its Asian heart, the British turned their attention to neighbouring countries—what they saw as potential Chinese satellite states. The Foreign Office and SIS contemplated building up espionage and resistance movements in these surrounding countries in much the same way as in Albania, Ukraine, and Poland. They combined this with a concerted effort to resolve political disputes, such as in Kashmir and Indo-China, and to improve the economic position of Southeast Asia as a whole.[143]

In truth, liberation was another false start. The early months and years of the Cold War saw a reactive and ad hoc approach to covert action. As the Russian threat became more apparent, diplomats found themselves under continued pressure from the military to engage in covert action and soften the Soviets in preparation for a future war, but constantly ran into Bevin's intransigence. Covert action developed slowly, incrementally, and reluctantly. It was defensive and portrayed as being forced on policymakers who simply tried to muddle through this period of transition. The Middle East served as testing grounds for operations, but action in Europe—where it most mattered—was delayed and watered down. The UK's cold warriors boldly talked of liberation from Europe to Asia, but any strategy only existed on paper. Bevin did not approve it and most supposed liberation operations served primarily to gather intelligence and prepare for a future war rather than dismantle the Soviet bloc. The only potential exception was Albania.

2

OPERATION VALUABLE
Defending Greece, Detaching Albania

One of the most powerful motives which actuate an agent is the hope of participating in or actively assisting a successful rebellion against the authorities in power in his own native country.

Horace Seymour, 1952[1]

Talk of liberating Eastern Europe excited those few civil servants in the know. Here was a chance not only to contain the spread of communism, but to take the fight to Stalin's backyard and denigrate the Soviet Union's capacity to fight a future war. Dramatic and ambitious top-secret reports circulated amongst Whitehall's elite planners. Yet Ernest Bevin only officially authorized liberation operations in Albania. And even these must be understood as much in the context of the broader Greek civil war as any supposed overarching liberation policy.[2] Albania served as a testing ground: a pilot scheme for a strategy that only ever existed in the minds of the few.

Bordered by Greece to its south and Yugoslavia to its north, with Italy across the sea to the west, Albania was a country the British knew well. Having fallen first to Italian conquest and then German occupation, it hosted a spirited resistance movement, aided by the Special Operations Executive (SOE), during the Second World War. Communist partisans took control in 1944 and the new leader, Enver Hoxha, soon allied with the Soviet Union.

An attractive target

As we have seen, the split between Yugoslavia and Moscow in 1948 left Hoxha's regime appearing vulnerable. But Albania formed an attractive target for another, perhaps even more important, reason. Planners did not initially have to frame covert action in the provocative lexicon of liberation. Instead, it could be presented to Bevin as limited guerrilla activity against Greek communists who had been using Albanian territory for logistical support and as a base to mount operations back into northern Greece.

As the axis powers retreated from Greece at the end of the Second World War, partisans began to fight each other for control. By 1948, a civil war was well underway. Although it was a long way from London, Bevin deeply feared a communist takeover of Greece. The country provided access to British positions in the Middle East and eastern Mediterranean and, as he put it, sat as the 'soft underbelly' of southern Europe. Greece fell within the UK's sphere of influence and losing it, Bevin feared, would have had a devastating impact on commerce, trade, and the spread of democracy. Despite opposition from sections of his own party, Bevin continued Winston Churchill's wartime policy of supporting any Greek regime so long as it was not communist.[3]

Accordingly, Britain supported government forces against communist fighters before discussions about liberation and Albania had even begun, including through remnants of the Special Air Service (SAS), black propaganda, and bribery.[4] Britain's meagre resources handicapped planning and so Bevin asked America for assistance. President Truman agreed to supply aid and, in doing so, began a broader policy of containment, whereby America would support peoples fighting the spread of international communism anywhere.

The Greek civil war forms an important moment in Cold War history for another reason too: it sparked covert action in Albania. Patrick Reilly, then a counsellor in the Athens embassy, had earlier reported that Hoxha provided safe havens for guerrilla fighters. He warned that 'Communist forces were being trained, equipped and organised in Yugoslavia and Albania and from these safe bases infiltrated into Greece'.[5] This remained the case into 1948. Framing any covert action within the context of the Greek civil war appeased the more cautious minds in Whitehall, and, by the end of the year, the Secret Intelligence Service (SIS) had drawn up an initial plan. First and foremost, SIS aimed to relieve pressure on Greece through sponsoring guerrilla operations directly targeting communist bases and lines of communication in southern Albania. Second, SIS would foment insurrection in other areas of the country, but only to weaken Hoxha's ability to cause trouble in Greece. Third, and more vaguely, SIS plotted to 'undermine the Communist position in the weakest of the orbit countries', hoping that any success would open up more exploitable weaknesses elsewhere in the Soviet bloc.[6]

Six weeks later, with American encouragement, part three of the SIS plan evolved into something more ambitious: detaching Albania from the Soviet orbit altogether.[7] The diplomats now balked. Despite the initial flurry of optimism from the Russia Committee, inspiring insurrection was incredibly dangerous. There was a very real chance of Soviet troops crushing a revolt, leading to wasted effort, money, and lives. Even if Moscow did not intervene, liberation risked creating a Tito-puppet government in Albania which may not have been any better for the West than the existing regime.[8]

Intelligence, or the lack of it, formed a core problem in evaluating these risks. Ultimately, planners lacked sufficient intelligence about conditions on the ground, levels of resistance, and the strength of internal security to formulate a political objective precise enough to justify preparations for insurrection. The part of the plan countering Greek communists was well defined, but the liberation elements were hopeful, speculative, and tagged on the end. Orme Sargent identified these problems and asked Ivor Porter, an ex-SOE officer now working in the Southern Department, to devise a counter-plan limiting activity to military operations against Greek rebel bases and lines of communication. But Porter and Sargent both knew that, first and foremost, it had to start with an intelligence-gathering operation.[9]

Stewart Menzies agreed that greater intelligence was necessary before proper planning could take place. Unfortunately, however, the Foreign Office's neat two-step approach of intelligence followed by covert action was flawed. Menzies was forced to point out that it was impossible to gather intelligence on resistance merely by inserting a few agents into the country. SIS could only know for sure whether there was substance behind the rhetoric of resistance by using what he called 'direct methods of probing'. Small-scale covert operations were therefore necessary to test local preparedness to take action, and these in themselves were a form of intelligence. Agents had a symbiotic dual role: intelligence-gathering and event shaping.[10]

Hitherto so sceptical of covert action, Bevin now became personally interested and followed developments closely.[11] Seeing Albania as an individual case rather than part of a broader liberation strategy, he was keen to use covert action to complement his Greece policy. After consultation between SIS and Porter, Bevin received a plan in March 1949. It was delivered by William Strang, the new permanent under-secretary at the Foreign Office, in the post for only a couple of months. Strang was loyal, highly disciplined, and possessed an impressively sharp and analytical mind. A shy but first-rate administrator, he took a deep interest in matters of Foreign Office organ-ization, establishing the Permanent Under-Secretary's Committee in 1949 in an attempt to provide a more holistic approach to issues of long-term policy, including the role of covert action. Events forced Strang to take a quick interest in intelligence matters. Albania landed in his in-tray almost immediately, whilst his tenure also saw the defection of Soviet moles Guy Burgess and Donald Maclean in 1951, as well as the covert operation to overthrow the Iranian prime minister two years later.[12]

On submitting the Albania plan to Bevin, Strang conceded apologetically that it 'was the best we can think of in present circumstances'. The foreign secretary did not dismiss it out of hand and promised to give the idea more thought. He then went quiet on the subject for a few weeks. With communist raids from Albanian territory against Greek forces intensifying, Strang pushed Bevin for an answer.[13] He told the foreign secretary that the Greeks interpreted these raids as a deliberate attempt by the Soviet Union to see how far Britain would go in defence of Greece.[14] This struck a nerve. Bevin now saw covert action as defensive and necessary. He consulted with Clement Attlee and agreed to establish an active intelligence organization inside southern Albania in April.[15] Meanwhile, Bevin was coming around to the idea of intelligence-gathering, if not subversion, behind the Iron Curtain more broadly—although he still banned it inside Russia itself.[16]

When it came to Albania, he went remarkably far. Spurred on by the importance of Greece and the Soviet challenge to Britain's position, he saw intelligence-gathering as only the beginning and hoped, if realistically achievable, to detach Albania from the Soviet orbit altogether. It formed part of a three-pronged covert campaign alongside discreetly supporting both Greece and Tito.[17] Feeling that 'if properly handled, the situation in Albania would pay dividends',[18] Bevin now advocated using 'any suitable means'.[19]

Attlee and his foreign secretary are usually portrayed as cautious cold warriors, reluctant to engage in dirty tricks and covert operations.[20] By late March 1949, however, the prime minister himself was pushing for SIS to bribe Albanian officials as part of the plans to instigate an anti-communist revolt.[21] He requested an assessment of key Albanian personalities and asked: 'Are they not possibly for sale?'[22] Attlee presumably felt bribery was a less provocative option than infiltrating agents. Either way, Strang replied that Albanian leaders were committed to Soviet communism, whilst junior and less fervent party members would not betray the government unless open resistance had broken out. There was a more practical reason too: SIS did not know whom to bribe. They simply had very little intelligence on Albanian personalities. If SIS could acquire the necessary intelligence for calculating the possibilities of bribery, then, Strang reassured Attlee, 'this is certainly one of the covert methods which we would bear in mind for possible use in due course'.[23]

Gathering intelligence to test local resistance required infiltrating agents by sea into southern Albania. They were to hide out in the mountains, make contact with resistance leaders in local villages, and assess willingness to revolt. Led by former SOE man David Smiley, who was employed under the cover of a cypher clerk, training began in Malta in the summer of 1949. Smiley, fresh from covert action to restrict illegal immigration to Palestine, was no stranger to this part of the world. During the war, he had parachuted into northern Greece, crossed the border on foot, and aided local resistance in ambushing Axis convoys.[24] Housed in an isolated Napoleon-era fort and disguised in British battledress, the Albanian agent class of 1949 received training from Smiley in radio operating, fitness, and using both pistols and sub-machine guns.[25] Six groups of twenty-nine Albanians left Malta in a discreetly armed fishing boat manned by former Royal Navy officers. When deep into the Adriatic, they switched to a light rowing boat which dropped them into a quiet inlet along a steep and rocky coastline. From there goat tracks led inland.[26] Smiley then left Malta for Greece to await news. If the intelligence proved that the conditions were right, then anti-communist guerrillas could be trained and unleashed. The plan was codenamed Valuable.

Working with Washington

The Americans also had plans for Albania, seeing it as a potential experiment to ascertain whether larger liberation operations would be feasible elsewhere.[27] These plans were ambitious, but had not yet been put into practice.[28] Given the size of the country, some coordination was required and the Foreign Office and SIS pressed for a joint operation. Roger Makins, a deputy under-secretary with great experience of Anglo-American relations, summed up the rationale: collaboration would 'keep American action under control'.[29] As Dean Acheson, secretary of state, informed Bevin: Cold War stalemate did not 'correspond to our people's conception of victory'.[30] The UK was happy to disrupt, but Washington seemed to want outright victory. The other, less noble, factor driving SIS into the arms of the Americans, lack of money, was left unsaid in Whitehall.

Codenamed BGFIEND, Washington pressed for liberation. For the Office of Policy Coordination (OPC), disrupting the attacks on Greece was only ever a corollary objective.[31] Instead, the OPC, a nascent and insecure organization, was desperate to liberate Albania—even if State Department officials remained unconvinced.[32] This was for bureaucratic as well as geo-political reasons. Success would have had significant impact on the development and perhaps even the existence of OPC. And yet they admitted to not being prepared organizationally or logistically to implement the operation, instead believing that the best thing was to learn on the job. Only the pressures of actual operations could, they thought, provide an impetus to develop America's covert action capabilities.[33] Even Frank Wisner, head of American wartime special operations in south-east Europe and now overseeing covert action, knew success was far from guaranteed. But he felt under pressure to launch probing operations against the Soviets, for which Albania formed the most promising target.[34] This headstrong, slightly reckless, approach did not inspire confidence across the Atlantic and allowed SIS to maintain its superiority complex.

The Americans had similar feelings about the British. Demonstrating a lack of clear objectives in Washington, Acheson thought the only difference between the US and UK positions was that the Americans were less inclined to precipitate trouble in Albania. The idea of fomenting insurrection, he told Bevin, made him nervous. It could encourage the Greeks and Yugoslavs to partition the country.[35] Likewise, a senior adviser in the State Department warned him to avoid the question of liberation when agreeing to support Valuable, on the grounds that the British were more likely to encourage it.[36] When Bevin shot back that they should 'bring down the Hoxha government', he suddenly appeared a veritable hawk.[37] This is quite striking, for it contradicts the British view that they were keeping the ambitious and provocative Americans in check. Regardless of who was restraining whom, SIS and the Foreign Office contacted OPC to suggest a joint operation.[38] Hayter believed that in spite of their differences, British and US policy was sufficiently vague to make joint action desirable.

Besides, he continued, 'it would always be possible for us to decline participation in any later activity which went beyond what we should think
desirable'.[39]

And SIS did need resources. They may have had the human assets and
expertise, but Britain relied on American money.[40] This automatically gave
Washington leverage. Wisner felt that the SIS plan selfishly focused on
Greece and on protecting British positions in the Balkans. After much dis-
cussion, he persuaded SIS to adapt their own plan in line with BGFIEND.[41]
The intelligence-gathering operation to disrupt communist supply lines into
Greece became the first stage in a broader and more ambitious coordinated
operation, in which Wisner fully intended to take the lead.[42]

In an early source of transatlantic tension, Washington pressed for the use
of émigrés in Albania.[43] The initial SIS plan, devised before Smiley began
training, had dismissed émigré groups as 'divided into many political factions
squabbling and intriguing among themselves',[44] yet the Americans got their
way and the agents sent into Albania were plucked from émigré camps.
On behalf of SIS, Julian Amery, accompanied by Harold 'Perks' Perkins
and Neil 'Billy' McLean spent three weeks in May 1949 making contact
with Albanian nationalists in Rome and Greece. Like David Smiley, Amery,
McLean, and Perkins all shared an SOE background. Perkins, who had
served with Smiley on the recent Palestine operation, spent much of the
war in Poland where he had headed SOE's section.[45] Amery and McLean had
served in Albania during the war. Julian Amery, once described as 'born with
a silver grenade in his mouth',[46] was an imperialist to the core with a lust
for romantic adventure and had accompanied Smiley on a parachute drop
into Albania in 1944.[47] McLean, a courageous, handsome, and charming
soldier, later received honours for his role in making contact with Albanian
partisans. Both he and Amery went on to become politicians—but, as we
shall see, neither gave up their passion for escapade and special operations.
Neither were ever far from covert action and, throughout their long careers,
both men operated as unofficial emissaries exploiting their dizzying array
of contacts spanning royalty, dissidents, and rulers across Europe and the
Middle East. Theirs would prove to be an address book of which even SIS
became deeply jealous.

For now, their main target was the nationalist leader Abas Ermenji. He
was, according to Amery, 'the key' and the whole plan hinged on the three
of them managing to convince him to take part. But Ermenji's group, the
right-wing Balli Kombetar, would not be enough. Amery, succumbing to

his romantic disposition, was thinking big—of 'rebellion everywhere'—and he sought to work with a range of resistance groups, including the royalists run by Abas Kupi.[48] The plan did not get off to the best start. Billy McLean had overslept, delaying the initial journey to Rome, and, once the trio arrived, Perkins seemed only to irritate Ermenji, leaving Amery having, in his words, to 'soften the worst gaffes' during their first meeting.[49] Moving on to Greece, the trio toured various refugee camps, where they faced intense lobbying to intervene in Albania.

The mission was successful, with Amery, McLean, and Perkins arranging for Ermenji to handpick the agents to be infiltrated into Albania.[50] The Foreign Office and SIS, they assumed, would supply Ermenji with false British papers to aid him in his mission.[51] Amery got a touch carried way, though, and spoke of having 20,000 rifles and £50,000 at his disposal, only drawing the line at Ermenji's request for tanks. As the scale of Amery's promises became apparent, Perkins's face was a picture. They reached agreement in principle and Ermenji left thinking he had been authorized to create a guerrilla strike force to topple the government.[52]

Meanwhile, the Americans created an exiled National Committee for a Free Albania (NCFA) as an umbrella to cover the anti-communist operations.[53] Still sceptical about using émigrés at all, Bevin was openly scathing about the idea.[54] But America needed British contacts and experience and so the Foreign Office, reminded that it had agreed to a coordinated plan, reluctantly agreed. The task once again fell to Amery and McLean who, in August 1949, helped establish the committee from Albanian émigré circles. A key part of the negotiations was to acquire King Zog's acceptance of any plans for a post-liberation government. Zog had ruled Albania from 1922 to 1939 successively as prime minister, president, and self-proclaimed king. His was a tough regime with little regard for civil liberties that had close relations with Italy before Mussolini invaded in 1939, forcing Zog into exile first in London and then Egypt.

A rather delicate situation greeted Amery and McLean when they arrived in Egypt in July 1949. The Americans had made parallel commitments to both Ermenji and Zog, and now expected the latter to surrender certain royal prerogatives in order to support the nationalists. Amery and McLean faced the problem of reconciling two irreconcilables and, as Amery put it, 'rather blundered in' to Zog's villa.[55] The self-declared king quickly became angry when they told him that an agreement for a government-in-exile had already been reached with others. He rose from his chair and shouted in

Albanian: 'It is I who made Albania. I left the country with the Parliament's authority and it is my duty to defend Albania.' Britain and America, he continued, 'have no right to make such appointments'. As his wife, Queen Geraldine, dutifully translated into English, Zog fixed a steely stare on Amery.[56] With a few well-chosen words, Amery won Zog over. According to the American representative present, 'his performance was masterly'. Although Zog refused to support the committee publicly, he would not oppose it.[57] Amery went on to visit various national leaders in Rome and Trieste to smooth over other disagreements between émigré factions.[58] The NCFA served both as a front and as a rallying point for subsequent activities.[59] It conducted propaganda; worked with other national committees and émigré groups; recruited agent teams; interrogated refugees; but most importantly, was a front for covert activities directed against the Albanian regime.[60]

Pilot schemes

Demonstrating a central theme in British approaches to covert action, Valuable was essentially a pilot scheme. Although its ultimate objectives proved more ambitious than later operations, they were still to be achieved gradually and incrementally. Despite this, Bevin's own thoughts raced ahead and, perhaps distracted by the simultaneous NATO negotiations, he was already thinking about the regime which would replace Hoxha. Sceptical of the NCFA, he told Acheson that any new leader had to be 'a person they could handle'. Capturing years of British thinking in one question, Bevin asked whether there were 'any kings that could be put in'. Acheson dodged the question, insisting the present situation was 'too fluid' to decide.[61]

Despite the grand ambition, any offensive needed to start small. As we have seen, the plan first involved establishing an intelligence organization in southern Albania to confirm whether conditions were favourable for further operations.[62] Pursuing an incremental approach had clear benefits. Untold damage and escalation could have unfolded had Britain moved directly towards inciting rebellion across Albania. A cautious approach made far more sense. Yet there were disadvantages, as Menzies himself pointed out. If the operation was not extended, then any losses incurred in the preliminary stages would have been in vain. He questioned whether it was worth incurring the risk of setting up an intelligence organization unless the operation was definitely going to be followed through.[63] With hindsight, starting on such a small scale probably saved many more lives than it cost.

Signals intelligence, gathered from tapping Albanian communications, offered some preliminary insight into the resistance towards the end of July 1949. The results were not particularly encouraging. There was virtually no evidence of the unreliability or misbehaviour of any Albanian authority, thereby offering little scope for blackmail or bribery. Some evidence suggested the regime was tied down with internal preoccupations, notably Titoism, giving some hope that authorities would be less alert to externally instigated subversion. Unfortunately, intelligence also revealed government suppression of opposition groups. To make matters worse, secret reconnaissance missions failed to spot any clandestine escape routes by land and only limited potential by sea. Most importantly, intelligence warned that the evidence of rebel activity was flimsy. Clutching at straws, the spies reported that one anti-government slogan had been written on a wall protesting against government treatment of the peasantry.[64] An effective uprising would need greater support than this. Bevin, however, remained keen to press on and awaited feedback from the infiltrated agents.[65]

He received the eagerly anticipated intelligence by the end of the year. It offered little encouragement. The six agent teams, nicknamed 'pixies' and infiltrated in the autumn of 1949, had made their way from the drop-off point and slowly travelled under the cover of darkness inland. The British watched from their boats as torchlights gradually grew fainter. As night turned to day, the agents sensed the communists were waiting for them. Local sympathizers warned them about government suspicions and that shepherds had been instructed to report any odd activity. One group was quickly ambushed by the Albanian military; another had to flee for their lives. Now based off the coast of Corfu, Smiley and his team grew concerned about the lack of news. When a message finally came through, the anxious agents explained that government patrols were everywhere, that they had to hide during the day, and that sceptical villagers doubted their claims to be the vanguard of a British-backed resistance. The operation had clearly leaked and created alarm amongst the Albanian government. Under intense surveillance, three of the parties were forced to withdraw to Greece a mere four weeks after landing in Albania.[66]

On a more positive note, there was evidence of resistance to Hoxha on a widespread, although not exactly heavy, scale. SIS were grateful for small mercies: the fact that some of the pixie teams had received enough support from the local population simply to survive in a dangerous mountainous region riddled with security forces was a success. Whitehall's relief at mere survival is quite striking. SIS and the Foreign Office callously treated the six Albanian parties as canaries in a mineshaft, infiltrated into a hostile area to see if they survived. If they did, then the plan could move on to phase two. Not all survived: one of the six groups was wiped out entirely, whilst the fate of another remained unknown. SIS planners were surprisingly pleased. They optimistically assessed that on these grounds it could be assumed that 'larger scale operations in the spring will at least most seriously embarass [sic] the Hoxha regime, and might at best touch off a revolt leading to its downfall'.[67]

Diplomats in the Foreign Office were also sanguine. In November 1949, they recommended to Bevin that 'preparation for the second or insurrectionary phase of the operation should continue without interruption'.[68] It was a classic case of policymakers, keen for success, emphasizing any intelligence which supported their plans. Bevin proved a more detached reader. Unconvinced by the intelligence reports, his initial support began to waver. Although he did not need to make any immediate decision, he toyed with the idea of cancelling the operation entirely.[69]

Covert action had achieved little by the end of 1949. The NCFA was successfully established in August, but the original chairman died, supposedly of natural causes, a month later. Propaganda had failed to extend beyond a few leaflets distributed amongst an illiterate population, whilst plans to equip a yacht with radio broadcasting equipment had ended in expensive failure,[70] and a proposed Anglo-American propaganda offensive had been delayed due to technical matters.[71] The SIS infiltration teams may have seen limited success, but the OPC had failed to recruit any agents for training at all.[72] Meanwhile, the international context had changed. Most importantly for Bevin, the Greek civil war was over, with victory for the government forces. To make matters worse, the OPC began to fear adverse consequences in the Balkans should the liberation go ahead. These included Soviet action against Tito on the pretext of aid to Albania as well as a potential Greek invasion if liberation had caused anarchy in the country. This, the Americans feared, would lead to complications and clashes with Yugoslavia. In short, it had the potential to become a dangerous flashpoint in an increasingly volatile Cold War.[73]

The disappointing end to 1949 did not spell the end of Valuable. The OPC modified its plan and, using intelligence acquired through the SIS infiltration mission, assessed that operations into central and northern Albania would 'have reasonable prospects of success in terms of survival and of profit in terms of reconnaissance and potential political action'. Approved by the State Department, the new plan involved eight parts. The first recommended that agents should gather intelligence under the cover of a mission to monitor Albanian abuses of international law. The second stressed continued support for the NCFA. Gradually becoming more provocative, number seven called for the infiltration of further agents into central and northern Albania to gather intelligence and exploit the situation. Finally, the plan advocated widening the operation and bringing in the French and Italian governments.[74]

Whitehall had to formulate a response. The Foreign Office was under pressure to agree. Future cooperation with Washington depended on it. Reassessing the pixie intelligence, diplomats accepted that the Albanian government had a larger counter-intelligence network than expected and that a revolt would only succeed if arms and ammunition could be provided on a large scale. The SIS agents had found that existing stocks were negligible in both quantity and quality. Moreover, internal security forces conducted prompt and effective sweeps wherever they expected resistance activity. To make matters worse, the Greeks, Italians, and French had gained an extensive knowledge of the operation through a series of leaks, most likely from the émigrés.[75] Anthony Rumbold, head of the Southern Department, sent a stark warning up to Bevin. The active promotion of rebellion would 'be a far more formidable undertaking than we had originally contemplated and the chance of His Majesty's Government's responsibility remaining undiscovered would be extremely small, indeed probably nil'. Rumbold recommended that Bevin abandon any concept of infiltrating 'fighting men' to lead a large-scale revolt.[76]

Failure

Whitehall's cold warriors now concluded that a broader liberation strategy was doomed to failure. The idea of freeing Eastern Europe proved no more than a romantic ephemerality. The end of 1948 had not opened the floodgates to a torrent of operations across the world. Neither did it signify any enhanced willingness to revert to provocative SOE-type operations. By 1949, those possessing the all-important veto stipulated that, in peacetime, SIS would only engage in minor operations which had been explicitly authorized.[77]

Four factors explain this. First, despite some initial optimism, the results of phase one showed that SIS had underestimated the strength of the internal security forces and counter-intelligence networks.[78] Second, the use of émigré groups—so integral to liberation operations—proved utterly limited. Bevin and Hayter had feared that émigrés were difficult to control, outdated in their views, lacking influence, and often leaky.[79] Despite these concerns, officials risked it in Albania but were not about to be stung twice. Observers have traditionally looked to the notorious traitor Kim Philby, who was SIS liaison officer in Washington until 1951, for exposing the operation.[80] He arrived on the scene too late to make a great impact, as the first wave of Smiley's teams entered Albania in mid-September and early October. Although Philby was stationed in Istanbul until August 1949, the Soviet intelligence station in London knew of the operation as early as June.[81] Blame must be shared with the loose-lipped and factional Albanian émigrés in the refugee camps of Turkey, Italy, and Greece, as well as the National Committee for Free Albania based in Paris.[82] Furious SIS planners and diplomats quickly blamed the whole failure on the NCFA and vowed never to work with émigrés again.[83] Whilst Whitehall's cold warriors had a point, they were keen to blame everyone but themselves.

Third, liberation was strategically flawed. Émigrés remained politically distinct from the state that was trying to use them, pursuing their own political goals and adopting their own respective strategic cultures.[84] Moreover, covert action alone was inadequate to roll back conventional Soviet military power from Eastern Europe. Unlike during the Second World War, Whitehall was never prepared to commit conventional forces to back up the resistance movements and secure liberation.[85] As SIS soon realized, encouraging liberation without offering ultimate support simply set resistance groups up to fail.[86] To make matters worse, liberation operations were inconsistent with broader foreign policy, which involved containing Russia and, as Bevin put it, 'holding the rim'.[87] Officials begrudgingly acknowledged that a lack of thorough planning and scrutiny had hampered the operation, and this was only accentuated by the ongoing bureaucratic tension.[88] Fourth, in August 1949, Moscow exploded its first atomic bomb. Although it had surprisingly little impact on military thinking,[89] it did raise concerns over covert action by dramatically raising the stakes. As a result, Whitehall's planners scuttled away from provocative operations. It is of little surprise that SIS's Directorate of War Planning, heavily involved in Albania, closed shortly afterwards.[90]

Still Valuable

In 1951, Britain ruled out liberation operations as well as any ideas of training a 'shock force' of approximately 1,000 armed Albanians.[91] And yet, despite common assumptions to the contrary, SIS covert action against Hoxha lasted until the middle of the decade.[92]

The CIA's Frank Wisner now refused joint operations. He had grown frustrated by what he saw as British errors and omissions, and was suspicious that SIS had secretly developed a relationship with Tito in Yugoslavia.[93] He had already forced Britain to drop plans to bring Tito on board once and worried that SIS was more disposed than the CIA to deal with the Yugoslav regime.[94] Always wary of London's desire to expand its influence, the CIA feared that the Foreign Office was using the plan 'as a stepping stone for penetration into the whole Balkan area'.[95] But Albania was too small for two separate operations and it made more sense to cooperate—and keep as close a watch as possible on each other's activities. Thus the Anglo–American relationship became one of so-called 'policy coordination and operational disengagement'.[96]

Propaganda, including running a black radio station, was closely coordinated between SIS and the CIA.[97] Broadcasts labelled Albania 'the pawn of USSR power interests' and Soviet collaborators as 'weak little men'.[98] By contrast, agent infiltrations were more operationally disengaged. The CIA continued to infiltrate agents to gather intelligence, spread propaganda, and promote a coordinated resistance movement. Thirty-nine men entered Albania between November 1950 and October 1951; one third did not survive.[99] A separate British infiltration team, codenamed TIGER, entered Albania by sea in July 1951. They lasted almost one month and faced nearly continuous ambush, including one ferocious attack which persisted for almost twenty-four hours and used up all their ammunition. Other British teams scurrying around the countryside were staggered by how quickly security forces tracked them. Surrounded, they ditched their equipment and fled across the nearest borders. In 1951, SIS infiltrated nineteen agents into Albania. Fourteen escaped to Greece, four died, and one was captured.[100]

Despite the problems, the CIA thought 'operations into Albania had produced tangible results'. The venture, they added, had also proved 'great
value in providing both the British Service and ourselves with a mass of
experience and knowledge obtainable in no other way'.[101] Moreover, the
ongoing Korean War provided further impetus to continue to make life difficult for the Soviets.[102] Plans for 1952 included two separate types of agent
operations: penetration and harassment.[103] By the end of the year, however,
the CIA and SIS had still achieved little. Allen Dulles, the incoming American
director of central intelligence, told John Sinclair, the new chief of SIS, that
the Albanian operation was 'now on trial'.[104] The CIA acknowledged that
although resistance activity had increased, most of the European intelligence services, including those of the Soviets and Albania, were aware of
connections between émigré groups and Western governments. The CIA
also sensed a decline in British determination, feeling that Whitehall
preferred the status quo in Albania to the risks involved in attempting to
establish a pro-Western regime.[105]

Tensions between the CIA, SIS, the State Department, and the Foreign
Office intensified. SIS refused to stress the idea of liberation so long as there
appeared to be no immediate prospect of success. It would, they explained,
'inevitably lead to eventual disillusionment and apathy on the part of the
Albanians'. By contrast, the State Department sought to 'continue to foster
the idea of liberation' so long as operations did not force revolutions prematurely. This led to British suspicions that the Americans were moving reck-
lessly fast, while the Americans felt that the British were unnecessarily
trying to restrain CIA activities.[106]

Security formed another source of frustration. American intelligence officers
running the Albanian operation had excellent access to SIS headquarters—
via a pass allowing them to come and go freely—and to information relating to Valuable. Indicative of growing suspicions about Soviet penetration of
British intelligence, the CIA did not respond in kind and insisted that the
SIS liaison officer had to make an appointment, always to be held offsite
to minimize access to CIA work environments.[107] This was not limited to
sensitive covert action. The Joint Intelligence Committee (JIC) representative
in Washington also complained about lack of access whilst his equivalent
in London seemingly had free reign.[108] The Americans were right to be
cautious, given that covert action in Albania overlapped with Kim Philby's
time in Washington.[109] Nonetheless, no matter how treacherous Philby may
have been regarding Albania, and plenty of ink has been spilt debating this,

the operation was betrayed by leaks from émigrés and Soviet agents elsewhere. Operations continued to be betrayed long after Philby left Washington under a cloud of suspicion in 1951.[110]

By late 1952, the CIA deemed coordination with SIS to be a 'major problem'.[111] They judged their own efforts to have 'been conspicuously more successful than British operations'. As a result, CIA operations, they believed, increased American prestige in Albanian circles, whereas British prestige had declined.[112] The balance in the relationship was shifting, and one CIA officer accused SIS of growing jealous of America's greater influence, capabilities, and accomplishments in Albania, as well as of free-riding off American funds.[113] Not that American smugness was particularly justified: Albanian security teams captured one highly regarded agent team and managed to launch a successful deception operation against the CIA lasting some two years in which they lured more rebels into traps.[114] The frustration was mutual, with SIS irritated by CIA infiltration teams operating outside of their assigned areas. On one occasion, American encroachment forced one SIS team to flee into Greece. Albania was too small a country for two operations and both intelligence agencies risked contacting the same individuals or compromising targets that the other was trying to cultivate.[115] For these reasons, and despite the differences, SIS continued unsuccessfully to press for closer relations—although both sides possessed a sense of superiority.

Despite transatlantic tension, operations continued throughout 1953. In February, the Americans began to plan for an Albanian coup instigated by the CIA, SIS, and Yugoslavia.[116] The Tito regime had stepped up its contact with anti-Hoxha rebels and, despite official denials, the CIA believed Yugoslav intelligence had been sponsoring the resistance for over a year.[117] It now made sense to coordinate. On 16 February 1953, two CIA officers discreetly slipped into Yugoslavia, where they held intensive talks on Albania inside a luxurious villa on the outskirts of Belgrade. The Yugoslavs laid on a cook, two waiters, and an abundance of food and drink for the occasion. Interestingly, the Americans held the meeting in secret and refused to tell SIS, as they remained suspicious about the relationship between British and Yugoslav intelligence. In Belgrade, the Americans told their hosts, known only as Mr B, Mr C, and Mr S, that the CIA knew all about talks between Britain and Yugoslavia.[118] And they were right: Anthony Eden had recently visited the White Palace in Belgrade, where Tito had encouraged greater liberation efforts in Albania—and indeed across the Soviet bloc—and accused the West of exaggerating communist strength. 'Europe', Tito argued, 'was mesmerised by the vast size of the Soviet Union and the thought of Soviet armies sweeping through to the channel ports.'[119] It was a remarkable message, and one which would have strongly appealed to the CIA had they been invited.

Yet Tito's demands for more action were contradicted by his own secret service. Yugoslav intelligence officers knew all about recent CIA and SIS operations in Albania. In fact, they were scathing about the whole thing, arguing that Western interference would not work. Hoxha publicly maintained that the rebellion was instigated by foreigners and would result in yet another foreign occupation of Albania. In that sense, the anti-communist propaganda spread by the CIA and SIS was flawed. It served only to alienate the masses who had fought against Nazi occupation and had since achieved substantial social progress, including land reform.[120] To make matters worse, SIS and the CIA failed to understand that the tribal politics, which had served the West well in the war, hampered a sense of national identity to which they were now appealing. Worse still, a large proportion of the local population were illiterate, making propaganda leaflets futile.[121]

The Yugoslavs argued that SIS and CIA attempts to infiltrate émigrés to lay the groundwork for resistance had unambiguously failed. They insisted that outsiders failed to understand the internal politics, whilst the agents were sending exaggerated reports back to their émigré leaders who, in turn, served only their own faction's interests rather than the broader cause. SIS, the Yugoslavs argued, had tried to launch a revolution prematurely and succeeded only in causing Hoxha to respond with repressive counter-measures. Resistance, they preached, must come from inside. The people would rise when conditions were ripe. Accordingly, Yugoslav intelligence favoured working with amenable elements inside the Albanian Communist Party to overthrow the government.[122]

The Yugoslav criticisms seem to have had some effect. From 1953, both SIS and CIA operations changed tack, attempting to infiltrate government circles rather than focusing purely on émigrés. Plans now involved developing small, secure underground networks to penetrate the army and the political establishment. These were to be 'gradually developed and expanded with the ultimate goal of undermining the Government and creating a resistance potential to be used in event of war or revolution'.[123] Operations also included a strong psychological warfare component involving a covert radio station in Greece, a semi-monthly propaganda newspaper, and leaflet drops.[124]

By 1954, Britain still had a covert liaison officer to the NCFA and continued to infiltrate agent teams. This season was to be the last.[125] A year later, President Eisenhower's special assistant, C.D. Jackson, sought to use psychological warfare to detach Albania once and for all.[126] Meanwhile, Foreign Office influence in the planning waned and became almost tokenistic, leaving Amery's circle angry with how Britain was 'prepared to stand by while the Americans handle the Albanians...with an almost inconceivable folly'.[127] Amery was deeply concerned that the CIA was making basic mistakes. Oddly, the CIA had attempted to put covert support 'on a business basis', as Amery put it, and even drew up—and signed—contracts for the dissidents. He feared this risked exposure of British financial support and the NCFA being branded as Western agents.[128]

By the middle of the decade, Anthony Eden, nearing the end of his time as foreign secretary, admitted that 'we are not in a position to control' the NCFA, but had 'done our best to influence them in the right direction'.[129] In 1956, the Americans terminated their support for it altogether, on the grounds that it had ceased to be operationally useful. Although it was replaced by a new émigré organization, the Free Albania Committee, formed under the sponsorship of the American–established Free Europe Committee, this too showed 'no promise of greater effectiveness', according to the CIA. There was no mention of consultation with SIS when doing so; British involvement had faded away.[130] Years of covert action achieved little and the CIA reported that the 'few isolated small guerrilla bands' were 'no more than a local nuisance which probably will be wiped out sooner or later by the security forces'.[131]

Albania remained a special case. In 1958, the Foreign Office still spoke airily of subverting—and even detaching—the regime. Frederick Hoyer Millar, its senior official, talked of forcing Moscow 'to acquiesce [sic] the loss of Albania to the Soviet bloc'. Whilst acknowledging that this would have had little impact itself, Hoyer Millar argued that 'it would have a tonic effect on the morale of the free world, which is beginning to suffer from the malaise of a purely defensive attitude, and on the other satellites'. With covert action limited elsewhere, Hoyer Millar and his colleagues were keen to discuss options with the US, France, and potentially Yugoslavia.[132] But despite revived British interest, the CIA had now grown pessimistic after years of failure. Although they knew that the Yugoslavs and Greeks were continuing to infiltrate agents and instigate subversion, the CIA assessed in 1958 simply that 'no organized resistance group is known to exist'.[133] The operation was formally terminated by the end of the decade.

Albania was a failure. British covert action had started as a means of defending Greece against communist takeover. It was a classic pilot scheme, beginning with intelligence-gathering and means of testing local resistance. Although SIS and the Foreign Office saw some glimmers of hope for broader insurrection, developments in Albania derailed any wider plans for a liberation strategy across Eastern Europe. It may have remained a special case throughout the 1950s, but Whitehall's cold warriors had to go back to the drawing board when thinking about how best to use covert action to undermine the Soviet position behind the Iron Curtain.

3

PINPRICKS

The Early Cold War

What could be done in the way of economic warfare or subversive activity or through other action which amounted merely to pinpricks?

Clement Attlee, 1950[1]

British covert action drifted aimlessly as Operation Valuable in Albania flailed in late 1949. Nobody in Whitehall knew what to do next. Scratching their heads, Britain's cold warriors could only agree on one thing: liberation had failed. And so a deep malaise—and some serious soul-searching—set in. The Russia Committee, suffocating under piles of paper, had proven inadequate for the prosecution of a more offensive campaign. Even its chairman, Patrick Reilly, dismissed it as 'pretty ineffective' and, by 1951, the chiefs of staff lost interest altogether. They gave it up, according to Reilly, 'in disgust'.[2] The most senior diplomats also floundered, with Gladwyn Jebb, now a deputy under-secretary playing a key part in formulating Britain's post-war global role, forced to trawl through dry ministerial statements in a vain attempt to decipher if any overarching approach to the Cold War existed at all.[3] Even then, he was only able to discern what policy might 'appear' to be.[4]

It is commonly assumed that, after a brief and reluctant flirtation with covert action in Albania, Clement Attlee shied away from such provocative tactics.[5] In reality, covert action continued to appeal. Britain nurtured remarkably ambitious foreign policy objectives: to remain a world power; to keep the relationship with America 'special'; to resist Soviet communism; and to ensure that the Middle East and Asia remained stable, prosperous, and friendly.[6] These objectives looked impressive on paper and soothed the

precious psyche of a country visibly in decline, but there was one rather
obvious snag. The diplomats begrudgingly admitted that these responsibilities now proved too great for Britain's economic and military strength.
Their impecunious colleagues across the road in the Treasury, ever keen to
balance the books, warned against carrying 'too heavy a burden'. Exasperated,
the Treasury accused the Foreign Office of underestimating the risks of
general economic collapse, pointing out that Britain was already seriously
overstrained. The diplomats therefore faced a trade-off: to sacrifice global
influence by revising ambition downwards or to sacrifice standards of living
in order to increase military strength.[7] Within this context, covert action
formed an appealing means of plugging the gap—of ignoring the trade-off
altogether and refusing to face up to the humiliation of decline. Why, planners wondered, commit troops somewhere when quieter, less direct, means
could shore up Britain's position more cheaply?

Egged on by Gerald Templer, vice chief of the imperial general staff, and
a number of other military heavyweights, Jebb now criticized his own side.
Well-built and forthright, he could be a formidable opponent.[8] Long sympathetic to the role of covert action because of his wartime position with
the Special Operations Executive (SOE), he criticized the Foreign Office's
approach as lacking 'co-ordination and central direction'. As a result, he
argued that officials had treated each covert operation in isolation and
wasted time on preparatory spadework which might have been carried out
by some central planning machinery.[9] The Secret Intelligence Service (SIS),
he continued, was the one body 'in a special position to participate actively
and purely offensively in the prosecution of anti-Communist or anti-Soviet
measures'. Yet its operations were restricted both by lack of clear policy
guidance and poor coordination with the military.[10] The British approach
was still too reactive and too ad hoc.

Other diplomats, led by William Strang, the new permanent under-
secretary keen on organization and forward thinking, attempted to fill the
vacuum with an approach they termed national deviationism. The idea was
simple: to 'weaken the Soviet grip on the European satellite States before
their peoples become so imbued with Soviet propaganda as to follow the
lead of the Soviet Government without demur'. Strang believed that the
end of the 1940s was a crucial time when the Soviets were most vulnerable
as they had not yet solidified power in Eastern Europe. This vulnerability
could be exploited by subtly highlighting the virtues of religion, nationalism, and personal freedom in order to supplant communist doctrines before
they took hold. As with all the best covert action planning, deniable measures

would quietly complement overt activity. In this case they supported a broader political strategy of splitting national communism from Stalinism.[11] Tactics involved diplomacy, economic inducements—and covert operations. Instead of liberation, therefore, Strang sought to undermine Soviet control subtly and 'to encourage the emergence of "national deviationism" in the other orbit countries'.[12] On 27 March 1950, Bevin endorsed the approach. Although it proved optimistic, not least because it was a theory based on the sole example of Yugoslavia,[13] the principles underpinning national deviationism formed the blueprint for a new phase in covert strategy.

Meanwhile, the Foreign Office established a new body in 1950 to energize Britain's flagging efforts: the benignly named Overseas Planning Section. Designed to provide the necessary drive behind possible actions,[14] it became the section of the Foreign Office most closely concerned with covert operations.[15] Drive was certainly an apt word as, upon formation, the Overseas Planning Section put out a call for covert action proposals to British missions across the world. It was 'ready to consider any scheme' from Ankara to Warsaw, from Bangkok to Santiago.[16] Indeed, one of its very first activities was to design and coordinate measures to loosen the hold of communism in Southeast Asia. Importantly, this included countries already under communist control, as opposed to those merely under threat.[17] Significantly, and learning from Albania, it also welcomed advice from missions overseas on 'pitfalls to be avoided'.[18]

Whitehall's planners informed heads of missions that for some time they had been thinking about extending the scope of anti-communist activities overseas beyond propaganda. They had 'been considering what could be done by economic and other means (not excluding subversive and clandestine operations) to forestall and counteract the spread of Communism, and to hamper the activities of Communist Parties and Governments'.[19] Despite the failure of liberation, covert action remained on the table. Schemes increased—but in number rather than provocativeness. Even so, compared to the intelligence-gathering aspects of SIS's work, covert action still encompassed a relatively small percentage of secret activities.[20]

Bevin sidestepped

This proliferation of small-scale operations formed a new approach: pinpricks. It was a product of recent trends, from acknowledging the failure of liberation to plans to drive a wedge between national and Stalinist communism.

It also resurrected some of the ideas that Stewart Menzies had originally put forward in 1948. Whilst assassination schemes fell by the wayside, his less controversial proposals to spread discord and nuisance now carried more weight.[21] By 1950, Jebb conceded that victory was not possible in the Cold War and disruption remained the core objective.[22]

Menzies had recently turned 60 and been chief of SIS since 1939. Despite some setbacks, the war enhanced his professional standing and, by 1950, he had gained a remarkable amount of experience in the secret world. Although he rarely left his red-carpeted fourth-floor office at Broadway, Menzies was an approachable leader with an informal managerial style, even allowing his senior secretary, Miss Pettigrew, to keep a parakeet in her room adjoining his private office.[23] At the pinnacle of British intelligence and a key adviser to a victorious government, Menzies had hoped to retire after the war, only to be persuaded by Alec Cadogan, then the Foreign Office's most senior official, to stay on and oversee the transition to peace.[24] With a reputation for sure-footedness and a keen sense of Whitehall politics, Menzies had become an unassailable player in shaping Britain's approach to covert action.[25]

His ideas now came to the fore. Indeed, it was Menzies who seemingly coined the phrase 'pinprick approach' in February 1950. It sought to test proposals for covert action by conducting small-scale experiments: pilot schemes with limited goals. Demonstrating the synergy between intelligence-gathering and covert action, operations gently tested, prodded, and poked the communists in order to determine whether conditions were favourable. The pinprick approach, which banned violent special operations and sabotage,[26] aimed to chip away gradually at Soviet control by exploiting weaknesses, targeting the economy, promoting dissension, and spreading distrust. Officials felt that there was nothing to lose and, if successful, 'they might well throw grit into the machine of the Communist regimes'.[27]

Pinpricks extended beyond the Iron Curtain. After Chinese forces entered the Korean War in October 1950, Clement Attlee expressed concern about aggressive plans emanating from Washington which seemed to involve starting underground wars around China's vast perimeter. He instead asked for smaller-scale economic warfare and subversive activities which could lead eventually to the settlement of the conflict.[28] This summed up the British approach nicely, but earned little approval in Washington, where the CIA continued to support paramilitary action against the Chinese mainland. Meanwhile, and indicative of Britain's global role, Whitehall attentions stretched as far afield as the USA's backyard. By late 1950, Britain had undertaken pinprick operations in Venezuela, Chile, and even Cuba, where intelligence officers worked with dissidents who refused to cooperate with the Americans.[29] Such operations included action taken by the Trades Union Congress, with which the UK, especially under the Labour government, was happy to liaise without American knowledge.[30]

The new strategy gained approval in another new and top-secret body: the Official Committee on Communism (Overseas). Although formally referred to as the AC(O), the few officials aware of its existence had a habit of calling it the Jebb Committee after its chairman, Gladwyn Jebb. This stuck when, later in 1950, Pierson Dixon took over chairmanship of the now Dixon Committee. It proved a short-lived tradition, as Norman Brook stamped out the nickname, fearing that, given the group's sensitive business, association with a particular person could cause embarrassment and potential security risks.[31] Indeed, its activities were so secret that even its mere existence has only recently come to light. More than sixty-five years on, the government is still battling to prevent historians from glimpsing many of its sensitive papers.

The AC(O) evolved directly out of a top-secret inter-departmental review into potential anti-communist operations conducted in 1949. Attlee and Brook were the driving force. Brook, an outstanding civil servant, organized and ever unruffled, had been cabinet secretary for two years but would serve for a total of sixteen.[32] It was a position which brought him into continued and close contact with the intelligence agencies and allowed him to shape how successive prime ministers approached, used, and funded the secret services. This gave Brook a highly influential, but perennially discreet, voice in the evolution of British covert action. Fed up with the bickering between diplomats and the chiefs of staff,[33] he advised that the most important thing was to satisfy the military that everything practicable was being done to prosecute the Cold War 'with vigour and efficiency, and to give them confidence in the organisation for conducting it'. Brook therefore insisted, against Bevin's protestations, that the chiefs of staff were properly represented on the new AC(O).[34] Attlee, having finally lost patience with Bevin's obstinacy, now felt he had little choice but to create some sort of inter-departmental machinery based in the Cabinet Office to resolve the lack of coordinated thinking on covert campaigns.[35]

Under Brook's guidance, Attlee charged the AC(O) with stimulating, initiating, and coordinating all UK anti-communist activities overseas. This included *inter alia* political, economic, and psychological warfare operations, whilst also providing proper scrutiny.[36] Quietly beginning its business around Christmas 1949, the AC(O) operated at the official level, met regularly, and maintained the very highest levels of secrecy. It brought together only a handful of the most senior cold warriors. Alongside the commanding presence of Jebb sat Patrick Reilly, also of the Foreign Office. A more modest and self-deprecating man with a penchant for Gregorian chant,[37] Reilly, at only 40 years old, had already served as wartime liaison between the diplomats and SIS. Now, he was beginning a new post as assistant under-secretary overseeing defence and security. Christopher Warner, one of the more aggressively anti-communist diplomats, also attended. Maurice Dean represented the new Ministry of Defence, where he was a slightly shy deputy secretary whose occasionally sharp opinions were softened by a keen sense of humour.[38] Stewart Menzies, chief of SIS, also had a seat. Last, but by no means least, was Arthur Sanders, deputy chief of the air force. Although the Foreign Office was still well represented in the AC(O), it crucially no longer enjoyed a monopoly. Persistence had paid off for the chiefs of staff.

Attlee wanted to keep a close eye on his new gang of cold warriors. Accordingly, he chaired a ministerial version, the Ministerial Committee on Communism, or AC(M), to oversee Jebb's work and approve various proposals. In doing so, Attlee, still frustrated by Bevin's obduracy, took this responsibility away from his foreign secretary and chaired the discussions himself.[39] Alongside him sat Bevin, now visibly ill and in decline; Herbert Morrison, Attlee's pugnacious deputy soon to become foreign secretary; A. V. Alexander, the minister of defence; and Hugh Dalton, the chancellor of the exchequer who had overseen SOE and worked with Jebb during the war. In the words of one rising diplomat, Attlee's government was finally 'turning towards the idea of competing with the Kremlin in the matter of subversion'.[40]

In parallel to all this, Brook recommended that 'restrictions on subversive propaganda to Communist-controlled countries and on seeking to provoke others into such actions should be removed'.[41] Bevin now agreed, on the condition that any proposals had to be approved by ministers and the shift in approach did not constitute a free-for-all.[42] Brook was a quiet advocate of unorthodox operations and, surprisingly for a man who valued order so highly, criticized SIS for becoming a career service in which university graduates could serve for life and enjoy promotions and a pension. This, Brook worried, would attract 'the average type of administrative civil servant' who was not interested in the 'more adventurous aspects of secret service work'. He added that SIS 'may be in some danger of becoming too respectable and losing, in the process, some of its former vigour, initiative and enterprise—in short, its buccaneering spirit'.[43] Stewart Menzies strongly objected to this dismissive description.[44]

In the middle of December 1950, Brook submitted the pinprick proposals to Attlee. He reassured the prime minister that they were on a modest scale and were 'the most likely activities to produce a reasonable return for the money and effort expended on them'. Demonstrating British proclivity towards pilot schemes, Brook also informed Attlee that, if successful, Jebb would make further proposals for an extension of covert action.[45] The prime minister met Bevin, Morrison, Dalton, and Alexander, and the quintet approved the proposals together.[46] After years of scepticism about covert action, Attlee had now become a reluctant cold warrior.

Undermining the Soviets in Europe

Covert action against the police in the Soviet zone of Germany was one of the first schemes approved.[47] In fact, Bevin had allowed SIS to discredit senior figures there as early as 1946.[48] According to the head of its German station in 1948, Germany was the 'nursery of SIS', the place in which the service learned to transition from wartime to the Cold War.[49] After the war, Germany was split into four occupied zones, with the Soviets controlling the east. This became the German Democratic Republic, more commonly known as East Germany, in October 1949. Britain, alongside America and France, occupied the rest of the country, thereby providing a useful base from which to launch operations to undermine Soviet rule.[50]

With the establishment of West Germany, SIS headquarters moved to the British embassy in Bonn, but the service kept outstations elsewhere, including West Berlin. The latter soon became the largest SIS unit anywhere in the world, surrounded by communist territory and the Soviet military. Before the Berlin Wall went up in 1961, SIS had easy access to plentiful targets and exploited this to the full.[51] Operations in Berlin benefited from another advantage. SIS activity was paid for by the Germans through occupation costs, thereby relieving the financial constraint which so often hampered British covert action.[52] SIS worked closely with anti-communist resistance organizations left over from the war and also recruited spies amongst the relatives of refugees arriving in the West. Agents working in mass organizations, government agencies, and the ruling Socialist Unity Party were the most prized targets.[53]

Echoing some of the earlier Menzies proposals, covert operations involved measures to lower morale and incriminate senior Soviet personnel. Specific tactics included whispering campaigns, forged documents, and planting evidence. Through this, the British hoped to 'undermine the confidence of the Russians in the loyalty and efficiency of this force'.[54] A lot had changed since Bevin had brusquely vetoed similar proposals two and a half years earlier. If Britain was to maintain its global role and convince the Americans of its reliability as a robust secret partner, the government could no longer afford to dismiss the potential advantages offered by covert operations. Bevin, despite his declining powers, did what he could to ensure they were limited and cautious.

By late 1950, SIS had established dissident groups, some of which were real and some of which were fake, to distribute clandestine propaganda.[55] One such group, established with the CIA in February 1950, was the Association of Victims of Stalinism.[56] Another with which SIS worked to gather intelligence and spread propaganda was a Russian resistance organization, the NTS, based in Frankfurt but with cells in Berlin.[57] Britain also collaborated with the West German Social Democratic Party, and particularly its Eastern Bureau. SIS received a great deal of intelligence from them and also recruited agents working on its newspaper in Berlin.[58] The Eastern Bureau, the head of which was an SIS agent according to East German sources, spread propaganda at the behest of British, American, and French secret services aimed particularly at industrial workers. Meanwhile, its agents rummaged through Soviet army rubbish dumps for anything which could be used to blackmail or discredit soldiers.[59] One operation involved forging Swiss bank account statements and posting them from Zurich to communist officials in East Germany, in the hope that censors would open the envelopes and ask questions. Others included the 'surfacing' of embarrassing documents for use as blackmail and forgeries designed to stimulate distrust among West German communists.[60]

Jointly drawn up by SIS and the Information Research Department (IRD), black propaganda intended to 'mislead and confuse' the Communist security services and encourage defections.[61] It had been British policy to induce defections since 1948, but SIS now had greater tools at their disposal. Targets often had a military or technical background and included Soviet scientists working in East German industry. Yet the new drive saw little success. The few defectors from East Germany came entirely unprompted and by late 1951 not a single scientist with knowledge of Soviet electronics, a highly sought-after prize, had come over.[62] Britain carried on trying though. Operation Dragon Return, persuading scientists in East Germany to defect, continued until 1958.[63]

The East German secret police, the Stasi, soon became aware of British covert action. They accused SIS of creating divisions, encouraging purges, and stoking tensions with the Soviet Union. SIS spies included railway workers on the lookout for military manoeuvres; an engineer monitoring military bases who hid his findings inside a razor with a hollow handle; a housewife watching troops on the West German border and equipped with a shopping bag with a false bottom in which she could hide her camera; and a Stasi informer tasked with seducing the daughter of a Stasi officer in order to gain influence over him. Other sources included a stenographer in the East German parliament, an officer in the energy programme, a deputy director in the Department for Planning and Statistics, someone in the East German state bank, and businessmen. They provided intelligence on military developments, economic policy, trade with Western counties, and relations with Soviet bloc states. Again, intelligence and action were closely linked, with SIS prioritizing high-grade information which could then be exploited. The Stasi believed that such intelligence had specifically enabled measures to disrupt the economy. A Stasi operation, codenamed Lightning, aided by Kim Philby and another Soviet mole, George Blake, in 1954 and 1955 successfully rounded up many of these SIS networks.[64] It was perhaps for this reason that the SIS man in Berlin targeting members of the Soviet armed forces, Roderick Chisholm, was withdrawn at short notice in June 1955.[65]

Meanwhile, the AC(O) coordinated secret channels of communication to permit disruptive operations in Czechoslovakia, Hungary, and Poland. Again, Jebb and Reilly envisioned black propaganda as being the key tool. They planned to disseminate material 'ostensibly produced by dissident elements inside the countries concerned' as well as 'publications produced by refugee groups and apparently disseminated by their own organisations'. On top of this, whispering campaigns sought to compromise communist officials.[66]

Importantly, Menzies, Jebb, and Reilly designed pinprick operations to support broader foreign policy. They complemented a longer-term attempt to enhance the authority of the federal government in Germany, develop popular affinity with the West, and ultimately reunify the country as a means of pushing the Russians back from Eastern Europe.[67] For Jebb, a strong West Germany represented 'a greater power of attraction than the miserable "Government" which the Russians were forced to set up in their zone'.[68] Taken together, the approach was to build up the West with one hand, whilst undermining the East with the other. Meanwhile, the Stasi felt that intelligence was playing a key role in Western containment policy. It informed economic policies and embargoes, but also enabled propaganda and subversion.[69]

The onset of the Korean War in 1950 intensified these efforts. The Foreign Office feared the same thing happening in Europe, namely East Germany being pushed to unify Germany by force. In response, Bevin promoted the independent status of West Germany and allowed it to accede to a plethora of international organizations. At the same time, covert action undermined the confidence of the Russians in the loyalty and efficiency of the East German police. This action was specifically designed to 'reduce the possibility of its being used to attack the Western sectors of Berlin or the Federal Republic'.[70] Bevin ignored the East German Socialist Unity Party and, as part of a broader diplomatic blockade against the East, treated the Soviets as the real authorities.[71] This was also complemented by covert action employed to chip away at communist and Soviet control in the East by splitting the ranks of the Socialist Unity Party, discrediting ministers, and spreading distrust between Soviet and East German authorities. Keeping in line with the diplomatic blockade of East Germany, covert action primarily targeted the Soviet occupying forces—again portrayed as the real authority.[72] Jebb summed it up neatly: British foreign policy, overtly and covertly, sought to 'strengthen the Western zones still further and to force the Russians into realisation that their position in East Germany is untenable'.[73]

Under the pinprick approach various means of covert action worked together. Propaganda sought to intimidate individuals; break their loyalty to the Soviet Union; play on irredentist or nationalist sentiment; and spread disaffection among the satellite populations. This propaganda then overlapped with, and was exploited by, more direct operations which included bribery and sought to shape ministerial statements, protests, and demonstrations.[74] As a joint Anglo–American meeting on political warfare concisely put it: 'mass target operations are useful not to encourage or foster open revolt but to create a suitable atmosphere and framework for carrying out specific operations'.[75] This was a two-way street, for operations also enabled propaganda. For example, Britain used covert action to overcome radio jamming and ensure that Western propaganda reached its intended audience.[76] Special operations were conceived, especially amongst the military, as a 'complementary and subsidiary means of action'. They formed a 'powerful adjunct to comprehensive political warfare plans'.[77]

The pinprick approach also worked hand in glove with deception operations. Although primarily engaged in preventing and preparing for open warfare, deception could play an active role in the Cold War if brought into the realm of political subversion, as one official put it, and coordinated with propaganda and special operations.[78] In return, Menzies promised that SIS would 'willingly give every assistance needed'.[79]

Operation Flitter offers a once top-secret example. It ran from 1950 until around 1955 and used fake radio signals to incriminate leading Soviet officials by linking them to subversive activity.[80] The plan was ruthless: to plant damning evidence on innocent and unsuspecting personnel operating in the West in order to spread suspicion amongst leaders back home, perhaps resulting in a purge. Again, the British felt that dissension at home would distract the Soviets from aggression abroad. General Aleksei Antonov was to be one of the unwitting fall guys, and Flitter set out to destroy his career. Or worse. Antonov, a Soviet general staff officer with dark eyes and slicked-back hair, had served with distinction during the war but was known to SIS as since having been involved in subversive activities. He had seemingly only survived by betraying some of his comrades—thereby crucially providing pre-existing suspicion which could be cleverly exploited. British officials engineered a situation whereby the Soviet Ministry of State Security would acquire, through intercepting a dummy radio transmission, incriminating evidence implicating Antonov in some dissident activity against Moscow. This was publicized alongside stories leaked to the press incriminating other Soviets. The deception plotters hoped these fake revelations would start a chain reaction of purges causing serious embarrassment. They were ultimately disappointed. Antonov was not denounced a traitor, purged and arrested, or murdered. Quite the opposite: he was promoted and went on to become chief of staff of the combined forces of the Warsaw Pact, eventually being buried in Red Square. Despite this particular failure, Operation Flitter continued throughout the first half of the 1950s.[81]

Clandestine economic action against the Soviet bloc also formed part of the pinprick approach. This was not especially new, though, as economic warfare plans to disrupt the Soviets in Austria had been in place since 1948.[82]

Such measures were less controversial than political warfare and presented a smaller risk of escalation. Jebb and his colleagues did not fear reprisals from the Soviets, instead believing that the communists were already doing everything they could to damage British economic growth anyway. Moreover, they deemed it unthinkable that Moscow would resort to a nuclear strike over small-scale economic operations in Central and Eastern Europe.[83]

Patrick Reilly may have been young but he had experience in special operations, having been attached to both SIS and SOE during the war. During the first five years after the war, he had grown deeply disillusioned by the infighting amongst Whitehall's secret departments.[84] Now though, Reilly had a chance to shape a more collegiate approach and, perhaps drawing on his wartime work, favoured covert economic action. Demonstrating the cautious approach, he called for a pilot scheme against one country. This was sensible in that it ensured efforts would not be overextended at the outset. In addition, economic operations were largely unchartered territory for the British in peacetime. Even the most senior officials planning covert action acknowledged that they could not have any real idea of what operations would be effective in the satellite countries until they tried. Pinpricks thus provided a valuable opportunity to teach the British, as one official put it, 'the technique and limitations of the business'.[85] SIS was still learning its craft.

Czechoslovakia seemed a good place to experiment. Prague had already accused SIS of subversion, sedition, and sabotage, forcing Pierson Dixon, the ambassador, to threaten disruption of Czech trade and communications with the West in retaliation.[86] Despite Dixon's repeated denials,[87] Czechoslovakia *was* a target for economic subversion by late 1950 because it was important to the Soviets, offered the easiest chance of success, and presented numerous exploitable fears. For example, the Czechs feared German reoccupation of the Sudetenland as well as Soviet distortion of their economic policy, from consumer goods to heavy industry, which had apparently damaged the Czech foreign exchange position and frustrated the local population.[88]

Economic covert action, combined with propaganda, sought to exploit these issues.[89] By 1951, Attlee had approved proposals 'to hamper the activities of Communist Governments in the economic field'.[90] Examples of operations, termed 'direct action' by Jebb, included launching 'go-slow' campaigns in factories, encouraging defections amongst technicians, attacking the currency, and making capital out of the government-sponsored return of Germans from the Eastern Zone of the Sudetenland.[91] SIS also discussed covert pre-emptive or selective buying. A tactic of economic warfare, pre-emptive buying involved obtaining material from neutral countries simply to push prices up and to deny it to others. Britain had done this during the war to deny the Nazis access to wolframite, used in munitions, from Spain, tungsten from Portugal, and chromite ore from Turkey.[92] Selective buying was associated with war rather than peacetime, and SIS knew that it was not an option to be undertaken lightly—especially given Britain's own weak finances—and, at least until the Korean War had broken out, economic concerns trumped strategic considerations for Britain's export policy.[93] Working covertly through reliable intermediaries, economic action did, however, offer a chance to 'cause considerable embarrassment to Eastern European purchasing agencies and upset the economy of the Soviet Orbit in Europe'.[94]

Planning brought together economic experts from across Whitehall's secret departments. It also involved officials from a shadowy group working with the European Purchasing Commission examining the implications of tightening and relaxing controls.[95] Set up by the Ministry of Supply, the commission held two functions, one overt and the other less so. First, it purchased material in various countries abroad to meet British requirements. Second, it provided the necessary cover to prevent the government from being blacklisted by dealers who threatened to sell products behind the Iron Curtain unless the UK bought them.[96] Intelligence compiled a list of seventeen commodities, none of which were in short supply to the Soviets, which may have formed targets for selective buying. Other targets included machine tools from Switzerland and Sweden, and rubber from Southeast Asia. This all formed part of a broader economic policy, known as economic containment, to impede the Soviet economy during peacetime. Aid, trade, and economic warfare were closely intertwined.[97]

Together, pinprick operations saw early, if intangible, success. They increased pressure on Stalin and contributed to his increasing paranoia. He feared that the operations uncovered by his security services merely formed a small part of a much larger Western subversion campaign. This, in turn, helped bring him into the Korean War. SIS operations, alongside the CIA, also helped instigate a series of purges across the Eastern bloc, notably in Hungary and Czechoslovakia. It is difficult to say how much impact covert action had and whether purges would have happened anyway, not least because Tito's split inspired its own wave of purges from 1948—before the pinprick approach had even begun. Nonetheless, covert action exploited divisions in the Soviet bloc and added to the pressure on Stalin.[98] As George Kennedy Young, an advocate of covert action when SIS station chief in Vienna, put it: 'keeping the Russians annoyed is a rather important part of intelligence work . . . we are trying to breed insecurity about their own people'.[99]

Beyond Europe

Pinprick ideas extended to China and Southeast Asia. As in Europe, propaganda formed the cornerstone of covert schemes and from May 1949 officials established what they called 'a covert propaganda organisation' for the region.[100] This was the Regional Information Office in Singapore, tasked with allowing propaganda to better service the Asian market. It allowed material to be drawn from more local sources and tailored for a local audience. It could therefore be far more credible than that concocted by the IRD in Whitehall, although, with a meagre budget, it got off to a slow start. Its first head was John Rayner, who drew on his wartime propaganda experience with both the SOE and PWE.[101] Meanwhile, Menzies pushed for the use of covert propaganda in southern China to promote dissension between various sections of the Communist Party.[102] Similar to material used in Europe and elsewhere, propaganda was made to look as if it had emanated from locals rather than the British. This was crucial given Britain's official policy of not attacking the Chinese communists or alienating the new government, not least because of any potential impact in Malaya, which had a large Chinese population and where British forces were involved in a gruelling counter-insurgency against local communists.

By mid-1950, officials felt that propaganda was having a considerable effect in Burma and making some contribution in Siam—although once hostilities in the Korean peninsula broke out, Britain was happy to let the Americans take the lead.[103] Extreme sensitivity existed inside Burma about collaboration with the West.[104] The situation here was particularly complex given that internal conflict had broken out after Burma achieved independence from Britain in 1948. The government faced resistance from the local Communist Party and from nationalists. To complicate matters further, the nationalists had been armed and trained by SOE to fight the Japanese during the war and, after independence, renegade Brits joined them in their fight against the central Rangoon government.[105] At the same time, in April 1950, SIS subsequently attempted to recruit agents inside Burma in order to penetrate the left-wing resistance.[106] Once inside, they would check moves towards communism and turn targets into nationalist opposition groups instead. Officials recommended similar action for Indonesia as well.[107] Meanwhile, the Foreign Office considered 'framing or denouncing' correspondents working for communist news agencies suspected of improper activities in the region or 'impeding their operations by Special Operations directed against their equipment, staff, paper, purchases, communications etc'.[108] Here, the approach in the Far East seemingly went further than that behind the Iron Curtain. Clearly advocating sabotage, the proposal was followed up a few months later by plans for covertly 'neutralising' the Vietnam News Agency in Burma.[109] It still fell far short of CIA activity, however, and the British confronted their American counterparts about dangerous special operations arming and supporting Chinese nationalists in Burma. This, they argued, risked pushing Burma towards chaos and communist rule, and dented hopes of drawing it back into the Commonwealth.[110]

Exploitation, both economic and political, also extended to the Far East. Arthur Sanders, deputy chief of the air staff, suggested that it might be 'possible to devise activities in China along the lines of those which were now being worked out for Czechoslovakia etc.'[111] This seems like a rather simplistic one-size-fits-all approach to covert action, and it implied the same exploitation of tensions between the periphery and the Soviet centre. Indeed, a primary objective by 1950 was to loosen the ties between China and Russia.[112] Focusing on the internal tension was perhaps more suitable. Optimistically arguing that the Communist Party were losing ground as the Chinese civil war drew to a close, Menzies sought to use covert propaganda to exploit differences within the party by promoting dissension. Diplomats advocated sitting back and letting the impetus come from inside the country, but ensuring that the UK was ready to exploit it when the internal dissension had developed to a suitable point.[113]

Accurate intelligence was, and remains, crucial to achieve exploitation. Without information about the various tensions, policymakers were clueless as to what to exploit and how. Having already hampered progress in Albania, this proved a fatal problem in the Far East too. The AC(O) admitted to being unaware of the extent to which communism was directed from Moscow and of the precise 'brand' of communism in each country (Titoist, Stalinist, nationalist, etc.).[114] And, by 1950, SIS's presence in China had all but disappeared.[115] Expanding SIS coverage was therefore a primary priority, and diplomats pleaded for more intelligence about the whole area, especially on exploitable conditions in China, what they called the 'Soviet Far East', and Korea.[116] One means of achieving this, aside from increasing secret intelligence capabilities in the region, was through enhanced cooperation with the Americans. The Overseas Planning Section therefore sought to intensify relations with the US to ensure that American intelligence was available to the British as swiftly and wholly as possible.[117] This would then inform covert action by offering an accurate impression of exploitable issues. Coordination with the Americans was easier said than done, though, not least because of Attlee's decision to recognize Mao's China—a move which led to serious problems in sharing intelligence prior to the Korean War.[118]

By 1951, and the end of the Labour government, the majority of British covert action conformed to this pinprick approach, half a decade in the making. It had been shaped by the intensification of the Cold War; the failure of liberation; supporting national deviationism; and consistent military pressure for a more coordinated and proactive anti-communist strategy. The pinprick approach and attendant machinery formed the apotheosis of this struggle. Meanwhile, Bevin lost his monopoly over covert action and Attlee had finally stepped in to ensure some sort of coherence. The result was more activity, but smaller in scale and ambition. Pinpricks sought to undermine Soviet authority and spread dissent, especially among the satellite states of Eastern Europe but further afield too. When conducting such activity, Whitehall's cold warriors combined the different measures in their arsenal, with propaganda often serving as an enabler of operational tactics. The approach also offered some synergy with broader foreign policy. It complemented attempts to strengthen Western interests and make Soviet-controlled areas appear a liability. It offered a sizeable step forward from the days of drift which preceded it and would dominate Britain's approach to covert action—in Europe at least—for years to come.

4

A LONG GAME

Exploiting Rifts Behind the Iron Curtain

Propaganda, to be effective, cannot be merely reminiscent. It needs fresh material, in this case new Communist crimes and contradictions.

Permanent Under-Secretary's Department of the Foreign Office, 1958[1]

Late 1951 saw the return of Winston Churchill to Downing Street. Old, ailing, argumentative, and 'gloriously unfit for government', many have seen this as a moment when Britain returned to wartime modalities.[2] It is commonly assumed that, with the Cold War turning hot in Korea and Vietnam, this extended to a romantic revival of Special Operations Executive (SOE)-style activity across Eastern Europe. Nothing could be further from the truth and in fact pinprick covert action bridged the Labour and Conservative administrations. A remarkable continuity existed as subterranean dealings rose above party politics. Fearful of provoking the Soviets and mindful of his public image, Churchill instead valued personal diplomacy and summitry as he attempted to end the Cold War.[3]

In December 1951, Patrick Reilly visited Washington. Just six weeks into Churchill's second premiership, Reilly, a key architect of the pinprick approach and still overseeing intelligence and security at the Foreign Office, outlined the gist of Britain's thinking to his American counterparts. He quietly warned that 'at this dangerous time the Soviets should not be "pushed too far"' in the satellite states.[4] Trying to manage expectations from the outset, Whitehall's representatives told Washington not to be quite so certain that, under Churchill, covert action would be any stronger than under Attlee. This was a blow to the Central Intelligence Agency (CIA), who had been expecting the opposite.[5] Reilly added that whilst the Secret

Intelligence Service (SIS) could take risks to obtain intelligence, these risks should not be added to by attempting subversion.[6] In doing so, Reilly reiterated the Foreign Office's neat, if unrealistic, desire for a clean distinction between intelligence-gathering and covert action.

Pinpricks therefore remained central to Foreign Office planning. As it had done since 1946, action remained couched within a counter-attacking mindset. According to senior diplomats, this now involved 'positive action designed to compress and disrupt the Soviet bloc' and 'covert action designed to bring about changes in the Soviet Union'. William Strang, still the bookish senior official at the Foreign Office, warned that instigating mass uprisings remained too dangerous. But, he continued, a series of specialist operations against specific targets to disrupt the Soviet economy and military, and to poison the relationships between bloc states and Moscow, could prove effective.[7]

Exploitation continued to feature prominently under the Conservative government. Using the terminology of the late 1940s, Anthony Eden, returning as foreign secretary for a third time, agreed to a series of limited 'psychological warfare operations' targeting 'known weaknesses and contradictions in the Soviet fabric'. These included extremes in wealth and poverty, tensions between nationalism and communism, and the unpopularity of Soviet systems.[8] Soviet 'sore spots' could be prodded to place pressure on Moscow—but this had to be at just the right level. Too little would be pointless. Too much risked war.[9] By the spring of 1952, SIS, in coordination with the CIA, planned to 'exploit suspicions and distrust existing in different parts of the Soviet administrative apparatus', especially relations between political and military officials.[10]

Much of this fell under the banner of the Lyautey principle or Operation Lyautey, held dear by SIS. It took its name from a French general who, seeking shade, had asked for a tree to be planted. When told it would not reach maturity for 100 years, Lyautey simply replied that it had better be planted right away. The SIS approach which borrowed his name involved a patient, long-term effort to undermine communist regimes. Espionage determined weak points and divisions within communist societies, which would then be exploited by carefully targeted propaganda, such as false information connecting communist officials with opposition groups. The aim was to instigate purges of satellite governments, encourage disaffection, and stoke public unrest. When rumours of Operation Lyautey first surfaced, they were dismissed as Soviet propaganda.[11] But now archival files reveal that they were true—and came from the very top of the Foreign Office.

Attempts at holistic thinking also continued uninterrupted, with open and deniable measures still complementing each other. In 1952, for example, Strang emphasized the importance of covert action to enable negotiation from a position of strength.[12] This complemented broader Cold War policy in which the Foreign Office kept negotiations alive, tried not to push Moscow too far into a diplomatic corner, but all the while sought to maintain advantages.[13] As the decade progressed, intelligence warned that Russia would only get comparatively stronger and that now was the time to reach a settlement over Eastern Europe and induce the Russians to withdraw their troops. Pinpricks were central in helping Britain to exploit its relative political strength.[14]

China constituted a lonely area of revised thinking. By 1952, the communists had solidified control and become active in the Korean War. Britain, intent on implementing its 'foot in the door' policy, emphasized a middle approach, involving containment combined with a search for a *modus vivendi*.[15] Within this policy, covert action held decreasing sway. 'Subversive operations inside China', Strang argued, may have had limited local effects, particularly on communications, but would not have been able to affect the Communist Party's policy. Moreover, no rival political force existed inside or outside of China which SIS could support.[16] Once more, despite some initial optimism, the Foreign Office judged engaging in covert action against the Chinese to be hopeless.

Conservative caution

Together, Winston Churchill and Anthony Eden oversaw a period of stability in Britain's approach to covert action in the early 1950s. Elected with a majority of just seventeen seats, the new Conservative government realized that it needed to be extremely careful regarding what could be perceived as warmongering.[17] This drew frustration from Tory hawks who had assumed a change of government would lead to a change of approach. By May 1952, familiar debates about the role of covert action had already resurfaced. Hardliners, including Julian Amery, who had entered parliament at the second attempt in 1950, continued to lament a lack of higher direction, strategic planning, or means of calculating acceptable risk.[18] Amery, aged just thirty-one, used his maiden speech in the House of Commons to argue that the Cold War 'cannot be won by remaining on the defensive' and that 'we must seek to break the communist monopoly on Eastern Europe, setting up resistance movements on the other side of the Russian front'.[19] The likes of Douglas Dodds-Parker, another former SOE-man-turned-MP, and Amery formed a group of a half-dozen Tories, all ex-professionals, who, in their own words, studied the 'Cold War in its widest terms' and tried 'to get something done'. They quickly impressed themselves upon members of the new Eisenhower administration in 1953, deliberately undermining official British policy in an attempt to ramp up anti-communist subversion.[20]

Four factors help explain Conservative caution. First, domestic party politics and electioneering influenced Churchill's thinking. During the 1951 general election campaign, the Labour Party had resurrected some of the narratives which saw them win in 1945. They portrayed Churchill as a belligerent leading 'a gang of war mongers'. The charge stuck and given that the Conservatives only held a slender parliamentary majority, Patrick Reilly recognized that the government could be 'hauled up in parliament on any day to account for its activities in foreign affairs'.[21]

Second, Churchill sought the Nobel Peace Prize. His was a premiership driven by ego and the increasingly frail old man hoped to go down in history as having won the Second World War and ended the Cold War. Partly for this reason, Churchill banned provocative special operations behind the Iron Curtain. Rather like Attlee and Ernest Bevin, he insisted on keeping a close eye on SIS. This proved frustrating given that, as one former official recalled, he was 'always in the bath or asleep or too busy having dinner' when urgent decisions were required.[22] In 1952, Churchill did approve continuing a high-risk operation begun under Attlee in which groups of agents parachuted into Poland and Ukraine. Their aim, however, remained to gather intelligence on Soviet intentions rather than engage in covert action, although the distinction easily blurred.[23] As foreign secretary, Eden was also reluctant to engage in special operations and approved the pinpricks plan he had inherited without enthusiasm.[24] Perhaps this was a hangover from the war, when he had been a determined enemy of SOE, largely owing to petty jurisdictional issues and a deep loathing of Hugh Dalton, the wartime minister responsible. Improbably, Eden would later become a cheerleader for the most aggressive covert actions available to SIS. For now, though, he remained cautious, fearing that such activity would undermine his carefully crafted foreign policies.

Third, continuity existed at the official level. Norman Brook's tenure as cabinet secretary was still in its relative infancy, and he remained unconvinced by American eagerness to confront Soviet Russia.[25] William Strang stayed in place as permanent under-secretary until 1953, setting the tone for much Foreign Office thinking. Likewise, Stewart Menzies stayed as chief of SIS until the middle of 1952 and inevitably continued the pinprick approach he had helped design. By 1952, covert operations accounted for around 15 per cent of SIS's efforts—equivalent to the work of ninety-five officers.[26] And senior SIS officers expected this only to increase.[27] The Foreign Office maintained a close eye on SIS business and whenever Menzies, or his successor John Sinclair, asked for space to engage in 'all of our peculiar illegal activities' without fear of making mistakes, they received short shrift.[28] The diplomats insisted on keeping an adviser inside SIS headquarters, whom intelligence officials disparagingly called the 'watchdog' behind his back.[29] Direct liaison on special operations continued through the Overseas Planning Section and Permanent Under-Secretary's Department, as did liaison on propaganda and suborning communists through the Information Research Department (IRD). In fact, relations between SIS and the Foreign Office became ever closer.[30]

Meanwhile, the Official Committee on Communism (Overseas), now chaired by Pierson Dixon, rumbled on. It charged SIS with what Menzies called 'political and economic warfare activities'.[31] In reality, however, its business was stymied by a lack of interest from Churchill in committees of any sort—even top-secret ones—and gridlock derived from constant bickering between the Foreign Office and the chiefs of staff.[32] Brook, dismissing the military argument as 'rather feverish and muddled', tried to resolve the problems but realized that only Churchill's retirement would suffice.[33] With little initiative to instigate any new approach, the AC(O) stuck to tried and tested pinpricks until its dissolution in 1956.[34]

Fourth, British continuity and caution derived from its role in the Anglo-American relationship, where diplomats hoped to become a restraining influence. Reilly, for example, believed it vital 'to deflect the Americans from unwise and dangerous courses'.[35] In the early 1950s the CIA was a relatively new and insecure organization in Washington with several eager competitors. It still had much to prove and was keen to make its mark.[36] Churchill visited President Truman in early 1952 to warn against provocative operations. He suggested that psychological operations were more appropriate and a lot less risky. Unfortunately for the British, the White House deemed Churchill's proposals feeble.[37] When Truman bluntly cut off the prime minister mid-ramble, it became painfully clear that Britain was now playing second fiddle.[38]

Restraining Washington

Much coordinated activity between Britain and America took place in Europe. By the end of his time in office, Attlee knew that all British covert action behind the Iron Curtain was carried out in full cooperation with the United States.[39] In 1952, a special Anglo–American working group was established to ascertain 'ways and means of discrediting and compromising Soviet and key Satellite officials abroad'.[40]

Despite this transatlantic discussion, rumbling divisions over the scale of covert action lingered. Senior figures, including Harry Hohler, of the Foreign Office's Northern Department, and Alvary Gascoigne, ambassador to Moscow, continued to express concern. They warned that the outbreak of a third world war most likely lay in 'the Americans getting too hot under the collar and taking action "off the cuff"'.[41] Consequently, senior diplomats, having restrained the British military, now targeted the CIA. They sought to 'exert a moderating influence so as to ensure that full account is taken at each stage of the risks involved'. Wary of being dismissed as negative and obstructive if constantly critical of American policy, they decided to indicate agreement in principle with a more aggressive stance, going further than they otherwise would have liked in order to generate as much influence in Washington as possible. Diplomats hoped that this Trojan horse approach would be more effective at shaping policy from the inside than snapping at the CIA's heels from the outside.[42] It may have been a similar strategy used to rein in the chiefs of staff, but the CIA would prove a much more ambitious target.

Once rumbled, Whitehall's deception did not go down well across the Atlantic. Leaders in Washington lamented London's timidity and were quick to use the politically loaded word 'appeasement',[43] lambasting what they saw as naivety and nervousness.[44] Amidst a barrage of criticism, Reilly had to confirm that, actually, yes his government really did oppose 'the encouragement of right-wing, separatist, anti-nationalist groups to engage in political activities looking forward to the eventual breaking up of the Soviet Empire into multiple independent nationalities.'[45]

This was all rather hypocritical, for the Americans had also been deliberately deceiving London. They knew full well that the concept of liberation terrified the British and so Winthrop Aldrich, the American ambassador, advocated a similarly devious, if reverse, posture. He accepted that 'lectures from us on the Russian threat will not dispel this "head in the sand" attitude' and recommended the US merely adopting 'an appearance of flexibility' without sacrificing any of its policies.[46]

Within this hall of mirrors, SIS limited its involvement in ambitious American operations designed to 'roll back' communism from Eastern Europe. Britain offered mere support measures, including providing aircraft to parachute agents into Ukraine from Cyprus.[47] Despite the disagreements, the Americans appreciated these efforts. Frank Wisner, still in charge of covert action at the CIA, once confided that 'whenever we want to subvert any place, we find that the British own an island within easy reach'.[48] Other examples of SIS support involved exchanging intelligence with Washington on the status of operations and sending modest subsidies to try to revive underground networks in Poland. The latter was particularly useful to the CIA given that many Polish émigrés lived in London.[49] Meanwhile, SIS continued to gather intelligence and make preparations for future warfare, including stay-behind networks, but this activity was not designed to constitute peacetime covert action and 'roll back' became a hollow slogan to appease Washington. Many inside SIS and the Foreign Office found all this rather confusing. In summer 1952, one senior intelligence officer recorded that 'at the moment no one knew whether HMG was in favour of the liberation of the satellite peoples or not'.[50]

To their credit, senior British officials were thinking hard about the purpose of operations. When designing covert action it was, and remains, crucial that planners clearly define objectives beforehand so as to avoid escalation, mission creep, and blowback. At every stage, Reilly and Hohler challenged the Americans on what they actually hoped to achieve by aggressive covert action. Was it to force parity with the East? Or was it to disrupt, or even defeat, the Stalinist orbit in Eastern Europe? Frustrated, Reilly accused the CIA of risking a preventative war being unleashed by the Kremlin.[51] These concerns came from the very top. Winston Churchill thought the American approach bankrupt and dangerous. He warned President Truman that it was wrong to encourage resistance forces if the West was not prepared to back them by force.[52] Although this stance was later vindicated by the failed uprisings in Czechoslovakia and East Berlin in 1953, the White House remained unimpressed by Whitehall's pinpricks. Officials felt that the British 'objective now may be to slow us down in carrying out our objectives in the field of political warfare'. In a sign of changing times, they insisted that 'We are going ahead with our general plans in this matter, regardless of British approval'.[53]

As the decade progressed, and with President Eisenhower in the White House, the CIA expanded its operations in Europe, knowing that the Foreign Office were still 'very sensitive indeed on anything that hints of armed liberation'.[54] Nonetheless, officials remained keen to work with SIS wherever possible, although they expected its operations to be focused predominantly on the Balkans.[55] Some within the White House optimistically thought that British covert action, specifically economic operations, would increase on the grounds that open criticism of the Soviet Union might serve as a pretext for Moscow to cancel diplomatic negotiations, whilst creating 'trouble in the Soviet back yard (or front yard) reduces Soviet bargaining power somewhat'.[56] Here at least the transatlantic partners converged, since British covert action did seek to disrupt in order to strengthen the Western diplomatic hand.

Exploiting divisions in Russia's backyard

Joseph Stalin died in 1953. Moscow now sought greater openness and reconciliation, creating tantalizing opportunities for détente. Yet, in a missed opportunity, Western leaders remained suspicious of Soviet motives, and the Soviets remained suspicious of Western policies. It was a fluid and dangerous era, characterized by swirling uncertainty and misperceptions.[57] Despite Stalin's absolute dominance of Soviet politics for two decades, his death had surprisingly little immediate impact upon Britain's use of covert action in Europe. The Joint Intelligence Committee (JIC) predicted that his successors would continue his policies, albeit in a more cautious manner. By 1955, intelligence suggested that Stalin's death had relaxed international tensions but that the Cold War would continue for some time and Nikita Khrushchev, the new premier in Moscow, would focus more attention on the Middle East and Asia.[58] The Foreign Office did conduct a review of likely Soviet reaction to Western activity in Soviet 'sore spots', including Scandinavia, Germany, Austria, Yugoslavia, and Albania. It concluded that Stalin's death allowed the West greater freedom of action without risking war.[59]

Despite this initially optimistic assertion, Churchill's successors shared his concerns about covert action in Europe. Nuclear deterrence was the strategic order of the day,[60] and this proved a double-edged sword for covert action: it pushed warfare underground by emphasizing political rather than military threats, but also increased the risk if covert action escalated into confrontation. In 1955, Anthony Eden, the new prime minister, and Harold Macmillan, then foreign secretary, agreed that now was 'not the time for any major covert anti-communist operations'.[61] Covert action in Europe was problematic: it risked ruining an opportunity for détente, provoking Khrushchev, and undermining Eden's reputation as a global statesman which he so relished. Having finally become prime minister after years of waiting for Churchill to step aside, Eden did not want anything to ruin his time in the spotlight. Instead, and as we shall see, he prioritized the Middle East and colonial territories as targets for covert action.[62]

In 1956, dramatic failures in Eastern Europe proved Eden and Macmillan right. In the summer, SIS headquarters had to accept that the Soviets had rumbled the long-running Operation Jungle. Run by Harry Carr, SIS controller northern area, over almost a decade, Operation Jungle infiltrated émigré agents into the Baltics along similar lines as had happened in Ukraine, Georgia, Poland, and Albania. The main aim was intelligence-gathering and war planning, but a fine line separated this from event shaping. Unfortunately for Britain, the Soviets executed some of the agents shortly after they had landed and turned others so as to launch a long-term deception campaign. It took years for SIS to realize. The operation ended in 1956 with a solemn message to the partisans: 'we can no longer help you. Will be sending no further physical or material help. All safe houses are blown... This is our last message until better times. We will listen to you until 30 June. Thereafter God help you.'[63] The KGB's lengthy and expensive deception operation had proved successful, but it was a rather pyrrhic victory given that SIS activity was more about gathering information than fundamentally challenging Soviet rule.[64]

Despite this bitter blow, other developments offered hope for further SIS intrigues. In February 1956, Khrushchev addressed the twentieth Congress of the Communist Party, and, in an extraordinary speech, denounced Stalin, heavily criticizing the dictator's brutality, his purges, his unlimited power, and cult of the personality. The delegates listened to him in absolute silence inside the huge hall as he spelt out the possibility of competitive coexistence with the West and his disinclination to micromanage local Communist Parties outside of Russia.[65] His remarks were supposed to stay private but Israeli intelligence officers managed to obtain a copy of the speech which they shared with a stunned CIA. Allen Dulles, its head, wondered if Khrushchev had simply been drunk. Either way, it offered too good an opportunity to miss and, with Eisenhower's approval, the speech was leaked to *The New York Times*.[66] The bombshell changed the way people inside the Soviet Union understood their political system, fostered a new wave of public opinion not seen since the 1920s, and created much confusion amongst the population.[67] Khrushchev's argument instigated a process of de-Stalinization which unwittingly gave hope to dissidents across the Soviet bloc, notably in Poland and Hungary. At the same time, the JIC assessed that the Soviet Union was reducing its armed forces in Eastern Europe. Even though West Germany was rearming, Khrushchev oversaw a dramatic decrease in the size of his army from over five million in 1953 to fewer than four million by the end of 1956.[68]

Britain's cold warriors sensed an opportunity, not least because they interpreted coexistence as code for an increase in subversion at the expense of conventional military pressure. Political cooperation would prevent war, but this would leave the Soviets and the West free to compete for relative influence, including through use of propaganda and covert operations.[69] Even before the speech, Ivone Kirkpatrick, who had since replaced Strang as permanent under-secretary, stressed the importance of detecting exploitable weaknesses and causing trouble at home for the Soviets.[70] After the speech, and always keen to attack the Soviets, he assured Britain's ambassadors to Eastern Europe that any ban on covert action did 'not exclude minor operations designed to embarrass Communist governments and keep alive a spirit of opposition to them as well as to foster rivalry and ill-feeling between the governments'.[71] In the mid-1950s, covert action targeted communist fronts and discredited Soviet officials, whilst unattributable propaganda repeatedly stressed the fraudulent nature of the satellite regimes.[72]

Much of this formed a continuation of Operation Lyautey, seeking to turn communists behind the Iron Curtain against each other. Khrushchev's address now allowed for a more discriminating approach to covert action, which had previously relied on mass propaganda and disappointing leaflet drops. The speech demoralized many within the communist elite who could now be individually targeted and exploited.[73] Some scope also remained for SIS to engage in unspecified—and inexpensive—disruptive measures inside Western Europe. In general though, Kirkpatrick accepted that there was 'little we can do by clandestine means to influence the situation in... highly developed European democracies', namely France and Italy.[74] 'Covert propaganda and special operations' in Western Europe, he acknowledged, were 'unlikely to be profitable'.[75]

Curiously, covert action did target Iceland and the Faroe Islands. In the wake of a fisheries dispute, intelligence assessments warned of a dangerous degree of communist control of the trade unions, leaving diplomats fearing that a forthcoming general election might return a pro-communist government.[76] This was made worse by reports that the communists sought to detach Iceland from NATO and spread neutralism across the region.[77] In response, Britain launched a wave of unattributable propaganda alongside a so-called 'cultural offensive' designed to demonstrate Western virtues of freedom and expression. Other operations included a combination of political and economic warfare, such as discrediting key communist officials and covertly funding the right-wing Independence Party. Unfortunately for the West, the 1956 election resulted in a leftist coalition, sending shock waves through NATO and leading to economic inducements to counter Soviet influence.[78]

At the same time, economic warfare targeted the fish trade, with the British legation in Reykjavik borrowing, in its words, 'communist methods'. The plan involved finding new fish markets, buying at a high price and selling at a loss in order to inflict financial damage on Iceland's own fisheries, forcing them out of business.[79] Given previous experience, it was likely that this activity was conducted by a shadowy front company to ensure deniability. This was not the first time covert action targeted Iceland. Owing to its strategic position, it had long been a target of British propaganda and, back in 1949, SIS and the CIA had even planned a counter-coup to be implemented in case of communist takeover.[80]

Eastern Europe, Russia's backyard, was the real prize, and fissures soon began to open. In Poland, Wladyslaw Gomulka, the reformist leader, sought a more national Polish socialism and, in doing so, distanced Warsaw from the international communism espoused by Moscow. Riots, driven by Western propaganda, poor economic conditions, and local reactions to Khrushchev's speech, broke out in June 1956.[81] In October of the same year, a spontaneous uprising erupted across Hungary, taking SIS by surprise. The British likely shared the CIA's assessment of the previous year that no broad resistance movement had emerged in Hungary and that Soviet control had restricted Hungarian resistance to passive, unorganized manifestations. 'Other factors', the CIA wrongly insisted, 'such as physically and psychologically exhausting work norms, material want, and compulsory political activities have further discouraged active resistance.'[82]

Neither SIS nor the CIA instigated the failed revolution in Hungary. Nonetheless, émigrés working for the CIA-funded Radio Free Europe did get overexcited in some of their broadcasts, leaving the station open to accusations of laying the ideological foundations for, and then directing, the uprising.[83] And America did accelerate the revolution by rebroadcasting local radio programmes which had called for rebellion, although the White House stopped short of allowing Frank Wisner to send in arms and rebels.[84] Less quantifiably, it is impossible to determine how years of SIS operations to sow dissension, discredit, and undermine indirectly impacted upon the uprising.

Across the country, rebels, some armed only with kitchen knives and petrol, won a string of small successes, even managing to disable tanks. With Soviet media promising negotiations, it appeared as if the rebels would achieve a miraculous victory. British diplomats and SIS officers looked on in hope but, in one of the darkest periods of the Cold War, at 4.15 a.m. on 4 November, Soviet troops rolled into Budapest and decisively crushed the rebellion with massive military force.[85] The uprising coincided with the Suez misadventure—when Britain, France, and Israel colluded to invade Egypt and reclaim the Suez Canal—and took place a month before an American presidential election. Perhaps unsurprisingly, Whitehall therefore did little as the bloody events unfolded. The JIC monitored the potential for discontent to spread beyond Hungary, whilst Rab Butler, the lord privy seal, explicitly informed parliament that the government had no 'intention of exploiting events in Eastern Europe to undermine the security' of the Soviet Union.[86] This angered some of the more hawkish proponents of covert action. Senior SIS officer, George Kennedy Young, fresh from planning operations across the Middle East, felt that, after attempting to maintain a spirit of resistance, the West had betrayed Hungary.[87] As an energetic vice-chief of SIS, he believed that spies had to remedy a moral stalemate created by the deficiencies of ministers, diplomats, generals, and priests. For Young, SIS was not constrained by the political and moral problems of others.[88]

Importantly, SIS did have the means to do something: officers had already trained bands of dissident Hungarians for stay-behind operations in case the Soviets invaded the West, and it seems that these agents did use British and American weapons hidden in woods around Prague and Budapest against the regime. Given the risks of escalating to a third world war, however, the new SIS chief, Dick White, decided not to deploy the stay-behind teams and watched helplessly from the sidelines.[89] From Washington, the Eisenhower administration conveniently blamed Eden's 'tragic' Suez policy for 'dampening the wonderful chain-reaction that Hungary's fighters for freedom, the living and the dead, began'.[90]

SIS did not lose interest in Hungary after the quashed revolution. The rebels who managed to escape had no intention of giving up the fight and formed an émigré group to continue the struggle from abroad. Usually, as we have seen, the CIA took the lead with such people. This time, however, the Hungarians were keen to avoid being associated with the CIA or any dissidents it sponsored. Again demonstrating the factionalism within émigré movements, they believed that 'the old crew which the Americans are nursing... though not being necessarily reactionary, are certainly somewhat obsolete'. They would therefore need some financial and diplomatic assistance from elsewhere—namely Britain.[91] The CIA was frozen out and, although it received some reports on Hungarian resistance, these were of dubious validity.[92] Meanwhile, young British academics, unaffiliated to the government, decided to help the rebels. M. R. D. Foot, the future SOE historian, and friends from Oxford planned to sabotage a Hungarian railway bridge in support of the dissidents. Foot even wrote to Colin Gubbins, once head of SOE, for advice. Gubbins suggested Foot abandon the amateurish plan.[93]

With Khrushchev's speech, the rise of national communism in Poland, and the Hungarian revolution fresh in British minds, the diplomats of the Foreign Office revisited their approach to covert action in Eastern Europe the following year. Although shaken by the Suez crisis, they smelt an opportunity and agreed on a surprisingly forward approach targeting Poland, Hungary, and Czechoslovakia. Suddenly liberation returned to cautious lips and Frederick Hoyer Millar, the new permanent under-secretary, approved a major counter-subversive campaign against communist-occupied countries.[94] The idea, akin to the Lyautey principle, was simple: to foster an evolutionary development towards Eastern European independence.[95] Whitehall's cold warriors looked to exploit schisms and go on the offensive to 'take advantage of what weaknesses it can find in the Communist camp'.[96] After all, the Soviets had long struggled to eradicate nationalist and ethnic sensibilities in these countries despite the strong presence of a Communist Party.[97] The Foreign Office just needed to find the right balance between fomenting change and provoking Soviet escalation.[98]

This approach maintained the familiar British caution and caveats. It was to be gradual, long-term, and excluded encouraging the use of force, sabotage, rioting, or guerrilla operations by the populations. Eastern Europe, according to Hoyer Millar, was 'an acutely sensitive spot. We must be careful how hard and how often we touch it.' He knew that Khrushchev had the tendency to hit back violently if attacked.[99] A further restriction followed the gruesome death of Buster Crabb, a diver working for SIS. His headless body washed up on a beach after an unauthorized intelligence operation to inspect a Soviet ship in Portsmouth harbour in early 1956. Combined with the Suez misadventure, covert actions now required even closer ministerial approval. Eden was livid at not having been consulted and at the damage done to his delicate personal diplomacy with the Russians. The debacle sparked a thorough review of intelligence operations and how to assess what Eden called 'political risk', ushering in greater political control over SIS.[100]

Hawks such as Julian Amery criticized the slowness and vagueness of the approach, lamenting that in practice it amounted to very little. Propaganda may have sought to keep hope alive, but few people inside the Foreign Office had seemingly thought much about the hope of what, or when, or about how to systematically measure risk and the dangers of provocation. It appeared that an array of ministers, diplomats, and intelligence officers were deciding operations almost on the basis of a coin toss.[101]

Senior diplomats rightly stressed that SIS activity could only support, and not replace, use of diplomatic and economic methods as the main instrument of foreign policy.[102] Overt means therefore included economic initiatives, normalization of political relations, and cultural and technical exchanges.[103] In terms of covert action, SIS channelled discreet support for the creation of national communist governments such as that run by Gomulka in Poland.[104] By the late 1950s, the Stasi noted that SIS was asking its agents in East Germany for any evidence of tension with Poland which could then be exploited.[105] In Czechoslovakia, Poland, and Hungary, SIS stimulated dissent and engaged in what the Foreign Office called 'discreet trouble-making'.[106]

As ever, unattributable propaganda was crucial. Recognizing that 'open Western trumpeting of Soviet misdeeds blunts their edge for neutrals', the IRD took the lead in emphasizing 'Soviet brutality and oppression to discredit the Soviet Union in the eyes of the waverers and neutrals'. But there was a problem. As the diplomats asserted, to be effective, unattributable propaganda could not just be reminiscent. By late 1958, Hoyer Millar recognized that 'we cannot live for ever on the propaganda capital provided by the Hungarian revolution of 1956' because 'in the eyes of the neutrals it has already lost most of its significance'. To be successful the IRD needed 'fresh material, in this case new Communist crimes and contradictions'.[107] Hoyer Millar had a reputation for being rather robust and, true to form, he then made a typically tough suggestion: 'it should be our task to provoke these'. He and his colleagues set about determining 'those targets which we can attack in the reasonable expectation that the risks involved can be limited and where we stand to gain a proportionate success'. In short, they recommended deliberately provoking repression for propaganda purposes. To minimize risk to Britain, the methods were to be 'indirect, gradual, and unspectacular', and in no instance giving any impression of pushing the satellites into revolt. Coming just two and a half years after the brutal suppression of the Hungarian uprising, this was a remarkable plan. Operations intended to compel the Russians to rely overtly on force as well as to grant concessions.[108]

However devious, British operations in Eastern Europe throughout the 1950s remained far less dangerous and dramatic than their Russian equivalents. SIS may have conducted pinpricks and provoked violence, but the Soviets had set up a special department in 1953 to engage in terrorism. Whilst SIS exploited divisions and spread rumours, the Soviet twelfth department provided for, as one recently declassified Soviet document puts it, 'terrorist acts against the most active and die-hard enemies of the Soviet Union and individuals in capitalist counties, especially foreign intelligence agents, leaders of anti-Soviet emigrant organisations and traitors to the Motherland'. The Soviets carried out or attempted—not all were successful—numerous assassinations and kidnappings in Europe throughout the decade.[109] The contrast is stark and it puts SIS covert action in perspective. It was hardly tit for tat. At the same time, the Soviets did use longer-term influence operations as well. They mirrored British activity by targeting the integrity of NATO and exploiting rifts within the alliance, especially the more independent policies espoused by France and the status of so-called second-class partners such as Denmark. Across Western Europe, black propaganda portrayed American troops in an unfavourable light, including spreading fake stories about them being involved in sexual offences and murders.[110]

The Lyautey principle, favoured by SIS, lasted at least until the 1970s.[111] However, the construction of the Berlin Wall in 1961 and the treachery of George Blake in the late 1950s severely hampered intelligence operations behind the Iron Curtain. SIS increasingly left spying in East Berlin to the West German intelligence service. When SIS opened a station at the new British embassy in East Berlin in 1973, it focused on recruiting agents in Third World countries, as it was here that the covert battle for influence now took place. GCHQ provided the bulk of intelligence on East Germany instead.[112]

★ ★ ★

By the 1950s, British covert action in Eastern Europe had achieved a relatively stable pattern. Its roots were firmly planted in the debates of the late 1940s and the ensuing pinprick approach. After much prevaricating and uncertainty, Clement Attlee's Labour government set a clear tone for the future of covert action in Europe. Winston Churchill, and then Eden and Macmillan, merely brought continuity. From Attlee onwards, four things characterized the British approach: exploiting contradictions; fostering national deviation from Soviet communism; trying to keep the Americans onside; and attempts to sow dissension and undermine Soviet authority in East Germany and the satellite states. Understanding how these states interacted with the Soviets and amongst themselves was crucial.[113] Britain had known this since the Soviet–Yugoslav split and continued to weave covert action into its broader Cold War policy. It was a long game, relying on evolutionary and incremental approaches. It was also a delicate game, balancing disruptive pinpricks against the danger of provoking the Soviets into a third world war. So much of the argument was about scale, since some Soviet repression was not necessarily deemed a bad thing, inasmuch as it offered propaganda value. This may have amounted to a British way in covert action in Eastern Europe, but the Middle East formed a different prospect altogether.

PART 2

END OF EMPIRE

5

Operation Boot

Regime Change in Iran

Individual and political parties could still be manipulated to advantage.
Anthony Eden, 1953[1]

As in Eastern Europe, covert action in the Middle East was marked by a striking sense of continuity between the Labour and Conservative administrations. Clement Attlee and Ernest Bevin, as we have seen, used the region as a testing ground for a more proactive approach, but the infamous coup d'état of 1953 in Iran forms the most important example. In the spring of 1951, the new Iranian prime minister, Mohammad Mossadeq, approved the nationalization of Iranian oil. In one blow, he overturned a long-standing agreement which had allowed Britain, through the Anglo-Iranian Oil Company, to enjoy the lion's share of profits.

Shortly afterwards, the Joint Intelligence Committee (JIC) noted that 'the situation in Persia has taken an unfortunate turn'.[2] This classic British understatement belied a growing panic in Whitehall. The government, still struggling with the financial consequences of the Second World War, simply could not afford to lose the revenue—judged to be some £170 million. At over £3 billion in today's money, this was an income stream on which Britain's fragile public finances depended. At a political level, the move was symptomatic of a rising tide of nationalism which threatened to sink Britain's long-held position in the Middle East. The JIC worried that events in Iran would encourage nationalism elsewhere, notably in Iraq, where the UK managed the Iraq Petroleum Company, and Egypt, where it controlled the Suez Canal. Meanwhile, the JIC also warned of the dangers of communist exploitation of the crisis, rendering nationalization a serious Cold War issue.[3]

To make matters worse, Mossadeq, at a stroke, single-handedly dismantled a top-secret Anglo-American plan to prevent Russian access to oil in the event of Soviet invasion. From 1949, the Secret Intelligence Service (SIS) and the Central Intelligence Agency (CIA) had plotted to transform oil production staff into a paramilitary organization, using flamethrowers and special grenades to destroy refineries and plug oil wells. The CIA had managed to insert five undercover agents into the Aramco oil company and took the lead in Saudi Arabia, Bahrain, and Kuwait. SIS, working alongside the Ministry of Fuel and Power, focused on Iran and Iraq. The plan relied on close cooperation with the oil companies and now nationalization scuppered the Iranian angle entirely. Eventually, the panicked chiefs of staff even asked the Americans to consider dropping tactical nuclear bombs on Iranian targets if Britain no longer had control.[4] This made it all the more imperative to deal with Mossadeq.

Whilst the coup in Iran is often seen as an American affair, the plan to overthrow Mossadeq originated in Britain. It was Herbert Morrison, Labour's pugnacious foreign secretary—albeit one with little experience of foreign affairs—who first sanctioned subversion against Mossadeq after Clement Attlee had vetoed military intervention.[5] For all the prime minister's love of committees and official machinery, it appears that the inspiration for this particular covert action came informally from the very top of government, namely Attlee, Morrison, and Richard Stokes, the lord privy seal.

Subversion

Morrison's early plan involved creating a political climate conducive to regime change. Diplomats, such as Eric Berthoud, overseeing economic matters at the Foreign Office, and James Bowker, head of its Eastern Department, first turned to Ann 'Nancy' Lambton. A renowned Persianist, she had served as a press attaché with the Ministry of Information in Tehran during the war. Advising the Foreign Office, Lambton, an austere and patrician academic, warned that it was impossible to do business with Mossadeq.[6] She therefore recommended covertly collaborating with sympathetic voices inside Iran in order to induce economic and social reform. At the same time, she advocated 'covert means' to undermine Mossadeq. This would, she hoped, 'create the sort of climate in Tehran which is necessary to change the regime'.[7] Similarly, Lambton and Geoffrey Furlonge, of the Foreign Office's Eastern

Department, agreed that propaganda should be used to demonstrate that any economic hardship in Iran was purely the fault of its own government, not the oil company or Britain.[8] Lambton's advice laid the foundations for the coup two years later.[9]

In June 1951, three months after the nationalization, Lambton recommended Robin 'Doc' Zaehner as the ideal man to conduct the subversive campaign.[10] An eccentric Oxford academic who had served in Iran with the Political Warfare Executive during the war, Zaehner was fluent in Persian, well connected in Tehran, and no stranger to peacetime operations. In line with the British tradition of turning to the same old faces, Zaehner had served as an interpreter alongside David Smiley training dissidents for infiltration into Albania back in 1949. Smiley remembered him as a 'most useful and entertaining member of staff'.[11] Indeed, Doc was a bibulous bon vivant who, when in Tehran, introduced the embassy staff to opium.[12]

Although Zaehner reported to the Foreign Office's Eastern Department, his brief came directly from Herbert Morrison himself and demonstrated a rare example of the Foreign Office rather than SIS taking the operational lead.[13] With access to closed files from this era, the official historian Michael Goodman has argued that Zaehner's 'sole purpose for being there was to foster regime change'; to overthrow Mossadeq and bring Sayyid Zia to power.[14] Zia, the initial British favourite, was a pro-Western former prime minister who had led a coup back in 1921. He too was personally recommended by Lambton.[15] Monty Woodhouse, head of SIS's Iran station, also felt British objectives were clear: 'to remove Musaddiq from power, to establish a pro-Western government, and to undo so far as possible the damage done to Britain's oil interests'.[16] As early as September 1951, Morrison and Attlee, along with William Strang, were busy preparing the line to be adopted once a more reasonable Persian government had been put in place.[17]

Like Lambton, Zaehner believed that Britain's best bet was covert support for factions who held similar interests to the UK and to create a network of disaffected opponents of Mossadeq.[18] This approach influenced wider Foreign Office thinking about how best to counter broader nationalism deniably. Strang later suggested using a combination of open and deniable measures to create a class with a vested interest in cooperation.[19] In Iran, the Foreign Office slowly and subtly set about constructing a climate conducive to revolution. By November, word from the embassy was that 'the chances of getting rid of Mussadiq within the next few weeks are reasonably promising'—although that did not mean that 'the operation of ousting him will be an easy one'.[20]

This programme of political action and manipulation was spearheaded by Zaehner's wartime anti-Nazi agents, the Rashidian brothers. Known simply as the brothers, they ran an influential network of associates in the bazaars, the press, and the parliament. Assadullah, Saifullah, and Qadratulla Rashidian were merchants who managed an import business supposedly dealing in British films. In reality, they used it as a means to channel SIS money to local supporters.[21] Zaehner tasked the brothers with mobilizing opposition to Mossadeq in the urban areas. Meanwhile, Sam Falle, oriental secretary at the embassy in Tehran, was busy cultivating the younger anti-Mossadeqists.[22] Galvanizing the opposition was crucial. As in Europe, propaganda remained a cornerstone of British covert action. It helped to create an atmosphere conducive to a supposedly spontaneous uprising.[23]

Bribery also formed a key means of exercising covert political influence. As we have seen, lack of local intelligence prevented Attlee's suggestion of bribery in Albania from coming to fruition. This time, however, SIS, working closely with the Foreign Office, knew exactly whom to bribe. As early as September 1951, there was talk of a fairly generous payment being made to Zia,[24] whilst Woodhouse estimated that SIS paid the brothers £10,000 every month.[25] Much of this went on merchants in the bazaar—a fulcrum of activity and rumour where public attitudes were constantly being shaped. SIS also bribed newspaper editors to place anti-Mossadeq material in the press, and were able to purchase a number of leading politicians inside parliament.[26] The latter was done as deniably, indirectly, and discreetly as possible.[27] What was clear, however, is that the British knew allowing free elections would eliminate moderate politicians and, as the chargé d'affaires put it, pack the parliament with 'emotional, ignorant national extremists and groups willing to look to Russia for leadership'.[28] As ever, British diplomats kept a close eye on the budget. Bribery and other political action was financed by the Secret Vote—money which Morrison rather tight-fistedly hoped the Anglo-Iranian Oil Company would reimburse if the operation proved successful.[29] When one dissident demanded a £2 million bribe from Julian Amery, Woodhouse remarked that the price was 'a bit stiff'.[30] Meanwhile, Zaehner offered advice on who was not to be entrusted with funds.[31] These activities seemed to be having some success by April 1952. Officials in the American State Department, seemingly unaware of British covert action, began noticing how the Iranian press had almost unanimously turned against the Mossadeq government, with bazaar merchants and politicians not far behind.[32]

The JIC insisted that the key to resolving the crisis was in finding an acceptable successor to Mossadeq and, although Zaehner was still cultivating Zia, an opportunity soon arose to support someone else's bid to topple the prime minister.[33] Mossadeq strongly suspected that British agents were manipulating elections held in early 1952 in order to undermine him and destabilize the country.[34] In response, he suspended the election, engineered a constitutional crisis by publicly demanding war powers from the young shah, and then dramatically resigned. His replacement was to be Ahmad Qavam—another tough, uncompromising, and pro-British politician who had also been recommended by both Lambton and Zaehner. Despite having some reservations about his support and venality, Anthony Eden, now foreign secretary, praised Qavam for being 'a strong man who will stand for no nonsense'.[35] Patrick Reilly, an architect of pinpricks in Europe, Julian Amery, never far from the action, and SIS were all involved in this manoeuvre, which likely involved applying pressure on the malleable shah to appoint Qavam whilst simultaneously bribing members of parliament to bolster his support there.[36] The British embassy in Tehran ruefully noted that 'the wheels of Islam need more lubricating than those of other faiths'.[37] Amery, revelling in clandestine diplomacy, secretly met Qavam in both Paris and London, encouraging his bid for power.[38] Meanwhile, Sam Falle asked Zaehner to contact Qavam discreetly to give him, in Falle's words, 'a little encouragement'.[39] Selwyn Lloyd, then serving under Eden in the Foreign Office, gave a 'green light' to Qavam shortly afterwards.[40]

Unfortunately for the plotters, protests soon erupted and the shah lost his nerve. British officials tried to persuade him to back Qavam more strongly, insisted that they and Qavam shared no secrets about which the shah did not know, and even pressured the BBC to play down reports of unrest which served only to weaken Qavam.[41] Nonetheless, within a week the shah had reappointed Mossadeq. Disillusioned, the British felt they had left too much to the Iranians, put too much faith in a civilian, Qavam, rather than a military strong man, and not acted jointly with the Americans.[42] It was the power of the mob as a political force, however, which served as the key lesson from this episode. Oliver Franks, the British ambassador in Washington, derided the rioters as hysterical 'psychoneurotics' and 'homicidal fanatics',[43] but George Middleton, the chargé d'affaires in Tehran, now knew that Britain would need the mob on its side if it was to instigate change. He argued that 'the only immediate hope is a <u>coup d'etat</u> with or without the knowledge or consent of the Shah'.[44] Although he was not advocating a coup engineered by the British,[45] diplomats back in London wondered what steps they might take to set one in motion.[46]

Eden sympathized with this view and hoped that 'a local Neguib could be found' for Iran. This was a reference to the Egyptian coup which, led by General Mohammad Neguib, had overthrown King Farouk in July 1952.[47] By this time, however, Mossadeq had got wind of British scheming and lost patience. He accused London of daily interference in Iranian affairs and even made allegations about intelligence agents planting bombs across Iran,[48] before breaking off diplomatic relations in October 1952, evicting all diplomats and SIS officers. For just over a year, the British strategy had been to create a climate conducive to regime change. Through bribery and propaganda, it sought to cultivate existing opposition forces and mobilize what was already there.[49] But this programme now came to an abrupt end.

Enter the CIA

Despite being banished from Iran, SIS managed to contact the brothers regularly via its station on Cyprus. On one occasion Norman Darbyshire, of SIS's erstwhile Iran station, even succeeded in meeting one of them in Geneva.[50] Nonetheless, orchestrating regime change from such a distance would have been practically impossible and so SIS turned to the CIA for help.

Unfortunately for Britain, Washington was unreceptive. Initially, the CIA was only interested in working with SIS on stay-behind activities in case of a communist coup. Back in 1951, they had agreed to support a 'rump' shah government under such circumstances.[51] As 1952 progressed, keen to challenge colonialism and preoccupied with his own election campaign, President Truman had consistently urged London to accept nationalization and cut a deal with Mossadeq, warning of the dangers of communism if a political vacuum emerged.[52] Frustrated that the British were stubbornly preoccupied with their oil interests, Truman and his secretary of state, Dean Acheson, saw Mossadeq as a potentially effective bulwark against communist penetration in Iran.[53] After Qavam fell, Acheson upped the pressure on London to settle the oil dispute. He warned that if Mossadeq lost power he would only be succeeded by a more left-wing government.[54] The Americans were amenable to using covert action, particularly propaganda, to bolster the shah's position,[55] but did not agree with the need for a coup.

In October 1952, the British half-heartedly raised the possibility of just such a coup with the State Department and CIA, but they dismissed it as impracticable. The following month, London's approach stiffened and, on 25 November, Bernard Burrows, representing the embassy in Washington, formally recommended a coup. The Americans assumed that, in the intervening weeks, SIS had reported that its contacts in Tehran were able to pull it off. The State Department was unconvinced. Rather than overthrow Mossadeq, its officials had been planning to support him openly. They wondered whether the timing of the British proposal was designed to forestall unilateral American assistance. To make matters worse, although the CIA deemed the project feasible and plausibly deniable, the State Department worried that 'many things could go wrong' and the Iranians would point the finger at the West with or without evidence. This could undermine the American position not just in Iran but elsewhere. Burrows acknowledged that the scheme would be risky but provided only general answers to US concerns. In response, the State Department politely declined the coup offer.[56] When Woodhouse lobbied Walter Bedell Smith in December 1952, the director of central intelligence simply responded that 'you may be able to throw out Musaddiq, but you will never get your own man to stick in his place'.[57] In return, Nancy Lambton speculated that American intelligence had long been supporting Mossadeq as a counter to communism.[58]

The State Department was particularly concerned about SIS attempts to instigate tribal uprisings in the south as part of the anti-Mossadeq plot. Since nationalization in 1951, the CIA had suspected that SIS—alongside the Anglo-Iranian Oil Company—had been bribing southern tribes who lived near the oil fields and promoting separatist activity across the region. Although Britain denied it, the Americans suspected plans were afoot for a repeat of SIS tactics from 1946 when coordinated tribal uprisings put pressure on the Tehran government. By late 1952, the State Department warned that such a revolt could only be instigated after a leftist coup and not to overthrow Mossadeq.[59] American diplomats also scotched risky British plans to leak false intelligence to Moscow implying that Washington was prepared to 'write off' Iran, seemingly in the dubious hope that this would feed back to Mossadeq who would then adjust his policies. Likewise, the Americans refused to consider a so-called 'big bluff', whereby the Russians would be enticed to believe that a leftist coup would be the signal for a

British counter-coup in the south. It was simply too dangerous and could have led to the split of Iran.[60]

In response to American caution, the British played their own anti-communist card. As early as 1951, long before Mossadeq severed diplomatic relations, the Foreign Office and SIS sought to emphasize that his staying in power increased the threat from communism.[61] In Tehran, Sam Falle suggested taking a deceitfully self-sacrificing line with the Americans by pretending to put communism ahead of the oil issue and opposing Mossadeq because he failed to take active steps against communism—not because he was anti-British.[62] Other diplomats emphasized the economic angle and attempted to highlight the potential repercussions for America. They warned that Venezuela might follow suit, thereby directly threatening American economic interests. Alternatively, Saudi Arabia or Iraq might nationalize their own oil industry, which could undermine Western defence postures that relied on Middle East oil.[63] These themes were emphasized at the highest level by Churchill and Eden too.[64] The objective, to draw the Americans into Britain's covert action, was clear but unsuccessful. In late 1952, the CIA insisted that, in taking a stand against Mossadeq, the UK was 'motivated primarily by considerations of prestige and precedent'.[65]

The inauguration of President Eisenhower in 1953 brought a more amenable ally. Churchill and Eden, pleased at the election of an old friend, sensed a change in the political landscape and, concerned that SIS's agent network in Tehran was going to waste, Woodhouse visited Washington just two weeks after Eisenhower's election.[66] After an initial show of reluctance, the new president agreed to overthrow Mossadeq—albeit in return for a share of the oil.[67] All the while, Churchill himself seemingly never bought the communist line he was trying to sell and, as late as May 1953, confessed that despite the State Department's irritating obsession, as he put it, 'there were no indications that Persia was nearer to Communism now, in spite of our refusal to give away everything, than she was 19 months ago'.[68] Although Churchill and senior diplomats found working through the Americans frustrating,[69] cooperation paid off in the long run. With the CIA taking the lead, the UK suffered far less criticism. Working with America increased Britain's plausible deniability. It allowed London to hide behind the actions of its larger ally and escape some of the long-term consequences.

Perhaps predictably, Anthony Eden soon developed cold feet. Despite initially backing Zaehner's efforts, he had already attempted to slow SIS planning once in late 1952, instead emphasizing negotiation and the need for

American support.[70] His Foreign Office followed suit and, according to Woodhouse, 'repented of its temerity in sending Zaehner to Iran on his subversive mission'. Cautious diplomats became alarmed by what they had started and had grown nervous about the risks. Eden happily handed operational responsibility for the brothers over to Woodhouse and SIS, away from his own Eastern Department. By the spring of 1953, Eden and senior Foreign Office officials, including Strang, as permanent under-secretary, and Pierson Dixon, as head of the AC(O), were mostly unenthusiastic.[71] Dixon panicked at the 'underhand action of uncertain effectiveness and doubtful morality'.[72] He feared it would be an embarrassing failure which would compromise Britain's reputation.[73] Similarly, Archibald Ross, new head of the Eastern Department, believed 'it was an illusion to think that we could influence events in Persia'.[74] In fact, Ross even tried to conduct his own last-minute negotiations with Mossadeq when travelling to the region. He did so without authorization and was bluntly told to drop the matter when he returned.[75]

Eden had many possible reasons for scepticism. Perhaps it was because, as he recalled in his memoirs, Mossadeq's position seemed at its strongest at this time and he had 'launched a violent attack on the court through every organ of his propaganda machine'.[76] Perhaps it was because, in early 1953, Eden agreed a new negotiation stance with Washington after a string of disagreements about compensation.[77] Or perhaps it was because the shah had become a nervous wreck keen to escape from Iran entirely.[78] Either way, Woodhouse and Zaehner met Eden in an attempt to change his mind. The meeting went badly and Zaehner, who also had grown disillusioned, oozed pessimism about the prospects of a coup. For Strang and Dixon, this settled it: the operation was dead. Eden remained negative, but left open the option of cooperating with the CIA. Visiting Washington in early March 1953, he had tentatively discussed the need to rally any assets which might support a replacement of Mossadeq, although, at this stage, there was no obvious candidate.[79] Foreign Office diplomats agreed to let Woodhouse try to bolster support across the Atlantic—presumably confident that he would fail. Amidst much prevarication in Whitehall, Woodhouse gave up on the idea of spending so much money and time on what seemed an unlikely prospect. He reluctantly recommended that the operation be wound up; Eden gladly accepted.[80] Boot was dead.

To everyone's surprise, the Americans were now becoming more eager for action. Although most discussion still revolved around covert action against the leftist Tudeh Party and liberation operations in the event of a communist coup, the focus increasingly turned towards Mossadeq as he ramped up the pressure on the shah. By February 1953, the CIA felt he was out to destroy the monarchy—long seen as a force for stability—altogether. He had over-played his hand.[81] As winter turned to spring, officials in the CIA and State Department began planning how best to ensure a smooth transition of power away from Mossadeq.[82] There was much relief inside SIS and, according to Donald Wilber, a CIA officer involved in the planning, 'the British were very pleased at having obtained the active cooperation of the Agency and were determined to do nothing which might jeopardise US participation'.[83]

In London, senior diplomats, including Dixon, quickly convened a top-level meeting on the 'non-oil aspects' of the crisis.[84] The political atmos-phere was changing in Whitehall too. By April, Eden was far from Whitehall recovering from a serious illness, leaving Churchill to take personal con-trol over the Foreign Office in his absence. It was, according to Strang, 'rather wearing'. Churchill relished the work, but brought unorthodox methods, resulting in 'a good deal of wear and tear' to the official machin-ery. He sometimes bypassed the senior diplomats altogether,[85] and on other occasions did business over three-and-a-quarter-hour lunches quaffing champagne, port, brandy, Cointreau, and a couple of whisky sodas to finish. The likes of Pierson Dixon could not keep up. When not lunching, Churchill found Foreign Office telegrams too numerous and too verbose—and thought the diplomats too prone to appease the likes of Mossadeq, whom he insisted on calling 'Mussy Duck'.[86] Most importantly, Churchill was far less inclined to accept the pessimistic judgement of officials than Eden and, according to Woodhouse, 'the idea of launching a coup against Mossadeq was much less distasteful to Churchill'.[87] It appears that, with Churchill at the helm, the operation was resurrected—and called Operation Heaven.[88]

Despite the uncertainty amongst senior diplomats, John 'Sinbad' Sinclair, the new chief of SIS, had quietly allowed his staff to continue drawing up plans with the CIA.[89] An upright military man and director of military intelligence during the war, he had taken over following the retirement of Stewart Menzies in 1952. Sinclair offered no great intellectual leadership but was humane, with a soft voice and kindly demeanour, and proved popular among his subordinates. Even Kim Philby expressed regret at having lied to him. For all his personal warmth, Sinclair was not a particularly strong per-sonality. He often deferred to Strang in the Foreign Office and failed to keep a close enough eye on his more buccaneering staff at SIS.[90]

Joint operational planning with the CIA, much of which took place on Cyprus, drew on SIS's impressive knowledge of Iranian personalities. They nominated Fazlullah Zahedi, a general and former chief of police known to be ruthless and manipulative, as the new prime minister.[91] SIS agreed to supply $25,000 to Zahedi, whilst the CIA paid $35,000. To support Zahedi's coup, SIS's agent network, led by the Rashidian brothers, would approach and bribe senior politicians. In the following months, money, around $11,000 per week, went to politicians and newspapers, whilst an unnamed terrorist group likely to have been the Fedayan-e Islam took direct action against Mossadeq and his circle. All monies were to be transferred using SIS assets inside Iran. SIS also proposed that Kermit Roosevelt, of the CIA, assume command in Tehran in the final phases of the operation.[92] Despite being removed from the field, British personnel remained heavily involved in the planning of an operation which, after all, they had started.

The negotiations and planning were tense. SIS representatives seemed envious of the financial resources available to the CIA, whilst the Americans knew they had to rely heavily on British assets but did not trust SIS enough to reveal their own sources. Darbyshire already knew that the CIA had two major agents in Iran and so, not willing to reveal their identity, Donald Wilber simply named a station agent and sub-agent instead. SIS seemingly never uncovered their true identities. As the planning continued, CIA staff met their SIS counterparts in Washington and London as well as Nicosia. In each case they met inside British premises, presumably to keep SIS out of CIA buildings, as they had been so keen to do regarding Albania.[93]

On 14 June 1953, the SIS/CIA planners submitted a final draft to Whitehall. Roosevelt and Wilber arrived at SIS headquarters the following day and, in a nondescript conference room marked only with a sign reading 'curb your guests', they met SIS officers including Norman Darbyshire and Monty Woodhouse. The SIS representatives apparently had high confidence in the plan,[94] which, drawing on British groundwork laid since 1951, involved building up the size and effectiveness of opposition groups through bribery and a massive propaganda campaign.[95] Propaganda themes included portraying the prime minister as pro-Soviet and anti-Islamic: a security threat, corrupt, and economically incompetent.[96] In doing so, Whitehall's planners built on the idea of exploiting so-called 'contradictions' which was simultaneously being employed across Eastern Europe. Accordingly, the Information Research Department and SIS covertly exploited rifts between various internal factions inside Iran. These included tensions between the rich and poor, communism and Islam, communism and nationalism, and modernization and traditionalism.[97]

Propaganda extended to false flag operations, a particularly provocative tactic seeking to incriminate targets so as to generate public hostility.[98] The plan included staged attacks against respected religious leaders, which others would then blame on Mossadeq. It also suggested that fabricated documents would 'prove' links between Mossadeq and the communists. It even appears that CIA agents made threatening phone calls, again in the name of the communists, and planned sham bombings. SIS was probably not directly involved in executing such activity by this time—but its officers certainly sanctioned and condoned it.[99] Meanwhile, Mossadeq accused British 'money and brains' of being behind a series of anti-American slogans, ostensibly painted by communists on walls across Tehran.[100]

By galvanizing opposition actors and disseminating provocative propaganda, covert action created an atmosphere in which overenthusiastic third parties were more likely to engage in assassination. Anti-Mossadeq factions committed a wave of kidnappings and murders prior to the coup. This had already included the tough and loyal chief of police, General Mahmoud Afshartus, murdered in April 1953. After he had been tortured to death, Afshartus's body was left outside Tehran to emphasize government vulnerability. Darbyshire has since claimed that the kidnapping of Afshartus was part of Operation Boot and was intended to provide a morale boost for the opposition. The actual murder, however, was conducted unbidden by a third party who had lost his temper with the authorities and become carried away. Afshartus's brutal death undoubtedly weakened Mossadeq's regime—and SIS had helped to lay the groundwork. A similar example concerns black propaganda planted inside a newspaper accusing Hessein Fatemi, Mossadeq's right-hand man, of being a thief, a homosexual, and a Christian convert. This, as one leading scholar argues, 'was an open incitement to murder'.[101] Not for the last time in the Middle East, propaganda and political warfare deliberately whipped the public into a violent fervour. This would soften the ground for Zahedi's power grab.

A simple military coup alone would not have worked, not least because junior officer grades in the army were seemingly riddled with communists.[102] After much discussion, SIS and the CIA agreed that the shah would have to be pressured into signing a royal decree sacking Mossadeq and replacing him with Zahedi, thereby making the coup more legitimate.[103] John Sinclair, Winston Churchill, and the caretaker foreign secretary, Lord Salisbury, all approved the plan on 1 July 1953, eleven days before the Americans followed suit.[104] With Moscow still preoccupied with the death of Stalin in March and the aftermath of the Berlin riots in June, both sides were confident that covert action in Iran would escape serious consequences.[105] At the last minute, Washington threatened to make their final agreement conditional on a more favourable post-Mossadeq oil deal. This threw Whitehall into a spin, with Salisbury warning that 'while we quite see the need for making matters easy for the new Persian Government', any deal could not be more favourable than that offered to Mossadeq.[106]

Coup and counter-coup

The cowardly shah was in a precarious position. He lacked a male heir, was criticized for his pro-Western stance, faced resistance from both the left and right, and often prevaricated. Woodhouse referred to him as 'a kind of Hamlet',[107] whilst the CIA noted that 'his indecision and susceptibility to bad advice were notorious'.[108] He had a lot to lose and needed convincing to play a role in Zahedi's coup. The shah was distrustful of the British, whom he feared were plotting to promote civil war to create a pretext for intervening and dividing Iran from the Russians.[109] On one occasion he had to be appeased by Churchill after reportedly ranting how 'the British threw out the Qajar dynasty; they brought in my father; they threw out my father; and they can throw me out or keep me as they see fit'. He continued, 'Do the British wish to substitute another Shah for me or to abolish the monarchy? Are the British backing present efforts to take away my powers and deprive me of my prestige in Iran and abroad?'[110]

The CIA's Kermit Roosevelt, with the help of Norman Darbyshire, managed to assure the shah that London and Washington would fully support his dismissal of Mossadeq and that the Imperial Guard and any street mobs would remain loyal.[111] Princess Ashraf, the shah's more assertive sister, was also instrumental in applying pressure on him. A grateful Darbyshire apparently presented her with a mink coat and a wad of cash, which only increased her willingness to help.[112] It took a covert message played over the BBC World Service to assure the shah of Churchill's personal support. Darbyshire arranged for the announcer to swap 'it is now midnight' for 'it is now [pause] exactly midnight'.[113] By 15 August 1953, the shah had signed the decree.

SIS maintained involvement right up until the moment of the coup. Officers in London, for example, offered detailed plans for disabling the central telephone exchange. Darbyshire even wanted to fly in to Tehran to help direct the operation on the ground. However, the Foreign Office refused him permission on the grounds that it would have been too embarrassing if anything had gone wrong. With no diplomatic personnel in Tehran, Assadullah Rashidian effectively ended up speaking on behalf of the British government.[114]

Having secured the shah's signature, the operation now needed to mobilize the population in support. Propaganda ensured that, just before the coup, public opinion would be fanned to fever pitch. Timing was crucial. If the propaganda and political warfare campaign peaked too early then Mossadeq might attempt a clampdown on the press, strangling the operation. And yet, its impact would have decreased the longer the campaign was drawn out.[115] Building on nearly two years of subversion, the effort peaked in mid-August 1953.

Conditions were now ripe for revolution. Unfortunately for SIS and the CIA, the initial coup attempt was betrayed.[116] After problematic experiences with leaky émigrés in Albania, this initial failure served only to remind Whitehall of the difficulties of operational security. This time the culprit was a young Imperial Guard captain and communist who had informed the leftist Tudeh Party.[117] Mossadeq evaded capture and arrested the key conspirators as his supporters flooded the streets in protest against the attempted coup. Bedell Smith warned Eisenhower that America would now have to 'snuggle up to Mosadeq if we're going to save anything there'—and braced himself for 'added difficulty with the British'.[118]

With his country in chaos, the shah fled, retreating, without warning, to the Caspian Sea. Not panicking, Roosevelt hoped that the Foreign Office would be able to get the shah on the radio, or at the very least broadcast a statement from him in Persian from a station in Baghdad, to declare his support for Zahedi. However, they failed to do so, leaving Roosevelt disappointed. He later reported back to CIA headquarters that 'the British let us down on that... They struggled. I think the British seriously struggled, but the Foreign Office was just thumbs down definitely.'[119] As for the shah, he promised to keep his involvement in the planning secret.[120] Resigned to exile, he even contemplated getting a job in America.[121]

Yet the CIA refused to be beaten. They mobilized mass demonstrations against Mossadeq in Tehran. Working, as Eisenhower later put it, 'intelligently, courageously and tirelessly',[122] they paid agents to create anti-shah havoc in the name of the communistic Tudeh, including tearing down statues of the shah and dragging them through the streets, in an attempt to incite anti-Mossadeq mobs to riot.[123] Agents looted shops with the objective of making it look as if 'this was the Tudeh in action'.[124] The CIA also worked with religious leaders to encourage yet more counter-protests against Mossadeq. Other agents, including the Rashidians, circulated copies of the decree, (real and fake) interviews with Zahedi, and statements by Zahedi to the crowds, journalists, and the army so as to undermine Mossadeq and remind Iranians that he had been sacked by the shah.[125] The Rashidian brothers also planned to instigate a large demonstration in support of religion and the throne.[126]

Meanwhile, Loy Henderson, the American ambassador, flew back to Tehran to offer Mossadeq, who blamed the British for the coup attempt, an ultimatum. Henderson questioned Mossadeq's legitimacy and claimed to 'have heard' that the shah had dismissed him as prime minister. Henderson demanded that Mossadeq, who had allowed anti-shah protests to take place, restore order to the streets. Mossadeq obediently did so, unwittingly clearing the stage for rival protests.[127]

Back in London, William Strang lost his nerve. Opting for damage limitation, he panicked and tried to call the whole thing off. One diplomat frantically cabled SIS in Cyprus: 'we must regret that we cannot consider going on fighting'.[128] In Nicosia, however, Darbyshire and his colleagues refused to give up hope. As Washington ordered a withdrawal of the CIA, SIS officers arranged a 'failure in communications' at the wireless relay in Cyprus, ensuring that their colleagues in Tehran did not receive the order to abort.[129] Despite the failure to get the shah on air, Darbyshire assured his CIA counterparts that they, personally, were doing all they could to convince London to continue to support their efforts. In doing so, he ignored requests from the Foreign Office to stand down, admit defeat, and cover British tracks. Whilst later appreciating this as admirable, the CIA knew full well that SIS 'had nothing to lose if the cause had been pressed to ultimate failure and disclosure'.[130]

On 19 August, pro-shah mobs began protesting in the bazaars of southern Tehran and made their way into the centre of the city. Some were paid to be there, whilst others had been swept up in the excitement.[131] Soldiers, influenced by the brothers' message, began to switch sides and join the protest. The improbable leaders of the street protests—a motley collection of weightlifters, wrestlers, and acrobats at the head of the crowd—were almost certainly put there by the Rashidian brothers. The CIA called it a 'brilliant stroke that showed a profound understanding of Iranian psychology', for the population apparently idolized such performers.[132] Having learnt from the riots that reinstated Mossadeq in 1952, Woodhouse and his SIS colleagues knew that street mobs formed a very powerful force in Iranian politics.[133] SIS/CIA planners had believed that they could muster up to 3,000 street activists.[134] The eventual crowd totalled nearly 4,000.[135]

Although small by Iranian standards, the mob provided a pretext for a military coup, similar to that originally planned by SIS. Mossadeq was finally arrested and Zahedi delivered a radio broadcast declaring that the shah had appointed him prime minister. Woodhouse, who had since been stationed elsewhere, tuned in to developments on a crackling radio from Southeast Asia—fending off the local ambassador's attempts to listen to the cricket from the Oval.[136] The same day, Pierson Dixon met Harold Gibson, a veteran SIS officer, also eagerly seeking an update.[137] On 20 August 1953, it became apparent that Mossadeq was no longer in power.[138] Darbyshire celebrated his secret victory in Cyprus.[139] Eisenhower thought it more 'like a dime novel than an historical fact'.[140] For Churchill, it was a 'great venture',[141] whilst Eden, still recovering from his operation, 'slept happily that night'.[142] Others in the Foreign Office remained anxious. They expressed considerable reserve about Zahedi and foresaw a period of grave difficulty ahead.[143] Dixon, still sceptical of the operation, added that 'we have no reason to expect that a Zahedi Government would be non-nationalist and pro-British'.[144] As for the Iranians, the shah, although mindful of British intrigues, swiftly promised closer relations between London and Tehran.[145] He did, however, remain sensitive about Anglo-American assistance during the coup for some time afterwards.[146] As for Zahedi, he had no love for the British but recognized the importance of establishing good relations with London, repeating again and again his desire to resume diplomatic relations and resolve the oil dispute.[147]

Cabinet ministers lied shamelessly to the British press, claiming: 'we had no prior knowledge of what happened. The first we heard was from the BBC Monitor on the morning of August 16.' They professed to be 'surprised at the strength of Royalist feeling'. Lord Salisbury, still acting foreign secretary, did clarify that 'the word "coup" is inexact as a description of the recent events. The initial attempt by the Shah to substitute Zahidi for Mussadiq was within his constitutional powers, although he was forced to have recourse to somewhat unorthodox methods.'[148] A masterpiece of understatement.

Kermit Roosevelt was smuggled out of Tehran to London. Here he met John Sinclair, the chief of SIS, and was soon engrossed in Whitehall's covert action politics. Sinclair, who often found himself dominated by the stronger personalities of the Foreign Office, told Roosevelt that 'SIS was grateful not only because of the success of the operation per se, but because of the effect the success had already had and would continue to have upon SIS's reputation and relations with its superiors'. Sinclair and his colleagues forgave Roosevelt for the lack of updates during those few confusing days.[149]

Roosevelt went on to brief senior diplomats. He got the impression that SIS was glad to be able to sell themselves amongst the upper echelons of the Foreign Office given that the relationship seemed rather strained. James Bowker, responsible for Near East affairs, was apparently particularly cold towards SIS covert action. Basking in the success, Sinclair paraded Roosevelt in front of William Strang. Through brains and persistence more than pugnaciousness, Strang had long imposed himself on Sinclair when it came to the Middle East, an area where Sinclair had little experience. This time, however, Strang must have detected a distinct glint in the blue eyes behind Sinclair's horn-rimmed spectacles.[150] Leaving Strang's office, Sinclair told Roosevelt that the Foreign Office had just approved another operation which it had previously turned down. This was as a direct result of the success in Iran.[151] Meanwhile, Churchill's team criticized the Foreign Office for having been too timid. What was needed across the Middle East was bold, decisive action such as that which, they believed, had worked well in Iran.[152] Churchill, whom Roosevelt found to be enthusiastic about the operation, hoped to use it as a springboard to ensure British influence across the Middle East. Buoyed by the romantic intervention, he was now keen to hang on as prime minister for as long as necessary.[153]

The overthrow of Mossadeq cannot be described simply as a CIA operation. Donald Wilber, who headed its psychological aspects for the Americans, later admitted that it could not 'have been carried through without the active cooperation of the United Kingdom and their assets'. Despite ongoing tension, including over security, the lesson for the CIA was clear: Anglo-American interests and activities had to be coordinated.[154] Roger Louis, a leading imperial historian, has also concluded that 'it is difficult to imagine how the 1953 operation against the Mossadeq government could have taken place without the Rashidian network'.[155] It must also be noted, however, that Operation Boot worked in conjunction with internal factors. SIS planning considered how best to work with and exploit existing local forces in order to bring about regime change. It would have been practically impossible to create a climate conducive to a coup from scratch.[156]

Although Operation Boot is a rare example of covert action where more is known about the execution on the ground than what was going on in Whitehall, the Foreign Office, as we have seen, became increasingly cautious in early 1953. In this sense, it mirrors to an extent Albania when, after some initial bombastic talk of regime change, caution set in. Remarkably in the Iranian case, committees were nowhere to be seen. Authorization relied more on Eden's illness and Churchill's subsequent personal involvement than bureaucratic machinery. In this respect, it was a deviation from the British way in covert action, but in other aspects, Operation Boot fitted an emerging pattern. First, it was a means of trying to control events where overt intervention was unfeasible. Both the CIA and Lord Salisbury recognized that doing nothing would have led to uncontrollable uncertainty and the risk of communist dominance.[157] Second, nationalism, where it compromised economic security and could be exploited by communism, could not be tolerated. Third, the British sought indirectly to foster a climate conducive to revolution. This involved using political warfare to cultivate allied groups alongside using propaganda and bribery to sow dissent, exploit 'contradictions', and discredit the target. Fourth, again echoing Albania, Britain sought to rely on a strongman. Fifth, Whitehall was content to take a circuitous approach to achieve these goals by letting the CIA execute the operation.

Covert action in Iran raises so many fascinating issues. It demonstrates just how long a successful operation can take from conception to execution. The overthrow of Mossadeq was the culmination of more than two years of planning and groundwork. Moreover, it provides a stark contrast, in terms of ambition and audacity, to the long-term pinprick approach then currently taking place in Europe. Operation Boot was therefore crucial in emerging British thinking about covert action. These ideas would be used repeatedly across the Middle East in the following decade. After the coup, the shah warned that British intrigue in Iran must now stop. Roosevelt reassured him that the 'steps that had been taken in this particular case were not in accordance with usual practice, but were due to the special importance of Persia'.[158] This was simply not the truth and Anthony Eden now realized that underhand manipulation could serve British interests effectively.[159] He soon turned his attentions elsewhere as British covert action sought to redesign the entire landscape of the Middle East.

6

EXPANSION

Covert Action before Suez

We should be ready to make more use of counter-subversion in the smaller countries
of the Middle East and in South-East Asia which are seriously threatened with
Communist infiltration.

Anthony Eden, 1955[1]

Success in Iran demonstrated the power of the hidden hand and gave
leverage to supporters of covert action. Under renewed pressure from
the chiefs of staff to take the initiative in subterranean warfare from the
Soviets,[2] Harold Macmillan, successively as defence minister and then foreign secretary, proved a key instigator. He had learned about Operation
Boot at Churchill's birthday party in December 1954 and championed the
idea of fighting the Soviets, as he put it, 'with our brains'.[3] The following
year, he pressed Prime Minister Anthony Eden for a clear and determined
policy to counter the twin threats of communism and nationalism. Britain,
he claimed, now needed to be proactive in disrupting subversive activities at
source and 'using covert means to protect our position'.[4] Developing this
theme, Evelyn Shuckburgh, overseeing Middle East policy in the Foreign
Office, wondered why Britain devoted so much effort to military pacts
and hydrogen bombs, when money could be better spent simply bribing
uncommitted countries.[5]

Norman Brook, the cabinet secretary, was furious at what he saw as
Macmillan's parroting of the chiefs of staff line.[6] Nonetheless, in late 1955,
Anthony Eden, with Brook's approval, did agree to 'undertake counter-
subversionary activities', especially in the Middle East and Southeast Asia.[7]
The Secret Intelligence Service (SIS), as we have seen, were already under-
taking operations in the Middle East, whilst in 1954 they had agreed to run

joint operations with the CIA in Indochina, Thailand, and Indonesia; SIS officers in the region, including future chief Maurice Oldfield, saw this as a licence to take the fight to the communists.[8]

Nonetheless, a step change took place in late 1955 as use of covert action expanded to become an integral part of foreign policy. By the end of the year, Ivone Kirkpatrick, now permanent under-secretary at the Foreign Office and long-time enthusiast of such activity, informed Whitehall's representatives abroad that 'we have decided, in view of the new type of threat, that counter-subversion, i.e. clandestine activities whether by propaganda or by special operations, will have an increasing part to play in support of foreign policy'. Just as they had done five years earlier, the Foreign Office asked for suggestions for covert operations.[9] And yet the military wanted to go further still: Eden's approach remained more cautious than the rambunctious chiefs of staff had hoped.[10]

Growing momentum

The growing momentum behind nationalism across the global South underpinned much of this thinking. Britain had been forced to withdraw from Palestine, insurgent uprisings were underway in Malaya, Cyprus, and Kenya, and Mossadeq had earlier nationalized Iranian oil. The Foreign Office worried these trends threatened worldwide speculation about Britain's readiness to maintain its position as a world power, adding that one 'particular blow may set off a chain reaction with incalculable results'.[11] To make matters worse, officials feared communist exploitation of nationalism and therefore treated it as an almost existential threat, with intelligence priorities diverted from capturing the Soviet order of battle towards monitoring subversion.[12] And the Kremlin was indeed courting Middle Eastern states, not least to exploit disagreements between London and Washington and as a means to counter Anglo–American attempts to create what they saw as an aggressive bloc of anti-Soviet states in the region. By the end of 1955, the Soviets were boasting about 'disrupting the influence of the imperialist Powers' across the post-colonial world.[13]

Britain's main opponent was Gamal Abdel Nasser. A long-time anti-colonialist, he had been instrumental in the 1952 overthrow of the Egyptian monarchy and ultimate elimination of British forces from the country. Although Egypt had been independent from 1936, Britain had continued to maintain a political and military presence there. Nasser formally became president in June 1956, remaining in office until his death in 1970. Praised for his intimate relationship with the Egyptian people and lack of corruptibility, he was a charismatic and skilled orator who worked eighteen-hour days and was determined to espouse Egyptian independence and achieve regional leadership—at the expense of British influence.

There are numerous factors explaining why Whitehall chose covert action to counter this challenge. World opinion forced British responses underground. As newly independent states joined the international community, diplomats felt that emerging ideas, including the condemnation of the use or threat of force, had severely limited Britain's ability to express its view.[14] By the end of the decade, the Foreign Office conceded that 'the use of U.K. troops in actual fighting, especially against Arabs, even with the consent of the Government concerned, acts as a red rag to nationalist opinion'.[15] Yet, ministers, mandarins, and spymasters alike were steeped in traditions of imperialism and had no intention of steering clear.[16] Perhaps the most important figure was George Kennedy Young, who dominated SIS activity in the region during the 1950s. Young was director of SIS personnel and operations in the Middle East, and went on to become vice-chief of the service. He was quick-witted, outstandingly bright, and, buoyed by the success in Iran, a firm believer in the power of covert action.[17] In this, Young, who became increasingly right-wing as he got older, was a determined operator unafraid to take risks. An imperialist to the core, he thought a sense of 'Britishness' was achieved through foreign adventures.[18] At the same time, covert action in the Middle East was far less risky than in Europe. The Foreign Office believed, for example, that the Soviets would not risk a war in Europe for the sake of Syria. Exposed SIS operations might result in Soviet propaganda, threats, subversion, and even assassinations of pro-Western leaders—but not nuclear war.[19]

Meanwhile, Brook and the diplomats shook up the covert action machinery in an attempt to inject a greater sense of urgency. They abolished the Official Committee on Communism (Overseas), which had long been gridlocked by inter-departmental fighting, in March 1956.[20] Brook agreed to a renewed covert action campaign but only through a so-called 'vertical' approach, in which the Foreign Office took the lead, to better integrate covert action into broader policy.[21] Unsurprisingly, this outraged the chiefs of staff. The AC(O) had served one important role until the end: as a forum into which the chiefs could air their hawkish views;[22] or, as Brook later put it, to engage in pointless 'sniping'.[23] Brook created a top-secret Political Intelligence Group, which included SIS, inside the Foreign Office in January 1956.[24] This, in turn, reported to a more senior body, known as the Overseas Planning Committee, which considered how best to bring covert action into broader policy, recommended proposals to the foreign secretary, and coordinated those which had been sanctioned.[25] Its main contribution, however, was in convincing the military that the Foreign Office was doing enough to wage the Cold War. Criticism of it in front of the chiefs of staff was banned and, by 1958, it met only once a year, remaining in existence mostly to head off military criticism.[26]

Perhaps most importantly of all, Britain, long struggling financially, now had the means to wage a covert action campaign. Operations involved ever larger sums of money, often spent on bribery, which had to be found from discreet sources. The Secret Vote was only so big, and public money funnelled to various strongmen could only be hidden so far. The answer came in the form of an SIS slush fund, codenamed HAM, so secret that only a select few ever knew of its existence.

When SIS chief Stewart Menzies retired to his twin pursuits of horse racing and shooting in the summer of 1952, he dropped a bombshell of an inheritance. During the war, he had acquired a secret and entirely unofficial fund which came not from the Exchequer but from subscriptions by well-wishers of SIS, including a particularly large sum from an unnamed American.[27] It totalled over £1 million.[28] The mere existence of this fund, not to be confused with official reserve funding granted by the Treasury, staggered the upper echelons of the Foreign Office. William Strang, then still its senior official, kept knowledge to as small a circle as possible. He and his private secretary knew, as did a couple of senior Treasury officials. Menzies and his successor, John Sinclair, obviously knew too. The following year, they let Rab Butler and then Harold Macmillan, as successive chancellors of the exchequer, in on the secret. But that was it. The prime minister did not know. The foreign secretary did not know. The JIC chairman, and link between the Foreign Office and SIS, did not know. Even the SIS financial director was kept in the dark.[29] It was a quite extraordinary situation.

HAM enabled the funding of covert action. On his retirement, Menzies revealed that SIS needed the money in case of 'a very large inducement to some person in an absolutely key position'. Bribery was integral to British covert action in the Middle East—so much so that beneficiaries were sometimes even asked to sign receipts.[30] The money was also needed in case a political emergency arose which could not be covered by the Secret Vote.[31] This proved the case in 1953 when Operation Boot was suddenly resurrected. Having received the political go-ahead, Sinclair quickly withdrew around £50,000, leaving Burke Trend, a senior Treasury official who looked after the Secret Vote, extremely relieved the fund existed. 1953 was an expensive year: on top of Boot, a mysterious Operation Trumpet also had to be paid for.[32]

The arrangements were simple and flexible. Sinclair, as chief of SIS, had easy access to the slush fund and could withdraw up to £25,000 each year without question from the Foreign Office or Treasury, so long as he informed them of his balance each March. This was a lot of money: some £700,000 at today's value. Anything above this had to be signed off by the permanent under-secretary at the Foreign Office.[33] This process continued when Dick White arrived as chief in 1956. He would not have been surprised by HAM because MI5, which he had previously headed, enjoyed its own—far smaller—fund. But in line with his broader desire to reform SIS, White sought to regularize the reserves. He was concerned that its existence had led to suspicions that the SIS chief possessed undisclosed funds which were in his sole control. This was not far from the truth, but such rumours were bad for morale and undermined proper accounting procedures.[34]

Faced with a perceived threat and armed with vigour and money, SIS launched a wave of offensive covert action after Iran in 1953. It spread across the region, targeting Yemen, Syria, Saudi Arabia, Iraq, Jordan, the Gulf States, Lebanon, and, of course, Egypt.[35] Led by Young, or GK as he was known, SIS thought big in the Middle East, while agreeing to leave covert action in other areas such as Latin America and, perhaps oddly, Antarctica to the Americans.[36] At the same time, MI5 conducted defensive covert action by bolstering the internal security forces of friendly regimes, such as Iran, Lebanon, and Turkey. They offered training courses, advice, and even had a role in setting up the notorious Iranian secret police, SAVAK. In doing so, they helped bolster non-communist parties and counter communist subversion. Conducted in secret and deniably, much of this had been recommended by senior Cold War planners back in London who tasked MI5, SIS, and the Information Research Department (IRD) to work in tandem.[37] One CIA operative admired the model. The British, he felt, only required two agents per country: the chief of police and the head of state. 'If you had them, you didn't need all those big political action ops.'[38]

From Yemen to Saudi Arabia

Special operations targeted Yemen throughout the 1950s. This was an area of immense strategic significance because of Britain's colony in Aden, lying on the south coast of the Arabian Peninsula. The territory, with its large natural harbour, facilitated the flow of oil between the Mediterranean and the Gulf, formed a base from which Britain could defend client states elsewhere in the Persian Gulf, and allowed London to project power into the Indian Ocean and beyond. Separating Aden from Yemen was the South Arabian hinterland which provided Britain with a protective buffer from the nationalist designs of the Yemeni imam.

Under Churchill's premiership, and at around the same time as Operation Boot was climaxing, British activity involved small-scale actions designed to destabilize the imam and deter Yemeni incursions across the frontier into British-protected South Arabia. It was all part of a wider game of tit-for-tat tribal raids across the border. The Yemenis, opposed to the British position in Aden, would regularly make a nuisance of themselves by encroaching on, or engaging in skirmishes along, the frontier. Churchill, and Eden after him, covertly sponsored retaliatory raids into Yemen by friendly tribes. They knew that overt retaliation, and inevitable condemnation for aggressive imperialism in the United Nations, was out of the question.[39]

Covert action in Yemen intensified as the decade progressed. One operation, codenamed Razzle, began in the summer of 1956 and cost around £860,000 at today's value. It was approved by the foreign secretary and Ivone Kirkpatrick, as permanent under-secretary. No details about Razzle exist in the declassified archives; it was discussed only orally by the few in the know. One Treasury official, however, jotted down just four tantalizing words in pencil next to a fleeting mention: 'Yemen. Imam Dying. Friends'.[40] 'Friends' likely refers to SIS involvement and Britain would certainly have wanted rid of the troublesome Imam Ahmad. He had long opposed colonial rule in Aden and, in addition to authorizing trade deals with the Soviets, by 1956 had signed a defensive pact with Nasser's Egypt. Perhaps there were plans to rig the system and ensure a more amenable successor. But whatever the mysterious Razzle entailed, Ahmad did not die until 1962, despite suffering regular bouts of ill health.

Syria formed a more urgent target. By the middle of the decade, the country had become increasingly entangled with both communism and the pan-Arabism espoused by Nasser. In October 1955, Harold Macmillan and Evelyn Shuckburgh stayed up talking until the small hours of the morning. Having exchanged war stories and political gossip, attention turned to the Middle East. They hatched what Shuckburgh described as 'a Machiavellian scheme' which allowed Iraq to absorb Syria in return for peace with Israel. Nuri al-Said, the pro-Western prime minister of Iraq, excitedly wanted to annex Syria right away, but Shuckburgh knew that such a move required preparation and had to appear to come from inside Syria.[41] Diplomats in the Foreign Office had grown increasingly concerned by Syria's anti-Western policies, whilst SIS officers, led by Young, pressed hard for regime change. This led to Operation 'Straggle, in collusion with the Americans and Iraqis, to overthrow the Syrian regime and undermine Nasserism in the region.

As in Iran, the British saw advantage in bringing the CIA on board, not least to finance the operation and shoulder the blame if things went wrong.[42] Moreover, Shuckburgh sensed that Allen Dulles, director of the CIA, was 'raring to start some new anti-Communist action' but did 'not seem to know just what'.[43] Unfortunately for London, Washington was again initially unreceptive. Dulles worried about the impact of covert action on negotiations with Nasser, whom he was trying to bring onside.[44] He also worried about the effect on Saudi Arabia, to which America was on the verge of providing arms in an attempt to keep Riyadh out of Moscow's clutches.[45] Others in the CIA thought the plan unrealistic and warned that the coup in Iran had not formed a precedent.[46] It was therefore SIS, with Young at the forefront, which made the running and worked hard to co-opt the CIA. Senior British personnel never missed an opportunity to emphasize to the Americans the dangers of communism in Syria and ongoing political warfare against Western interests in the region.[47]

Eden approved regime change in March 1956, and his cabinet ordered the Foreign Office and SIS to 'establish in Syria a Government more friendly to the West'.[48] Shortly afterwards, Selwyn Lloyd, the foreign secretary, was assured that 'covert action to diminish Nasser's influence in other Arab countries is being actively prepared'.[49] The plans centred on Iraq where Nuri al-Said, a staunch ally of the British, feared Egyptian and Saudi subterfuge in the region.[50] He had suggested creating 'a situation in Syria in which an appeal would be made by non-Communist elements for help from Iraq to rid themselves of alien domination'. Lloyd agreed but left the option of attaching Syria to Iraq in a so-called fertile crescent for a later date.[51] As an alternative, the Pakistani government, keen to cement its relationship with the West whilst India remained a leader of the non-aligned movement, suggested simply giving Syria a bribe of £1 million to entice Damascus away from Nasser. This could, according to Pakistan, be paid by the oil companies, allowing the British government to stay in the background.[52]

Operation Straggle, at a cost to the Foreign Office of £150,000,[53] ultimately went down the Iraqi route. Borrowing tactics from Boot, G. K. Young and his team attempted to unite and back certain factions. As early as October 1955, SIS and the CIA agreed that leftists had gained ground in Syria because conservatives were divided into small groups and too busy fighting each other. Any covert action had to unite these elements and create a harmony of interests amongst themselves—and with the West. The Foreign Office was also on the hunt for any Syrian group which sought alignment with Iraq, and which could then be manipulated to support the Iraqi coup.[54] The White House eventually agreed to influence friendly Syrians to put aside their differences, whilst also promoting rivalries among communist and other anti-Western leaders.[55] Kermit Roosevelt, who had led operations in Iran, accompanied by his cousin Archie, arrived in Beirut in July to assess the conditions for covert action and begin mobilizing the opposition across the border in Syria.[56]

Again as with Iran, Young, who drafted the plan,[57] was unafraid to ally with unsavoury people. This time SIS worked with an extreme right-wing party, the Parti Populaire Syrien, who, having swelled their number with infiltrations from Lebanon, would start to riot.[58] This was to take place alongside Iraqi-instigated border agitation and coordinated uprisings by Iraqi-trained tribesmen.[59] The Voice of Britain radio station was later accused of giving the signal to begin.[60] For Britain, no coup plan was complete without a strongman at the helm. This time, however, the nominee threatened to undermine nascent American support, which was still far from wholehearted. Deviating from Washington's wishes, SIS consulted the Iraqis about returning a former dictator, Adib Shishakli, to power even though Washington doubted his levels of support and worried about his heavy drinking. Not to be dissuaded, Britain then explored the possibility of Shishakli's brother.[61] The CIA, favouring a coup from within, grew ever more frustrated by British scheming with Iraq.[62]

SIS and the Foreign Office also turned to another mainstay of the covert action playbook: bribery. Geoffrey Arthur, a Middle Eastern specialist at the Foreign Office, advocated what he called a 'Machiavellian scheme' for an

Iraqi–Syrian union to be achieved through propaganda and bribery.[63] Arthur had long sought to work secretly with Nuri to extend Iraqi influence across the Fertile Crescent and now recommended *inter alia* 'bribery in Syria, by or on behalf of Iraq', targeting the Syrian army.[64] Similarly, John Gardener, the British ambassador to Syria, although sceptical about a coup, had been boasting for a year that he could bring about the merger of Iraq and Syria whenever he wanted if given enough money.[65]

With Young's plans progressing, SIS worried about neighbouring states suddenly engaging in their own uncoordinated covert action against Syria. In fact, Britain had to block aggressive proposals, including setting up a Special Operations Executive (SOE)-type body, from other regional allies for fear of undermining its own plan.[66] Even the Americans were trying to do their own thing, in providing a wealthy conservative politician some half a million Syrian pounds to launch a coup internally, and did not inform him of the simultaneous Anglo–Iraqi collusion plans.[67]

Nonetheless, the plot collapsed in October 1956, not least because of concurrent events in Egypt, where Britain and France had colluded with Israel to invade. The White House thought operations in Syria no longer wise or feasible, and the CIA planners and their assets angrily feared they had been set up by SIS, who had supposedly orchestrated Straggle to coincide with the confusion in Suez, thereby allowing Iraq to take control.[68] Although SIS still wanted to press ahead regardless, the Iraqis feared simultaneous action might make them appear in league with Israeli intervention in Egypt. The Syrian security services uncovered the plot shortly afterwards and arrested forty-seven conspirators.[69] Harnessing Iraq's ambition paid off for the British, though, as Nuri shouldered the consequences and Syria referred to Operation Straggle as the Iraqi Plot. Meanwhile, Iraq itself was not immune from Britain's hidden hand. An operation, referred to by Patrick Dean as 'covert action' and likely involving unattributable propaganda and bribery, worked simultaneously to prop up Nuri by undermining Nasser-inspired opposition forces.[70] Any such defensive operations could only have worked in the short term, however. Nuri was overthrown in 1958 and Britain lost a key ally in the region.

Saudi Arabia also worried Britain's Nasser watchers. Oil, only discovered in 1938, had dramatically increased the importance of the country in the eyes of the West, but in 1955 Saudi Arabia signed a military agreement with Egypt. Both also opposed the Baghdad Pact, a treaty signed in the same year promising mutual cooperation and protection amongst its members—Britain,

Iran, Turkey, Pakistan, and Iraq. Saudi Arabia and Egypt feared it gave too much power to Iraq, a key British ally. From London, Eden ranted to President Eisenhower about Saudi bribery subsidizing leftist newspapers and paying off ministers across the region. He stressed that the Saudis, the Russians, the Egyptians, and the Syrians were conspiring to redraw the political landscape in the Middle East.[71] And Eden was not alone. By April 1956, Selwyn Lloyd increasingly feared a Nasserite coup in Riyadh, whilst SIS officers warned of growing Egyptian influence within the existing Saudi regime. Amidst discussions of a coup, covert action to prevent an Egyptian–Saudi axis soon got underway.[72]

It was not Britain's first attempt to covertly meddle in Saudi affairs. In the autumn of 1953, the Saudis had attempted to expand into the Buraimi region, which bordered the Sultanate of Muscat and Oman and the Trucial Sheikhdom of Abu Dhabi. Claiming the territory as its own, Saudi Arabia sent a small party under Sheikh Turki to occupy a village in the Buraimi Oasis. Britain, bound by treaty to protect the small Gulf States, planned to kidnap Turki in order to, in the words of the Foreign Office, 'demonstrate our strength in the Persian Gulf'. The military confirmed that the 'escapade' of 'kidnapping, repeat kidnapping' Turki was 'perfectly feasible'.[73] However, the remarkable plan was overtaken by events when King Ibn Saud died, allowing hope of 'an amicable settlement of the frontier dispute'. Therefore, Britain held the operation in abeyance in case the situation deteriorated.[74]

The new Saudi leadership cannot have held British confidence for long. In late 1955, with the Buraimi dispute rolling on, Bernard Burrows, political resident in the Persian Gulf, struggled to find a way to 'scupper' Saudi designs in the region without Britain 'seeming to be very dirty dogs indeed'.[75] The following year, British diplomats on the ground warned Eden of the 'disquieting ease with which Saud has apparently forgotten his previous apprehensions about Nasser's ambitions and Communist infiltration'. They felt it possible to 'bring him to the boil again on both issues', but warned that this would take 'time and energy.'[76] Young, together with Nigel Clive, in charge of SIS's political action capabilities, planned another regime change. They hoped to exploit splits within the Saudi royal family and use the British position in the Trucial States to hasten the fall of King Saud in revenge for his reneging on British oil interests and developing closer ties with Egypt and Syria.[77] Young also believed that Saud would need to be removed because of inevitable adverse Saudi reaction to the proposed coup in Syria, which was supposed to have happened first.[78]

As in Syria, SIS tried to bring the Americans on board.[79] Even if it was merely a pipe dream, Young regaled CIA representatives with his ambitious plans at SIS headquarters in Broadway. He argued Nasser had to be stopped, pointed to Egyptian subversive propaganda undermining Western influence across the region, and angrily blamed the CIA, in covertly supporting Nasser's rise in 1952, for creating 'a monster'.[80] But the Americans were alarmed—and not only by Young's liberal use of phrases such as 'wogs' and 'Gyppos'.[81] Although the White House had long expected that success in Iran would cause the British to take a strong line elsewhere in the region,[82] Wilbur Eveland, of the CIA, thought he had 'entered a madhouse'.[83] The shabby conditions, rain-damaged conference room, identically dressed but hostile SIS officers, and lack of anything James Bond-esque left him disappointed and bemused. Another CIA representative was struck by the vengeful, irrational tone, later reporting back that SIS had openly spoken of assassinating Nasser.[84]

The American ambassador in London, Winthrop Aldrich, slammed Britain's 'emotionalism' over the region and later recalled that the British, fanned by inaccurate intelligence, had suggested a 'number of immoderate and obviously impractical courses of counter-action'.[85] It took another two years before the Saudis, concerned by Nasser's anti-monarchism, broke links with Egypt and Syria. The extent to which covert action played a part in achieving this remains unknown, although SIS clearly never achieved its coup.[86] By 1958, however, King Saud had become sufficiently anti-Egyptian to offer a £1.9 million bribe to the head of Syrian intelligence, Abdel Hamid al-Sarraj, to assassinate Nasser.[87]

Talk of covert action was everywhere—even inside Buckingham Palace. In Jordan, King Hussein had recently married, and the British ambassador in Amman hoped this would offset the influences of his uncle, Sharif Nasser.[88] Britain saw Nasser, a close adviser to Hussein, as a damaging force who had lobbied against British interests in Jordan, notably General Glubb, British commander of the Arab Legion.[89] Evelyn Shuckburgh, in charge of Middle Eastern affairs at the Foreign Office, updated Queen Elizabeth on the 'machinations of the wicked uncle, Nasser', over lunch in July 1955. In an unguarded moment, she said that 'she was surprised nobody had found means of putting something in his coffee'. Shuckburgh agreed

taking out Nasser was 'a good idea which ought to be applied to a number
of people in the Middle East', and promised to keep her updated about
developments in Jordan. He had wanted to tell the Queen that her comment
was 'dangerously like a remark made on a famous occasion by her predecessor
King Henry II', who, before the murder of Thomas Becket, the Archbishop
of Canterbury, had asked, 'will no one rid me of this meddlesome priest?'[90]

Egypt

SIS and the Foreign Office might have plotted regime change in Syria and
Saudi Arabia, but removing Nasser from Egypt was the biggest prize. Eden,
increasingly neurotic and obsessive, had been planning to topple him as
early as 1955—long before the nationalization of the Suez Canal in July the
following year which set the stage of the Anglo–French–Israeli invasion.[91]
After his earlier botched operation, Eden was now an exhausted and ill
man surviving on little sleep and a potent combination of prescription
drugs and amphetamines. All of this sorely affected his thought process and
judgement, perhaps explaining the shift from foot-dragger to advocate
when it came to the apparent panacea offered by covert operations.[92] On
at least one occasion, Norman Brook had to act as a calming force to balance Eden's increasingly wild emotions, reminding the prime minister of
something he had said in quieter days before entering Number 10: Britain
should 'harness nationalist movements rather than struggle against them'.
Eden did not take the pointed reminder kindly.[93] He thought the time was
right for action, as not only did Nasser oppose British interests, but Egypt
was seemingly the lynchpin of Soviet penetration in the region. Yet, as Julian
Amery put it, the Soviets were not so deeply committed as to be unable to
accept a setback there.[94] Rather like Albania before, Egypt therefore presented a seemingly ripe target.

Unsurprisingly, Amery was amongst the most vocal in calling for positive
steps to create a 'friendly Egypt'.[95] He was now secretary to the Suez group
of Conservative MPs, had the ear of his father-in-law Harold Macmillan,
and continued, in his deep and plummy voice, to act unofficially as Whitehall's
emissary to dissidents. Attempts to achieve this friendly Egypt included
fomenting regime change, creating a government-in-exile, and even assassination. Sawdust and Scant were two such covert operations. The former,
targeting Nasser between 1956 and 1958, was approved by successive foreign

secretaries and cost Britain a vast £375,000 (around £8.7 million today and much greater than Operation Boot).[96] It is unclear what Sawdust actually encompassed but, as discussed below, myriad covert operations likely fell under its banner. Scant was more clearly defined: a black radio station established in April 1956 at a cost of £60,000.[97]

Intent on removing the president from power, Eden, Young, and Amery were willing to consider any means necessary. Initially influenced by the Iranian success and a similar American operation in Guatemala the following year, Eden's circle sought to encourage the Egyptian opposition, identify a suitable replacement, and instigate a military coup.[98] Revelling in the direct comparison, Young boasted to the CIA that SIS would '"do a Mossadeq" with Nasser'.[99] In 1954, just a year after Iran, Amery was working with Egyptian dissidents to plan a coup, but this fizzled out after Britain promised to withdraw its armed forces from the Canal Zone.[100] He did not give up though and in 1955 made use of his excellent network of contacts inside Egypt, which dated back to his wartime service there, and was soon holding secret discussions with an apparent shadow government. These dissidents agreed to take control of Egypt after Britain had overthrown Nasser. SIS was then able to exchange lists of rebel officers with the CIA.[101]

Amery, travelling with Adam Watson, head of SIS's Africa Department and an old friend from the war, met King Zog, the self-proclaimed ruler of Albania, at a villa on the French Riviera. A friend since Amery's days serving with SOE in the Balkans, Zog was a ruthless strongman.[102] He was also distantly related to the Egyptian royal family and, this time, Egypt was on Amery's agenda. Sitting in a high-backed armchair in a dimly lit room, drinking coffee served by a henchman, Zog regaled his old friend with stories of his recent contacts with the Muslim Brotherhood, the Egyptian royal dynasty, and opposition political leaders. He spoke keenly of their apparent willingness to unite, overthrow Nasser, and restore a king to Egypt.[103] On hearing this, Amery suspected Zog of making a dramatic and unlikely bid for the Egyptian throne himself, not least because Zog had been on the verge of doing so back in 1954 before the Americans found out and told him to stop. Either way, Amery later informed him that the British government would not oppose a coup d'état against Nasser.[104] When reporting back to Whitehall and the Suez group, he talked up the benefits of a royalist coup but insisted that British aid may be necessary to achieve it.[105]

Amery and his friends, including Billy McLean and Norman Darbyshire, held further talks with Egyptian dissidents in France before travelling to

Switzerland. McLean had accompanied Amery on secret trips before, notably regarding post-war operations in Albania. He too was now a Conservative member of parliament but refused to give up his other, more exciting, life and personally asked to be sent on a delicate or dangerous mission.[106] Darbyshire, of course, was a veteran of Operation Boot. In Geneva, they met representatives from the Muslim Brotherhood. With a history of violence, including against British troops, the Brotherhood were unusual bedfellows. Nonetheless, these covert efforts resulted in the establishment of a shadow, undemocratic, and potentially ruthless regime ready to seize power.[107] Talk now moved towards a government headed by General Mohammad Neguib, currently under house arrest, but who would emerge once Nasser fell.[108] By the start of August 1956, Amery was meeting with Douglas Dodds-Parker, an SOE man turned politician, Patrick Dean, and SIS's George Young and Adam Watson at the Foreign Office. Having heard them out, Amery felt that there was little difference between their activity and his more unofficial manoeuvrings and so introduced his chief Egyptian contact to SIS's Biffy Dunderdale. When Egyptian authorities rounded up SIS's agents, including a stay-behind resistance network, in early September, British intelligence had to ask Amery for more of his personal contacts.[109]

Bribery was essential in cultivating these opposition groups and creating a climate conducive to regime change. One SIS officer on the ground in Cairo, John Farmer, promised vast sums of money to Isameddine Mahmoud Khalil, deputy chief of Egypt's air force intelligence, in an upmarket Beirut hotel room overlooking the Mediterranean. Like many of the key players in the 1950s, Farmer also had experience in special operations. During the war he had worked for SOE in France, hunting out suitable fields for supply drops. More recently, he had liaised with the CIA during Operation Boot.[110] His money was now destined to fund a group of officers who promised to mount a coup. In return, Farmer offered Khalil secret intelligence on Israel to prevent Khalil's colleagues from becoming suspicious about his travels and subterranean activities. Maurice Oldfield, briefly stationed in London before becoming SIS chief in Singapore, warned that it was a dangerous game which would backfire if Israeli intelligence found out.[111] And backfire it did. Khalil had received around £165,000 before the British realized he was actually a double agent, loyal to Nasser.[112]

Meanwhile, Amery reported to Young that two plans had arisen from his covert diplomacy. One involved the overthrow of Nasser, replacing him with a monarch. The other envisaged Nasser assassinated and then replaced with a former deputy foreign minister.[113] Unsurprisingly, it is the assassination plans that have attracted the most attention. Michael Goodman, official historian of the Joint Intelligence Committee (JIC), has unequivocally stated that 'nothing recorded in the open or closed papers indicate that assassination was ever considered as an option'. But this is not necessarily the full story, for Goodman also notes significant gaps in the Suez records and that Norman Brook, who had privately supported the operation as cabinet secretary, admitted to taking 'damned good care' to ensure 'that the whole truth never does emerge'.[114] Eden personally instructed Brook to destroy all the relevant documents and the cabinet secretary complied, although, torn between his duty to the prime minister and the official record, he made a note that he had done so.[115] After the fall of the Eden government, two mid-ranking Foreign Office officials collected all of the sensitive papers on Egypt and put them in a file marked 'SUEZ'. When Brook left the Cabinet Office, the files disappeared and were never seen again.[116]

Eden famously telephoned Anthony Nutting, his minister of state for foreign affairs, and blustered: 'what's all this nonsense about isolating Nasser or "neutralising" him as you call it? I want him destroyed, can't you understand? I want him murdered, and if you and the Foreign Office don't agree, then you'd better come to Cabinet and explain why.'[117] Similarly, Young informed Dick White, the new chief of SIS, that he had been personally selected to implement Eden's orders to 'bump Nasser off'.[118] The maverick Young relished what he saw as a licence to kill and excitedly drew up plans to assassinate Nasser.[119]

The rumoured plots—some of which may well have never escalated beyond loose talk amongst SIS officers—range from the ludicrous to the sinister. They include disseminating nerve gas throughout the ventilation system of Nasser's headquarters; killing him with a poison dart; injecting poison into his favourite chocolates; sabotaging his electric razor to make it explode; and resurrecting the wartime practice of outsourcing assassination to third parties.[120] Candidates for the latter supposedly included Nasser's doctor, the Muslim Brotherhood, a group of dissident military officers, a German mercenary, and even the SAS.[121] The Muslim Brotherhood had attempted to kill Nasser back in 1954, after which Churchill had rather ironically written to Nasser congratulating him on his escape.[122] From 1955, it certainly seems that Eden wanted Nasser removed by any means necessary. Miles Copeland, a CIA officer stationed in London at the time, recalled frequently discussing assassination plots with him and senior SIS officers. The CIA had even enjoyed a running joke throughout 1956: that they 'would have to restrain Sir Anthony physically to keep him from going down to Cairo to shoot Nasser himself'.[123]

In reality, there were serious divisions at the top on this subject. Dick White informed Eden that he would sanction no further SIS involvement in assassination plans,[124] whilst Selwyn Lloyd declared that a secret file on the subject had no business in the Foreign Office.[125] Intelligence officers from GCHQ expressed further doubts. Driven by practical rather than ethical considerations, they warned the Foreign Office that assassination would make Nasser a martyr. It would be counterproductive and serve only to reinforce anti-British feeling in Egypt.[126] Officials had taken the same line when Eden suggested killing Muhammad Neguib, Nasser's predecessor, back in 1953.[127] Maurice Oldfield appreciated the new-found opposition to assassination under White and, when asked to sanction a £10,000 payment to an assassin to kill a Thai leader at around the same time, happily responded: 'Forget it. We don't do that kind of thing anymore'.[128] Nonetheless, even if not directly authorized, there was always a danger of SIS officers going off-piste. As Geoffrey McDermott, Foreign Office adviser to SIS, recalled, officers in the field 'would be saints rather than human beings if, in the occasional burst of inspiration, or of exasperation with the official diplomats, they did not deploy a little private enterprise'.[129]

Despite the fascination with assassination, as in Iran, it was unattributable propaganda which formed the backbone of British covert action. Such activity had been in place long before the actual Suez crisis erupted and remained staunchly anti-Nasser, rather than anti-Egyptian, throughout. This was an important distinction given that, as Amery pointed out, 'one day we may need a friendly Egypt'.[130]

Douglas Dodds-Parker played a leading role. Another veteran of the SOE, he had served with distinction in the Middle East and Mediterranean. Drawing on his wartime experience, Dodds-Parker chaired a committee from July 1956 to examine non-military ways to influence the Middle East. Just a day before Nasser announced the impending nationalization of the Suez Canal, Norman Brook was considering how best to divert military funds to support Dodds-Parker's proposals.[131] Dodds-Parker determined themes for black propaganda and scrutinized both political and economic covert operations. On the latter, he recommended encouraging discussion in Egypt about the possibility of alternative government, thereby complementing the work being conducted by the likes of Julian Amery, as well as undermining confidence in Egypt's financial credit.[132] Dodds–Parker also oversaw a highly secretive Information Co-ordination Executive for Political Warfare in the Foreign Office. Its first meeting set about brainstorming ideas that ranged from sabotaging the transmission of Cairo Radio to hitting Nasser with economic sanctions.[133] He advocated both official BBC channels and 'other means',[134] warning that open attacks on Nasser would likely strengthen him but 'covert attacks attributable to Arab Moslem sources will tend to weaken him'.[135] Black radio programmes, including *Voice of the Arabs* and *Voice of Free Egypt*, continuously sought to destabilize Nasser by subverting and misleading the general population.[136]

The most important operation was Scant. From April 1956, a black radio station based in Cyprus broadcast six hours a day. Although London had an imperfect picture of its impact, officials were confident that locals were listening and felt it helped 'to blacken Nasser and other regimes hostile to us in the eyes of fellow Arabs'.[137] Black propaganda broadcast a number of pre-determined themes, mostly along the lines that Nasser was an intransigent coward firmly under the thumb of the godless Soviets.[138] One plan, which bizarrely started out as a genuine course of action but was later reduced to a piece of black propaganda, was that Britain intended to divert the waters of the White Nile at Owen Falls in the British colony of Uganda. Officials soon realized that this was impractical but recognized the propaganda value of convincing the Egyptian population that Nasser was putting the Nile at risk.[139] Scant transmitted towards Egypt, Syria, Iraq, southern Jordan, Saudi Arabia, Lebanon, and the Gulf, with the programmes also drawing comment from as far afield as Zanzibar and Yemen.[140]

It appears that Britain kept radio operations secret from the Americans. In 1956, the CIA reported hearing an unidentified radio station broadcasting propaganda against Nasser. On top of familiar lines about Nasser, the CIA spotted coded messages within the broadcasts, including 'wait until the dawn breaks'; 'do not move until you hear the birds sing'; 'watch the even numbers at full noon'; and 'the lighthouse flashes for the third time'. These may have related to British attempts to liaise with the rebel factions inside Egypt under Operation Sawdust. Unsurprisingly, the CIA traced the transmissions back to Cyprus and its monitors 'reported having recognised the voices of two Sharq-al-adna announcers when a microphone was inadvertently left live'. Sharq-al-adna was known to be under the control of SIS.[141]

SIS continued to press the CIA for covert action against Nasser. By September 1956, it looked like they might have been making progress when the CIA agreed to Operation Mask. This was to be an attempt to remove Nasser through 'peaceful means'. Although a working group, which unsurprisingly included Young, met to discuss ideas, there was little momentum, not least because Eisenhower still disapproved of targeting Nasser. Young's ebullience and impatience contrasted starkly with American caution, and the CIA was reluctant to commit anything to paper. These discussions and tensions ultimately counted for little, as the Suez crisis erupted shortly afterwards.[142]

★ ★ ★

Back in 1955, Anthony Eden, ill and erratic, had ordered a drive for more covert action in support of British policy. Recently unearthed files reveal the remarkable scope of deniable interventions in Yemen, Syria, Egypt, Saudi Arabia, and elsewhere. And many more operations were turned down. 'I've had to stop a lot of operations in the Middle East,' Jack Easton, deputy of SIS, told incoming chief Dick White in 1956. 'Too many are suspiciously unsafe.'[143]

Waged under the shadow of Nasser and fear of British decline, covert action experienced a high point in the early 1950s. It became almost mainstream. By spring 1955, SIS had practically taken over the regional MI5 headquarters, known as SIME or Security Intelligence Middle East, with almost four times as many staff working there as MI5's paltry twelve. From here they launched covert operations across the region—much to the concern of MI5, which was conducting a more defensive type of action by developing security liaison relationships with local governments.[144] When he became chief of SIS, Dick White, often seen as a sceptic, went on to standardize such activity rather than eschew it. Even Queen Elizabeth was talking about covert action. Then, in late 1956, Israel attacked Egypt and provided a pretext for British and French military action to secure the Canal Zone. The disastrous operation is seen by many as a key moment in British decline. If Britain had used covert action as a means to protect global interests, then the humiliation at Suez asked serious questions about what these would now entail.

7

INTERDEPENDENCE

Covert Action after Suez

A special effort should be made to eliminate key individuals.
Anglo–American Working Group on Syria, 1957[1]

Eden's conflict with Gamal Abdel Nasser came to a head in late 1956. On 26 July, the Egyptian president nationalized the Anglo–French Suez Canal Company. Eden was livid, for Britain had now lost control over the shortest route between East and West, with potentially damaging consequences for trade and global influence. Recalling the appeasement of Hitler prior to the Second World War, he plotted action. With a string of covert operations already underway, Eden met French and Israeli counterparts in October. Secret discussions, held at Sèvres just outside Paris, lasted three days and led to an agreement that Israel would attack Egypt, thereby providing a pretext for Anglo–French intervention and the reclaiming of Suez. Israel did so on 29 October and, as agreed, a week later Britain and France launched their assault. Despite achieving military successes, American and world opinion forced the British and French forces to withdraw. It formed the pivotal event in the decade and served as a humiliating and visible marker of British decline.

The Suez misadventure had little impact on British covert action. Norman Brook privately confided that he thought Suez to have been 'a folly', but expected Eden to return and assume charge again as if nothing had happened.[2] Regarding covert action at least, he was correct. Failure in Egypt did not put Eden, or indeed his successor Harold Macmillan, off the idea of covert action. Nor did Dick White, the chief of the Secret Intelligence Service (SIS), eschew such activity, despite having been brought in to clean things up and tame the buccaneering style epitomized by senior officers such as George Young. If anything, the central driver underpinning deniable interventions, the gap between perceived responsibilities and actual capabilities, only increased after Suez. Diplomats maintained that Britain had no alternative but to maintain interests in many parts of the world and that these should be protected with the best use of available resources.[3] The public failure in Egypt cruelly exposed British decline and American ascendancy, but Britain still turned to covert action in an effort to hang on and maintain influence.

Just one month after retreat from Suez, Eden was frantically asking for updates on Yemen and pushing for more special operations against the imam.[4] When Macmillan became prime minister the following year, Britain continued to sponsor raids and plotted uprisings on a much larger scale. There were even discussions about arming tribes inside Yemen and planning a coup to overthrow Imam Ahmad.[5] Deniability remained crucial throughout and Whitehall ensured that supplies of weapons to tribes along the frontier could not be traced back to SIS. Officials pointed out that the 'necessary arms and funds have been supplied and will be supplied in such a manner that it will be impossible to bring home the operation to our agency or instigation'.[6]

The Foreign Office authorized at least three other covert actions across the Middle East in 1957. Britain had been distributing propaganda throughout the Persian Gulf from early 1956 and, in July 1957, extended this to Operation Tutor in Oman.[7] Elsewhere, SIS simultaneously embarked on Operation Scream in Lebanon, targeting Nasser's encroachment in the aftermath of Suez and shoring up the position of the pro-Western President Chamoun.[8] Britain, along with France, lobbied the Central Intelligence Agency (CIA) to fund sympathetic candidates in the elections that summer— and the CIA hesitantly agreed, delivering briefcases full of cash to the presidential palace.[9] Britain had earlier launched a concerted, but covert, effort to shape Lebanese internal security policy and replace French influence in the country. They did so without telling Paris and by drafting instructions in French so as to disguise the British hand.[10]

SIS continued operations against Egypt too. George Young carried on devising means to assassinate Nasser,[11] whilst Scant continued to broadcast propaganda throughout 1957. Patrick Dean felt optimistic that the Foreign Office could 'get a lot more money out of the Treasury for propaganda' and could continue to target Nasser across the region.[12] SIS—seemingly under the leadership of the CIA and alongside Iraqi, Jordanian, and Lebanese intelligence—also authorized Operation Sipony in 1957. Conducted from Beirut, intelligence officers aimed to use the Egyptian army to overthrow Nasser in a palace coup. It clearly failed, not least because the movement of so many shadowy intelligence figures in and out of the CIA station in Beirut was so obvious that the Egyptian ambassador in Lebanon apparently took bets on where and when the next anti-Nasser coup would take place.[13] Either way, any coup attempt, whether a success or failure, was good news for Britain. As one diplomat put it, 'next best to a plot against Nasser that succeeds is a plot that fails. Even the latter shows that the former stability of the regime has been shaken.'[14]

By now, though, Nasser's position was more secure. He enjoyed public Soviet support and there was far less hope of encouraging an opposition to take over. Amery and his co-conspirators were left deeply frustrated when the Suez invasion failed to instigate an uprising. That said, Operation Sawdust, the broader plan to undermine Nasser, also continued until 1958, as did black propaganda.[15] After the Iraqi coup of 1958, Khrushchev, ever keen to stoke tensions, warned Nasser that he remained a target for British assassination. Nasser had been holidaying in Yugoslavia before meeting Khrushchev, who warned him not to travel on an unarmed yacht back across the Mediterranean after the coup: 'It would be easy' for the West 'to sink your ship at sea and impossible for anyone to prove what happened'. Nasser heeded the warning and flew via Syria instead.[16]

Meanwhile, the Information Research Department (IRD) did not call off its grey propaganda campaign against Nasser, known as Transmission X, until late 1959.[17] In the same year, the British Regional Information Office in Beirut discussed a fairly small-scale operation to undermine the union between Egypt and Syria, known as the United Arab Republic, which had taken place in 1958. Targeting the Gulf and Aden, it sought to use unattributable propaganda disseminated by what officials called 'untraceable methods' to warn of the dangers of getting too close to Nasser.[18] By this time, however, diplomats back in London put the brakes on anti-Nasser operations.[19] Any kind of covert action risked spoiling recent efforts to resume diplomatic relations with him. The Sharq-al-adna radio station was handed over to the BBC and opted to play more bazaar music in a lighter approach to propaganda, which proved popular for years to come.[20] In return, the Soviets inserted agents inside the United Arab Republic to channel disinformation produced in Moscow and Prague. Targeting America and, to a lesser extent, the UK, forged material implicated the West in subversive activities against Arab nationalism. Eastern bloc intelligence collected signatures of senior diplomats, which could then be used in forged documents, by sending out Christmas cards to the Whitehall and Washington elite and eagerly awaiting the replies.[21]

British covert action in the Middle East followed a remarkably similar pattern. SIS worked with unsavoury allies and used bribery and unattributable propaganda to create an atmosphere conducive to a coup. All this activity was expensive and still funded by SIS's top-secret slush fund, codenamed HAM.[22] By 1958, so-called special political action projects cost around £455,000 each year—and were predicted to increase up to £1.5 million.[23] White maintained access to the annual £25,000 no-questions-asked allowance, but for anything above this he needed Foreign Office permission to withdraw and all monies had to align with a schedule of covert actions agreed between SIS, the Foreign Office, and the Treasury.[24] By 1958, White had amalgamated the unofficial money into SIS's official reserves, combining it with a sale of SIS gold secretly held by the Bank of England, a hoard of Deutschmarks, and a stash of other foreign currencies held in SIS stations around the world. This formed one large—and still very secret—pot. By this time, with the accrual of interest the fund reached around £1.4 million (more than £30 million today).[25] These arrangements came in useful throughout 1957 and 1958 when the secret account proved the only means of funding numerous covert operations.

White regulated covert action spending further. Special political operations had become, according to White, 'a regular part of the secret effort'.[26] With his schoolmaster character and lack of experience in agent-running, he is often thought to have curtailed covert action. In reality, he actually expanded and formalized it. Brook agreed that, given its regular use, covert action should be funded by the Secret Vote but, because 'the essence of SPA is improvisation', this had to be flexible. A margin from the Secret Vote was therefore kept back each year to be used for short-term covert actions, which Brook and White preferred to more ambitious long-haul operations. As covert action became a more commonplace means of executing government policy, Brook also called on the permanent secretaries to meet, as a steering body, every summer to discuss it.[27]

Britain continued covert action uninterrupted after Suez. The biggest potential snag had been relations with America, where President Eisenhower was furious about the invasion and refused to deal with Eden afterwards.[28] Frank Wisner also felt furious and betrayed, having been stood up by Dean for dinner and port in October 1956. Little did Wisner know that his absent friend was busy on a secret mission in France.[29] Yet intelligence relations remained remarkably unscathed and Macmillan increasingly sought to coordinate covert action with Washington.

Transatlantic cooperation

With Britain in decline, it became ever clearer that the Americans held more of the cards. But, their global reputations on the line, British policy-makers drew very different lessons from Suez than did their co-conspirators, the French. Whilst Paris saw Washington as an unreliable ally and went off to build its own independent nuclear weapons, London, by contrast, learnt that maintaining a global role necessitated staying on the right side of American foreign policy.[30] Despite this, Tracy Barnes, the CIA's liaison with SIS after Suez, was struck by the world-weariness of the British. One senior SIS officer told him that it was all 'a lot of shit' and that Britain was now 'just playing games'.[31]

Harold Macmillan, who succeeded Anthony Eden as prime minister in early 1957, was an increasing enthusiast of covert action—and saw it as more than games. He knew that responding to a range of global threats with force risked political condemnation in the United Nations, and that the Americans were expanding their own programme of covert action at an alarming rate. Macmillan had maintained good personal relations with President Eisenhower since their time in North Africa during the war. Well liked in Washington generally, he thought the two of them were 'thick as thieves'.[32] With Macmillan, or Handsome Harold as Eisenhower's political warfare chief referred to him,[33] Anglo–American covert action was back on the table as early as 1957.

By this time, SIS was eyeing up regime change in Syria once more. The US State Department reported in the spring that Britain favoured 'active stimulation of a change in the present regime in Syria'. This was out of step with Washington's thinking, which did not yet consider the situation irretrievable.[34] Gradually, though, as Britain lobbied for a coup and the CIA revised its assessments, the Anglo–American positions aligned.[35] In May, Patrick Dean thought it still possible to 'overturn the leftist regime in Syria', although, as his lunching companion, Evelyn Shuckburgh, noted, he had 'been thinking that for a long time'.[36]

Britain and America agreed Operation Avalon in autumn 1957, at a cost of a further £50,000 on top of the Straggle money.[37] The plan had three parts. First, SIS and the CIA would promote unrest within Syria. Second, they would provoke border incidents between Syria and Iraq or Jordan. Third, the border incidents would trigger Iraqi or Jordanian military intervention alongside an Anglo–American coordinated tribal rebellion within Syria.[38] Drawing on external assets in Iraq and Jordan was vital because, as Allen Dulles, director of the CIA, noted, the opposition inside Syria was too weak to launch a coup on its own—especially after the government crackdown following earlier failures.[39] Turkey, as the most militarily powerful neighbouring state, and one which had been running its own dangerous subversion campaign against Syria in recent months, would also have to become quickly involved. Indeed, fear of Turkish aggression causing a Cold War flashpoint was one of the factors encouraging Anglo–American covert action in the first place.[40] For the intervention to be credible, however, it could not be led by Turkey, which was of course a NATO ally.[41]

The CIA saw Iraq as the most likely proxy to intervene first, not least because of previous collusion between SIS and Baghdad.[42] Selwyn Lloyd, Britain's foreign secretary, meanwhile suggested that 'Jordan must give the first push, to be followed by Iraq'. Both agreed that Turkey had to be able to follow up quickly as Iraq and Jordan were unable to carry out the operation alone.[43] This time, however, the CIA was more ambitious than SIS. Dulles hoped to use the operation to eventually create a union between Jordan and Iraq, believing that Jordan was not a viable state anyway and that such a union would offer assurances to Israel regarding a share of Jordanian waters. Lloyd stayed quiet on this latter aspect.[44] Privately, senior policymakers, including Macmillan himself, now rued what they saw as American recklessness in the region, fearing that unleashing Turkey might provoke war with the Soviets. It was ironic that it was SIS, rather than the CIA, which had made all the initial running in the region.[45]

The plan had some clear, if cynical, benefits. If these were uncovered, these neighbouring states, rather than the West would take the blame. Indeed, the White House refused to give any appearance that the Arab states were colluding with America and Britain.[46] Yet it was also a dangerous plan. Involving so many countries complicated the operation and created multiple variables to control. As Dulles put it to Selwyn Lloyd: 'we must perhaps be prepared to take some serious risks to avoid even greater risks and dangers later on'.[47]

In late September 1957, Lloyd proposed that the identification of prospective members of a new government should start at once. Harold Beeley, a senior official at the Foreign Office, told Lloyd to be patient and that the composition of any new government would depend on which regional states actually intervened. If Turkey ended up going in alone, he warned, then many Syrians would refuse to participate in the new government. To reduce uncertainty, planners in the CIA and Foreign Office decided to tip off the various governments and discreetly passed messages to Turkey, Iraq, and Jordan, paving the way for them to intervene in Syria. The Americans also passed a reassuring warning to Israel.[48] Deciding whom to tell, what to tell them, and how to tell them was diplomacy at its most intricately secretive. Dulles and Lloyd even discussed how best to deal with the inevitable UN vote on a ceasefire of military actions which had begun with their own covert blessing.[49] At a lower level, officials considered how best to get their files in order in case they had to explain their common positions to Parliament or Congress in the future.[50] The covert action essentially involved collusion remarkably similar to the Suez episode which had so angered America the year before; it is therefore of little wonder that Dulles dramatically warned those around the table, including Lloyd, that this was excruciatingly secret and to protect it with their lives if necessary.[51]

Like most covert action, Operation Avalon drew heavily on unattributable propaganda. Lloyd and John Foster Dulles, his American counterpart, agreed that the psychological and internal subversion programmes should be started at once, even before agreement had been reached on the ensuing Arab intervention. Propaganda highlighted the dangers of communism and provided much of the groundwork for revolution. It argued that the pro-Soviet regime in Syria lacked popular support and that the Soviets at heart were supporters of Israel willing to double-cross their supposed friends.[52] At the working level, SIS and CIA planners felt it 'impossible to exaggerate the importance of the "psychological warfare" aspects'. Demonstrating a wider pattern in Middle Eastern covert action, this was because, as they put it, 'an appropriate climate for Arab military action against Syria had to be created for success to be achieved'. Both SIS and the CIA mobilized their press assets in the region, whilst clandestine British short- and medium-wave transmitters were to spring into action.[53] Ralph Murray, a former head of the IRD, left his day duties overseeing Soviet policy to head the overt and covert propaganda programmes.[54]

Propaganda was rarely an end in itself. It was designed to create an atmosphere conducive to the success of a broader operation. This time, the plan involved propaganda in conjunction with internal disturbances inside Syria, including sabotage. Lloyd suggested using the Muslim Brotherhood to cause internal disturbances. State Department officials consented, but warned against expending assets prematurely. Accordingly, Dulles and Lloyd agreed to 'minor sabotage'.[55] False flag operations formed another important tactic. SIS and the CIA stressed how the Syrian regime had to be 'made to appear as the sponsor of plots, sabotage and violence against neighbouring governments'. They also planned for special operations ascribable to Syria to be mounted in Iraq, Jordan, and Lebanon, including 'sabotage, national conspiracies and various strong-arm activities'.[56] False flag sabotage, conducted against a backdrop of hostile propaganda, would help incite violence both within and against Syria. The original plan involved using what looked like Syrian planes to attack Iraqi forces in an attempt to further stoke violence and disorder. Lloyd vetoed this as being fraught with danger.[57]

Assassination was also on the agenda. Remarkably this was agreed in unambiguous language:

> A special effort should be made to eliminate key individuals. Their removal should be accomplished early in the course of the uprising and intervention and in the light of the circumstances existing at the time.[58]

SIS and the CIA even named 'those who should be eliminated': Abd al-Hamid Sarraj, the leftist head of Syrian intelligence; Afif al-Bizri, army chief of staff and a suspected communist sympathizer; and Khalid Bakdash, leader of the Syrian communists.[59] Perhaps demonstrating an indirect approach to assassination, SIS and the CIA had previously commented that plans for minor sabotage should not be such as to increase the personal protection measures of key figures in the Syrian government, thereby leaving them open to attack by opponents—perhaps without SIS and the CIA ever having to give an order directly.[60]

SIS and the CIA thought that the Soviets would not respond with military force and that they would essentially get away with the operation,[61] but the local CIA station chief was less sanguine. He strongly advised against the whole coup idea and was confident that the Syrians had penetrated the plot. Washington clumsily, as he later rued, overruled him.[62] He was right and the plans soon fell apart.

As Egypt offered more direct military support to Syria, and Iraq increasingly turned to diplomatic engagement, the CIA accepted that the proposed operation would not succeed. Any covert action would have had to rely solely on the Turks, which, to growing relief within SIS, was too dangerous.[63] Meanwhile, the French intelligence services turned to Syria too. Not put off by their own experiences in Suez, they suggested instigating a coup, with Shishakli, the former dictator, tapped up to take the lead once the conditions were ripe. Ivone Kirkpatrick, outgoing head of the Foreign Office, was evasive in response: now was not the time for more Anglo–French collusion.[64] And Paris had no idea that SIS had tried—and failed—more than once themselves in recent months. It was not a wasted experience, though; the cooperation provided a model for joint Anglo–American planning which defined covert action under Macmillan. It demonstrated that transatlantic covert action relationship had survived Suez. Amidst fears that the Soviets were winning the Cold War in the region, a new era of pragmatic transatlantic competitive cooperation began.[65]

Working groups

Aware of the shifting balance of power and keen to harness American strength in order to uphold British influence, Macmillan prioritized an interdependent relationship with Washington.[66] For the US State Department, interdependence meant Britain no longer had the strength to pursue its own approach on major international issues and instead sought to make its voice heard through influence on Washington.[67] This was a fair assessment. The Foreign Office rather desperately advocated involving themselves so closely with the Americans that 'withdrawal on either side ceases to be practical policy'.[68] This inevitably extended to covert activities leaving secret service liaison, together with nuclear weapons, as the twin pillars of any remaining special relationship.[69]

Macmillan did not think his personal ties with Eisenhower would be enough and worked hard to institutionalize the relationship through an Anglo–American working group system.[70] After seeking assurances that a successor Labour government, if elected, would essentially adopt the same foreign policy as the Conservatives, Eisenhower and Secretary of State John Foster Dulles agreed in October 1957.[71] They had been very impressed by the secret cooperation over Syria, and the personal role of Macmillan in instigating it. The relationship had been far more 'genuine, intimate and effective' than under Eden, Dulles noted gladly.[72]

Macmillan and Eisenhower committed themselves to achieving maximum practicable coordination across a range of fields including politics, economics, defence, and psychological warfare.[73] Working groups therefore covered nuclear matters, trade, intelligence issues surrounding Hong Kong, the insurgency in Algeria, as well as covert action. On the latter, they brought together SIS, the Foreign Office (and the Ministry of Defence, Colonial Office, and Commonwealth Relations Office where appropriate) along with the CIA, State Department (and Pentagon when necessary) to consider sensitive topics including psychological and economic warfare, Syria, Lebanon, Indonesia, and Yemen.[74] Norman Brook enthused that there was 'now full co-ordination between United Kingdom and United States authorities over S.P.A. objectives and targets'. This was helped in no small part by American willingness to bear the major financial responsibility.[75]

Secret collaboration went to the very top. The following summer, Macmillan and Brook met the Dulles brothers in the White House to discuss anti-communist policy. Allen Dulles, still head of the CIA, explained that there were two types of situation in which a country had been so badly penetrated by communists that it risked a communist takeover. The first was through paramilitary activity, as in Cuba, and the second involved what he called 'a creeping spread of Communism through the electoral process', as threatened Italy. Accordingly, Dulles proposed initiating counter-action in numerous countries including Burma, Indonesia, France, and Italy. He also suggested that differences between Tito and Moscow might give the CIA and SIS a new opportunity for operations, most likely in Albania.[76] As his British guests listened intently, Dulles warned that communist penetration of the labour movement even in countries where they were weak in parliament, such as Japan, was also dangerous.[77] It is unclear whether SIS knew that the CIA was covertly supporting the Japanese Liberal Democratic Party in what became one of the more successful, and little-known, anti-communist operations of the Cold War.[78] Dulles also criticized the British position within the International Confederation of Free Trade Unions, urging the UK to take a leading role in aiding it fight communism. This had the potential, the CIA believed, to counter communism in places like India and Japan, but at present merely amounted to 'a kind of "lowest common denominator" of the fears and prejudices of its members.'[79]

The first working group priority was Syria. It was through similar machinery, chaired by the CIA's Kermit Roosevelt, that SIS had approached Operation Avalon in the autumn of 1957.[80] By the following year, the Syria Working Group covered the Middle East in general and coordinated propaganda and psychological warfare.[81] It even considered manoeuvres against the imam in Yemen, an area where SIS had traditionally taken the lead.[82] Although the State Department neither thought the imam a lost cause nor placed Arabia at the top of its hectic foreign policy agenda,[83] American diplomats knew that Britain sought 'to undertake political action to facilitate the transfer of power to a more friendly Yemen Government'.[84] The imam, still alive after numerous assassination attempts and having successfully fended off attempted coups by family members, continued to refer to Aden and the south as 'Occupied Yemen'. He beheaded or imprisoned those threatening his position, made overtures towards joining Egypt and Syria's short-lived United Arab Republic, and interpreted Yemen as including all lands south of Mecca, from the Red Sea to the Persian Gulf. In short, he could still cause trouble for the British imperialists and threaten the strategically vital position in Aden.[85] Driven by Whitehall, the working group subsequently considered whether a major subversive operation was possible.[86]

Once again, Harold Macmillan took the lead. Discussing Yemen with John Foster Dulles, he agreed to build up intelligence assets and then to work through Prince Hassan, the imam's brother, to, at the very least, subvert the Yemeni government. In an ideal world, Macmillan and SIS hoped to overthrow it. Time, he emphasized, was of the essence. It was a risky strategy, though, not least because Hassan also opposed the British presence in Aden and American officials warned any operation would be difficult.[87] Ultimately, the working group struggled to agree on an action plan.[88] Communications soon broke down and British diplomats complained to their American counterparts about a lack of intelligence-sharing. After checking with the CIA, the State Department sent a snide note back and professed to being mystified by British irritation.[89]

Meanwhile, Britain launched another discreet operation, this time in Oman and without American support. In fact, and demonstrating the pragmatic nature of any so-called special relationship, the Americans—or at least the American oil company, Aramco—actually supported the opposing side instead. In 1958, Julian Amery, now secretary of state for war, offered his old friend David Smiley command of the Sultan's Armed Forces in order to quash a rebellion in the Omani interior. Exploration for oil had begun and the British held clear interests in helping the sultan stabilize his territory. For similar reasons, the Saudis and Aramco, keen to extend their own stake, supported the Omani rebels in what became a shadowy proxy conflict.[90] The Foreign Office felt that large military intervention was too expensive and would attract negative attention. Therefore, it was the Special Air Service (SAS) that worked quietly alongside Smiley's local forces.[91] Secrecy surrounded the mission. SAS men, travelling from Kuala Lumpur, did not know even where they would be fighting until they changed planes at Colombo.[92] It was a swift mission. British-led forces recaptured the rebel stronghold in early 1959 and, in doing so, claimed a decisive victory not just for the UK, but also for the SAS, the future of which had been in doubt.[93]

Oman aside, by the end of the decade covert action looked to have been a mistake. Despite attempts to hide behind allies and maximize plausible deniability, British policy, including Suez and the plots against Syria, according to the Foreign Office's Sam Falle, himself a veteran of Operation Boot, had 'sown the deepest suspicion of us and our motives'. He worried that Britain had played its hand so badly that it might be impossible to recover without a drastic rethink to 'save something from the wreck'.[94] A more constructive, forward-thinking attitude to Arab nationalism was needed. Falle was perceptive, for people and governments across the Middle East began to see conspiracies everywhere as trust in the West plummeted. Manipulation—and, equally importantly, suspicions of manipulation—left its mark on a generation of writers and activists. The fallout can still be felt many decades later and, arguably, has held back development and modernization across the region.[95] The British hand may have been as indirect as possible, but ultimately it did not remove London from suspicions of conspiracy.

Turning attention to Asia

By 1956, Patrick Dean was calling for more counter-subversion, both open and deniable, in Burma and Indonesia. He noted that action in Indochina was already in hand thanks to a secret agreement between the CIA and the chief of SIS.[96] It was instead Indonesia where an Anglo–American working group would be more successful, coordinating covert support for a rebellion against its President Sukarno.[97] President since the end of the Second World War, Sukarno had played a prominent role in Indonesia's independence from the Dutch. As the 1950s progressed he took greater personal control, nationalized hundreds of Dutch companies, and allowed left-wing movements greater influence. While he was not a communist, he was viewed favourably by the Communist Party—which was one of the strongest in the non-communist world. All of this drew concern from SIS and the CIA, who feared that if one state fell to communism others would soon follow.

Wasting little time, the working group met to plot Sukarno's fate five times during January 1958 alone.[98] This time the Americans, who had spent millions trying to fix the 1955 elections and had been working on this particular plan since summer 1957,[99] drove the planning and thought it practical to bring the British up to speed after the CIA had approached an ex-Special Operations Executive (SOE) officer, John Galvin, now a businessman with considerable shipping activities in the area, to help supply arms to the rebels.[100] Dubbed Operation Haik, the CIA plotted to repeat the successes of the overthrow of President Arbenz in Guatemala four years earlier by using a psychological campaign to allow a contrived military offensive to strike fear into the regime.[101] The plan also involved encouraging non-communist factions to work together and install a new government on the island of Java, whilst also building up anti-communist forces across the outer islands.[102]

Demonstrating interdependence in action, the State Department and CIA needed British cooperation, namely access to bases in Singapore. Macmillan was initially sceptical, but heeded the advice of Robert Scott, the commissioner-general for Southeast Asia, over more cautious voices in the Foreign Office.[103] Believing that Sukarno had 'irredeemably identified' with the communists, Scott lobbied Macmillan directly to offer the rebels covert support.[104] The prime minister knew that overt military intervention risked international condemnation or escalation to a limited war,[105] and so covert action alongside the Americans offered a discreet and politically appealing solution. He agreed to help the CIA build up the rebels' military capabilities and unite various dissident factions so long as the origins of that support remained concealed.[106] But, in practice, he and Lloyd limited assistance to making facilities available for refuelling undercover CIA planes and for use as staging posts for supplies sent to the rebels. They would not allow arms to come through Singapore.[107] At the same time, British diplomats worked through the legal implications of recognizing a new rebel government.[108]

Unfortunately for London, the working group model failed to live up to Macmillan's high expectations. Cooperation was seriously hampered by four factors. First, the CIA and State Department had a difficult relationship and, as Macmillan was told, neither side trusted the other. Second, the Foreign Office grew frustrated with Washington's inevitably selective approach to intelligence-sharing. Third, lack of intelligence on the ground severely hindered planning.[109] Fourth, the CIA remained cautious about British security, especially given the perpetual spy scandals hounding Macmillan's premiership. In response, diplomats sneered snobbishly at the Americans' failure to 'live up to public school traditions'.[110] Both sides feared leaks and pressed for ever smaller and more personal meetings.[111] Intense secrecy hindered coordination and dissemination, with diplomats soon realizing that the secret had been kept too well.[112] Accordingly, working groups had all but vanished by 1959, replaced by a renewed emphasis on informal consultation.[113]

The failure of Operation Haik in Indonesia demonstrated many of these issues. As decisions were taken by ever smaller groups of people, covert action became increasingly divorced from broader policy, leaving those on the ground frustrated.[114] Robert Scott, for example, became increasingly troubled by the lack of policy guidance coming from his superiors in London. Similarly, Commander-in-Chief (Far East) Francis Festing complained to Gerald Templer, chief of the imperial general staff, about how events in Indonesia had been allowed to drift.[115] Feeling frozen out of the planning and lacking policy guidance, the military resurrected its familiar complaints about a lack of drive in covert action and there was even talk of summoning Dick White, chief of SIS, to the next chiefs of staff meeting to explain himself.[116] To make matters worse, the covert action planners also lacked accurate intelligence on which to base their operations,[117] whilst a retrospective American assessment attacked the operation for exhibiting 'no prior planning on the part of anyone' within Washington.[118] With his presidency drawing to a close, Eisenhower scolded Allen Dulles, insisting that the CIA was badly run and badly organized.[119]

Although signs had appeared promising at first, with a rebel administration formed on Sumatra in February 1958, the Indonesian uprising failed. By March, Macmillan privately conceded that Britain was 'losing out in Indonesia, in spite of as much "covert" help that we and the US can give them quietly'.[120] Western support ultimately came to an abrupt end in May after an undercover CIA plane was shot down following the accidental bombing of a church. Although Washington ruthlessly hoped to disown the captured pilot as a mere soldier of fortune, deniability was no longer plausible. The following month, and after a string of rebel defeats, the Foreign Office told Macmillan that the Indonesian rebellion had failed and that it was too dangerous to try to salvage it.[121] Britain had been swept up in an American failure. Planners in the State Department soon realized that they had over-estimated the power of anti-communism to unify various groups in armed opposition to the central government. In a moment of candid self-reflection, US diplomats privately admitted that they had been too quick in unques-tioningly assuming that rebels possessed intelligence, maturity, and political sagacity just because they opposed communism.[122]

America and Britain needed a new approach and Harold Caccia, British ambassador in Washington, suggested to the Dulles brothers that they could 'try to open chinks on the government side'. Robert Scott, an early supporter of covert action, favoured this and advocated working through Abdul Nasution, a senior general soon to become Indonesian defence minister. Although the Dulles brothers were unconvinced, the broader idea of dividing Sukarno's government was more sensible.[123] Instead of covertly supporting anti-government rebels, SIS and the CIA decided to aid non-communist elements inside the government—notably in the army—instead.[124] Interestingly, this formed a similar pattern to covert action in Albania earlier in the decade when, after instigating a failed rebellion, SIS and the CIA switched support to more internal targets. Covering all bases, the Foreign Office nevertheless deemed it prudent to maintain discreet contacts with the dissident leaders as well.[125]

The era of working groups and, by extension, of formal Anglo–American interdependence on covert action was short-lived and marked by disap-pointment. It involved operations in Syria, Yemen, and Indonesia—all of which failed. Yemen did not even get off the ground. Sensitivities surround-ing security and intelligence-sharing combined with bureaucratic rivalries severely impeded formal cooperation. The demise of the working groups gave rise to a period of as much tension with America as there was cooper-ation when it came to covert action. As the 1950s gave way to the 1960s, Britain's policy in the Middle East and Southeast Asia was at odds with that of the State Department and the new president, John Kennedy. It spawned an unhappy period of drift for Britain's covert action planners.

8

DECOLONIZATION AND DRIFT

The Battle for Influence after Empire

From my point of view there is no doctrinal objection to the use of clandestine and covert activities.

Alan Lennox-Boyd, 1955[1]

Britain's colonial rule was built on information management and it is no exaggeration to describe the British Empire as an 'empire of intelligence.'[2] Swathes of information, gathered as part of the process of colonial governance, were vital to allow a few administrators to govern vast territories such as India. Intelligence in the colonies had developed differently from intelligence in Whitehall: it remained more informal, less glamorous, part of the quotidian administration. Relying more on the autonomous activity of local authorities, the Colonial Office traditionally enjoyed relatively little interaction with the rest of Whitehall's intelligence and security machinery.[3]

This began to change from the late 1940s, when policymakers in Whitehall saw the empire as a new front line of the Cold War.[4] Britain had granted independence to India, Pakistan, Burma, and Sri Lanka by 1950 and nationalism swept across remaining territories in Africa and Southeast Asia. By the mid-1950s, Britain had faced an insurgency in Palestine and was fighting rebellions in Malaya, Cyprus, and Kenya. Each of these relied on covert operations, involving black propaganda and deception, to supplement conventional political and military counter-insurgency techniques.[5] In Cyprus, for example, propaganda portrayed nationalist fighters as paedophiles, whilst in Kenya plans were afoot to stage an outbreak of disease by spreading rumours, planting dead bodies, and using fake doctors to lower insurgent morale and force them out of the forests.[6]

Policymakers and intelligence analysts alike feared nationalist unrest would be exploited by Moscow and these fears grew as more colonies neared independence, creating a potential power vacuum. This was the era of competitive coexistence and an enticing opportunity for Khrushchev to intervene in parts of the world previously out of reach. Whitehall braced itself for a subterranean battle for influence, although much Soviet activity targeted American ascendency rather than the old colonial powers, for Moscow was already confident of British decline.[7] Policymakers had already pressed MI5 to take a closer interest in colonial security and help train local services to be ready for independence.[8] But this was not enough. Faced with a growing threat and already waging prolonged counter-insurgencies, Prime Minister Anthony Eden called for preventative covert action in the colonies from 1955.[9]

A new front line?

Imperial and Commonwealth territories complicated covert action. Officials hotly debated whether it was right to subvert populations; whether local ministers should be consulted; and whether the Secret Intelligence Service (SIS) should be involved. Most contentious of all was who should be in charge. Alan Lennox-Boyd, the colonial secretary, signed up to covert action in principle, but intended to assume control.[10] Unsurprisingly, this angered senior diplomats who had spent the best part of a decade persistently fending off military designs and had no intention of relinquishing authority—even in the colonial sphere. Ivone Kirkpatrick, the permanent under-secretary, made the point characteristically bluntly—'we wish to have a finger in the Colonial pie'—and insisted that governors could not veto covert action.[11] Norman Brook complicated matters further by insisting that SIS remained responsible for all covert action, including in the colonies. This challenged the status quo whereby MI5 traditionally enjoyed jurisdiction over British territory, including the colonies and extending to the Commonwealth.[12]

When the Official Committee on Communism (Overseas) disbanded in 1956, Brook created a new one specializing in colonial security: the Committee for Counter-Subversion in the Colonial Territories. Chairing it himself, it became known simply as the Brook committee. Once more Norman Brook found himself at the centre of British covert action planning.

In his sixteen years as cabinet secretary, the great technician and unflap-
pable backroom coordinator advised successive prime ministers on these
most sensitive matters. Some called him the 'best mind in the civil service',
others 'the grey eminence'. Nobody in Whitehall knew more British secrets
than he.[13] Dick White, vastly experienced in colonial security from his time
running MI5 and now the new chief of SIS, was another prominent member.
Their aim was to consider where covert measures could support British policy
in individual territories, especially those moving towards independence.[14]

The Brook committee came up with a range of ideas targeting colonies
from the Gold Coast to the Caribbean, Nigeria to Malaya. As usual they
revolved around all shades of propaganda but extended to bribery, blackmail,
and political action designed to encourage more favourable leaders emerging
amongst nationalist movements. British Guiana forms the most important
example.[15] In the absence of an effective moderate political party, Brook
tried to secure what he called 'better leadership' of the People's Progressive
Party, led by Cheddi Jagan, a dentist turned politician whom Britain feared
possessed communist sympathies. Plans involved discrediting Jagan and
building up his rival Forbes Burnham. This was despite acknowledging that
Burnham was bitterly anti-European and would have been a deeply flawed
leader.[16] Brook and his colleagues also talked about training foreign nationals
on imperial territory to support covert action as well as arrangements for
'stay-behind' networks in colonies approaching independence.[17]

Unfortunately for Brook, the entire approach was an utter failure. Despite
the gathering momentum in Whitehall and Westminster, covert action
achieved little in the colonies. Four reasons explain this. First, many officials,
from Alex Kellar, MI5's expert on colonial security, to the governors of
British Guiana and the Gold Coast, strongly believed that it was morally
wrong to engage in covert activity against colonial or Commonwealth citizens. It was simply un-British and unbefitting of Britain's global status.[18]
Kellar argued that even suspicion of covert action would erode trust and
undermine the entire approach underpinning decolonization.[19] Second, the
Colonial Office resented encroachment by the Foreign Office and justifi-
ably accused diplomats of misunderstanding the threat by obsessing over
communism.[20] These two factors caused colonial officials to express far
greater caution about covert action than their counterparts elsewhere in
Whitehall. More familiar with trying to restrain the overactive chiefs of
staff, Patrick Dean, overseeing intelligence and security matters, and
Kirkpatrick now attempted to stimulate the somnolent Colonial Office and
grew increasingly frustrated with their reservations and lack of experience in

covert action.[21] This played out on the ground across Africa, where George Young sent an SIS officer, Frank Steele, to tour colonial capitals. He was welcomed by a great deal of 'over my dead body' responses.[22]

Third, Britain did not necessarily need to engage in risky covert activity. Colonial authorities had the power to introduce reforms to counter subversion. Britain had no power to change the Albanian constitution and had to resort to covert intervention. By contrast, Britain could—and did—simply suspend the constitution in British Guiana in 1953 after Jagan won an earlier election.[23] Fourth, the fluidity of colonial security impeded centralized management by senior officials in London. With so many territories at different stages of independence, with differing constitutions, and facing a spectrum of threats from communism to nationalism, strategic planning proved difficult.[24]

Covert action in these constitutionally complex areas therefore proved to be a damp squib. The cumbersome committee soon fell by the wayside. In its place, Brook strengthened SIS's top-secret Special Political Action (SPA) section, created in late 1953 or early 1954 and responsible for conducting covert action. From July 1958, he established an SPA Group allowing representatives from the Colonial Office, Commonwealth Relations Office, and the Ministry of Defence's deception planners to work with SIS for the first time—albeit on a part-time basis.[25] Underscoring Foreign Office dominance, the diplomats maintained full-time liaison. As for ministers, they were to be told as little as possible about specific operations, and, if one did gain knowledge, Brook noted that he should be warned not to discuss it.[26] Brook and the Committee of Permanent Secretaries on the Intelligence Services met every summer to oversee the special political action programme.[27] The idea was to streamline covert action, ensure political control, and redress the balance between inter-departmental discussion whilst maintaining broader departmental policy.[28] This pleased the new senior official at the Foreign Office, Frederick Hoyer Millar, who ominously noted that 'we expect there to be a growing need for this form of activity rather than the reverse'.[29]

Transition to independence

Whitehall had two objectives as more colonies moved towards independence in the late 1950s and 1960s: to preserve as much post-colonial influence as possible and to prevent Soviet encroachment into Africa. Accordingly, and despite the failure, officials did not give up on covert action and tried to fix certain election results.[30] This involved prioritizing indigenous groups deemed more reliable, inserting them into local institutions as a mechanism of political control, and accommodating moderate nationalist movements.[31] Officials attempted most of this overtly through aid, trade, defence agreements, threats of coercion, and political reforms to generate goodwill.[32] Deniable activity supplemented these measures and both the Colonial and Commonwealth Relations Offices sponsored covert action themselves.[33] In the Gold Coast, Governor Charles Arden-Clarke helped Kwame Nkrumah, the nationalist leader with whom he had an excellent working relationship, to win the 1954 elections to such an extent that he was dubbed Nkrumah's 'propaganda secretary'.[34] Interestingly, it seems that Britain later discussed with the CIA the possibility of overthrowing Nkrumah in spring 1961 and again in 1964. A coup—in which Western foreknowledge is at least suspected—took place in 1966.[35]

Meanwhile, in Singapore SIS inserted an agent into the entourage of Lee Kuan Yew, the future prime minister. Amidst fears that Lee was collaborating with known communists, a freelance writer, Alex Josey, began spending a great deal of time with him. Josey's attendance of left-wing meetings in the region worried some in the CIA, until its Far East Division chief, who knew that Josey was ex-SOE, reassured them that he was 'great at the vagabond leftist act' and was, in fact, 'working on' Lee.[36]

Sudan gained independence in 1956, but enjoyed little stability thereafter. The following year Britain launched not one but three covert operations to manipulate political developments. The first, Operation Scion, targeted the forthcoming elections at a cost of £98,000 (with another government putting in £102,000). The second, Operation Aileron, targeted Sudanese newspapers for two years at a cost of £10,000 up front followed by £3,000 each year. The third, Operation Alismah, somehow involved the nationalist political and religious leader Abd al-Rahman al-Mahdi. However, in what appears to be another case of Britain hiding behind someone else—likely Israel—to maximize deniability, the plan merely involved SIS giving a guarantee of up to £250,000 while hoping not actually to spend anything.[37] Al-Mahdi had long been a thorn in the side of colonial rule but was seen as the lesser evil after a Nasserite People's Democratic Party established itself in 1956. Details of the covert action are sparse, but the Umma Party, of which al-Mahdi was a leading figure, won the most seats in the 1958 elections. In November, a military coup overthrew the civilian government altogether. Al-Mahdi supported this, whilst the Sudanese Communist Party opposed it and went on to attempt a series of counter-coups.

In Tanganyika in May 1959, Governor Richard Turnbull advocated using deception to, in his words, 'tame' and promote the nationalist leader, Julius Nyerere.[38] The following year, Britain rigged the Nigerian election. The governor-general, James Robertson, allegedly asked a colonial officer, Harold Smith, to ensure that the northern region of Nigeria, the most conservative and traditionally closest to the UK, held the balance of power upon independence in 1960. Unfortunately, the party which dominated the north, the Northern People's Congress Party, lacked power to govern the whole of an independent Nigeria alone. Therefore, Smith claims to have co-opted a nationalist party, the National Council of Nigerian Citizens, in the east, seemingly through blackmail of their leader, Nnamdi Azikiwe, to do a deal with the Northern People's Congress Party.[39] Britain continued to use similar tactics into the 1960s. In Zambia, Daphne Park, SIS's redoubtable officer on the ground, channelled funds to support Kenneth Kaunda's election campaign, as the least undesirable of the available candidates, after independence in 1964.[40]

Given the underwhelming performance of British covert action in the colonies, it is hardly surprising that the largest operation on imperial territory was not conducted by SIS at all. Instead, the US took charge and covert action dramatically shaped British Guiana's transition to independence in 1966.[41] Washington had long coveted a role in British territories, so much so that a decade earlier Patrick Dean had flown to Singapore to try and convince the governor there to liaise with the CIA on matters of counter-subversion. Doing so, he claimed, would have prevented the CIA from embarking on dangerous unilateral covert actions.[42] The Colonial Office mandarins were horrified;[43] yet liaison had little impact anyway, as CIA officers continued to run their own operations on British imperial territory regardless. Working from Singapore, they developed political warfare schemes in such a way that, if SIS found out, they could present the operations as being merely exploratory.[44] One CIA officer worked by the dictum, 'liaison with the British is one of our greatest assets; don't tell the bastards anything important'.[45] Unlike covert action elsewhere, the colonial and Commonwealth context formed a rare case in which Whitehall chose to distance itself from the Americans.[46] Britain and America were increasingly in covert competition, with the CIA looking to shift its focus from Europe and cultivate new leaders in independent countries.[47]

In April 1961, British and American officials met to explore means of influencing the forthcoming election in British Guiana and prevent Cheddi Jagan from winning. The local MI5 representative, stationed in Trinidad, was sceptical about the prospect of covert action and warned that it risked unintended consequences for little chance of success.[48] Under pressure from Washington, Alec Douglas-Home, the foreign secretary, instead favoured working with Jagan to gently shape his outlook by supplying technical, economic, and financial aid.[49]

When this failed and Jagan's party won a clear majority, the White House tried again. They knew that Britain opposed covert action in the colonies, but hoped British Guiana would be an exception and pressed hard for a coordinated operation to politically destroy communists there whilst building up locally acceptable non-communist leadership.[50] When Douglas-Home again refused, Dean Rusk, secretary of state, brusquely informed him that Washington simply would not 'put up with an independent British Guiana under Jagan'.[51] In a particularly blunt letter, Rusk demanded that Britain join the CIA in overthrowing him.[52]

Douglas-Home and Harold Macmillan were taken aback by what Macmillan described as Rusk's 'pure Machiavellianism'. Douglas-Home replied with a snide dig at previous American covert action, pointing out that the president of Guatemala was using language reminiscent of Hitler to press his claim for control of British Honduras and urged the Americans to 'prevent another misadventure' on their doorstep.[53] President Kennedy felt the exchange was a bit sharp, to which Douglas-Home retorted: 'it was lucky I had not sent my first reply'.[54]

Macmillan and Douglas-Home soon gave in to American pressure. British Guiana became increasingly troublesome, held little strategic value compared to the likes of Aden, and fell into America's sphere of influence.[55] But Macmillan thoroughly enjoyed making Washington squirm over the prickly issue of colonialism. He later admitted that it was 'rather fun making the Americans repeat over and over again their passionate plea to us to stick to "Colonialism" and "imperialism" at any cost'.[56] Macmillan may have enjoyed teasing Americans over their hypocrisy, but his sense of humour was not shared in the Colonial Office, where officials variously described Washington's position as 'ambivalent, schizophrenic or just two-faced',[57] and bitterly derided Puerto Rico, New Mexico, Wyoming, Alaska, Louisiana, and elsewhere as little more than colonial territories.[58] British Guiana allowed Whitehall to make a point.

After Macmillan consented to covert action, President Kennedy swiftly authorized a covert $2 million CIA operation to drive Jagan from power before British Guiana attained independence. In October 1962, Duncan Sandys, as colonial secretary, gave the CIA the green light to approach Jagan's foremost political opponents, Forbes Burnham and Peter D'Aguiar. Both received funding and advice from the Americans. Throughout all of this, Roger Hollis, the director-general of MI5, instructed his staff to steer clear of the planning.[59] Over the next two years, the CIA executed a striking array of plots to destabilize Jagan. They rigged elections, bribed trade unions, organized strikes and riots, and apparently even orchestrated bombing campaigns.[60] The latter may have been to justify a return to British direct rule, the pretext for which, the State Department accepted, had to withstand public scrutiny.[61] Harold Wilson, upon entering Number 10, continued to sanction the use of covert methods in British Guiana from 1964. Ultimately, Jagan lost the 1964 election and was succeeded by a coalition headed by Forbes Burnham—the target simultaneously built up by the CIA as 'Washington's man'.[62]

Cooperating with the CIA

Informal cooperation between Britain and the CIA was easier outside of the imperial context. After the failure to overthrow Sukarno in Indonesia, Macmillan turned his attention to American covert action in Cuba, where in early 1959 Fidel Castro had assumed power after a dramatic insurgency. The following year, Eisenhower left Macmillan in no doubt that he wanted to be rid of Castro and was prepared to use covert methods to establish the conditions necessary for a counter-revolution. As in Indonesia, Eisenhower again sought British assistance—this time in the form of economic pressure and support at the United Nations.[63] It was the covert elements, however, which worried the British embassy in Havana. Officials insisted that deniable financial and political support to émigré groups intent on overthrowing Castro was futile. In a hard lesson learned in Eastern Europe, such groups would be unable to succeed without being backed up by conventional military forces.[64] It appears that Maurice Oldfield, future chief of SIS and travelling around the Caribbean at the time, told the CIA that there was no evidence that a popular uprising would take place.[65] Norman Brook raised a wry smile and saw parallels with Britain's manoeuvrings against Nasser in the mid-1950s. He noted it was all too 'easy to offer a cynical comment'.[66]

Macmillan pressed Eisenhower for more details of CIA schemes and tried to offer advice. 'After all,' he added, 'we have been through it all ourselves.' The prime minister warned that covert action was fraught with difficulties and dangers, not least because the Cubans had grown suspicious about American interference and would rally around Castro as a martyr. Nonetheless, Eisenhower hoped he could count on British cooperation and shortly afterwards approved planning for what would become the disastrous Bay of Pigs operation under President Kennedy.[67] In April 1961, 1,400 Cuban exiles—covertly trained by the CIA—landed along beaches in the Bay of Pigs on the south of the island. With covert American air support, they hoped to inspire a popular uprising and overthrow Castro. It went spectacularly wrong. Castro gained advance warning of the operation, the CIA bombers missed most of their targets, bad weather hampered the invasion, and Castro launched a swift counter-attack. Watching from across the Atlantic, Macmillan was unimpressed by what he called 'a gross error of judgment' on Kennedy's part and professed to having had 'not great hopes of their winning'.[68] CIA failure also affected Whitehall's cold warriors. They realized that at some point most covert action will inevitably become undeniable.[69]

Meanwhile, the Americans plotted wider covert action from Tibet to Panama, China to the Dominican Republic. There is little evidence of British involvement, comment, or even knowledge,[70] but SIS did offer active assistance to regime change in Congo, where Patrice Lumumba had become the first democratically elected prime minister in 1960. Congo gained independence from Belgium in June of that year. It had been a messy process, with pressure for speed leaving many issues unresolved. As prime minister, Lumumba proved provocative, showed little appetite for a smooth transition, and immediately began attacking Western colonialism.[71] He was an avowed nationalist, a shameless opportunist, and inherently unpredictable. According to one Belgian official, Congo was a country of Groucho—rather than Karl—Marx and there is little evidence that Lumumba intended to align with the Soviets. But, as the newly independent country quickly slipped into chaos following army mutinies and attacks on Europeans, the White House feared that the Soviets would exploit the situation to gain a foothold in central Africa. Meanwhile, the CIA labelled Lumumba a communist sympathizer and interpreted developments as a classic communist takeover.[72] He had made overtures to Moscow and received favourable, if hollow, reassurances from Khrushchev. Russian intelligence was sorely under-represented not just in Congo but the whole of sub-Saharan Africa at the time,[73] yet Congo now became a flashpoint in the Cold War. Many feared the future of a continent was at stake.

Leaders in London held similar worries. Macmillan described Lumumba as 'a Communist stooge as well as a witch-doctor'.[74] Britain's ambassador, Ian Scott, compared him to Hitler and Mussolini.[75] Alec Douglas-Home wasted little time in promoting covert action. He reported to his Cabinet colleagues that Lumumba had obtained considerable support from the Soviets but knew that opposing him openly would be counterproductive. Douglas-Home therefore suggested doing so 'privately'. Macmillan, ever keen to preserve Anglo–American relations, agreed and authorized SIS to work with the CIA's Project WIZARD to destabilize and overthrow Lumumba.[76]

SIS turned to its increasingly familiar playbook of dirty tricks honed over the previous decade. As ever bribery was an obvious option, and leading politicians soon found themselves on the SIS payroll.[77] It is difficult to demonstrate the impact of bribery, but shortly afterwards the Congolese Senate began to balk at Lumumba's requests for Soviet intervention and considered a resolution censuring Lumumba for pro-communist and dictatorial acts. One opposition leader even called for a coup.[78] Meanwhile, the local SIS and CIA stations penetrated parliamentary opposition groups and began engineering a vote of no confidence in the new prime minister. Lumumba easily countered this through simple intimidation, surrounding the Senate with troops.[79]

Unsurprisingly, black propaganda was also on the agenda. SIS and the CIA both inserted forged letters into newspapers to discredit Lumumba and spread rumours of corruption and witchcraft. On the economic front, they organized go-slow campaigns in the workforce—another standard tactic used back in the late 1940s. In terms of political warfare, they instigated 'spontaneous' demonstrations and, as on the streets of Tehran, engineered mob protests and scuffles. This, according to Larry Devlin, the local CIA chief of station, would 'undermine Lumumba's image of a man loved by his people and in full control of the nation'.[80] In a further parallel to the overthrow of Mossadeq, the CIA, again supported by SIS, pressured the head of state, this time President Kasavubu, to remove his prime minister and then briefed him on how best to do it.[81]

Demonstrating remarkable continuity from early Cold War pinprick operations, Daphne Park, SIS's head of station, even used stink bombs to disperse crowds and perpetuate a general atmosphere of uncertainty and anarchy.[82] More sinisterly, SIS knew full well that if it was possible for their agents to detonate a stink bomb, it would be possible to detonate a real bomb.[83] Sabotage, including blowing up bridges, was also undertaken, likely by the CIA—although Park and Devlin worked very closely together.[84] By August 1960, rumours of coups against Lumumba swirled around Léopoldville.[85] Actively encouraged by both Park and Devlin, Joseph Mobutu, head of the Congolese army, seized power in September 1960. The following month, SIS and CIA manoeuvrings saw further success when twenty-five politicians from Lumumba's party retracted their support for him.[86] The general idea, as Park later explained, was to use 'really good intelligence' to 'set people directly against one another. They destroy each other, we don't destroy them.'[87]

High-level discussions between Britain and America continued, with Douglas-Home leading the charge. Replying to President Eisenhower's wish that Lumumba fall into a river full of crocodiles, he lamented how the West had lost many of the techniques of what he called 'old fashioned diplomacy'. The following week, he again stressed to Eisenhower the need to remove Lumumba.[88] Responding to Ian Scott's desire to make Lumumba disappear,[89] one tough diplomat—and future MI5 director-general—Howard Smith suggested killing him: 'This should in fact solve the problem, since, so far as we can tell, Lumumba is not a leader of a movement within which there are potential successors of his quality or influence.'[90] Although this was more a wish than a proposal, it found some support in the Foreign Office. Archie Ross, an old-fashioned and straight-laced veteran of Operation Boot, scribbled that 'there is much to be said for eliminating Lumumba, but unless Mobutu can get him arrested and executed promptly, he is likely to survive and continue to plague us all'.[91]

Lumumba was executed by firing squad in January 1961. It was an improvised and bungled job, resulting in his mangled corpse being dissolved in acid.[92] Daphne Park has since claimed responsibility.[93] A formidable woman and a strict keeper of official secrets, she supposedly made the uncharacteristic comment to a fellow peer over tea at the House of Lords in 2010. Most likely a dry joke, it is rather unlikely that SIS did it. SIS did not even directly organize it. Despite talk of killing leaders in Egypt and Syria a few years earlier, the British were not generally in the business of assassination. Macmillan had even worried about the precise circumstances of Lumumba's execution, fearing that troops loyal to Mobutu would 'kill him (and perhaps eat him!)', thereby undermining the Congolese government.[94]

By contrast, the CIA's Larry Devlin *was* tasked with assassinating Lumumba—using poisoned toothpaste provided by the CIA's appropriately named Health Alteration Committee which would have masked Lumumba's death as polio. 'Jesus H. Christ!', Devlin exclaimed when he received his order, before dragging his feet and cabling back: 'don't you know the Belgians are going to kill him?'[95] He was right. Congolese rebels eventually killed Lumumba at the Belgians' command, although the CIA had encouraged both parties.

SIS was guilty of indirect complicity. Throughout the preceding decade, Britain had developed a dubious track record of creating atmospheres conducive to the murder of problematic individuals and this now extended to Congo and Lumumba. After being sacked by the president and put under house arrest, Lumumba tried to escape but was soon captured by Mobutu's forces. He was beaten, humiliated, and handed over to secessionist rebels in the full knowledge that they would kill him. SIS's campaign of destabilization whipped the population into fervour and created conditions in which murder was practically inevitable. Moreover, Ian Scott, the British ambassador, had suggested that the UN stop protecting Lumumba and leave Mobutu to deal with him.[96]

It is distinctly possible that Park knew about the operation in advance. She was close to one of the men who handed Lumumba over to his executioners, having previously saved his life by bundling him into the boot of her small car and smuggling him to freedom when chased by Lumumba's followers.[97] There is one further intriguing point. Arch conspirator and long-time covert actioneer, Billy McLean, a man who revelled in such activity, just happened to be in Congo meeting various ministers in the secessionist Katanga government at the same time they executed Lumumba.[98] Like so much British covert action, SIS was twice removed from the assassination itself. As Daphne Park's biographer concludes, 'Britain, it seems, was quite comfortable with this as long as its hands were not actually dirtied'. Inadvertently summing up Britain's approach to assassination more broadly, he continued: 'neither Park nor Devlin pulled the trigger or gave the order to the firing squad, but they conspired to bring about a situation where the most logical, indeed the only possible outcome would be the death of Patrice Lumumba'.[99]

Failure to coordinate

Covert action remained high on the British agenda during the opening years of the 1960s. With Britain still in decline and imposing cuts on the defence budget, military planners believed that the value of counter-subversion had assumed even greater importance than before.[100] They saw it as a silver bullet allowing Britain to punch above its weight around the world. As such, covert action targeted Indonesia and Yemen, areas where nationalism and decolonization threatened long-held British interests, but SIS discussions extended to Nigeria, Iran, Finland, and Venezuela.[101]

Despite the perennial appeal of covert action, it had once again begun to drift. With Britain's position in Asia and the Middle East under severe pressure, a great deal was at stake but, echoing the early years of the Cold War, lack of clear ministerial direction left those in charge of planning covert operations flailing. This had damaging results which risked undermining what was left of Britain's global role and even the relationship with Washington.

Macmillan's attempts to conduct covert action in conjunction with the CIA could not hide a lack of coordination within Whitehall itself. Despite enjoying initial praise, Britain's special political action (SPA) arrangements, in place since 1958, soon ran into problems. Requests for covert action came from the political department concerned, usually the Foreign Office, but sometimes SIS itself. The SPA section then worked out the details, keeping in constant touch with the Foreign Office through a diplomat seconded to SIS headquarters.[102] Whilst this allowed integration into broader policy, it hindered liaison with other departments. Moreover, covert action suffered from a lack of coordination, especially regarding funding, between the Information Research Department (IRD) and the SPA (Prop) section, which conducted black propaganda.[103]

Although Norman Brook allowed the Ministry of Defence, alongside the Colonial and Commonwealth Relations Offices, to send part-time liaison officers to the SPA, they lacked any real input. John Drew, overseeing deception, waxed lyrical about the military's new-found voice at the heart of Whitehall's covert action planning;[104] not for the first time the deception expert was himself being deceived. Brook and Patrick Dean never saw the new arrangements as inter-departmental. For them, covert action remained firmly within the realm of SIS and the Foreign Office, with the military having just enough of a voice to prevent them sniping from the sidelines.[105] Whitehall's battles rumbled on.

A Counter-Subversion Committee (CSC) emerged in January 1962 as an informal Foreign Office body—but one which also included representatives from the Colonial Office, Commonwealth Relations Office, Ministry of Defence, MI5, and SIS. Possessing an exciting remit, the CSC considered how both open and deniable measures could counter subversive threats. Means available included unattributable propaganda, 'covert activities of all kinds', cultural and educational activities, and technical aid.[106] Familiar ructions soon dogged the set-up, with the military criticizing a lack of drive and the Foreign Office cleverly stacking the bureaucracy in its favour (this time by lying about which departments its people represented).[107]

Yemen presented an early challenge to the new system. In September 1962, a republican coup overthrew the imamate and established a Yemen Arab Republic. The plotters, however, botched the job. A palace courtier, the would-be assassin, failed to kill the imam, who, escaping with his life, fled for the mountains to wage an insurgency against the new regime. So began a long and bloody civil war between republican and royalist factions. To complicate matters, the conflict swiftly escalated into a proxy war with Egypt and Saudi Arabia supporting the two sides respectively. Nasser, who had himself come to power after military officers overthrew a monarchy, saw an opportunity to influence a neighbouring country. Saudi Arabia, in return, feared Egyptian designs on its own monarchy.[108] The coup, and Nasser's subsequent flooding of Yemen with tens of thousands of troops, alarmed Whitehall. It not only threatened a chain reaction of republican revolutions across the area, but specifically threatened British interests to the south in Aden and the Federation of South Arabia—an area of strategic importance owing to oil exports and the projection of power east of Suez. Much was at stake.

As well as aiding the Yemeni republicans, Nasser also supported underground rebel groups, such as the National Liberation Front, which launched a series of vicious attacks on Aden. In December 1963, Kennedy Trevaskis, the high commissioner, was waiting to board a flight at the local Khormaksar airport when an assailant threw a grenade from the crowd. Trevasksis escaped the assassination attempt with only minor injuries to his hand—but his deputy, George Henderson, was killed as he bravely tried to shield Trevaskis from the explosion.[109] The high commissioner immediately declared a state of emergency, but nationalist violence in Aden only intensified. In addition to fighting a colonial counter-insurgency campaign, Britain turned to covert action against the Yemeni republicans to ease the pressure on Aden and give Nasser a bloody nose.

Jack Nicholls, the chairman of the Counter-Subversion Committee, and his colleagues plotted the response. However, it amounted to little more than half-hearted propaganda and the committee's weaknesses quickly became clear. The extensive membership led to a natural unwillingness on the part of SIS's special political action team to discuss more sensitive and controversial measures.[110] Harold Macmillan offered only cautious support for the royalists channelled indirectly through the British-protected tribes on the frontier.[111] After much drifting, Whitehall's Yemen policy imploded amidst tension between those in favour of intensification and those against. In one corner, diplomats in the Foreign Office, backed by Joint Intelligence Committee (JIC) assessments, expressed scepticism that covert action would work: the rebels could not be trusted and it risked escalating into a dangerous arms race.[112] In the other corner, an alliance between Julian Amery, only in his early forties but already one of Britain's most experienced covert operators, Duncan Sandys, the hawkish colonial secretary, and local Adeni authorities offered competing assessments and lobbied Macmillan personally to authorize more aggressive covert action.[113]

A bitter, ultimately futile, Whitehall battle ensued and policy drifted as frustration and mistrust engulfed both sides. The diplomats were especially jumpy, trying, for example, to ban an unofficial party of men on leave from the Special Air Service (SAS) from entering Yemen. This was in the wake of the 1963 Profumo affair and they feared Macmillan's government could not take any more embarrassment should details leak. And leak they almost did when one of the team's briefcases broke open at Tripoli airport spilling plastic explosives all over the floor, which the security guards helped repack without realizing what they were.[114] Indicative of the confusion and lack of control, when Whitehall called the operation off, the team went ahead regardless.[115] On other occasions recommendations for covert action got lost or took so long to be approved that they were no longer viable.[116] Trevaskis did acknowledge that London had provided funds for bribing local officials, infiltrating subversive organizations and enabling friendly tribal leaders to intimidate enemies and organize mob riots. But he criticized the money as 'pathetically inadequate' and demanded £50,000 to cover the next six months.[117]

The Americans, who had little sympathy for British imperialism, further complicated matters. President Kennedy thought it more profitable to renew relations with Nasser as a means of preventing him from stirring up trouble.[118] As usual, eager British officials started lobbying Washington to support covert action instead. Trevaskis insisted that the republican position had begun to crumble and the West had a chance to militarily embarrass the Egyptians. Patrick Wright, in the British embassy, nuanced this message by pointing out that the JIC did not share this view.[119] Neither did the State Department. The Americans dismissed accounts of royalist capabilities as exaggerated and outright false.[120] They warned Wright that covertly supporting the royalists was a dangerous folly, which would merely escalate Nasser's aggression, strengthen nationalism in Aden, and radicalize moderates.[121] President Kennedy urged Macmillan directly to stop his futile support of the royalists.[122]

The following year, with Kennedy abruptly removed from the scene, Rab Butler, the foreign secretary, tried again. This time he played up Nasser's threat to Israel as well as international communism, before asking for American support. He presented his proposal as a compromise, telling Dean Rusk, the secretary of state, that if he were 'in the hand of the extremists in the Cabinet' then he would have expounded a far more radical position.[123] Rusk now lost patience. In a remarkably undiplomatic put-down, State Department officials thought Britain grossly over-reacting to a threat which was 'more talk than anything else';[124] denounced 'Sandysism', the aggressive approach advocated by Colonial Secretary Duncan Sandys, as dangerously provocative and prone to escalation; and strongly criticized the lack of proper coordination, scrutiny, and planning taking place in London.[125] Rusk's regional specialists despaired at Britain's drifting policy, and threatened Butler that America would 'bite back' if he started attacking its Middle East policy.[126]

The State Department had detected the malaise, but its warnings did little to rescue Whitehall's quagmire as pro-British rulers in the South Arabian hinterland grew angry at British inconsistency and constant prevarication over covert support for the royalists.[127] Disagreement at home severely undermined Britain's operations in Yemen. Nasser, who plotters hoped would be forced to withdraw, remained utterly untroubled and even sent those running the tame covert action his official Christmas card.[128]

Similar problems surfaced elsewhere. As the small East African island of Zanzibar staggered towards independence in the early 1960s, it became a playground for covert foreign intervention. Different countries, from Egypt to Israel, backed different factions vying for power.[129] But Whitehall and SIS were nowhere to be seen. They had established a working group in early 1962 but it became bogged down in bureaucratic gridlock, passing proposals back and forth between a parade of prevaricating officials.[130] In the end, the predictable rebellion broke out before any British counter-subversion could be undertaken. In January 1964, a bloody revolution overthrew the Sultanate leaving up to 20,000 people dead and over 100,000 exiled as murderous rebels plundered their way through the countryside publicly executing any opposition and dumping their bodies in mass graves. 'It is no credit to the rebels', John Drew bluntly observed, 'that they apparently moved faster than we did.'[131]

Covert action in Indonesia also proved a damp squib. It had remained on the agenda following the failed rebellion in 1958, but Anglo–American policy oscillated between backing the rebels and backing government insiders.[132] In 1959, the CIA considered assassinating (or, euphemistically, 'biologically immobilising') Sukarno and ran operations to see if an agent could get close enough to achieve it. Hopes fell on an airline stewardess who was willing to exploit Sukarno's famous sexual appetite, but the planning progressed little beyond that.[133] In 1962, Macmillan and Kennedy apparently agreed to 'liquidate President Sukarno, depending upon the situation and the available opportunities'.[134] Opportunities for liquidation did not arise and Sukarno survived to vigorously oppose the creation of Malaysia in 1963. In response, he launched Confrontation—effectively an undeclared war encompassing subversion, propaganda, and minor military operations—against it.[135] As in Yemen, Britain struggled to respond openly. Officials knew they would be condemned as imperialists in the UN, whilst defensive patrols along the jungle frontier to prevent Indonesian incursions were prohibitively expensive and drained military resources at the expense of Britain's other global commitments. Covert action offered a useful means of plugging a gap between responsibilities and material capability.[136]

Once more, a great deal was at stake. Britain committed to defending Malaysia on more than altruistic grounds. Bases in Singapore, then part of the nascent federation, could sustain large air, sea, and land forces. They formed an integral means of projecting power across the Far East and meeting military commitments to the South East Asia Treaty Organization, or SEATO, to defend the region from communism. Equally importantly,

Britain's position sustained links with Australia and New Zealand, and, above all, offered influence with the US.[137] By late 1963, Britain had over twenty battalions in the Far East and more than a third of the Royal Navy, whilst the following year Number 10 feared having to cancel the annual Trooping the Colour ceremony at Horse Guards Parade if any more soldiers were transferred to the theatre. Britain was desperately overstretched. And all for a war that did not officially exist.[138]

As Confrontation intensified, many across Whitehall warmed to the idea of covert action. The new prime minister, Alec Douglas-Home, had long supported the idea.[139] Meanwhile, Duncan Sandys called for operations in Sumatra and, despite different emphases, both Rab Butler and Peter Thorneycroft, the foreign and defence secretaries, also saw covert action as part of the Confrontation strategy.[140] For the cash-strapped chiefs of staff it unsurprisingly formed the key solution.[141] They called both for subversion designed to pin down Indonesian soldiers and for unattributable propaganda to undermine Sukarno.[142] Similarly, local military personnel pressed for operations to be 'carried out either by unidentifiable agents or, better still, by indigenous dissident agents'.[143]

The wish list of the chiefs of staff went much further than the Foreign Office had agreed and, as ever, the diplomats braced themselves for a Whitehall battle. Meanwhile, military authorities in the region, such as General Walter Walker, heading Borneo operations between 1963 and 1965, lobbied Whitehall to allow British forces to engage in cross-border operations designed to press the Indonesians back and deter their raids into Malaysian territory. Policymakers slowly agreed and, in April 1964, sanctioned deniable operations within a range of 3,000 yards across the border but refused anything more. Meanwhile, Britain and Malaysia began giving some limited covert assistance to dissidents inside Indonesia.[144]

The Counter-Subversion Committee secured £50,000 from the Secret Vote in November 1963. The money—close to £1 million at today's value— was discreetly channelled to the Malaysian government through the British High Commission.[145] It was not enough and the CSC continued to struggle. Nicholls lacked the funds to have his better ideas implemented and the work proved underwhelming and mundane.[146] Meanwhile, too many other concurrent but hermetic plans were being formulated in isolation. The chiefs of staff and local military personnel drew up their own schemes; so too did the Foreign Office's Permanent Under-Secretary's Department and South East Asia Department, whilst SIS concocted contingency plans.

In addition to a lack of cross-departmental thinking, clashing personalities and departmental jealousies hampered this effort.[147]

The British response was predominantly defensive in 1963 and early 1964, aiming simply to contain Indonesian irregular operations against Malaysia. Tactical covert operations disrupted the Indonesian infrastructure across the border, thereby taking the fight to Sukarno but maintaining a defensive and attritional approach. It fell short, however, and military chiefs pressed for conventional as well as deniable responses, as without the former the latter had little impact. Deniable operations on their own were not enough to disrupt the enemy sufficiently.[148] Struggling to link means and ends effectively, policymakers pursued the least worst option in a similar manner to the compromise over Yemen.[149] This time, problems emanated less from Whitehall's own deficiencies and more from external developments which dramatically shaped Confrontation, including the increase in Indonesian military activity in September 1963 and the expansion of operations from Borneo into Malaysia the following year. Each put much pressure on Britain's limited and defensive objectives.[150]

★   ★   ★

Nicholls and his Counter-Subversion Committee suffered from a lack of ministerial policy directives and strategic clarity. He and his colleagues lamented how their work would have been more useful 'if the Government's objectives could be stated more clearly'.[151] As early as 1962, the committee's then chairman, Leslie Glass, admitted to being unsure what he was even supposed to be doing in the first place.[152] 'Projects', he moaned, 'cannot be dreamed up in a vacuum.'[153] The situation did not improve and a dearth of ministerial guidance allowed policy to drift in both the Middle East and Southeast Asia. Meanwhile, the committee engaged in activities that bordered on the underwhelming, including countering Sino–Soviet penetration in West Africa by sending the England football team on a tour of the region.[154]

Between the late 1940s and the early 1960s, one committee succeeded another with any progress sporadic at most. Despite trying to institutional-ize covert action and expecting to conduct ever more of it, the UK's approach during the late 1950s and early 1960s was effectively bankrupt. A lack of coordination allowed policy to drift and prevented a coherent strategy to counter subversion which integrated both open and deniable means. As civil servants feuded and prevaricated, opportunities in Yemen, Indonesia, Zanzibar, and elsewhere slipped by. What is particularly striking is that this period resurrected so many of the same old arguments and debates that had broken out a decade earlier. Lacking institutional memory, officials were going around in circles.

Whitehall was forced to accept that it was failing on covert action. The CSC found itself unable meet its terms of reference and had hardly dealt at all with specific projects.[155] Not the for first time, the Foreign Office turned to an old boy to sort things out and brought William Strang, a former permanent under-secretary and stickler for administration heavily involved in planning covert action in the late 1940s and early 1950s, out of retirement. Strang wasted little time elevating the CSC to Cabinet committee status and, after interviewing nearly 100 people—many of them twice—recommended better integrating the IRD into the Foreign Office. Regular diplomats did not know about its work and could not use its resources to best effect.[156] The military thought the changes did not go far enough,[157] but now even the Cabinet Office had grown frustrated at Foreign Office dominance.[158] Further change was on the horizon. In July 1964, the British approach to covert action was revolutionized. After fifteen years of rehearsing the same old arguments, the military and the diplomats finally agreed on a new idea: a joined-up and integrated approach allowing a dramatic intensification of secret wars in both Yemen and Indonesia.

9

MILITARIZATION

Secret Wars in Yemen and Indonesia

MI6 is adequately equipped to undertake <u>untraceable</u> operations.
Joint Action Committee, 1964[1]

The hapless Counter-Subversion Committee (CSC) plodded along throughout the second half of the 1960s. It spent most of its time collating information on subversive activities and, when it did venture into the realm of action, focused on police training, trade, and cultural relations. It sent cheap books to Latin America, enhanced the role of the British Council, and despatched professors to Africa to lecture on international law. Covert activity was limited to unattributable propaganda used, for example, to expose Egyptian subversion in Sudan and to exploit Tanzanian disillusionment with Chinese investment.[2] Its most important function was perhaps, as its chairman once pointed out, to give the Ministry of Defence 'the opportunity of letting off some steam about inadequacies of the Foreign Office'.[3]

This set-up lacked the capacity to fight simultaneously not one but two covert wars: in Yemen and Indonesia. Meanwhile, Whitehall had also agreed to send special forces teams to intervene surreptitiously in the Vietnam War. This was a delicate matter and in order for ministers to stick to the line that no British troops were involved, men from the Special Air Service (SAS) and Special Boat Service (SBS) were secretly seconded to Australian Special Forces.[4] There have been allegations that the Secret Intelligence Service (SIS) also helped by quietly shipping arms to the theatre.[5] This may well be true, although any impact would have been negligible compared to the American effort. Nonetheless, most of Britain's deniable involvement in Vietnam came from intelligence-gathering. SIS officers on the ground passed material to the Americans throughout the 1960s, whilst GCHQ analysts shared their data too.[6] Britain's deception organization loaned a lieutenant colonel to the Americans working from Bangkok from 1962.[7] With Vietnam, Yemen, and Indonesia all escalating, Britain lacked the machinery needed to think carefully about its covert responses.

Sick of the Whitehall malaise, Prime Minister Alec Douglas-Home instructed Rab Butler, his foreign secretary, to appoint someone to take a grip of the competing Foreign Office, Colonial Office, and Ministry of Defence interests.[8] At around the same time, Bernard Burrows, overseeing intelligence and security at the Foreign Office, pinpointed the key flaws in the existing arrangements. SIS officers were unwilling to discuss particularly sensitive topics in the Counter-Subversion Committee, whilst the Joint Intelligence Committee (JIC), which Burrows chaired, was an inappropriate forum because covert action would, in his words, 'endanger the purity of its intelligence function'. Burrows therefore suggested a new body to allow secret intelligence to inform deniable action. Guided by the new cabinet secretary, Burke Trend, Douglas-Home enthusiastically agreed and approved the formation of the Joint Action Committee (JAC).[9]

Created in July 1964, the JAC formed part of a broader reorganization of the joint intelligence machinery.[10] Bernard Burrows chaired it himself. Tall and handsome, Burrows enjoyed an eventful diplomatic career and has been described as one of the five most powerful men in the Foreign Office at the time. An old Etonian, he radiated an air of natural authority but possessed a kindly demeanour and lacked self-importance. Outside of public life, he cultivated eccentric interests in crop circles and square-dancing.[11] Burrows was a sensible choice for chair, not least because the JAC drew heavily on Joint Intelligence Committee assessments and shared its secretariat.[12] Burrows' colleagues on the new body were, at Trend's insistence, hand-picked.[13] Trend had become cabinet secretary at the start of 1963 and, like Norman Brook before him, took a close interest in intelligence. A shy, serious man with a formidable intellect and famous poker face, Trend had long experience of the secret world, having superintended SIS and MI5 spending during his time at the Treasury. When he replaced Brook, he brought with him responsibility for overseeing intelligence finances. The first cabinet secretary with access to a new door between the Cabinet Office and Number 10, he went on to serve four prime ministers, advising each on covert action and intelligence. A keen reader of John Le Carré novels, Trend enjoyed this aspect of his job the most.[14]

Trend picked Leslie Glass, an assistant under-secretary, as the other Foreign Office representative alongside Burrows. An unconventional diplomat, Glass looked not dissimilar to Ernest Bevin with a rumbustious laugh and generous girth. His specialism lay in propaganda and disinformation work.[15] Dick White, as chief of SIS, was a prominent member, as was Kenneth Strong, the director general of intelligence at the Ministry of Defence. Others included representatives from the Colonial and Commonwealth Relations Offices, the Counter-Subversion Committee, and the Ministry of Defence.[16] Demonstrating the scale and urgency of British covert action, they met surprisingly regularly: fortnightly with extra ad hoc meetings as required.[17]

The JAC's task was simple. It coordinated inter-departmental plans for covert operations in areas of military interest, thereby enabling closer relations between the military, special forces, and SIS.[18] It allowed the government to evaluate covert action options through the full inter-agency process, including consultation with intelligence analysts, not just covert action specialists, whilst also ensuring that the chiefs of staff and ministers were adequately informed.[19]

Large-scale deniable operations

Burrows and White appraised the covert action landscape, noting that competitive coexistence and decolonization had created conditions for a new kind of undeclared war.[20] Britain was losing out in this area because, unlike the CIA, SIS was a small service and future operations were likely to be on such a scale that it would need military support.[21] SIS had some paramilitary capabilities, but could not operate on anywhere near the same scale as the Special Operations Executive (SOE) had during the Second World War.[22]

There was abiding nostalgia for the war; it was a time when Britain did not need to deny committing hostile acts in enemy territory. By contrast, these new secret conflicts necessitated plausible deniability given that London was formally at peace with the adversary. To achieve this, White, who despite his reputation for caution was not averse to covert action, accepted that SIS had to work more closely with the military. Whilst it could undertake small-scale untraceable operations without help, SIS was simply 'not equipped to carry out large scale deniable operations on its own'.[23] Moreover, some of the former SOE operatives who had transferred into SIS were getting older and the service's paramilitary capabilities deteriorated further still.

This was not an entirely new issue. SIS had worked closely with the military over the previous decade on certain operations such as the daring mission, led by David Smiley, to defeat Omani rebels in the late 1950s when the Foreign Office feared open military intervention on behalf of the sultan would lead to repercussions at the United Nations. Before then, however, the SAS had been an unknown quantity within Whitehall. When Winston Churchill received a memo on irregular warfare in 1952, he circled the letters SAS and scribbled 'meaning?'.[24] Likewise, the SBS had been underemployed after the war, which the Admiralty put down to its highly specialized nature. Aside from limited patrolling and reconnaissance, the SBS carried out one partially successful operation in 1952 in the Eastern Mediterranean, likely involving Egypt.[25] Despite SAS success in Oman, neither of Britain's elite forces was particularly well integrated into Whitehall thinking in the early 1960s.

In this new era, SIS's role in larger deniable operations, some of which would later become known as special military operations, was twofold. First, it provided the specialized manpower and services required. Second, it maintained responsibility for safeguarding the deniability of joint operations. SIS was responsible for liaison with overseas intelligence services, especially the CIA, where required.[26] At the same time, Burrows and White recommended that more use should be made of the Defence Planning Staff. Although it would have had to be modified to take account of security demands, political risk assessment, and the all-important Foreign Office veto, this was something the military had consistently pressed for since the end of the Second World War.[27] For twenty years his predecessors had been thwarted at every turn, so Lord Mountbatten, chief of the defence staff, greeted the JAC with delight.[28]

Burrows and his colleagues enjoyed an instant impact. They coordinated and scrutinized planning, attempting to arrive at some sort of consensus before putting covert action proposals to ministers—and not forcing them to choose between wildly different designs as poor Harold Macmillan had to do over Yemen.[29] Once an operation was sanctioned, they coordinated the military supplies, as well as other departments and agencies involved. Burrows now provided a clear framework setting parameters for covert action in Yemen, where the civil war had intensified. Since the revolution in 1962, the royalists had stifled repeated Egyptian offensives, preventing them from delivering a fatal blow. Intent on securing a republic in

Yemen, Nasser escalated the conflict and, by summer 1964, had posted some 40,000 troops to the country.

Couching operations in defensive terms, the JAC agreed that to maintain Britain's position in Aden, Egyptian and Yemeni subversion had to be contained and the authority of friendly federal rulers upheld. Covert action was designed to hit back at the dissidents and their bases across the frontier, thereby scotching subversion at an early stage. This, planners hoped, would avoid the need for politically tiresome and expensive military operations.[30] In doing so, Burrows successfully moderated more aggressive proposals emanating from local authorities in Aden, certain Colonial Office officials, and sections of the Ministry of Defence. The JAC accommodated the military, whilst serving as a balance to ensure that operations were examined in detail and conducted in a less gung-ho fashion than they otherwise might have been.

Late in the summer of 1964 for example, hawkish ministers hoped to ramp up the covert British intervention. Familiar faces such as Billy McLean and Julian Amery, never far from a special operation, pressed for direct aid to royalist forces inside Yemen via clandestine parachute drops. They found support amongst Peter Thorneycroft, the defence secretary, and Lord Mountbatten.[31] Despite this pressure, the covert action sanctioned, code-named RANCOUR, was more defensive, involving merely indirect aid. The JAC agreed to send arms and money to British-sponsored tribes along the frontier, allowing them to attack Egyptian targets inside Yemen, so long as this remained deniable.[32] Special forces teams passing themselves off as political officers then distributed these supplies, which usually amounted to 30,000 riyals, thirty rifles, and thirty boxes of ammunition each month.[33]

Meanwhile, in Aden itself SAS teams, disguised as local Arabs, patrolled the streets looking to engage with terrorists. Others inserted small bombs into elaborately framed portraits of Nasser before sending them as gifts to terrorist leaders.[34] Outside of Aden, the most sensitive—and deniable—work was conducted by an unofficial force comprised of former SAS men. Back in April 1963, David Stirling, a founder member of the SAS, had met the usual suspects including Amery, McLean, and David Smiley, alongside Alec Douglas-Home, then foreign secretary, in White's, the exclusive gentleman's club on St James's Street, to discuss Yemen. With Douglas-Home aware that it would take SIS too long to insert agents into the theatre, he asked Stirling what help the SAS could offer the royalists. The answer: a small and unofficial force headed by SAS veterans Smiley and Johnny

Cooper, funded by the Saudis, and comprising Englishmen, Frenchmen, and Belgians.[35] Working from London, McLean, who visited Yemen numerous times, helped recruit extra volunteers, whilst Paul Paulson, SIS's Middle East controller, managed to get another SAS veteran, Jim Johnson, excused from his day job at Lloyd's to help run the operation.[36]

Although the force was unofficial and deniable, SIS officers in the region knew exactly what they were up to and increasingly assisted them. One of the covert actioneers even described the whole operation as being overseen by SIS, although that was a stretch. As operations progressed, Smiley's motley crew did gain respect from British intelligence who rated them as a professional outfit, but SIS were not in control.[37] The extent to which the JAC endorsed this mercenary activity is unclear. Some of its operations fell within the JAC framework laid down in London, but many went beyond it. Besides, it was multinational, externally funded, and consequently difficult to control. Operations included the covert supply of bazookas, ammunition, and money to friendly tribes, as well as organizing small-scale retaliatory operations carried out by local tribesmen.[38] Operating in intense heat and with minimal food and water, they directed and received arms drops, intercepted arms supplies heading from Yemen into South Arabia, and ambushed infiltration routes across the border. It certainly seems that, from October 1964, Harold Wilson's government, despite continuing JAC-sanctioned activity, was less sympathetic to Amery's unofficial activities. The Foreign Office denied him RAF transport to Aden and Yemen, arguing that his presence was complicating efforts in the region.[39]

Deniability remained key throughout. The mines used to blow up roads were American-made leftovers from the Second World War laid only by local tribesmen. British personnel instead offered instruction and payment: two gold coins in advance and three more on proof of explosion. Other targets for sabotage included Russian-built tanks which, when bombed out of service, would expend Egyptian time, resources, and morale fixing them. Occasionally the covert warriors did have to get their own hands dirty. Fighting insurgents in the Radfan area of South Arabia, an SAS team, hiding behind a cluster of rocks, saw two Arabs, one with a rocket launcher, the other with an AK47, descending a ridge towards them. Before the locals could fire, an SAS soldier felled them both with a scatter of bullets. The shooter deemed it retribution, for the republican fighters were a vicious bunch and had earlier decapitated an SAS corpse and paraded the severed head on a stake through the streets.[40]

Meanwhile, the Information Research Department (IRD) and SIS maintained the propaganda campaign against the Egyptians and Yemenis. The
problem, however, was that local audiences assumed that any material attacking Nasser and the republicans in Yemen was *de facto* British propaganda
and treated it accordingly. At the same time, Britain could not launch overt
propaganda attacking the republicans because official policy dictated not
taking visible sides but instead helping to facilitate a peaceful resolution. In
the end, Britain distributed unattributable leaflets across Yemen and South
Arabia to discredit Nasser, increase the unpopularity of the Egyptians in
Yemen, and relieve pressure on the South Arabian frontier. Much of this
involved spreading truthful information, for the Colonial Office warned
that 'scurrilous or dishonest propaganda can only do harm in the long run
and should not be undertaken'.[41]

JAC scrutiny of the British effort continued throughout. Led by Burrows,
officials back in Whitehall considered the impact of halting operations on
the morale of local leaders, as well as how political developments in Egypt
would shape the effectiveness of covert action.[42] They asked the vital 'what
if' questions, whilst also assessing what exactly should be sent to the rebels;
how to ensure costs were kept low; how deniability could be ensured; how
British agents could be protected; the likely political consequences; and the
dangers of British weapons ending up in enemy or Soviet hands. Given the
seduction of cloak-and-dagger activity, advocates can develop an intense
personal commitment to a particular covert operation and lose perspective.
Burrows, with his strong and inter-departmental forum, was able to maintain objectivity and rationality in a politically charged atmosphere.[43]

Before long, British-backed tribesmen had become engaged in larger-
scale operations along the Yemeni frontier. The border between South Arabia
and Yemen formed a vital flashpoint for Whitehall because it marked a buffer
zone protecting British interests in Aden and because Britain was treaty-
bound to protect local rulers. Policymakers may have wanted to drive Egyptian
forces out of Yemen, but their first priority was to prevent the conflict from
spilling across the border. The likes of Amery still called for more aggressive
operations inside Yemen itself,[44] but the JAC made it clear that none of the
RANCOUR operations had 'any direct connection with the Royalists versus Republican struggle in the Yemen', but were rather 'part of an economical system for protecting the frontier of the Federation for whose defence
we are responsible'. Moreover, it insisted that the high commissioner seek
inter-departmental clearance before conducting covert action beyond the

agreed level.[45] The JAC also ruled that covert action stop during ceasefires, but allowed dissident organizations to be maintained in case—or for when—the conflict resumed.[46]

Demonstrating a remarkably smooth transition from Conservative to Labour governments, Harold Wilson and his most senior ministers approved this approach on accession to office.[47] A man fascinated by the mysterious and murky world of intelligence, Wilson evidently shared his predecessor's belief in the value of special operations and approved covert action along the lines set out by the JAC.[48] He was, however, less sympathetic to mercenary activity and the extent to which, if at all, he endorsed Smiley's activities remains unclear. There is no declassified documentary evidence suggesting active cooperation or any attempt to integrate them into the JAC system. It seems that, as a forerunner to later private military operations in the post–Cold War period, the unofficial force communicated with the state but was not under state control.

As late as April 1966, ministers agreed to maintain RANCOUR.[49] Operations continued until British withdrawal from Aden in 1967, including, for example, the supply of ammunition from Czechoslovakia to local rulers in South Arabia via Parker Hale, a Birmingham-based company, at the request of the high commissioner.[50] Yet officials continually made a distinction between aiding frontier tribes so as to alleviate pressure on British interests in Aden and directly intervening in the Yemeni conflict, with the latter proving a step too far for most in London. Despite heavy military representation around the table, careful scrutiny ensured victory for Bernard Burrows and Dick White, although the mercenary force on the ground—funded by the Saudis—did breach this official line, to the fury of the Foreign Office. By 1965, the CIA assessed that the unexpected durability of the royalists—buoyed by covert British support—was frustrating Nasser, denting his prestige, and forcing him into a costly stalemate. Despite earlier American scepticism, the CIA now believed that Nasser would be forced to agree to a compromise settlement.[51]

Confrontation

The same approach simultaneously applied to Indonesia. Confrontation had continued into 1964 after Indonesian 'volunteers' escalated sabotage activity along the jungled border with Borneo and President Sukarno's forces began to cross the Malacca Straits and infiltrate the Malaysian Peninsula. From the summer of 1964, Burrows and his Joint Action Committee approved a number of defensive measures including deniable operations to disrupt bands of Indonesian guerrillas within an initial limit of 3,000 yards across the border.[52] Shortly afterwards, the SAS moved into a new role as local military operatives pressed for more sophisticated reconnaissance and a special offensive force.[53] Meanwhile, SIS and special forces busily trained Malaysian instructors in the art of subversion. These operations proved more difficult in Sumatra, which was under strict police control, but enjoyed some success in Celebes, where a strong independence movement had developed.[54]

Within this framework, SAS and SBS teams patrolled the jungle, protecting posts on the front line. This was intense work involving days of creeping through dense undergrowth and swamps with no maps and little food or water. Soaking wet and covered in mud, they suppressed their hunger with cigarettes. The soldiers carried no British identification and wore boots with an unusual tread to disguise their footprints. Around his neck, each man carried a syrette of morphine whilst 'escape money' was kept in two separate places on his body to enable him to buy his way out of danger if necessary.[55] In an operation known as Claret, teams infiltrated across the border, launched ambushes, and laid mines on Indonesian infiltration routes. It was a tense mission: each man lived in a state of heightened awareness, concentrating intensely on the trees for any sound that might indicate enemy presence. Under such mental strain, one SAS team ambushed—and killed—a group of wild pigs rustling through trees by mistake.[56] Another team, retreating after a successful ambush, found themselves eyeball to eyeball with a king cobra, reared up aggressively. Shooting it would have alerted the Indonesians to their presence and so the men stood there nervously, relieved when it eventually slithered away.[57] The SBS, for whom operations came thick and fast after a slow start, grew frustrated by the limitations and so-called golden rules underpinning the early months of Operation Claret, some of which were set locally as well as from London. SBS men predominantly engaged in intelligence-gathering work, but raids had to be approved.[58]

Meanwhile, Patrick Dean, now ambassador to the United Nations, denied Britain was engaged in covert operations at all. Despite his recent personal involvement in such activity, Dean officially knew little of current activity. Even if he had, he would have misled the United Nations. Bernard Burrows and Dick White had little problem obfuscating the truth—or even lying to the United Nations and the House of Commons—when it came to deniable operations. They agreed that an operation could be classified as deniable if 'Her Majesty's Government considers it politically feasible to deny complicity in public statements, e.g. in the House of Commons or the United Nations or in answer to official representations'.[59] Other operations officially denied during the autumn of 1964 included creating an organization to transfer arms and money to rebel groups in Kalimantan, as well as training dissident Indonesians in handling weapons, psychological warfare, and inciting insurrection.[60]

As with Yemen, Harold Wilson took an interest in Indonesia on coming to office. He wanted to know how Britain could influence the Indonesians and asked the JAC to help establish a framework for covert action. Burrows submitted this to ministers in January 1965 and, the following month, spelt out Britain's aims: to force Sukarno to call off Confrontation and recognize Malaysia. To achieve this, the JAC recommended 'taking every possible step to ensure, and demonstrate, that "confrontation" is a failure', whilst also being 'ready to examine any formula which might make it possible for the Indonesians to abandon or at least modify this policy'. The most important thing was to avoid getting dragged into an open and attritional military campaign.[61]

Covert action formed an appealing alternative and Wilson approved a three-pronged approach. First, it undermined the will of Sukarno's forces to attack Malaysia, both by portraying China and the Indonesian Communist Party as their real enemies and by stressing the futility of Indonesian raids into Malaysia. Second, covert action encouraged dissident movements inside Indonesia on the grounds that creating trouble at home for Sukarno would prevent him from attacking Malaysia. This was dangerous, though, for it risked impairing the capacity of the army to fight a potential communist uprising and could even have led to a civil war inside Indonesia. To prevent this, the JAC recommended that ministers discreetly tell the Indonesian army that any support for dissidents was merely a tactical response to Confrontation. Third, covert action targeted any potential successor to Sukarno whose accession to power might benefit the communists. To achieve this, the JAC advocated all possible measures to discredit him.[62]

Burrows and his colleagues then continued to ensure that covert action did not escalate into more dangerous activity.[63] The approved framework did ease restrictions on special forces activity giving them, in the words of one SAS solider, 'carte blanche to cross the border, ambush enemy patrols and kill as many Indonesian soldiers' as possible.[64] Shortly afterwards an SAS team watched from the undergrowth as two longboats sailed up a river towards them. After a two-minute firefight, every Indonesian on board was dead and one of the boats had sunk completely. It was not always so straight-forward. Another ambush team stumbled upon a luxury yacht but, seeing women on board, chose not to attack and it later transpired that the colonel commanding the Indonesian Parachute Regiment, a crucial scalp, had been present.[65] As with Yemen, the CIA assessed that by 1965, the campaign against British interests was floundering. And Sukarno knew it.[66]

Those in the military aware of the operations praised the SAS's contribu-tion as invaluable.[67] In reality, however, the SAS made little impact; their skills were woefully underused by theatre commanders lacking imagination and flair.[68] The majority of SAS activity from 1964 involved reconnaissance, with ambushes targeting Indonesian forces forming a sizeable minority. The SAS conducted eighteen ambushes between 1964 and 1966, of which they deemed seven successful, one partially successful, and ten failures: not a par-ticularly impressive rate. These tactical failures can in part be blamed on the strategic context outlined in the JAC. As with many post-war SAS operations, special forces leaders had to lobby hard for a role in Indonesia, and Whitehall struggled to integrate their capabilities into broader planning. In this instance, SAS involvement only came about because of active lobbying by its com-manding officer, John Woodhouse.[69] The JAC set out the broader framework but paid less attention to its tactical implementation, and so did not engage closely with special forces.

Use of special forces struggled to align with the broader political objectives. Deniability was important insofar as policymakers thought conventional mili-tary action would alienate international opinion and make any agreement with Indonesia more difficult. However, covert action could only ever be attri-tional and consequently struggled to force Sukarno to abandon Confrontation. The constraints imposed from above, and discussed within the JAC, limited the amount of damage special forces could inflict on the ground.[70] This, according to a leading historian of Confrontation, meant that 'SAS oper-ations were often unsuccessful tactically because they were subject to the constraints believed necessary to promote effective strategic performance'.[71] As in Yemen, those on the ground always wanted more leeway to engage in more lethal—and less deniable—force.[72] Again as in Yemen, the JAC stuck to its more limited framework and, in doing so, constrained the effect of special operations. That said, the JAC did not intend special operations alone to succeed in persuading Sukarno to abandon Confrontation. The idea was always for such activity to complement diplomatic negotiations, allowing the Foreign Office to negotiate from a position of strength.

Officers from SIS's special political action section also worked within the JAC's covert action parameters. Aiming to influence targets through black propaganda and bribery, 'we did', according to one former operative, 'everything we could do to make life difficult for the communists'. For example, one SIS officer bribed a contact in the Malaysian government to establish a radio station which, in a classic black operation, broadcast as if coming from Indonesian sources when it was actually being run by British intelligence.[73] The transmissions sought, amongst other things, to spread disaffection amongst the Chinese population in Indonesia.[74] Another idea, this time vetoed, was to acquire—or create—compromising photos of Sukarno with underage girls. Spreading the image of Sukarno as a paedophile, some in SIS hoped, would undermine and ridicule him.[75] It was for the best that this was rejected, for it would not have been the first time an intelligence service had tried to exploit Sukarno's famous libido. The CIA had already produced a pornographic film supposedly featuring a Sukarno lookalike or an actor in a mask. And the Russians allegedly held footage of Sukarno participating in an orgy with which they hoped to blackmail him. All attempts failed, though, not least because he was proud of his promiscuity.[76]

The JAC also worked with military deception planners, headed by John Drew.[77] In early 1965, Harold Wilson considered a mysterious deception plan put forward by Burrows, White, and Drew—but rejected it for being too hazardous. It risked putting Indonesian forces on heightened alert.[78] One plan involved convincing the military that Indonesian waters were haunted. Reprising the Q boat system from the First World War, warships, manned by the Special Boat Service, were to be disguised as old steam- or tugboats before sinking Indonesian ships, seemingly from out of nowhere. Drew hoped that sinking four or five vessels in this manner would act as a deterrent; it would play on Indonesian superstitions by creating the impression of lethal ghost ships appearing ominously from the mist.[79] Drew went back to the drawing board and, teaming up with local deception officers in Singapore, examined how best to intensify the war of nerves. In February 1965, the JAC agreed that the local commander-in-chief could use deception to 'deter and if necessary repulse all Indonesian attempts at invasion, infiltration or sabotage in Malaysia'. Harold Wilson gave his blessing and various operations got underway.[80]

Meanwhile, the Soviets launched their own deception and misinformation campaigns against the British. Intelligence officers thought Sukarno was 'ripe for accepting any new proof of American conspiracy' and concocted a supposed Anglo–American plan to invade Indonesia from British bases in Malaysia. Czech intelligence forged a document, supposedly from the British ambassador in Jakarta to the Foreign Office, to serve as the evidence. They then sent it to Sukarno's foreign minister in the summer of 1965.[81] The plot amounted to little though as, at the end of September, Sukarno faced an attempted military putsch as army trucks whizzed around Jakarta rounding up and executing his most loyal generals. Amidst a flurry of confusion, demands, and counter-demands, the putsch collapsed anticlimactically the next day. The Indonesian military, likely having been fed forged documents, wrongly blamed the coup on SIS covert action conducted jointly with the Chinese.[82]

Other rumours fingered the communists. Britain's propagandists unsurprisingly preferred this version of events and quickly moved to exploit them. Officials in Singapore wasted little time in lobbying London: 'we should not miss the present opportunity to use the situation to our advantage'. They had 'no hesitation in doing what we can to surreptitiously blacken the PKI [the Indonesian Communist Party] in the eyes of the army and the people of Indonesia'.[83] The Foreign Office was receptive. Propagandists in the IRD suggested a few themes to be stressed, including that the Communist Party was brutal, having murdered the chief of staff's six-year-old daughter alongside various army generals; that Indonesia was becoming a client state of Russia and China; and that the PKI had virtually kidnapped Sukarno during the coup. Keen to act quickly whilst Indonesia was still off balance, diplomats emphasized that propaganda would be made to appear as if it came from Pakistan or the Philippines. They added that 'British participation or cooperation should be carefully concealed'. This contrasted fiercely with Britain's publicly professed approach of strict non-interference.[84]

Norman Reddaway took up the position of political warfare coordinator in November 1965. An expert in propaganda, he had helped found the IRD back in the late 1940s and had since headed propaganda activity across the Middle East. Now based in Singapore, he led a renewed propaganda offensive with simple terms of reference: to get rid of Sukarno.[85] Reddaway worked with the IRD and SIS to target the Indonesian communists and in the process taint Sukarno as a communist by inserting articles into the local press and broadcasting from a black radio station. At the same time, the

Indonesian army launched a widespread campaign to destroy the Communist Party, encouraging mass killings of communists in Sumatra and Bali whilst massacring thousands in Java. By the end of December 1965, the PKI was no longer a political force and around half a million people had been murdered. Officials in London watched with satisfaction.[86] Whilst the massacres were underway, the Foreign Office, whose propaganda ignored the killings, admitted to 'blackening the PKI's reputation within Indonesia and outside by feeding into the ordinary publicity media news from Indonesia that associates the PKI and the Chinese with Untung's [a leader of the coup] treachery plus corresponding covert activity'. Propaganda also presented the generals as Indonesian patriots and in no way Western stooges.[87] British operations did not cause the massacres, but Whitehall did covertly exploit them to its advantage. As the propaganda accelerated, Britain deliberately restrained its Confrontation policy to allow the Indonesian army to devote its attention to targeting communists. The Foreign Office chose to discreetly pass a message to the generals indicating willingness to refrain from attacks so long as the Indonesian military continued to clamp down on the PKI.[88]

The impact of British covert action on the massacres is difficult to assess. The army may well have travelled this brutal route regardless and the generals actively advised Britain on potential propaganda themes themselves. It was more than a mere subplot of the Cold War, as internal forces and complex local factors drove the killings.[89] As the CIA recognized, the army had a long record of opposing the PKI, with some military leaders deeming communism as alien to the Indonesian way of life.[90] Rather modestly, the propagandists in London believed that their work 'may have contributed marginally towards keeping the Generals going against the PKI and causing friction with China'.[91] But the propaganda had a greater effect on the public. Local media, churning out British material, consistently supported the army's stories and incited the population against Sukarno. In the summer of 1966, Alec Adams, the political adviser to the commander-in-chief (Far East), thought Reddaway's activities had had considerable impact.[92] The commander-in-chief himself, John Grandy, thought the propaganda had made 'an outstanding contribution to the campaign against the Indonesians', whilst Andrew Gilchrist, the British ambassador, noted that it 'has had no small effect in breaking up' Sukarno's regime.[93] The president had been utterly discredited and lost power in 1967, whilst, according to the CIA, 'the danger of a PKI takeover in Indonesia has been dissipated, probably for many years'. Communism was a 'spent political force'.[94] As with so much British covert action, the idea was only ever to mobilize existing local forces and help create a climate in which near-inevitable developments would suit British interests.

Through the JAC and its sponsored activities, Britain was able to intervene without a full-scale military presence. It demonstrated the value of deniable operations. Britain's covert war in Indonesia is often seen as a success. This may be so, but it was far from inevitable. As one historian has written, 'British policy makers were trapped by the need to defend vital interests and, influenced by powerful political and economic factors, chose the least bad means to do so, knowing that the relationship between the means and ends was unclear.'[95]

★ ★ ★

By the mid-1960s, Britain's approach to covert action had become increasingly inter-departmental. Larger operations and secret warfare necessitated closer cooperation between SIS, deception experts, and special forces, whilst political warfare continued its integral role. This gave rise to a period of closer coordination overseen by the JAC. After two decades of sniping from the sidelines, the military had finally secured a place at the top table. The system provided an overarching framework for covert action, set the parameters, asked the important 'what if' questions, and kept a close eye on objectives—often tempering calls for more aggressive operations coming from local actors.

Covert action in both Yemen and Indonesia enjoyed successful coordination between policy, intelligence, and military actors within Whitehall. In both cases, however, the SAS was deployed at the tactical level seemingly with little higher political involvement or direction, and only after its leaders had lobbied vigorously for a role.[96] In its defence, the JAC provided the framework rather than the tactical detail of how operations would work on the ground. Nonetheless, and despite their best intentions, Burrows and his military colleagues on the JAC perhaps did not yet properly understand the role of special forces quite as well as they might. It would take a few more years before a director of special forces was brought into the inner circle of covert action planning to ensure that tactical means were properly aligned with broader objectives. The JAC was an important development and one which brought many benefits at a time when Britain increasingly relied on covert action in playing its hand. This was probably a reflection of declining military capabilities, but also a recognition that the nature of the Cold War required a more subtle and deniable approach to pursue British interests.

The JAC approach did highlight a strategic problem, however. The covert action it sponsored and the broader secret warfare waged suited attritional campaigns. This was certainly the case in Yemen where Nasser faced a lengthy stalemate in the civil war. Similarly, special operations in Indonesia protracted the conflict. The problem was that JAC-sponsored activity was not necessarily enough on its own to inflict sufficient harm to force opponents to withdraw. Without conventional force, special operations extended rather than ended conflicts. This could be beneficial; forcing opponents into a lengthy quagmire could inflict great damage. For example, Lord Shackleton, Labour peer and son of the famous explorer, concluded that operations in Yemen were extremely successful because they caused Nasser considerable inconvenience by tying down a disproportionate number of Egyptian forces.[97]

If, however, Britain's objective was to force withdrawal, then covert action struggled. In addition, an attritional approach risked indefinite and expansive missions. It could be argued that covert action in Yemen proved insufficient given that Britain ignominiously withdrew from Aden in 1967, although this did not stop Stirling and his new mercenary organization, Watchguard International, from playing a private sabotage role inside Yemen, funded by Saudi Arabia, afterwards.[98] That said, policymakers rarely saw covert action as an end in itself. Instead, they used covert action to disrupt, frustrate, and allow negotiations from a position of strength. The same principle spanned from Eastern Europe to Yemen and Indonesia. In this, the JAC was successful, for operations kept pressure on an adversary, multiplied force, and created space for diplomacy to work. As the 1960s gave way to the 1970s, Britain became directly embroiled in an even more secret war. Testing Whitehall's inherent caution, developments in the Gulf led to not one but three coups. Suddenly, and for the first time, the Foreign Office became the driving force pushing the military into risky covert manoeuvres.

PART 3

AGE OF ILLUSIONS

10

OPERATION STORM AND BEYOND

From Latin America to Oman

The Omani coup would be 'presented as an internal matter with the British hand concealed or at least deniable'.

Stewart Crawford, 1970[1]

The end of the 1960s brought much change to the UK, its global role, and its adversaries. In 1967 President Sukarno lost power in Indonesia and Britain withdrew from Aden. Sukarno and Nasser died from kidney failure and a heart attack respectively three years later. In a broader, more realistic, evaluation of Britain's global objectives, Harold Wilson famously announced, at the start of 1968, plans for Britain's withdrawal from bases 'east of Suez', heralding what many historians see as the final phase of a long retreat.

Dick White, a quiet enthusiast for well-organized covert action, retired as chief of SIS in 1968. Many expected his replacement to be Maurice Oldfield, White's deputy. They were disappointed when Oldfield was overlooked in favour of John Rennie, a career diplomat widely viewed as a Foreign Office cast-off.[2] Rennie had some experience of the secret world, having previously headed the Information Research Department (IRD), but his appointment as an outsider was a deliberate choice and can perhaps be interpreted as a reassertion of Foreign Office control. Rennie, a shy man and a talented painter, had no ambition to become chief and his reserved manner, combined with his outsider status, caused frustration within the Secret Intelligence Service (SIS) and made life difficult for him personally.[3] He tended to submit every minor operation to the foreign secretary for approval, although

Oldfield and others inside the service simply responded by not always bringing Rennie their proposals in the first place.[4]

The year before Rennie's appointment, unaccustomed public debate had broken out over the organization of British intelligence. *The Economist* called for SIS to be more independent like the Central Intelligence Agency (CIA) and criticized the foreign secretary's control. Patrick Dean, now ambassador to Washington but who, as we have seen, was well acquainted with the secret world and had a lengthy track record preserving Foreign Office primacy, defended the present arrangements in a personal letter to his close friend, the cabinet secretary Burke Trend. Foreign Office primacy was essential, he argued, because it was 'the largest producer, assessor and user of intelligence of all sorts'. Trend wholeheartedly agreed that the CIA model, in which intelligence was completely divorced from policy, was inappropriate. When such a divorce extended to the field of covert action, he added, results could be disastrous.[5] Rennie's appointment can be seen in this context.

Maurice Oldfield, who finally took over as chief from 1973, was almost as sceptical as Rennie about the SIS event-shaping role. He was pudgy-faced, a great raconteur with an impish sense of humour, and a devout Anglican. Occasionally his deeply held religious beliefs conflicted with his role as chief of SIS, not least when it came to the more controversial and aggressive covert actions.[6] Despite being an internal candidate and not someone imposed from the Foreign Office, he insisted that his staff knew the difference between intelligence-gathering and operations which involved sabotage and assassination. Oldfield, who had witnessed the Bay of Pigs fiasco when serving as SIS liaison officer in Washington, strongly believed that no intelligence service would be respected if it descended to these levels and that covert action should not become normalized: it was too risky, prone to escalation, and unnecessary. Public exposure of failure, Oldfield believed, would only further increase political control over SIS and damage officers' morale.[7] Putting his ideas into practice, he closed the Special Political Action section in late 1973, when only a few months into the job. He also thwarted suggestions by both Harold Wilson and later David Owen, James Callaghan's foreign secretary, that it might be desirable if Ugandan dictator Idi Amin were killed. Oldfield issued a memorandum reassuring his staff that SIS did not do assassinations.[8] His response to Owen was that 'we prefer more cerebral solutions these days, Foreign Secretary'.[9]

It is worth noting that 1973 also brought in a new cabinet secretary. John Hunt, who replaced Burke Trend in the autumn, was less intellectual and

more practical. He was demanding, direct, and determined. He had experience of the secret world as secretary of the Joint Intelligence Committee
(JIC) in the early 1960s and maintained the role as accounting officer for the
Secret Vote, but he was rather dovish on international relations.[10] Meanwhile,
and indicative of the age, Julian Amery, although promoted from the wil-
derness of minster for public works to a junior minister in the Foreign
Office and operating as the main ministerial liaison with SIS, was banned
from receiving information from Patrick Wright, the head of its Middle
East Department. Alec Douglas–Home, foreign secretary under Edward
Heath, personally insisted that Amery was not allowed to go 'off-piste' on
Arabia. Consequently, he did not resurrect his covert role from Suez
when the Yom Kippur War broke out between Israel and the Arab states in
October 1973.[11]

Much intelligence focus at this time was on domestic affairs. As the economy
faltered, subversion and industrial militancy at home dominated the agenda
and policymakers established new groups, such as Subversion in Public Life,
to develop methods to counter subversive activity, including through covert
operations.[12] Despite this changing climate, Britain still turned to covert action
overseas in the late 1960s and into the 1970s, albeit not to as great an extent as
the heyday a decade earlier. Europe remained off limits for anything beyond
pinprick operations as part of the evolutionary approach towards Moscow, but
opportunities for larger-scale deniable interventions still existed after those in
Yemen and Indonesia wound down. Intelligence actors continued to work
closely with the military to meet British interests in the Gulf. Indeed, the
decreasing military presence enhanced the appeal of covert action as a discreet
force multiplier. The Joint Action Committee (JAC) still existed inside the
Cabinet Office and a former chair, Denis Greenhill, became permanent secretary at the Foreign Office in 1969. Elsewhere, policymakers discussed a role
for less ambitious influence operations from Africa to Latin America.

Global thinking

Throughout the summer of 1966, Harold Wilson considered using covert
action against Rhodesia, which had unilaterally declared independence the
year before. On Christmas Eve 1965, Trend and his deputy, Philip Rogers,
arranged a small ministerial group to plan how best to encourage an alternative government. Much of their work seems to have been above board,

including finding a suitable emissary to convince Ian Smith, the Rhodesian prime minister, to resign.[13] More underhand operations complemented these efforts. Trend established a covert action group working in conjunction with the JAC.[14] The group had a clear objective: 'to bring about the downfall of the Smith regime and a return to constitutional government and the rule of law in Rhodesia, with a view to the resumption of progress toward majority rule as quickly as possible'. Any operations, Trend insisted, had to distinguish between Smith's rebel regime and the constitutional elements in Rhodesia, principally target the white community, and must not stimulate a racial conflict.[15] Much of this activity involved psychological warfare and covert economic operations to complement Wilson's reliance on sanctions. Meanwhile, Whitehall's plotters drew up plans to instigate a coup d'état to replace the hard-line regime with a more liberal and amenable—but still white—alternative. The idea was rumbled when the Rhodesians discovered British paratroopers practising capturing Luqa airport in Malta as a dry run for a strike on Salisbury.[16]

Between 1967 and 1970, Britain covertly intervened in the Biafran War in Nigeria. Determined to prevent secessionist rebels from breaking up the country, Britain sold weapons to the federal government on a far greater scale than it admitted. More muted than special operations, arms sales formed—and still form—a central part of low-key British intervention in foreign affairs. Britain also offered propaganda assistance, another mainstay of covert action, throughout the conflict.[17] In January 1970, *The Telegraph* exposed details of the deniable scheme drawn up by the High Commission's military adviser to help the federal government destroy the secessionist state of Biafra.[18] Shortly afterwards, in a Middle Eastern country, likely Jordan where a civil war had broken out between the government and Palestinian guerrilla fighters, Britain helped persuade the CIA to establish covert supply routes through Turkey to help defeat the rebels. For its part, Whitehall sent the Special Air Service (SAS) to patrol with and train local special forces.[19]

At around the same time, some in SIS hoped to instigate covert action in Libya against Colonel Muammar Gaddafi, who had overthrown the king in 1969. SIS officers plotted to restore the royal family, which had enjoyed excellent relations with Britain, to the Libyan throne. The plans withered though, not least because of mistaken American assumptions that Gaddafi would be anti-communist. With John Rennie reluctant to pursue covert action, operations were outsourced to David Stirling and his mercenary organization at the formal request of the exiled Libyan monarchy. The plan involved freeing political prisoners from a Libyan prison, nicknamed the Hilton, who would then help launch a counter-coup against Gaddafi. Despite supporting the operation's objectives, the Foreign Office and SIS eventually warned Stirling off. It was too dangerous and too easily traced back to British personnel—even if they were operating in a private capacity. But the warning came too late and the Libyans detained one of the boats chartered by the mercenaries, while two others were wrecked off the North African coast.[20] The failure did little to change Rennie's mind about the virtue—or lack thereof—of covert action.

Meanwhile, rumours circulated about SIS officers working with the CIA to help mercenaries elsewhere in Africa, including in southern Sudan. If true, such operations would unlikely have had official blessing, initially at least, given that mercenary activity deeply concerned Harold Wilson who worried what would happen if right-wing soldiers of fortune ever turned their attention to a coup back home.[21] Perhaps Edward Heath, prime minister from June 1970, was more amenable. Any mercenary or covert activity in southern Sudan may have also related to suspected SIS involvement in the 1971 Ugandan coup, in which Idi Amin ousted Prime Minister Milton Obote. An SIS officer, Beverly Barnard, allegedly supported the coup by coordinating these same southern Sudanese rebels with whom Amin had affinity and connections.[22]

After a spate of nationalizations echoing Mossadeq's earlier activity in Iran, the British government was undoubtedly glad to see the back of Obote. Shortly after the coup one diplomat enthused, 'General Amin has certainly removed from the African scene one of our most implacable enemies in matters affecting Southern Africa'. Yet British complicity in the coup, if any, was likely overshadowed by the involvement of Mossad, the Israeli secret service. Amin had long been facilitating large-scale Israeli support for the rebels in southern Sudan as punishment for Sudanese involvement in the Six Day War, and Israel lost a key ally when Obote sacked him in 1970. The British high commissioner in Kampala seemed genuinely surprised by the coup, although he swiftly pointed out that Amin and the Israeli defence attaché had spent the morning of the coup together.[23]

Much uncertainty remains about British covert action in Africa at the turn of the decade. Rumours and intrigue abound. We can say with more confidence that British covert action extended to Latin America. Kidnapping for ransom, intertwined with the rise of political terrorism, had become increasingly common in the late 1960s and early 1970s.[24] In September

1969, the American ambassador to Brazil was kidnapped and held for five days by a guerrilla group known as the Revolutionary Movement of the 8th of October. Following a spate of high-profile kidnappings, the Ministry of Defence sent an SAS team to Brazil to train local forces in close protection skills.[25] This became a growing role for the SAS which remains important today.[26]

Meanwhile, SIS and the Foreign Office drew on their own skills to counter kidnappings. In May 1971, SIS launched what diplomats called a 'covert campaign of disinformation' against the Tupamaros in Uruguay. A leftist urban guerrilla group, the Tupamaros had kidnapped British ambassador Geoffrey Jackson in Montevideo in January and his colleagues back in London turned to black propaganda and disruption to secure his release. Disinformation aimed at sowing doubts among the fighters about the continuing value of holding Jackson.[27] The IRD produced an article by a French journalist with a suitably authentic revolutionary background to promote self-criticism among the Tupamaros. As diplomats in the Foreign Office's Latin American Department explained: 'After a properly revolutionary introduction, it questions the whole principle of kidnapping diplomats and suggests that in particular the Tupamaros are now losing support with ordinary people in Uruguay by the continued detention of Mr Jackson.' The article also made the point, subtly so as not to raise suspicions about British authorship, that the UK did not pay ransoms for diplomats. It sought to reinforce doubts amongst the guerrilla leadership, which intelligence sources had said already existed, and to aid negotiations being undertaken by President Allende of Chile. Demonstrating levels of scrutiny involved, Thomas Brimelow, a senior official in the Foreign Office, personally read—and amended—a draft of the article before giving the IRD the go-ahead.[28]

The propaganda had little immediate effect. By August, the Foreign Office rather bizarrely considered using psychics—or 'experts in extra sensory perception'—to locate Jackson. The Latin American Department had received no fewer than three separate recommendations on this case alone. They ignored the first because they doubted this particular psychic's respectability. They turned down the second because they refused to share classified information with this psychic. The third came via Colin Crowe, Britain's permanent representative to the United Nations in New York. In London, the diplomats worried about the media fallout if the press got hold of this bizarre story. However, and despite assuming Jackson's wife would be distressed by the idea of using a psychic to find her husband, the

Foreign Office refused to rule out the idea and began vetting one potential medium.[29]

Neither black propaganda nor psychics had much effect. Jackson was released following eight long months in captivity after Edward Heath quietly negotiated the ransom using President Allende of Chile as an intermediary.[30] Two years later, Britain's secret operatives would deal with Chile again; this time SIS helped to exfiltrate CIA personnel involved in a botched coup against Allende from the country.[31] Diplomats also sought to use covert tactics to sow doubts amongst another South American leftist group, the ERP, who had kidnapped Stanley Sylvester, an honorary British consul in Argentina, around the same time.[32] As we shall see, Whitehall consistently turned to this *modus operandi* against terrorists in Northern Ireland in the late 1960s and early 1970s and in the Middle East from the 1980s. Discrediting, dividing, and sowing doubts were common—if covert—responses. Sylvester was released a few weeks later after his company paid a ransom of $250,000.

Coups in the Gulf

Between 1970 and 1976, the largest British covert action took place in Oman. Leftist rebels in the Dhofar province, in the south of the country, had threatened to break away and establish a Marxist republic. London reacted with horror as the Omani counter-insurgency effort flailed. If Dhofar fell, many believed, so too would the rest of Oman, leaving the oil-rich states of the Gulf vulnerable.[33] The insurgency had begun in 1967 but the sultan made no attempt to win over the hearts and minds of the Dhofari population. He governed harshly, even concreting over wells as a devastating form of collective punishment.[34] British intelligence castigated the despotic ruler, Sultan Sa'id, in increasingly exasperated terms, realizing that his personal flaws were powerful obstacles to progress.[35]

Fortunately for the counter-insurgency effort, the sultan's son, Qaboos, assumed power in July 1970. It was a near-bloodless coup—although the old sultan managed to shoot himself in the foot while firing blindly from behind a locked door deep inside his palace. Back in Whitehall, the British government reacted with relief, not least because it had covertly helped plan and execute it.[36] In order to understand Britain's role in the coup, it is first necessary to examine its track record of orchestrating regime change in the

Gulf, an area of informal empire in which Britain maintained a strong, if sometimes hidden, hand.

In June 1965, British officials on the ground helped remove Sheikh Saqr of Sharjah, a small emirate in the Persian Gulf. He had become too nationalist for London to stomach and allowed the Arab League, and by extension Egypt and Iraq, too much sway in his sheikhdom. This, in turn, threatened Britain's position in the Trucial States more broadly. Accordingly, the political resident, William Luce, had long lobbied to undermine Saqr and even suggested colluding with neighbouring Dubai in a takeover. As pressure grew on Saqr, Luce and Glen Balfour-Paul, Britain's political agent in Dubai, urged London to depose him. Minister of State George Thomson supported their tough stance and suggested stimulating a revolution in Sharjah. Between 23 and 24 June, Saqr was swept from power after his family presented a letter to Luce's deputy expressing their wish to depose him. British personnel then swiftly escorted Saqr to the airport and flew him to Bahrain on an RAF plane. Publicly insisting that the coup had been an internal family affair, the Foreign Office braced itself for a wave of anti-British propaganda blaming Britain for engineering it.[37]

Although the relevant files remain classified, British involvement was more direct than the Foreign Office admitted. As those involved in Operation Boot in Iran could have attested, this was not the first time Britain covertly ensured a letter demanding a change of leader be written. Balfour-Paul had heard of three different conspiracies to overthrow Saqr in the fortnight preceding the coup. The day before the coup, Denis Healey, the defence secretary, decided not to resist any regime change and, in doing so, demonstrated Britain's power to choose whether to allow or block a coup in an ostensibly independent territory. The extent to which Britain encouraged or exploited these conspiracies remains unknown. As noted above, however, Luce and Balfour-Paul had lobbied for a coup against Saqr for months and Thomson congratulated them both for their hard work afterwards.[38]

The following year, British officials in the Gulf grew frustrated with another local leader: the unpredictable Sheikh Sakbout of Abu Dhabi, whom they accused of impeding Western development plans. Much to the delight of the Foreign Office, Sakbout's brother Zaid deposed him in early August 1966. Echoing events in Sharjah, British diplomats had been plotting this for quite some time. As early as May 1963, Alec Douglas-Home, then foreign secretary, approved a plan to replace Sakbout with Zaid, working through influential members of the ruling family. The Foreign Office's Arabian Department intended to deny any British input and instead point to an internal family squabble. Britain's role was to be presented as merely the messenger. The plan, however, was abandoned after Sakbout heard rumours of an impending coup and bribed his scheming relatives to back him over his brother.[39]

Over the following two years, William Luce pressed successive foreign secretaries for regime change in Abu Dhabi. Patrick Gordon Walker, the new Labour foreign secretary, was initially cool, arguing that 'I will need a lot of persuading that this James Bond scheme is a good one',[40] before secretly agreeing to depose the sheikh. But, again reminiscent of the Iranian shah in early 1953, Luce struggled with the ruling family's continued loss of nerve. After consultation with the oil companies, he continued to press his case whilst Zaid continued his own campaign to undermine Sakbout, even going so far as to offer a written statement formally confirming his readiness to depose his brother. Eventually, Zaid overthrew Sakbout in August 1966, having received the necessary assurances to act during a private visit to London in June. Zaid then returned to Abu Dhabi and asked Balfour-Paul for assistance. Luce, Balfour-Paul, and Zaid managed to obtain a letter from the ruling family allowing the coup to go ahead. Meanwhile, Britain put the Trucial Oman Scouts, the local military force, on standby to help if needed. In line with similar operations, this allowed the Foreign Office to appear to be responding to Zaid's initiative whilst stressing non-interference in internal affairs.[41]

This historical context is essential for understanding the 1970 coup in Oman. Deep inside the Ministry of Defence, thoughts had turned to regime change that February. Planners knew that it would be risky, though, not least because Qaboos, the most likely usurper, was an unknown quantity.[42] This was not necessarily a prohibitive problem and he did have support elsewhere in Whitehall. The JIC praised him as having a potentially greater appeal amongst Dhofaris than the sultan himself,[43] whilst Antony Acland, the head of the Foreign Office's Arabian Department, agreed Qaboos was 'likely to be a much better bet than the present Sultan' and that a coup was desirable.[44] The bigger obstacle was that it would put British officers seconded to the Sultan's Armed Forces, or SAF, in the unenviable position of having to overthrow their commander-in-chief.[45]

With this in mind, and considering that the sultan had been a loyal friend to the British over the years, Michael Stewart, the Labour foreign secretary, offered to give him one last chance.[46] Unfortunately for both sides, Sa'id remained stubbornly unreceptive and, after another revolutionary group, modelling themselves on Che Guevara, attacked SAF positions inside northern Oman in June, British officials, under pressure from the Shell oil company, accepted that the beleaguered sultan would now be overthrown come what may. It made sense, therefore, to install a friendly replacement.[47] The time for watching and waiting was over.

At around the same time, a British intelligence officer in Dhofar, Tim Landon, reported that Qaboos had expressed interest in overthrowing his father. Despite strong warnings from the JIC that a coup would be unlikely to succeed without external support,[48] eager officials in the Foreign Office took Qaboos's talk seriously and allowed it to serve as a catalyst for action.[49] Rather than exposing the planned overthrow of a supposed ally, Peter Hayman, a senior official at the Foreign Office, chaired a meeting to discuss a deniable British role in facilitating the coup. Despite being fully aware of the problems—and the illegality—of using the sultan's own armed forces against him, Hayman recommended a top-secret plan to help, or at the very least protect, Qaboos. No stranger to deniable interventions, the returning Conservative foreign secretary, Alec Douglas-Home, agreed that Qaboos could take refuge with the SAF or be discreetly flown out of the country if things went wrong. The diplomats went further still and pressured Colonel Hugh Oldman, the Briton seconded as the sultan's defence secretary, to reluctantly agree to a remarkable move if the coup failed: SAF would be used to assist Qaboos 'in gaining control of Salalah town and in deposing his father'.[50] Oldman knew that a failed coup would have damaging consequences and so accepted, albeit with a heavy heart, the argument in favour of ensuring it succeeded.[51] Stewart Crawford, the political resident in the Persian Gulf, followed by ministers in London, then approved a specific plan.[52]

For once, the military were more cautious than the diplomats. Use of seconded British military personnel in a coup created deep unease in the Ministry of Defence. Aside from the ethical and legal issues involved, removing a leader whom Britain still recognized as being head of state would have threatened the standing of other seconded forces around the world.[53] In a marked contrast to earlier decades, Edward Peck, now chair of the Joint Action Committee and overseeing intelligence and security in the Foreign Office, had to convince the military to support the plan. He promised that it would not be traced back to London. Similarly, Stewart Crawford also stressed that the coup would be presented as an internal matter with the

British hand deniable. 'We would', he argued, 'of course maintain the position that we had no foreknowledge.'[54] It was the same line used in Sharjah and Abu Dhabi. Meanwhile, it appears that someone asked Julian Amery, still minister of public works, for his views on deposing the sultan.[55]

In the end, the operation was plausibly deniable. Deliberately coinciding with the anniversary of the 1952 Egyptian revolution, a prominent date in the liberation calendar and a time when British officers loyal to Sa'id were on holiday, the coup was arranged by John Graham, commander of the sultan's armed forces.[56] A dozen Omanis forcibly entered the palace to depose the sultan, thereby creating an impression of local action, but were led by Ray Kane, a British officer acting on direct orders from his British commanding officer. It was Kane, armed with a machine gun, who apparently chased the sultan into a locked room and forced the bullet-proof glass by repeatedly firing at the same spot.[57] The sultan, who received four gunshot wounds, soon surrendered. Speaking to the BBC some forty years afterwards, Antony Acland reflected that he had hoped the coup would go well, 'and in the end it didn't go badly'.[58] There was no need for the controversial contingency plan of using the SAF to take control of Salalah.

Sa'id, who took refuge in the UK, formed one last loose end. Senior ministers wanted to make sure he kept quiet, expecting him to feel sore about the coup, which, as he had already protested from his hospital bed, could not have succeeded without British assistance.[59] Douglas-Home intended to warn him off 'engaging in embarrassing political' activity, and prevent him from writing a book or giving interviews about events surrounding the coup.[60] Fearing contravention of asylum obligations, Reginald Maudling, the home secretary, settled on a more subtle threat: 'to say no more than that we look to him not to abuse our hospitality by embarrassing HM Government in any way'.[61]

Storm and beyond

Within hours of the palace coup, the Foreign Office agreed to send an SAS team to Oman to invigorate the counter-insurgency effort now that Sa'id was out of the way.[62] The SAS were pleased at the deployment, ever conscious of the need to find small wars and keep the regiment alive.[63] Special forces involvement (the Special Boat Service joined later but it was predominantly an SAS show), to which Qaboos was more receptive than his father, was codenamed Operation Storm. It brought together clas-sical counter-insurgency thinking, including psychological operations to break morale and encourage surrenders, improved intelligence-gathering, and economic and health inducements such as providing fresh water.[64]

Initially, Whitehall refused to support covert action inside rebel territory. It was too dangerous—and politically damaging—if uncovered. The SAS therefore began Operation Storm by trying to win hearts and minds, partly through offering medical and veterinary services.[65] Such restrictions were lifted as the insurgency intensified and throughout the first half of 1970s special forces played an important role in training, managing, and leading guerrilla units consisting of turned enemy personnel known as *firqat*.[66] SAS-led teams engaged in aggressive patrolling, climbing steep tracks up the mountains at night to lay ambushes. They directed air supply drops, which proved vital in allowing operations to be extended.[67] The initial idea also involved using the SAS to form groups of so-called 'pseudo gangs' of rebels launched, according to the plan, 'to hunt down and eliminate specific rebel leaders and Chinese advisers'.[68] It is unclear whether this ever came to fruition but, as we shall see, it did form part of British operations elsewhere, includ-ing in Northern Ireland. Special forces activity had to remain deniable, not least because politicians back in London feared publicizing a war which risked turning into another Aden. Oman was, according to one historian, 'the least publicised of any war in which British forces have been involved'.[69]

Led by the SAS, *firqat* consisting of 600 guerrillas engaged in one of the turning points of the war in October 1971. They retook a mountainous region from the rebels and constructed a new base, known as White City, and an airstrip. This allowed SAS teams to patrol the region, gain extra supplies, and cut off supply routes feeding the insurgency from Yemen. The following spring special forces established another base, this time on the Yemen border.[70] In July, SAS soldiers fought a battle which has gone down in folklore: the Battle of Mirbat. Just before dawn on a misty morning, more than 250 insurgents, armed with automatic rifles and machine guns, launched an ambitious assault against the town. Vastly outnumbered and lacking ammunition, a small SAS team of just nine men managed to hold their position under heavy fire until reinforcements arrived—inflicting a humiliating defeat on the rebels.[71] This was British covert action, in pursuit of British interests and, for once, there was little American involvement. Nonetheless, Washington still knew what was going on and claimed influence.

White House officials told Henry Kissinger, the secretary of state, that Britain had assumed 'the primary military role with our approval and encouragement in the context of our policy of maximum regional self-reliance'.[72]

At the same time, Britain launched another covert operation in conjunction with Oman. Between 1972 and 1975, SAS teams recruited, trained, and sponsored tribesmen exiled from what had become South Yemen to conduct cross-border raids, codenamed Operation Dhib, into Yemeni territory. Although the initiative came from Oman, defence officials in Whitehall knew that as long as South Yemeni support continued, the insurgency in Dhofar could not be defeated.[73] The plan recommended harassment, raids, guerrilla warfare—and even a rebellion in the Mahra region of South Yemen—to embroil Yemeni forces in their own backyard. This, in turn, would relieve pressure on the Sultan's Armed Forces fighting in Dhofar.[74] Sultan Qaboos shared the enthusiasm and, in October 1972, asked the British government to help him raise a *firqa* for unattributable guerrilla operations inside South Yemen.[75]

In London, Michael Carver, chief of the general staff, was optimistic. He agreed that Yemeni rebel activities had been allowed to go 'entirely unmolested'. Sabotage, demolition, mining, and ambushing, Carver felt, could cause significant disruption.[76] The main problem would be political, rather than military—and ministers thought the plan extremely sensitive, stipulating that it would have to be entirely unattributable.[77] The ambassador to Oman, Donald Hawley, initially rejected the idea, but, after further reflection, and still worrying about the difficulties of maintaining plausible deniability if any British-trained tribesmen were caught and interrogated, he reconsidered.[78] Hawley realized that the Omanis intended to do the operation anyway and so thought it stood a better chance of success with SAS assistance.[79] Likewise, officials in the Foreign Office thought it risky, not least because it could distract Qaboos from fighting his own rebels in Dhofar,[80] but accepted that Britain would probably get the blame regardless, so they might as well make the operation as effective as possible. Ministers authorized Operation Dhib towards the end of November 1972, albeit with caveats. First, it had to remain completely deniable. Second, ministers forbade SAS soldiers from accompanying the tribesmen across the border. Third, the sultan had to know that this was a limited operation and liable to be cancelled abruptly if uncovered.[81] Masked by the ongoing Operation Storm, an SAS team swiftly moved into position.[82]

Most raids were sporadic and small-scale, engaging in sabotage and ambushes. They also generated a great deal of intelligence on enemy forces.[83]

One of the larger raids, in May 1973, saw the SAS-trained tribesmen attack six trucks in a Yemeni military convoy, killing twenty-two people and taking one prisoner.[84] The following year, ambushes and minelaying supposedly killed around twenty Yemeni fighters, destroyed two vehicles, and damaged machinery.[85] Fearing escalation to war with South Yemen, Whitehall planners kept the situation under constant review and initially balked when Qaboos insisted on extending the raids. After some consideration, though, Prime Minister Edward Heath agreed, again on the basis that Qaboos would do it anyway and so it was better to maintain quiet SAS involvement to prevent unprofessional raids from becoming an embarrassment.[86] Nonetheless, when one *firqa* showed ill-discipline, cautious officials quickly removed the SAS and redeployed the offending rebels to a less sensitive area. Likewise, they temporarily suspended operations in late 1973 when violence provoked a marked reaction from Yemeni forces.[87]

Operation Dhib continued until 1975. Carver thought it had proved a success at both inflicting casualties and producing intelligence,[88] whilst Donald Hawley noted with relief how little attention it attracted from the outside world.[89] Perhaps most importantly, SAS control directly restrained *firqat* operations, preventing military escalation, whilst also disrupting supply routes to the Omani rebels from South Yemen.[90] As with much British covert action, officials in London, partly through the JAC, ensured that operations were adequately scrutinized, coordinated, and carried out within a framework agreed at the highest level. As had happened in South Arabia and Indonesia in the 1960s, tightly controlled covert action sought to temper the more aggressive demands from leaders in the region. Operations in Oman demonstrated improvement in managing covert action. In 1973, the Ministry of Defence formed a Special Forces Operations Sub-Committee which reported to the assistant chief of the defence staff (operations)— himself a JAC member. It advised on the 'higher direction and employment of Special Forces'.[91] This helped to ensure that tactical means properly aligned with broader objectives, a problem which had impeded operations in the 1960s.

★   ★   ★

Covert action in Oman came against a backdrop of the Watergate scandal playing out in Washington and a season of congressional inquiries, the most famous being led by Senator Frank Church, into intelligence excesses. Ministers, officials, and intelligence operatives alike were horrified, fearing that details of British covert action would seep into the public domain as journalists and senators rummaged through CIA secrets. The febrile atmosphere rippled across the Atlantic and British investigative journalists began to search eagerly for the British equivalent of the CIA's global misdeeds. More than ever, planners in the Foreign Office, Cabinet Office, and Ministry of Defence feared the risks of covert actions becoming common knowledge and the damage this would do to London's supposed reputation for fair play and decency in international affairs. The need for secrecy dominated discussions of operations in Oman. Whilst SAS activity increased, political covert action appeared to move in the opposite direction, not least because Maurice Oldfield had closed SIS's Special Political Action section in 1973. Nonetheless, the phrase continued to be used within SIS for at least another decade afterwards as functions dispersed elsewhere.[92] Meanwhile, some in the Foreign Office thought that détente and the freer movement of people it brought facilitated the spread of Western values. There was, they argued, now less need for government-sponsored influence operations.[93]

Against this background, David Owen, the Labour foreign secretary, closed the IRD in 1977. Some in the Foreign Office had grown increasingly frustrated with it. David Lipsey, an adviser to Owen's predecessor Anthony Crosland, thought that the IRD had turned into, as he put it, 'a sort of mini-CIA, a propaganda machine campaigning everywhere against communist policies'. It was crude and, despite its recently broadened agenda, still focused too narrowly on communism. On one occasion Lipsey asked the IRD's head, Ray Whitney, who would later become a Conservative MP, for unattributable material on South Africa, where the liberation struggle was putting increasing pressure on the white regime. The IRD came back with a report linking the rebels to international communism. This was not what the foreign secretary had in mind, and Lipsey thought the whole thing hilarious.[94] Giving its covert functions to SIS and replacing the research side with a small Overseas Information Department,[95] Owen argued that it was necessary to 'end the grey area, which for far too long escaped proper scrutiny, falling neither in the open area of our diplomacy nor in the closed area of spying'.[96] He ensured that the head of the covert aspects was not accountable to the head of the conventional research wing.

Meanwhile, under Maurice Oldfield, SIS covert action seemingly focused on disruption continued through a new General Support Branch, which operated in conjunction with special forces. The Branch provided tactical support for SIS operations, including infiltrating and exfiltrating officers and agents, although not all of these constituted covert action. Defence officials sat in the drab SIS headquarters at Century House and oversaw the use of SAS and SBS personnel almost as contract labourers.[97] Whilst the more ambitious campaigns against Albania, Iran, Egypt, and Syria fell out of favour, special forces, working alongside SIS, became a useful means of pursuing British interests where conventional military force was impossible.

Covert action in Oman, like that in Indonesia and Yemen before it, took place a long way from home, thereby aiding deniability. Meanwhile, violence had broken out on the streets of the UK itself. The long-simmering sectarian conflict in Northern Ireland had come to the boil once more. With protests, riots, and terrorist killings on the rise, Whitehall's planners, more used to plotting operations in faraway lands, had to turn their attention closer to home. With constraints limiting both the use of conventional military force and the willingness to negotiate with terrorists, Britain turned to covert action as part of its response. Doing so inevitably proved highly controversial and, operating so close to home, deeply challenging.

11

TROUBLES

Covert Action in Northern Ireland

It felt like we were all effectively licensed to kill for that short time, dodging in and out of the shadowy murky streets, spying on and hunting down terrorists.

Military Reaction Force member[*][1]

The Troubles in Northern Ireland remain a particularly controversial era of British history. The sustained use of political violence by the Irish Republican Army (IRA) pushed state responses to their limit, raising difficult questions about employing covert tactics so close to home. Activities that Whitehall's planners deemed acceptable in some far-flung colony or against the mendacious Soviets now appeared much less appropriate on the streets of the UK—against British citizens.

Although Northern Ireland had long been a hotbed of sectarian tension, the streets turned violent in 1969 following a series of civil rights marches by the Catholic minority and counter-protests by loyalists. In August, the British government sent troops to restore order and keep the peace. The nationalists may have initially greeted them as protectors, but, as the security situation deteriorated, they soon saw the army as occupiers. As British forces increasingly came into conflict with the IRA, violence escalated during the 1970s. The government sent more troops to Belfast and Derry, whilst paramilitary organizations from both sides engaged in ever more sectarian killings. In 1972, Edward Heath, the prime minister, imposed direct rule from Westminster on the six counties but violence continued to spiral despite attempts to normalize the situation from the middle of the 1970s.

---

* From *MRF Shadow Troop* by Simon Cursey. With permission from Thistle Publishing.

Policymakers in Whitehall found themselves in a difficult position. On the one hand, escalating the use of military force was problematic. Terrorists hid among the population, thereby making conventional strikes difficult. Civilian casualties served only to increase sympathy for the IRA. On the other hand, political constraints made policymakers reluctant to negotiate openly with terrorists. As in the Cold War and colonial counter-insurgency, planners therefore wondered if covert operations might play a role. Terrorist groups were already playing dirty, and covert action against the IRA could, they hoped, allow negotiation from a position of strength while supporting the military offensive.

Black propaganda

Unattributable propaganda, conducted by both military psychological operations, or psyops, teams and the Foreign Office's Information Research Department (IRD), formed a key part of British activity in Northern Ireland. Back in 1969, at the outbreak of the Troubles, the army, which initially took the lead in this area, defined psyops as 'the planned use of propaganda or other means, in support of our military action or presence, designed to influence to our advantage the opinions, emotions, attitudes and behaviour of enemy, neutral and friendly groups'.[2] Such activity covered black, white, and grey propaganda and it is important to remember that the vast majority of information work was overt public relations activity. Covert propaganda formed a smaller-scale and complementary activity, used when attribution would undermine credibility.

By July 1970, the army wanted to create a dedicated psyops unit in Northern Ireland.[3] In October, it sent a lieutenant colonel to its headquarters at Lisburn to run an Information Liaison Department. This achieved little and, in September 1971, a new Information Policy Unit, headed by Colonel Maurice Tugwell, replaced it. Through holding unattributable briefings with journalists, Tugwell sought to wage a propaganda war.[4] Although those working in Lisburn deny any involvement in black operations,[5] one retired colonel has stated that 'if one wanted to convey a message to a particular group, you can make it appear as if it was coming from somebody else'.[6] At the same time, psyops specialists sent army personnel onto the streets to distribute leaflets disguised in Beatles wigs.[7]

Civilian propagandists also targeted Northern Ireland.[8] In fact, IRD staff were particularly keen to find a role in the conflict given that the receding communist threat had placed their jobs under threat. Whitehall managers slashed the IRD's budget by more than half in 1971, leaving those who survived the axe anxious to safeguard their careers.[9] From Downing Street, Heath also called for unattributable propaganda. He had been fully briefed that officials, including Norman Reddaway, now overseeing all cultural and information work at the Foreign Office, were working 'overtly and covertly, to blacken the IRA' by placing propaganda into the British press.[10] Stewart Crawford, chairman of the Joint Action Committee (JAC) and overseeing intelligence and security work at the Foreign Office, argued in favour of applying IRD techniques, including, in his words, 'covert propaganda', to Northern Ireland. He sought to 'expose the extremists, discredit their methods, and isolate them, and to counter their efforts by damping down inter-communal tensions'. Echoing a long-held British theme, propaganda would 'exploit any tendencies to disagreement and rivalry among the extremist groups'.[11]

In August 1972, Heath piled on more pressure. The government was losing the propaganda war in the aftermath of internment without trial and the killing of unarmed civilians on Bloody Sunday. Heath insisted that a massive propaganda counter-attack was needed to refute IRA allegations and discredit the terrorists, and that experienced staff should be drafted in from wherever possible to achieve this. He even advocated bribery: 'using money freely' to gain information and influence people.[12] Ministers, civil servants, and the military all pressed for a counter-propaganda offensive.[13]

That the British state was subverting its own people raised serious problems. Hugh Mooney, the IRD's man on the ground, recognized that 'the department saw Northern Ireland as a poisoned chalice. It promised salvation but would probably end in disaster.'[14] Propaganda and manipulation at home, however, were nothing new. As early as December 1951, the Secret Intelligence Service (SIS) had suggested using satire to ridicule communism, sparking a conversation with Norman Brook, as cabinet secretary, about whether Noël Coward was a suitably reliable comedian to spearhead the new campaign.[15] In the same year, the IRD created a small Home Desk or English Section, which focused on subversion and industry, and remained in place into the 1970s.[16] As part of the so-called cultural Cold War, the IRD bolstered purportedly independent domestic writers and presses through moderate trade unions, the BBC, several daily newspapers, and the non-communist left.[17] Beyond the Cold War Heath's drive for British membership of the European Economic Community in 1970 required discreet support. Stepping up, the IRD planted material in the press and drafted letters for MPs to send to newspapers.[18] As Thomas Barker, the head of the IRD, explained in the context of Northern Ireland, the IRD 'have had for many years a responsibility both in the <u>home</u> and overseas fields'.[19]

Nonetheless, the government attempted to circumvent potential criticism about covert propaganda in Northern Ireland in three ways. First, officials portrayed the IRA as a subversive organization, thereby allowing them to fall within the IRD's recently broadened remit.[20] Second, they portrayed the nationalists as foreign, mainly from Ireland, but also linked to the Vatican.[21] Third, IRD appointments had to take place under deep cover, especially because the Northern Irish prime minister, James Chichester-Clark, had resisted propaganda operations against his own people.[22] Accordingly, IRD officers took on Home Office cover.[23]

From 1971, the IRD placed anti-IRA material in the British and foreign press.[24] As Hugh Mooney reported to London, 'The darker side' of propaganda had 'not been neglected'.[25] Examples of unattributable propaganda in Northern Ireland are endless. They range from planted stories of IRA embezzlement and fraud, to Soviet shipments of rocket launchers into Ireland; from spreading rumours that making explosives caused cancer, to rumours that explosives hidden in women's clothing risked being ignited by friction in their underwear. Propaganda also accused terrorists of dabbling in witchcraft and black magic, with the British even going as far as planting 'black altars' and placing upside-down crucifixes in parts of Belfast. Colin Wallace, an army intelligence officer, claimed that 'we used to collect chicken blood from the cookhouse at the army barracks and put that on the altars so it looked like there had been a sacrifice or something'. Other allegations include the smearing of members of parliament seen as having unhelpful views on Northern Ireland.[26] One journalist covering the Troubles remembers how 'in our various newsrooms we were being overwhelmed by a blizzard of facts and atrocities, lies and propaganda, from all sides, and it was simply impossible to tell truth from fantasy, fact from fiction'.[27]

Recently declassified files reveal remarkable IRD activities. One scheme countered terrorist use of bazookas. These heavy weapons were difficult to handle and the IRA wondered why the shells had not been exploding when, in fact, the safety cap was still on. British propagandists deliberately concealed this explanation and instead issued a dummy army order stating that shells should be tested electronically. This, Mooney hoped, 'would have the effect of exploding the shell in the tester's hands'. Similarly, two young nationalists died while making a bomb during what happened to be the coldest night of the year. The British swiftly issued misinformation stating that gelignite reacts to changes in temperature. This had the desired effect when the IRA quickly disposed of what they thought were suspect stocks against soft targets.[28]

Covert propaganda emphasized familiar themes. It portrayed the IRA as having links to international terrorism, especially Libya and the Gaddafi regime,[29] as well as being part of a broader international communist movement.[30] Both themes, but especially the latter, were reminiscent of attempts to discredit insurgents during the wars of decolonization. Propaganda also exploited divisions and fostered rivalry amongst targets. Mooney set the Provisional IRA against the Official IRA by suggesting that the latter were 'seriously considering assassinating the dozen or so leading Provisionals in Belfast'.[31] He spread further rumours that the Provisionals had betrayed the Officials in the aftermath of internment.[32] Finally, propaganda was intended to undermine the IRA in the eyes of ordinary people—and portray them as ruthless killers divorced from the concerns of the local community they were supposed to represent. The British authorities sought to expose what they saw as the IRA's 'total ruthlessness and disregard for the lives and property of either section of the community'.[33]

Many propaganda operations were outlandish and ultimately backfired.[34] British intelligence lacked a nuanced understanding of why people joined paramilitary groups in the first place,[35] whilst black propaganda was particularly difficult to run in Northern Ireland, where nothing remained secret for long.[36] Gradually, the British realized that Ireland could not be treated as a mere extension of colonial counter-insurgency strategy and the army handed responsibility over to the Royal Ulster Constabulary in the mid-1970s.[37] Even before then black propaganda was on the decline, as locals referred to Lisburn as the Lisburn Lie Machine.[38] In 1973, Britain removed IRD staff altogether,[39] although they continued to take a keen interest from London. Shortly afterwards, the army's Information Policy Unit was closed.[40]

That is not to say that unattributable—even black—propaganda ended. In late 1974, the government continued to press for a determined information policy, including 'unattributable briefings to press and "leaders of opinion"', alongside 'the creation of [apparently] independent organisations which will support moderate policies, peace festivals and other uncommitted groupings'. Moreover, MI5 later called for a 'sustained and structured propaganda war' to disrupt terrorist recruitment and encourage defections. Although this did not happen in the way MI5 hoped, the service did engage in a limited propaganda initiative in the 1980s against Provisional IRA leaders, some of which was conducted without proper authorization.[41] MI5 propaganda set out to discredit terrorists publicly, leaving the head of its Operational Section with misgivings and warning that such activity should not include anything that 'might be taken as incitement' to murder. Similarly, the head of MI5's agent-running section pointed out the obligation not to exacerbate the sectarian tension. Despite this, he described the 1980s campaign as both 'talented and clearly successful'.[42]

In truth, MI5 initiatives lacked focus and control. They ended up targeting individuals who were not members of terrorist organizations but prominent figures in the broader nationalist and republican community. This, as we shall see, led to allegations of collusion or incitement when loyalist paramilitaries murdered some of these people. The operation designed to unnerve and expose key IRA members finished towards the end of 1989. In a post-mortem, MI5 acknowledged executing 'CA', or counter-action, 'activity before we had developed either a controlling mechanism for it or a means of fuelling it with suitable CA material'.[43] Nonetheless, as late as 1990, Defence Secretary Tom King implied that disinformation was still used in Northern Ireland for 'honourable security reasons'.[44]

Hit squads

Propaganda formed the backbone of broader deniable activities. In Belfast, Hugh Mooney considered himself involved in 'all SPA', or special political action, projects.[45] In London, Heath demanded more than just propaganda action and complained to Burke Trend, the cabinet secretary, about the timidity of the intelligence services. In turn, Trend, perhaps simply to appease Heath's desire for action, instructed the secretary of the JAC, then seconded SIS officer Brian Stewart, to come up with a list of possible responses. Much like Stewart Menzies' menu to counter communism over two decades earlier, it included the entire gamut of covert operations. Stewart, who described himself as the last of SIS's 'robber barons' in a time when special operations had gone out of fashion, particularly advocated black propaganda in the form of forged letters to incriminate and undermine terrorist leaders.[46] In summer 1971, the Joint Action Committee invited IRD representatives to participate in its top-secret discussions on Northern Ireland.[47]

Stewart also recommended sabotaging IRA weapons and ammunitions. He suggested keeping booby-trapped weapons inside poorly guarded British depots from where the IRA could steal them.[48] The JAC likely sanctioned this operation, whilst another former JAC representative remembers more 'hairy' schemes, which will never see the light of day.[49] JAC-sponsored activity on the streets of the UK alarmed officials in the Home Office. Philip Woodfield, heading its Northern Ireland department, was particularly concerned and accused Denis Greenhill, the senior official at the Foreign Office and himself a former chair of the JAC, of driving covert activity. Woodfield reassured his own permanent under-secretary, Philip Allen, that he would personally attend any JAC meetings on Ireland to keep emphasizing the political risks involved.[50] The military, as was so often the case, proved the most vocal proponents of such operations, although, as one person involved recalls, 'nobody wanted to touch Ireland so everyone passed the buck. Northern Ireland was the graveyard of reputations.'[51] Formal JAC involvement was relatively short-lived and took a back seat after the creation of the Northern Ireland Office in 1972—perhaps unsurprisingly given the earlier Home Office caution. In fact, the Northern Ireland Office knew nothing about the JAC at all.[52]

In the meantime, assassination also featured on Brian Stewart's list. Dick White, now Whitehall intelligence coordinator and the most experienced secret servant in the land, had little enthusiasm for special operations in Ireland. His face went ashen grey when he saw the reference to assassination, but he passed the whole paper up to Heath regardless.[53] The prime minister's reaction is not known. When Alec Douglas-Home, the foreign secretary, saw Stewart's proposals he shook his head and wisely said that after hundreds of years of the Irish problem, Britain did not need more blood on its hands now.[54]

Nonetheless, the alleged use of extrajudicial killings in Northern Ireland has sparked particular controversy, with much criticism focusing on the Military Reaction Force (MRF), a top-secret unit operating in 1972. Britain had long used subterranean teams to fight terrorists and insurgents across the empire. These units operated undercover, disguised as the local or insurgent population in order to gather intelligence and engage in proactive measures to eliminate the enemy, including ambushes, armed assaults, and false flag operations intended to provoke discord within an insurgent movement.[55] Some of these groups, known as counter-gangs, also comprised former insurgents who had switched sides to work with the security forces.

Britain had turned to counter-gangs when fighting Zionist guerrillas in Palestine after the Second World War. Posing as terrorists, teams drove around in battered civilian cars modified to hide weapons and ammunition. Their task was to provoke contact, but without firing first.[56] Similar tactics, sometimes known as Q patrols, were then used in Malaya, Kenya, and Cyprus in the 1950s to uncover and eliminate enemy fighters.[57] The following decade in Aden, SAS teams masqueraded as locals, wearing Arab dress but carrying concealed weapons, in order to snatch, arrest, or kill terrorists.[58] They even used soldiers as bait to draw out terrorists before launching into action from the shadows. The purpose, according to one military historian, 'was to meet terrorism with terrorism'.[59]

An equally risky game played out on the streets of Northern Ireland. Around Easter 1971, the army had formed plain-clothed units, run jointly with the Royal Ulster Constabulary, known as Bomb Squads. When, owing to problems of intelligence-sharing, these proved unsuccessful, MRFs took over later in the year.[60] In October, Michael Carver, the chief of the general staff, called for 'more aggressive tactics against gunmen, such as the formation of Q squads in special areas, to mystify, mislead and destroy the terrorists'.[61] By this time MRFs had already quietly begun their activity and each of the three brigades in Northern Ireland had an MRF under its command.[62] In Belfast, 39 Brigade, initially under Frank Kitson, who had pioneered counter-gangs in the colonies, ran the most active MRF. It consisted of three sections, each containing three non-commissioned officers and nine men. At any one time, three teams were on duty in Belfast and a further three remained on standby.[63] The Belfast MRF operated out of a corrugated iron compound, which looked like a builders' yard, deep inside the Palace Barracks in Holywood on the outskirts of the city. Despite sharing the base with regular troops, the MRF compound was off limits to everyone else.[64]

Engaged in sensitive and deniable work, MRF men fully expected the government to deny all knowledge of their existence if caught by paramilitary groups. Their disguises included masquerading as road sweepers—hiding machine guns inside dustcarts—and as meth addicts lying on the pavement with a pistol strapped to each leg. They knew that, if caught, they would probably be killed.[65] Like colonial counter-gangs before them, MRF 'covert operations', according to the Ministry of Defence, 'included surveillance, protection, counter-hijacking and arrests'.[66] Like those in Palestine and Aden, this extended to generating arrests.[67] The offensive and surveillance roles often merged. MRFs' main duty was to react to intelligence but in doing so their operations often gained further information themselves.[68]

Offensive operations involved spoiling, disrupting, and compromising terrorist attacks.[69] Echoing SAS tactics in Indonesia, they involved as brief a contact with the enemy as possible, known as a 'shoot and scoot' approach.[70] It was, as one former member stated, a 'hard-hitting anti-terrorist' role. MRFs did not operate as a traditional army unit. Instead, they acted 'like a terror group' and played by 'their own rules'—although they deny shooting innocent civilians.[71] Another former MRF man remembers, 'we had to overwhelm them right from the start' before targets could fire back or detonate a bomb.[72] MRF teams drove around Belfast in adapted Hillmans and Ford Cortinas, some of which had been stolen or confiscated from the IRA,[73] and carried a range of weapons. These included pistols and sub-machine guns, some with silencers, as well as at least one Thompson machine gun—a favourite of the IRA. Although the MRF officer commanding, Hamish McGregor, has said that policy dictated tommy guns be used for training purposes only, an MRF team used one in action at least once. For them, it was simply part of the disguise.[74]

MRF teams drove around the city responding to intelligence and looking for terrorist suspects. In the words of one member, they felt that they had been 'sanctioned to go out and specifically hunt down the IRA'.[75] Although senior soldiers stressed to Lord Carrington, the defence secretary, that MRFs could only use lethal force as a last resort,[76] the nature of their work meant last resorts occurred regularly. By the deputy chief of the general staff's own admission, MRFs often sought to instigate a situation that would result in an arrest or terrorist shooting.[77] Teams looked to provoke action and, as the SAS had done in Aden, apparently even used uniformed military colleagues as bait to draw terrorists out of the shadows.[78]

Over 10,000 shootings took place on the lawless streets of Belfast in 1972. Many killings therefore attracted relatively little attention; others were more controversial. In May, an MRF team fired a sub-machine gun from an unmarked car and killed a man at an unauthorized checkpoint operated by the Catholic Ex-Servicemen's Association. The coroner heard that the dead man had not fired his weapon. The following month another MRF team in another unmarked car shot and wounded three black-cab drivers standing at a bus stop.[79] The army covered up MRF shootings, blaming loyalist para-militaries for the violence.[80] Nevertheless, one MRF man, Clive 'Taff' Williams, was charged with three counts of attempted murder after attacking a group of men with a tommy gun. As his trial began, officials back in the Ministry of Defence frantically sought to hide the existence of the MRF.[81] Williams was acquitted and later promoted. In 2014, police in Northern Ireland began investigations into eighteen shootings in Belfast between April and September 1972, in which the MRF might have been involved. One, on 7 May, involved the shooting of a 15-year-old boy outside a school disco.[82]

MRF operations apparently included snatches too. As had happened in Aden and, as we shall see, would again happen in the Balkans, suspects were bundled into unmarked cars. Bystanders assumed the MRF was just another terrorist kidnap squad operating in the city.[83] Turned IRA members, known as Freds, helped to identify some of the targets. Although Freds and MRFs were separate plain-clothed units lacking proper coordination,[84] MRF teams occasionally used a Fred as a spotter hidden inside an unmarked car to identify potential suspects.[85]

MRF-style operations drew plaudits in Whitehall. Heath knew they existed whilst William Whitelaw, secretary of state for Northern Ireland, stressed the need to 'do everything we can to disrupt' terrorist activities. 'This means taking off the streets those men who lead and direct their activities, together with some of the more vicious bombers and snipers.'[86] Similarly, senior soldiers believed MRFs showed 'real value in both offensive and defensive operations'. Even when they failed to draw terrorists into the open, 'the mere knowledge itself of covert forces acting in an area has a deterrent effect'.[87] Carver explained to Heath that 'the importance of this type of work will increase as force levels are reduced'.[88] As so often in the British experience, covert action filled a capability or manpower gap.

Unsurprisingly, the MRFs proved deeply controversial. When ministers in the new Northern Ireland Office found out about such activity in May 1972, they were unenthusiastic to say the least.[89] Amateurism increased the risk of controversy further still. As early as February 1972, soldiers on the ground had called for greater continuity within MRFs,[90] whilst in November, Carver informed Heath that MRFs lacked the expertise, experience, and security consciousness necessary for such sensitive operations. At the same time, the MRFs as a whole lacked a unified command and control structure. This, Carver warned Heath, meant that there was a relatively high risk of mistakes and exposure.[91] Predictably, Frank Kitson swiftly became a hate figure amongst republicans. Fuelled by IRA propaganda, MRF excesses, and his very real experiences of running colonial counter-gangs, nationalist communities accused Kitson of leading, or at least establishing, covert death squads.[92] It should be noted, however, that Kitson refuted the idea of 'death squads' and understood MRF tactics more in terms of gathering intelligence than using lethal force. He felt that successful counter-insurgency had to take place within the confines of the law.[93]

Although McGregor, the officer commanding, has since accused critics of sensationalizing routine operations,[94] the MRFs did need professionalizing. In practice, this meant bringing in SAS assistance. Carver and Carrington agreed that replacing the MRF with a new undercover unit of 'volunteers with SAS training' would greatly reduce the chances of mistakes.[95] It would ensure a higher standard and move away from the trigger-happy excesses of 1972 towards a more disciplined defensive and surveillance unit.[96] Bringing in the SAS, with its robust reputation, however, presented a problem. Heath rightly predicted uproar if the nationalists realized that SAS personnel operated in elite undercover units on the streets of the UK. Accordingly, Carver assured him that he would do all he could to hide SAS involvement.[97]

Formed with Heath's agreement in early 1973, the new unit was originally going to be called the Special Reconnaissance Squadron, or SRS. However, officials deemed this too similar in name to the SAS and feared it would raise suspicions.[98] Instead, they named it the SRU, or Special Reconnaissance Unit. Heath insisted that 'every attempt would be made to conceal SAS involvement' and so, whilst allowing SAS men to train the new recruits, he placed a three-year embargo before SAS troops could sign up to serve with them.[99] In practice, a lack of suitable men forced Carrington to reduce the embargo to two years, before Harold Wilson abolished it altogether.[100] Despite the changes, the Ministry of Defence stuck to the line, technically true, that 'no SAS unit' was serving in Northern Ireland.[101]

After the excesses of the MRFs, officials in Whitehall were pleased with the Special Reconnaissance Unit. Within a year, they thought it had 'proved extremely effective, achieving successes out of all proportion to its size'.[102] It had also provided greater coordination and control over undercover military operations, taking overall command of the Fred units that had hitherto existed separately.[103] As operations gradually became more about surveillance than offensive action, SRU morphed into 14th Intelligence Company from late 1973.[104] It engaged in surveillance—planting bugs and tracking devices—but patrols were still armed with sub-machine guns and silencers.[105] One former Special Boat Service man serving in 14th Intelligence Company remembers it as being 'one of the biggest steps you can take on the SF ladder'. It was 'the ultimate challenge'.[106] 14th Intelligence Company operatives formed detachments to the British Army's brigades, and so the unit most commonly became known as the Det. The constant name changes were a deliberate attempt to confuse the enemy.[107]

Despite taking the blame for many nationalist deaths on the streets of Northern Ireland, SAS involvement was limited in the early 1970s. Instead, former members—alongside former members of the Special Boat Service—operated in the Military Reaction Forces and the Special Reconnaissance Unit, allowing Heath to truthfully deny SAS presence. Besides, the SAS was tied down in Oman whilst SBS activity was limited to its traditional strengths of tracking and intercepting terrorist gunrunners off Ireland's west coast.[108] This changed in early 1976.

On 5 January, IRA gunmen stopped a minibus driving textile workers home from a factory near Kingsmill, County Armagh. They ordered eleven Protestant passengers to line up on the roadside and unleashed over 100 cartridges at point-blank range. Only one man survived. Shortly afterwards, Harold Wilson publicly despatched the SAS to Northern Ireland in a patrol and surveillance role. It was a reactionary political, rather than strategic, decision and sent the government's public relations team into a spin: they now had to be as open as possible about SAS activity, but also needed to disguise its movements and involvement when necessary. Communications teams admitted that the SAS operated in plain clothes but dismissed any talk of assassination squads as nonsense.[109]

SAS activity was initially amateurish, poorly directed, and convinced many military leaders that they had been saddled with a 'gang of amateur cowboys'. However, the SAS gradually became more sophisticated as its local experience grew. Roy Mason, the outgoing defence secretary, praised the impact of what he called 'SAS-type operations', especially after the 1976 public announcement, and lobbied his successor, Fred Mulley, to intensify them.[110] By 1977, SAS activity had expanded beyond its initial remit of South Armagh and into Derry and Belfast. Although the government hoped to 'use them offensively whenever there was a possibility of confrontation',[111] the SAS continuously operated under severe political restraints.[112] Comparing Belfast to Aden, one former SAS soldier lamented how 'there were to be no exploding portraits of Irish revolutionary heroes in this conflict'.[113] Turf wars between the various arms of the British security state, including the army, Royal Ulster Constabulary, MI5, and SIS marginalized and constrained SAS operations further still.

Meanwhile, a series of SAS killings in 1978, including of a 16-year-old boy, provided a propaganda coup for the IRA and led to a moratorium on offensive ambushing. Instead, the local special branch took the lead in the subterranean conflict.[114] By the end of 1980, 14th Intelligence Company and the SAS had been combined under one commanding officer,[115] and throughout the early 1980s continued to engage predominantly in surveillance activities. This lasted until around 1983 when, under Margaret Thatcher, SAS ambushes increased dramatically, with nearly thirty terrorists dying at the hands of the regiment over the next decade.[116] As police surveillance units took on a greater role, the SAS were freed up for more dynamic operations, including ambushes and other attempts to disrupt terrorist activity. Moreover, visibly heavy-handed police operations, leading to accusations of their own shoot-to-kill policy in the early 1980s, also allowed the pendulum to swing back towards the SAS. Special forces worked closely with 14th Intelligence Company and military Close Observation Platoons to launch undercover operations known as counter-ambushes which sought to eliminate IRA active service units. Although consistently denied by the government, these select forces had authority to aggressively pursue suspected terrorists and, guided by detailed intelligence, ultimately engage in targeted killings.[117]

In 1987, the SAS launched one such counter-ambush against an IRA active service unit in the process of bombing a police station in Loughgall, killing two innocent bystanders in the process. The following year an SAS team killed unarmed IRA targets in Gibraltar in another counter-ambush operation. Both cases proved controversial and reopened allegations of an SAS shoot-to-kill policy, handing the IRA yet another propaganda victory.[118] Political restraints fluctuated throughout the 1970s and 1980s, but it does appear that undercover units, starting with the MRFs, had authority to lure and then lethally engage terrorists. This would certainly have been in line with earlier covert action experiences.

Collusion

Controversies over extrajudicial killings and supposed undercover death squads gradually gave way to allegations of collusion. Covering a broad range of activity, collusion spans from turning a blind eye to unlawful or improper action to actively facilitating it.[119] Collusion between the security forces and the loyalist para-militaries in Northern Ireland did happen. Inquiries led by Sir John Stevens, a former commissioner of the Metropolitan Police, unearthed 'the wilful failure to keep records, the absence of accountability, the withholding of intelligence and evidence, and the extreme of agents being involved in murder'. These actions and omissions, Stevens concluded, 'meant that people have been killed or seriously injured'.[120]

According to the Northern Irish police's historical inquiries team, senior Royal Ulster Constabulary officers failed to investigate murders and became aware of broader collusion in the early 1970s. From two farms in South Armagh and Tyrone, RUC officers and members of the Ulster Defence Regiment (UDR) operated as part of a gang responsible for the deaths of 120 people between 1972 and 1976.[121] Collusion became more prominent as the conflict wore on, and some of the more notorious cases fell in the mid- to late 1980s when loyalist violence increased dramatically. Allegations focus on the RUC Special Branch and the Force Research Unit (FRU). Formed in 1981, the FRU served as the covert military intelligence body responsible for handling British agents inside paramilitary organizations.[122] Despite being part of 14th Intelligence Company, in practice the FRU operated as an independent unit and, although it also recruited republican informants, is alleged to have been involved in a number of murders, often through providing intelligence files and weapons to loyalist terrorists.[123]

The most infamous example is the case of Pat Finucane, a solicitor known for representing republicans. In February 1989, loyalists burst into his family home in north Belfast with a sledgehammer and shot him dead in front of his wife and three children. The family had been enjoying Sunday lunch when the attack suddenly began. Bullets flew around the kitchen as the assailant shot Finucane fourteen times. John Stevens unambiguously concluded that 'the murder of Patrick Finucane could have been prevented', that 'there was collusion'.[124] More recently, judge Desmond de Silva, in another inquiry, found that 'a series of positive actions by employees of the state actively furthered and facilitated his murder and that, in the aftermath of the murder, there was a relentless attempt to defeat the ends of justice'.[125]

Fingers pointed towards the FRU, which had used Brian Nelson, the intelligence chief of the Ulster Defence Association (UDA), as an informant at the height of the Troubles. Nelson used this relationship to provide loyalist terrorists with intelligence to help them target their victims, including a dossier on Finucane, and served ten years in prison for conspiracy to commit murder. Finucane was hardly a one-off. Desmond de Silva, who described Nelson as a direct state employee, found that 'the net impact of Brian Nelson's activity as an agent of the FRU materially increased the UDA's capacity to target republicans'—and the British knew it. Even the Ministry of Defence later admitted that Nelson's proliferation of targeting material had 'greatly enhanced the UDA's potential for murder'. Some of this had come from the FRU itself and, according to MI5, by the mid-1980s around 85 per cent of UDA intelligence came from the security forces. In 1988, Nelson attempted to enable the UDA to murder another man, Alex Maskey, a local Sinn Fein leader. [126]

The RUC have also faced accusations of collusion. In 2007, the police ombudsman for Northern Ireland found that the Ulster Volunteer Force (UVF), a loyalist paramilitary group, committed up to twenty murders in North Belfast whilst several of its members were simultaneously employed by the RUC Special Branch—including the commander of the terrorist unit concerned.[127] Moreover, investigations have linked one particular police informant to another ten murders between 1991 and 2000.[128] This is a damning picture and an increasingly familiar pattern. Some commentators have alleged collusion at the highest levels of government, almost forming a state policy.[129]

This is highly unlikely. There was no policy of collusion. De Silva found no evidence suggesting that ministers tasked intelligence agencies with assisting terrorist groups in any way.[130] Briefed only at the strategic level, ministers had no involvement in tactical aspects or knowledge of the actions of specific agents. Neither is there any evidence that ministers knew about the plan to kill Finucane. Instead, they were kept unaware of intelligence leaks from security forces to loyalist para-militaries.[131]

Importantly, however, other policies did create the perfect climate for collusion to take place. The first, dating back to the mid-1970s, was Ulsterization, which sought to disengage the army from Northern Ireland as far as possible and to replace it with local forces, such as the RUC and the Ulster Defence Regiment. This growing reliance on local recruits allowed for increased collusion, especially in the border areas,[132] not least because of the close and historic relationship between the Protestant community and the security forces.[133] Even before Ulsterization, Edward Heath had agreed that 'unofficial "civil defence" groups set up in the Protestant areas could be tolerated and might be allowed to assist the army with intelligence, though on a purely unofficial and local basis'.[134] Indeed, the British government did not proscribe one paramilitary group, the Ulster Defence Association, until 1992 despite the fact that it had killed hundreds of people. Back in 1972, officials had praised the UDA precisely *for* cooperating with the security forces,[135] whilst ten years later, the government played down the UDA as 'little more than a drinking and welfare club'.[136] Meanwhile, UDA members easily infiltrated the ranks of the Ulster Defence Regiment and vice versa, with such dual membership facilitating loyalist violence.[137]

Paramilitary groups encouraged their members to join the security forces, including the Ulster Defence Regiment, to gain access to training in weaponry, tactics, and intelligence. Accordingly, there are numerous cases of loyalist terrorists using their membership of the UDR to facilitate serious crimes—such as the Miami Showband massacre of 1975 when five people, including three members of a popular cabaret act, were murdered in County Down.[138] There is even evidence that members of the UDR provided para-militaries with weapons held in their own barracks. Indeed, one of the guns involved in the murder of Finucane was a UDR weapon sold to the terrorists in 1987.[139] Likewise, terrorists murdered Loughlin Maginn in 1989, after wrongly identifying him as IRA. Facing criticism from Maginn's family and the local community, the UDA shared a video showing the wall of a police briefing room covered in photographs of suspects, including Maginn. The video was shot by soldiers from the Ulster Defence Regiment.[140] Importantly, British intelligence and the Force Research Unit were both aware of the widespread links between the UDA and local security forces.[141]

Second, Britain had consistently used local surrogate forces to battle a common enemy in earlier colonial campaigns; this approach lingered into Northern Ireland. The 1969 army manual for counter-revolutionary operations tasked the SAS with 'liaison with, and organisation, training and control of, friendly guerrilla forces operating against the common enemy'. In the Irish context, this could only mean loyalist para-militaries. In this sense, collusion perhaps formed an extension of proxy warfare—a means to increase deniability and distance the state from violence. Collusion formed an intangible extension of the counter-gang tactic that had featured across

British counter-insurgency experience, but with Northern Ireland so close to home an even more deniable version became necessary. As the security forces came under greater scrutiny for alleged shoot-to-kill operations, collusion increased. The effect of this was as if the state outsourced killings to loyalist proxies because they lacked the means to engage in the action themselves.[142]

Third, British security personnel operated in a grey zone. When the military failed to defeat the IRA swiftly and conventionally, a covert and subsidiary goal arose: to hurt the IRA by deviant means. The perception of exceptional circumstances created a certain amount of rule bending aided by the large amount of operational freedom afforded to the security forces on the ground.[143] The FRU, SAS, and Special Branch not only competed with each other but also operated largely as autonomous units, with little coordination or accountability.[144] As Desmond de Silva judged, rivalry and competition for results allowed greater scope for deviance.[145]

In the case of Brian Nelson, MI5 and the FRU offered contradictory accounts, both passing responsibility for his handling on to the other.[146] Whilst there is no evidence of MI5 collusion in the Nelson case, the service failed in its advisory and coordinating duties.[147] One senior intelligence officer expressed his concerns to Patrick Walker, the MI5 director-general, about the 'lack of legal and political responsibility and management control'.[148] At the same time, army officers continually failed to monitor the chain of command adequately, even after MI5 raised concerns about the targeting of Gerry Adams in 1987.[149]

Meanwhile, the government was fully aware that no adequate framework existed for agent handling, but did little to address it.[150] The result, as journalist Mark Urban acutely observed, 'was one of those compromises, typical of British government, in which real power is exercised by those who are not responsible to parliament or the electorate who, in return, shield those who *are* responsible from painful decisions'.[151] Lack of intervention by Whitehall offered negative confirmation and tacit encouragement of local actions. Overall, de Silva found that 'the system appears to have facilitated political deniability in relation to such operations, rather than creating mechanisms for an appropriate level of political oversight'.[152] Operational autonomy, divisions and rivalry, and a lack of accountability in the system created a context in which collusion could occur—without formal ministerial approval. By late 1990, John Major's cabinet were discussing the impending prosecution of Nelson, with some, including Defence Secretary Tom King and Secretary of State for Northern Ireland Peter Brooke, arguing that the whole case should be forgotten. The attorney general favoured prosecution, but others questioned whether doing so would divulge sensitive information or even lead to attempts to kidnap MI5 officers. Robin Butler, the cabinet secretary, also attempted to persuade Major that prosecution was not in the public interest. It was, of course, a legal, rather than prime ministerial, decision, but Major, who was very torn, continued to take great interest in the case.[153]

At the same time, British propaganda enabled collusion. Prior to his murder, MI5 had spread information referring to Finucane amongst the loyalist community. De Silva found that MI5 material 'effectively involved fanning the rumours and speculation linking him to the IRA'. The aim was to discredit and unnerve him rather than to incite violence, but it ensured that loyalists associated Finucane with the activity of his clients and could also have legitimized him as a target. According to de Silva, MI5 was aware 'that the propaganda was reaching loyalist paramilitaries' and acknowledged that they were treading on 'dangerous ground'. Special Branch and FRU were also aware of the propaganda and appeared to endorse it.[154] MI5 spread damaging propaganda about other solicitors, Oliver Kelly and Paddy McGrory, too, despite knowing that both were under threat from loyalist para-militaries.[155]

Covert action is always a sensitive matter. Covert action so close to home was especially sensitive. Newly released documents and recent inquiries cited here reveal black propaganda discrediting the IRA, undercover disruption operations authorized to use lethal force, and a context in which collusion with loyalist para-militaries thrived. Senior policymakers, from the Foreign Office to the prime minister, actively endorsed the first two of these in the 1970s and early 1980s. They were not the work of rogue agents but can be traced back to Whitehall and Number 10. Both also fitted neatly into previous British experience of covert action elsewhere, from the Cold War to countering nationalist subversion. Collusion was more intangible and there is no evidence of it being a government policy. That said, Whitehall, unwittingly or otherwise, did preside over a system conducive to collusion. Once again, this fitted into a broader British approach of maximizing plausible deniability, and shielding politicians and the most senior civil servants from making direct orders. Moreover, Thatcher clearly pressed for tougher action against the IRA after she assumed office and throughout the 1980s. A fan of covert action, she found fewer restraints presiding over deniable interventions further away from Britain's well-scrutinized shores.

12

containment

The Second Cold War

We are looking at a variety of possibilities for covert action.
Margaret Thatcher, January 1980[1]

Despite extensive operations in Northern Ireland and Oman, British covert action declined in the latter half of the 1970s. Withdrawal from east of Suez, the rise of investigative journalism, and the reverberations of the Watergate and Church Committee revelations from across the Atlantic, forced a re-evaluation of commitments and injected a sense of caution. As we have seen, the Secret Intelligence Service (SIS)'s Special Political Action section closed in the first half of the decade—its functions dispersed amongst SIS area controllers—and the Information Research Department (IRD) followed suit in the second, although SIS maintained an ability to launch covert propaganda.[2] Foreign Secretary David Owen kept SIS on a tight leash and praised its scrupulousness in gaining his political consent.[3] However, such caution—even aversion—towards the subterranean side of international relations coincided with a period of renewed communist expansionism. It would not last forever.

The Second Cold War

The Soviets and Cubans targeted Africa. They supported guerrillas fighting Mozambique's war of independence against Portugal, before aiding leftists in the Angolan civil war from the middle of the 1970s. Meanwhile, Moscow helped to sustain new Ethiopian rulers, known as the Derg, who had deposed the long-serving Haile Selassie in 1974. These troubling developments asked questions of the West, and the Angolan civil war soon became a proxy conflict between America and the Soviet Union.

Foreign Office diplomats remained reluctant to deploy SIS or special forces. As one minister, who had resigned from the diplomatic service in protest against Suez before becoming an MP, put it, 'the last thing I want to see is a return to the days of the cold war, with the CIA and other para-military forces plotting coups and counter-coups in every capital of the world'. This, he argued, would only ever be counterproductive.[4] Nonetheless, the prime minister, James Callaghan, was not entirely averse to using assets of the secret state. He was the first resident of Number 10 to work closely with the Special Air Service (SAS), personally authorizing daring counter-terrorist missions around the world. In May 1977, he despatched the SAS to assist Dutch security forces in resolving a train hijacking. The SAS had been developing its capabilities in this area since the 1960s and the oper-ation was a success. The following October, Callaghan again called on the regiment, this time sending them to assist the Germans with an airplane hijacking in Somalia. Special forces teams forced open the doors as the plane sat on the tarmac and used stun grenades to temporarily blind the hijackers, before killing two and injuring two more.[5] After various successes, officials within both the Ministry of Defence and Foreign Office soon braced themselves for an onslaught of requests for SAS assistance and increasingly saw special forces as a useful means of executing British foreign and defence policy.[6]

Callaghan turned to SIS too. In 1976, he allowed Maurice Oldfield, as chief of the service, to blackmail an influential, but previously hostile, French official into supporting Greece's application to join the European Economic Community.[7] Three years later, as the shah of Iran faced mounting challenges in the months preceding revolution, Callaghan instructed David Owen to explore the possibility of cultivating alternative leaders in case a coup became necessary. This was against the advice of the British ambassador in Tehran, who warned such plotting would succeed only in undermining the shah's regime further.[8] Shortly after the Iranian revolution in early 1979, Julian Amery met members of the exiled royal family and their supporters in Paris, including the former Iranian commander-in-chief, General Oveissi. He listened attentively as they discussed the possibilities for a counter-revolution. Oveissi felt that the British understood Iranian politics better than the Americans did and suggested that Whitehall guide an American response, just as they did in 1953. Reporting back, Amery specifically called for SIS action. The plotting amounted to little, though, as Oveissi was later assassinated.[9]

Meanwhile, on Ethiopia, Callaghan insisted that Britain should 'get rid of the Derg and get Ethiopia back from Soviet clutches'.[10] For its part, the Derg accused Whitehall of actively plotting to overthrow them and of helping the exiled crown prince to establish a government-in-exile. These ideas would have been commensurate with the traditional British playbook—and Amery and Billy McLean, both veterans of such activity, were sniffing around the Horn of Africa at the same time—but diplomats in the Foreign Office's East Africa Department seemingly knew nothing of any covert action.[11]

In May 1979, Margaret Thatcher replaced Callaghan as prime minister and ushered in a new era. She was besotted with the intelligence services, became the first premier to attend a Joint Intelligence Committee meeting, and evinced a romantic enthusiasm for special forces not seen since Winston Churchill's heyday.[12] With Thatcher at the helm, the Foreign Office soon accepted that Britain needed to take a stand against Soviet expansionism, otherwise populations around the world would accept that history was, after all, on the side of Marxism–Leninism. The response was to be predominantly conventional, encompassing cultural exchanges, trade, aid, white propaganda, and military assistance (including Special Air Service training). Importantly though, and echoing British thinking throughout the Cold War, covert action, or 'subversion' as officials put it, would complement these open measures to form a broader counter-expansionist policy.[13] The role of British subversion was again deemed important and London's cold warriors worked hard on proposals for 'destabilising the USSR and its clients within the Bloc and the Third world'.[14] The problem came in deciding what actions to take and how far to go.

Despite Thatcher's love of intelligence and special forces, many in the Foreign Office expressed their traditional caution. Diplomats warned against being seduced by the cheap financial costs as 'subversion can be politically disastrous if it is detected or otherwise fails'. They continued: 'The creation by the West of instability (from which in the past the Russians have usually benefitted) needs very careful consideration.' Diplomats did acknowledge the need to consider, as they put it, 'attempts to destabilise Soviet power' in Ethiopia, Angola, North Yemen, and even Cuba,[15] but soon ruled them out. As ever, this was about practical factors rather than ethical considerations.

Promoting stability rather than insurgency, they argued, would be more likely to decrease reliance on Cuban support in Africa, whilst any 'plot to oust the Russians' from North Yemen was deemed unlikely to succeed.[16] According to Christopher Mallaby, head of the Eastern Europe and Soviet Department, there was little use in backing insurgency in the Gulf because North Yemen was 'a country of venal, untrustworthy intriguers and attempting to influence them was a lottery'.[17] On Angola, the Foreign Office ruled out covert military support for rebels on the grounds that they lacked enough popular support to make a difference and that increasing rebel activity would merely result in more Cuban intervention, thereby dramatically escalating the conflict.[18] Staff in its Research Department agreed that 'the idea of our being able effectively to do an Iago on Carlos Rafael or Castro seems to me frivolous'.[19]

The Foreign Office was even more cautious when it came to covert action in the Soviets' backyard. Any attempts to foment unrest in communist countries by supporting dissident nationalists, they warned, would merely engender repression and set back the cause.[20] Accordingly, British staff based behind the Iron Curtain were prudent when contacting dissidents. In Moscow, they feared the Soviet reaction if contact with dissidents was uncovered and so merely maintained discreet relations without offering direct encouragement.[21] Britain's embassy in Belgrade thought dissidents had 'widely differing aims and weak support', and rarely made contact with them,[22] whilst in Sofia dissident groups had made it clear that 'they would feel safer if we kept our distance'.[23] London's ambassador to Poland warned against increasing contact on the grounds that £260 million of British exports were at stake if the government found out; British interference would drive Poland closer to the Soviet Union; and 'to over-encourage dissidents risks making everything worse for the Polish people and their human rights'.[24] Cool on covert action, the Foreign Office pursued its traditional approach of identifying and gradually exploiting the diversity of Eastern Europe by positively discriminating in favour of countries which showed some independence from Soviet thinking.[25]

Although such Foreign Office caution was nothing new, an interesting change had occurred. In the early Cold War, its cagey approach to covert action had been countered by hawkish voices within the chiefs of staff and Ministry of Defence. By the late 1970s and early 1980s, however, informal advisers, private intelligence networks, and an older generation with experience of special operations lobbied the Thatcher government from the sidelines. They made the chiefs of staff look positively dovish. In many ways, Thatcher welcomed outside voices and, since her time as leader of the opposition, had sought unconventional advice which supported her own positions on Soviet policy. According to one of these advisers, George Urban, she had a 'less than overwhelming confidence in the wisdom of the Foreign Office' and was frustrated that their voices did not 'represent a wide enough spectrum'.[26] Less than a year into office, she moaned to Robert Armstrong, the cabinet secretary, 'they're all against me, Robert, I can feel it'.[27] Finding outside advice was easy for Thatcher: a group of intelligence old boys, sensing an opportunity for influence and action, were emerging from the shadows even before Callaghan's Labour government had fallen.

From 1976, Thatcher attended a few meetings of the unofficial Shield Committee, comprised of like-minded private citizens. Its chair, Brian Crozier, was perhaps rivalled only by Julian Amery for the title of ultimate cold warrior. A journalist by training who became a political vigilante, he had earlier worked with the Central Intelligence Agency (CIA) and the Information Research Department (IRD) disseminating anti-Soviet propaganda. Never doubtful of his own abilities, nor shy in telling others about them, he cultivated contacts inside SIS and courted both Thatcher and Ronald Reagan. Belligerently persistent in his approach, Crozier's aim was simple: to counter Soviet subversion, which he described as 'the political equivalent of Aids'.[28] Alongside Crozier on Shield sat former intelligence officers such as SIS's Nicholas Elliott and the Special Operations Executive (SOE)'s Harry Sporborg. Together, they sought to advise Thatcher, who was initially receptive, on subversion.[29] A year before Thatcher came to office, Crozier even attempted to create a Counter-Subversion Executive, along the lines of the SOE, to, in his words, 'conduct a clandestine offensive against Soviet power'.[30] But this time he had gone too far and Lord Carrington, Thatcher's foreign secretary in waiting, refused point-blank.[31] Worried about Crozier's scheming, Carrington quietly plotted against him and even Thatcher gently warned him off his more ambitious secret activities.[32]

Once in office, Thatcher sought more private advice, including from the Centre for Policy Studies, a think tank to which she had close links. Affiliated academics Hugh Thomas, Elie Kedourie, Leonard Schapiro, and Michael Howard recommended she undertake a more determined propaganda effort as well as covert action in Afghanistan, Angola, and Morocco, where tension had broken out over the Western Sahara. On Europe, they criticized Foreign Office fears about being too provocative as unnecessarily cautious and pressed for both propaganda and broader political warfare. Importantly, the academics advised that Britain could exploit the CIA's ongoing difficulties in the aftermath of Watergate and various inquiries into its earlier excesses to make a substantial contribution in the sphere of covert action. Britain could 'offer something to the US in order to compensate for the inevitably small scale of our military effort'.[33] This would become a key driver of British covert action throughout the 1980s and Thatcher took a personal interest in the academics' suggestions, using them as an independent measure against which to judge proposals put forward by the Foreign Office.[34]

Thatcher also received a great deal of unsolicited lobbying to intensify British covert action. By 1980, Julian Amery, a wartime veteran of SOE but still only in his early sixties, had become chairman of the mysterious 'Cercle' organization. His friends, Brian Crozier and Nicholas Elliott, were also leading figures within the group, whilst other intelligence figures, such as Billy McLean, Frank Steele, Anthony Cavendish, R. V. Jones, Tim Landon, and SOE's Peter Tennant, also attended meetings.[35] The Cercle comprised, according to one member, 'the friends and fans' of Amery himself.[36] Founded in the early 1950s by French statesmen Antoine Pinay to promote European reconciliation, the Cercle had since become more Atlanticist in focus and served as a discreet forum in which to hold off-the-record discussions about anti-communist action.[37] In 1982, it decided to play a more active political role and Amery instructed members to lobby their government contacts to support all forces resisting Soviet expansionism, from Afghanistan to Nicaragua.[38] All the while, as Amery sternly reminded colleagues, the group did not officially exist.[39]

Shortly after becoming chairman of the Cercle, Amery, now a backbench MP, began lobbying Thatcher and Francis Pym, her defence secretary. He suggested that 'old hands from the SOE and PWE' should be 'consulted about building up our strength for covert operations'. Although Thatcher tried to ignore him, the idea sparked alarm within official circles, and Dickie Franks, the chief of SIS and himself an SOE old hand, thought the idea disastrous.[40] In response, Pym tried to reassure Amery that 'counter-subversion and counter-propaganda' remained a 'proper function for the civil authorities',[41] whilst Thatcher told him it was a field in which Britain already had 'certain flair' and politely declined his assistance.[42] Amery never made it into Thatcher's select inner circle and was passed over as a potential foreign secretary in 1982. He was too risky, even for Thatcher.[43]

Amery did not give up. Over the next few years he clamoured to resurrect the SOE in its entirety, urged Thatcher to stop worrying so much about investigative journalism and plausible deniability,[44] and even designed a new secret team charged with contacting British citizens, from engineers to academics, to conduct 'actual sabotage activity' in areas where trouble flared.[45] Many of these arguments echoed those being rehearsed behind the closed doors of the Cercle. Despite asking even Alec Douglas-Home to have a word with Thatcher on the subject, Amery's pleas made little impact. Thatcher effectively told him to stop living in the past and leave covert action to SIS and special forces. The Second World War had long ended and such activity was now much riskier.[46]

Meanwhile back in the Cercle, Brian Crozier encouraged fellow members to 'provoke the disintegration of the Soviet system and the Soviet empire'.[47] Their plans included rigging the 1980 West German election through bribery and black propaganda to ensure the anti-communist Franz Josef Strauss became chancellor, as well as influencing the situation in Rhodesia and South Africa from what Crozier termed 'a European Conservative viewpoint'. They lobbied support for rebel groups in Africa, Asia, and Latin America and specifically worked with anti-communists in Angola, Namibia, and Mozambique. Throughout the decade, the Cercle tried to wage propaganda operations against the Soviet Union and across Western Europe, playing a key role, for example, in one international campaign blaming the KGB for controlling international terrorism. Some of this linked the famous terrorist Carlos the Jackal to Moscow, in a move that confused Eastern bloc intelligence services which had long grown wary of the Jackal's unpredictability. As late as 1989, and despite growing financial problems, the Cercle was still planning influence operations, such as organizing demonstrations, to combat what they saw as Western reconciliation towards the Soviets. Despite much lobbying and access to senior policymakers, it is not clear how much influence they actually had—although at the end of the Cold War, President Reagan acknowledged that he and the Cercle were 'allies in the fight against the evil Communism and it looks like we scored'.[48]

The constant lobbying of Thatcher created extra work for the Foreign Office. Its head, Antony Acland, remembered the range of people visiting Number 10: 'She had politicians, she had cronies, she had journalists, she had businessmen...she had crooks, all sorts of strange people who had got access.'[49] But one area where the Foreign Office and the privateers did agree was the need for propaganda. Thatcher's advisers urged Britain to 'shoot back' through 'clandestine broadcasting to the Ukraine, the Baltic States, Georgia, Central Asia, Cuba, Libya and Afghanistan' overseen by a new Office for Information Policy. Revelling in his role as a personal adviser to Thatcher, George Urban gleefully noted that these recommendations would strike the Foreign Office as 'wildly out of tune with the ways of sedate government'.[50]

Just three years after the IRD had been shut down, the diplomats did acknowledge that propaganda, both overt and unattributable, should play a role. They agreed that the West 'should be prepared to "take on" the Russians' in this field by stressing Moscow's false promises and poor track record of providing aid to the developing world.[51] Diplomats commissioned wide-ranging studies on the best means to counter Soviet propaganda,[52] and argued that Whitehall needed more funds and better arrangements to 'disseminate this material, if appropriate by covert means'.[53] Machinery for 'counter-propaganda' had, they argued, been run down. Whilst the Foreign Office did not need and could not afford the 'elaborate or extensive arrange-ments' of the IRD, its officials did need better 'arrangements to produce high quality and carefully tailored material angled towards audiences in the Soviet bloc and the Third World'.[54] The Overseas Information Department (OID), which had assumed the IRD's research and briefing role, was a mere shadow of its forerunner; its briefings were clearly attributable.[55] Although some modest work along these lines had been done by the OID and SIS's covert propaganda wing, especially after the invasion of Afghanistan by Russia in late 1979, it needed streamlining and coordinating with the American propaganda effort. Diplomats even suggested using specific action to destabilize states in the Soviet orbit and examined how best to consult with allies in this most secret of fields.[56] Thatcher was a receptive audience, arguing that 'we must answer back and take the offensive'.[57]

Maximizing Soviet discomfort

Within this context of official advice, unofficial lobbying, and an erosion of boundaries between state and private intelligence actors, Thatcher's government tackled two simultaneous crises. In December 1979, the Soviet Union invaded Afghanistan, beginning a civil war which would last much of the next decade. Closer to home, strikes and discontent in Poland led to the creation of Solidarity, an independent trade union, in 1980. By December

1981, the Polish government had declared martial law. Both crises would play an important role in the demise of the Soviet Union. Developments in Afghanistan took the JIC by surprise, although it fared much better on Poland.[58]

The CIA had actually begun covertly supporting Afghan rebels before the Soviet occupation, even trying to entice an invasion and tie Moscow down in its own Vietnam-style quagmire. Reversing the Anglo–American story of the 1950s and 1960s, this time it was the Americans who hoped to bring SIS on board. In October 1979, Zbigniew Brzezinski, President Carter's national security adviser, met Nicholas Henderson, the British ambassador to Washington, for breakfast and hinted that the White House was prepared to make life difficult for the Russians in Afghanistan.[59] Two months later, a senior group of American officials committed to exploring 'with the Pakistanis and the British the possibility of improving the financing, arming, and communications of the rebel forces to make it as expensive as possible for the Soviets to continue their efforts'.[60] Stansfield Turner, head of the CIA and a man who tended to get what he wanted, was confident that the British would be most forthcoming in supporting American action.[61]

Despite SIS being the poor relation in financial terms, there were two reasons why the CIA was keen to work with them. First, the CIA still operated under strict constraints after the Watergate scandal and Church Committee revelations. SIS, by contrast, had a greater freedom of action. Whilst CIA officers were banned from setting foot inside Afghanistan itself, for fear of mission creep and escalation, SIS teams could do just that. Likewise, Britain could, in theory at least, support the use of lethal force in ways that the CIA could not. The Americans therefore sensed an opportunity to work through SIS in order to bypass restrictions. SIS impecuniosity and eagerness to please made them an easy target to exploit.[62] Second, SIS knew the region and some of the key players better than the CIA did. British intelligence officers went on to help the CIA by activating long-established networks of contacts, in a manner not dissimilar to Britain's role in the 1953 Iranian coup.[63]

This time, however, it was the British who needed persuading. SIS was short of money and out of practice aiding insurgencies. When the CIA later requested 400 million rounds of ammunition for imperial-vintage British rifles, the resulting offer of 500,000—and some old winter coats—seemed rather paltry.[64] Meanwhile, the Foreign Office exhibited their characteristic caution about covert action, especially regarding something as risky as arming rebels. One diplomat sagely wondered: 'wouldn't we be better off with a socialist regime rather than a reactionary Islamic type that is giving us problems elsewhere?'[65] Even the Ministry of Defence had reservations. Staff worried about material, in this case operating manuals for Soviet weapons acquired by the rebels, going to fighters over whom Whitehall had little control.[66] According to one official, Britain's civil servants had to be 'dragged kicking and screaming' into the operation.[67]

But the Americans held a trump card. In the words of the CIA officer running the Afghan operation, Margaret Thatcher was 'to the right of Attila the Hun'.[68] Her foreign secretary, Lord Carrington, was also keen to engage in the covert action in Afghanistan. After the Soviet invasion, the Cabinet quickly agreed that a strong stance was necessary over Afghanistan, noting that 'the west had too often given an appearance of weakness in the past', for example over Angola, 'and that there were serious dangers involved' in not giving the Americans adequate support. This, however, came with a caveat: overt measures, especially sanctions, risked harming Britain's economy, which relied on exports.[69] A deniable response therefore looked appealing and Thatcher reported to Carter in January 1980 that Britain was examining various means of covert action.[70]

After a quick tour of the region, Carrington reported to Cyrus Vance, his counterpart in Washington, that the rebels would benefit substantially from anti-tank weapons and mines, suggesting that Anglo-American officials work together to deliver them.[71] Brzezinski also visited the region and, lobbying Britain for support, told Cabinet Office intelligence officials that he had been 'impressed by the determination of the Pakistanis, and also with the Afghan resistance fighters'. Buoyantly he told the British: 'I am convinced that we have something solid to work with in frustrating Soviet ambitions toward the south.'[72]

Carrington's tour piqued his interest in broader covert action against the Soviets in the Gulf and Middle East. He warned about the dangers of communist subversion in places such as Iran and South Yemen, before floating the idea of Western counter-subversion across the entire region.[73] Going further, Carrington, the last surviving member of Churchill's post-war government, even recommended considering the practicability of promoting insurgency in South Yemen, Ethiopia, and Afghanistan.[74]

In fact, SIS and special forces had been undertaking covert action in South Yemen since the late 1970s. It was a paramilitary support operation designed to undermine and disrupt the Marxist government. It involved training Yemenis to engage in sabotage by, for example, blowing up bridges. Britain, which had been conducting covert operations in the region since the 1950s, took the lead but the CIA offered support. This was under a programme in which the CIA engaged in covert activities with allies such as Britain and Saudi Arabia primarily as a means of cementing intelligence relationships rather than achieving strategic goals. Stansfield Turner, the director of central intelligence, described the operation as 'harebrained' and left it to his deputy to oversee. He thought the British were receiving too much intelligence support from the US, could not be trusted with the most secret information, and had too much leverage over the relationship.[75]

Afghanistan formed Carrington's immediate focus. He aimed to 'create a situation in which the Soviet Union concludes that it has much to lose from further adventures'. This would involve overt diplomacy and attempts to isolate the Russians, alongside 'the covert supply of arms and training' to Afghan patriots.[76]

Despite the early enthusiasm at the top of government, it is unclear what British covert action actually amounted to in the first two years of the Afghan insurgency. There was progress on the propaganda front, with Dickie Franks convincing media editors to portray the rebels as freedom fighters and Moscow as aggressively violating international law.[77] In addition, the Foreign Office quietly commissioned a film on the Soviet occupation. It cost £34,000—'good value for money' according to those involved—and government sponsorship was kept unattributable.[78] To ensure the rebels' story got out, fighters were equipped with small video cameras and SIS used its contacts in the Islamic world to keep the war on television screens. Thatcher heartily approved.[79] By autumn 1980, some twenty-six cameramen had been trained, equipped, and despatched. It was dangerous work. As one report to Number 10 stated, the latest cameraman returned 'bloody and tattered having lost everything except his cameras and film after being involved in a heavy Soviet attack'.[80] More provocatively, SIS allegedly also funded the leader of a right-wing Islamic Pakistani group, Jamaat-i-Islami, to spread Islamic literature inside the Soviet republics of Tajikistan and Uzbekistan to incite rebellion amongst local religious circles, thereby distracting the communists from Afghanistan.[81]

Beyond propaganda, which formed the backbone of its operations, confusion surrounds Britain's early role. This is largely because of Carrington's deliberate obfuscation of the issue. By the summer of 1980, Thatcher had agreed to meet the American request for assistance to the rebels,[82] and Carrington admitted to being 'satisfied that arms are getting through to the Afghan resistance'.[83] The extent to which Britain was involved in supplying these arms is another matter. CIA intelligence suggested that the rebels received the bulk of their weapons from retreating or deserting Afghan troops and by ambushing supply convoys. Beyond that, the rebels looked to the local arms market in western Pakistan, where they purchased locally manufactured or imported weapons stolen from the Afghan or Pakistani armies, as well as from disillusioned Afghan soldiers keen to sell ammunition for cash. Whilst the insurgents did receive a few arms from outside sources, including Pakistan and China, this had made little impact so far. Exiled leaders also apparently purchased some small arms in Western Europe through arms dealers.[84] This included British firms, one of which, running out of Richmond, had delivered consignments of Soviet-made equipment to Pakistan paid for by the Saudis—and against the wishes of the Foreign Office.[85]

Brzezinski described the British effort as merely 'mobilizing resources from as many directions as possible'.[86] This was a fair assessment, as Carrington himself limited involvement to encouraging the non-aligned and Muslim world to support the resistance.[87] By October, Pakistan had grown frustrated by Britain's lack of support and pressed for more. President Carter supported any new initiative along these lines and asked the CIA to liaise with SIS to 'pursue this matter on a more active and tangible basis'.[88] In response, Thatcher rather dismissively told Muhammad Zia, the Pakistani president, that the status quo was working satisfactorily.[89]

Britain's role in the covert action began as an indirect facilitator. In a classic case of ensuring maximum deniability, the Foreign Office and SIS lobbied other nations to support the resistance rather than doing it themselves. It suited Carrington that Islamic countries appeared to be at the forefront.[90] Remarkably, however, Carrington publicly hinted that British covert action was underway and, more remarkably still, that it was on a larger scale than was really the case. Sometimes a covert action is paradoxically designed with an audience in mind. It can show resolve. Carrington believed that if he denied sending arms then 'we remove an incentive on the Soviet Union to look for a political solution and lay ourselves open to domestic criticism for being unwilling to back our words with deeds'.[91] He therefore advised his colleagues to stick to a prearranged public line: 'it is desirable that the Afghan resistance should have the wherewithal to oppose the Soviet invasion; that arms appear to be getting through; and that it is not helpful to the Afghans themselves to speculate about the sources'.[92] If pressed, officials and ministers were allowed to explain 'unattributably to trusted contacts that we are not saying whether we are or are not supplying arms to the freedom fighters', before adding, 'though it is not necessary for every possible supporter country to become involved'.[93] Carrington used this approach himself in front of the Foreign Affairs Select Committee in late 1980, ending with a deliberately teasing line: 'I think I would rather leave it at that.'[94] It was almost as if he wanted people to think Britain was sending arms, without actually admitting to it—the diplomatic equivalent of a nudge and a wink.

Meanwhile, a potentially more serious crisis emerged in Poland. A wave of strikes and discontent put pressure on the Polish government and, by extension, on Moscow. Centred around Solidarity, demands for reform grew louder and louder, sweeping the country. In contrast to Afghanistan, the CIA initially offered little support and Carter agreed only to channel some $150,000 to Solidarity through trade union networks. In spring 1981, the CIA's new director, Bill Casey, warned against planning covert action prior to any potential Soviet invasion and did not become particularly enthusiastic about such activity until December, after the declaration of martial law.[95] The Foreign Office shared these cautions, preferring to stick to the long-standing gradualist approach to Eastern Europe. President Reagan took a more assertive stance. His National Security Council examined what covert action could be taken if the Soviets invaded Poland. Options included dramatically increasing covert action in Afghanistan, Angola, Libya, and Ethiopia. The idea was to 'roll back Soviet expansion and to capitalize on Soviet preoccupation with Poland', thereby maximizing difficulties for Moscow.[96] By contrast, British contingency planning for a Soviet invasion centred on aid, trade, and debt reconstruction.

With Reagan keen to make life as difficult for the Russians as possible, the CIA admitted that its current political warfare operations in Eastern Europe were 'a pale shadow of their programs in the 1950s'. CIA analysts pointed to a similar, if not worse, attitude across the Atlantic, criticizing European governments for being 'just as derelict as we in terms of efforts designed to help democratic forces in communist countries'. They bemoaned the fact that there was not 'even much study being done of how communist regimes can be changed—even though it is clear that the potential exists (witness Solidarity, Yugoslavia, thousands fleeing Cuba, etc.)'. The West, including

Britain, needed to undertake more 'covert political action', combined with political programmes, as, the CIA argued, 'we will never have a permanent, stable peace until these systems are transformed from armed-camps to democracies'.[97]

Fearing the Reagan and Thatcher effect, the KGB grew concerned about Western intelligence operations in Poland. Its resident there was convinced that Solidarity was funded by the CIA, SIS, and French intelligence. Unsurprisingly, the Polish security service shared this view, accusing the CIA and SIS of infiltrating agents into the Solidarity movements.[98] The deputy head of Polish intelligence warned that he knew what they were up to and that the KGB had demanded they be stopped.[99] Russian intelligence accordingly stepped up its own covert action and propaganda campaign, largely focused on discrediting the Solidarity leadership and undermining the Vatican, from where Pope John Paul II took a close interest in his homeland.[100]

Shortly before the imposition of martial law in December 1981, American covert action intensified. Reagan's national security team advised that it was in US interests to 'institutionalize, or at least prolong' the unrest in Poland. Doing so would undermine the Warsaw Pact's military potential, increase the chances of resistance spreading across Eastern Europe, and deter against another Afghanistan.[101] After martial law forced Solidarity underground, the CIA stepped up support as part of the broader effort to maximize Soviet disadvantages.[102]

Although Thatcher was delighted by the rebellion in Poland,[103] Britain was slow off the mark. SIS ploughed more resources into Eastern Europe in the early 1980s and East Germany had recently re-emerged as a priority after opposition movements sprung up there. As in Poland, many of these groups formed within Protestant churches in order to gain some protection from the regime, and SIS, which had particularly good contacts with the church in Berlin and Brandenburg, gained much intelligence on their activities.[104] However, in East Germany as in Poland, Thatcher's government remained hesitant about covert action.

A rather defeatist Carrington wondered: 'when one sits down and thinks about it, I mean what is there we can do? There's nothing we can do to help the wretched people' other than saying 'nasty things'. Although Thatcher expected Solidarity to continue passive resistance—because, in her words, 'there's nothing any government can do about it'—Carrington supported her prioritization of aid and trade, agreeing that 'one doesn't want to encourage them to think they are going to get help from us and then let them down and really incite them to have a fight'.[105] Others in the Foreign Office feared that supporting the dissidents would destabilize the system too far, causing chaos and inviting Soviet intervention.[106] Based on intelligence advice, Thatcher thought the crisis an internal issue and therefore that it was unwise to provoke the Russians if they were not directly involved.[107] Meanwhile, in contrast to the growing role of American trade unions in supporting Solidarity, British equivalents were initially less receptive. Some in the Transport and General Workers' Union thought Solidarity anti-socialist,[108] whilst Len Murray, general secretary of the TUC, underestimated the strength and organization of Solidarity altogether.[109]

The likes of Brian Crozier, who passed intelligence on Solidarity to Western capitals through the Cercle, privately briefed Thatcher on the subject. Echoing the arguments of earlier covert action cheerleaders, for example over Yemen, Crozier urged the prime minister to 'stiffen the back-bone of the Foreign Office and the Foreign Secretary' behind the scenes.[110] It was Reagan, however, who made the running. In June 1982, he met the pope in the Vatican library and agreed to undertake a clandestine campaign to destabilize the Polish government and keep the outlawed Solidarity movement alive.[111] Britain, by contrast, seemed to be out of the loop, having spent much of the previous year expecting the pope to exercise a moderating influence on Solidarity, on the grounds that whipping up dissent would lead to Soviet repression.[112] The CIA and the Vatican used a secret network of intermediaries, agents, and priests to smuggle in equipment such as printing presses, fax machines, radios, photocopiers, and computers.[113]

Britain played a less direct role. Solidarity had its own network of personnel who did not need to be recruited or run by SIS. Its representatives in London, Marek Garztecki and Artur Swiergiel, liaised with the Solidarity headquarters in Brussels and developed links with British trade unions.[114] The Foreign Office allowed Solidarity to operate from London and publish subversive leaflets as well as newsletters, with diplomats regularly reading the latter.[115] Officials in the Eastern Europe and Soviet Department also held discreet discussions with Solidarity's representatives about the latest developments in Poland and how Britain might help.[116] Meanwhile, one of the leading exiled dissidents, Miroslaw Chojecki, travelled frequently to London to coordinate various activities and add contraband supplies of humanitarian aid destined for Poland.[117]

Britain, led by Thatcher and Carrington, facilitated covert action to counter communist expansionism in the early 1980s. Under pressure from private interests and intelligence old boys, they considered launching a concerted effort to undermine the Soviets across the Gulf, Middle East, and parts of Africa. But when confronted with the reality of action, much of this proved a step too far even for Thatcher. And, despite agreeing to an intensification of propaganda activity, diplomats inside the Foreign Office expressed their usual caution. Afghanistan, and to a lesser extent Poland, therefore became Britain's prime focus. In both cases, covert action generally involved facilitating the work of others to disrupt the adversary. Thatcher was generally more than happy to use unconventional means to support anti–communist movements.[118] In Poland, though, agency came from within, from a pre-existing movement, and SIS helped coordinate illicit supplies and networks where it could. While Reagan's White House deliberately copied Eisenhower's East European strategy of 'low cost, low risk indirect assistance',[119] Britain seemingly plumped for even lower cost, lower risk, more indirect assistance. Indicative of the more limited British role, some in the Foreign Office thought Solidarity dead by 1982 and even began writing its obituary.[120] SIS and special forces soon stepped up activity, especially in Afghanistan, but nobody inside government, not least in the intelligence services, realized that the end of the Cold War and the fall of the Soviet Union was on the horizon.

13

Transition

The New Agenda

Moscow could hardly complain if a handful of British volunteers exercised what Prime Minister Salisbury called 'the Englishman's right to get his throat cut where and when he likes'.

Julian Amery, 1983[1]

British covert action in Afghanistan became more direct and intense as the first half of the 1980s wore on. This was partly because the Americans still valued British access and contacts; partly because the Afghan insurgency was enjoying some success and seemed able to give Moscow a bloody nose; and partly because covert action in Afghanistan was far less risky and prone to escalate to a third world war than that in Eastern Europe. Despite decreasing levels of plausible deniability, covert action offered Margaret Thatcher's government a means of pressing Russia and creating space for more conventional diplomacy to end the occupation of Afghanistan and place pressure on the Soviets more broadly.

If Britain was to step up its efforts, though, the Foreign Office and the Secret Intelligence Service (SIS) needed to decide which of the chronically disunited rebel factions to back.[2] The original British favourite, Ahmed Gailani, a moderate pro-Western politician, was proving ineffective, whilst Gulbuddin Hekmatyar, the more successful fighter already funded by Pakistan, Libya, Iran, and Saudi Arabia, was an Islamist dictator-in-waiting.[3] Not that this dissuaded the British too much; they had earlier backed the Muslim Brotherhood in Syria and Egypt, and now remained happy to give Hekmatyar the benefit of the doubt. Besides, intelligence suggested that his was the most organized faction and that the fundamentalist Islamic groups were the best fighters.[4] In true British pro-monarchy fashion, there was also talk of working through the unpopular former king, Zahir Shah.[5] Deciding which faction to back was a difficult task and, in reality, planners had little intelligence to go on. One official from the British embassy in Islamabad admitted that 'no-one knows nearly enough about the Afghan leadership, potential or existing'.[6] Accordingly, Gerry Warner, SIS's controller for the region, asked his staff to work out once and for all where Britain's best bet lay. They recommended Ahmad Shah Massoud, an insurgent leader in the north nicknamed the Lion of Panjshir.[7] The phoney war was over and British covert action could now begin in earnest.

Shortly afterwards, British teams carrying wads of cash secretly met Massoud inside Afghanistan. They included special forces personnel seconded to SIS's General Support Branch, sometimes known as The Increment.[8] By this point, special operations which drew on both SIS and military assets were known as special military operations and came with their own clearance procedures—and fights about who would pay for them.[9] A team of seven or eight, carrying fake IDs, travelled to Afghanistan twice a year, spending up to three weeks in the mountains. Whilst there, they trained rebels in using explosives, snipers, and silencers, as well as in bomb-making. They also provided secure radios so that the insurgents could better coordinate their efforts.[10] These British teams could even move supplies to Massoud independently of the Pakistanis, who insisted on maintaining control. This was a capability of which the Central Intelligence Agency (CIA) were deeply envious.[11] Increment teams also used these trips to gather intelligence on Soviet weapons and military technology, successfully extracting helicopter parts on the back of donkeys.[12] It was a dangerous business, though, for KGB units were simultaneously hunting down any foreigners assisting the mujahideen.[13] Once the operation was set up, the Joint Action Committee, first under Patrick Wright, who had long experience in dealing with the Middle East, then Antony Duff and the formidable Percy Cradock, who simultaneously served as Thatcher's foreign policy adviser, maintained annual reviews on progress. They did not get involved in the tactical issues, but kept a watchful eye over the costs and benefits, always asking if covert action was worth the risks.[14]

As it turned out, SIS backed a strong horse and the CIA became increasingly interested in Massoud. The Americans, often drawing on intelligence shared by the British, noted that Massoud was politically savvy, 'a brilliant resistance leader', and a 'genuine folk hero'.[15] At the same time, the CIA grew frustrated when he agreed to a ceasefire in early 1983, and criticized him as selfish.[16] On both counts, the CIA knew they needed a meeting with SIS. A familiar tension lingered in the air as Gust Avrakotos, a CIA officer running the Afghan programme, arrived in London for talks. Drawing on decades of hang-ups about which service was best, the CIA quickly felt SIS's superiority complex and sensed that SIS thought they knew more about Afghanistan than the CIA did and wanted to be involved if only to 'play Athens to our Rome'.[17] The tension was not helped by Avrakotos's frustration at the SIS tradition of interrupting meetings for afternoon tea and biscuits.[18]

Avrakotos wanted Massoud back fighting, but SIS officers insisted that their man would need more supplies and money. They assured Avrakotos that SIS could secretly funnel weapons to Massoud without Pakistani knowledge but lacked the funds to do this on a large scale. This was not a problem for the CIA and Avrakotos agreed that both agencies should work together. He sensed an opportunity not only to circumvent the Pakistanis, but also to use SIS to bypass American legal restrictions on covert action. Without ever asking for proper confirmation, he fully expected SIS to use CIA money to channel silencers to Afghanistan, effectively funding assassination. He later recalled that SIS 'had a willingness to do jobs I couldn't touch. They basically took care of the "How to Kill People Department"'. This, he figured, would not be illegal so long as he never specifically discussed what he was doing. Demonstrating the dense layers of smoke involved in covert action cooperation, the CIA simultaneously created its own independent channel to Massoud to ensure that America was not dependent on Britain.[19] Throughout the insurgency, Massoud enjoyed much success in the Panjshir Valley. Time and again, Soviet forces swept in and took territory but could not inflict a final defeat because of his evasive tactics. The Soviets would then pull out, leaving the Afghan armed forces to hold the territory, at which point Massoud would reappear and retake his land.[20]

At around the same time as Avrakotos met SIS officers in London, attitudes back in Washington stiffened. The Reagan administration feared that the Soviets had effectively annexed Afghanistan to use it as a military springboard into the Gulf and pressed the CIA to do much more to prevent this.[21] In London, Thatcher also upped the ante. She insisted on sending heavier weapons, such as Blowpipe missiles, to the rebels, despite knowing that doing so would dramatically decrease plausible deniability. Her aggressive attitude and apparent disregard for covertness alarmed her officials, but would have pleased the likes of Julian Amery constantly lobbying for a more offensive approach. Under intense pressure, Whitehall's planners worked hard to implement her orders whilst concealing the British hand as much as possible. According to Rodric Braithwaite, then in the Foreign Office, the Blowpipes, left over from the Falklands War, 'found their way to Afghanistan through a variety of covert sources so that their provenance could not be proved'.[22] It was part of a toughening stance from Number 10. As the decade progressed, leaders of armed opposition groups from El Salvador, Iran (through intermediaries), and Eritrea, as well as Afghanistan, all met British officials.[23]

The Soviets were rattled. British diplomats in Kabul reported a KGB campaign to intimidate Western officials by using the Afghan secret police to conduct aggressive surveillance measures against them. Up to three cars followed them whenever they left the embassy compound—day or night. This made it difficult to meet intelligence sources.[24] At the same time, Pakistani intelligence told the British about an underground cell within the Afghan secret police engaged in murder, sabotage, and subversion operations targeting rebels. It was, according to the Pakistanis, advised by the KGB.[25]

As Thatcher approved intensification in Afghanistan, she received a private briefing from Winston Churchill, member of parliament and grandson of the wartime leader. Churchill had sent Lieutenant-Colonel Colin 'Mad Mitch' Mitchell, famous for his brutal counter-insurgency exploits in Aden, to Afghanistan and Pakistan to examine how more assistance could be sent to the resistance. With echoes of the private briefings on Yemen received by Harold Macmillan and Alec Douglas-Home twenty years earlier, Churchill talked up the rebels' chances and pressed for greater British covert action. Ever his grandfather's grandson, Churchill requested that Thatcher fund a mercenary mission, under Mad Mitch's command, to train the resistance in using mortars, mines, and Blowpipes. He sought £10,000 a month for nine months, plus radio sets.[26] Thatcher was unimpressed. She struggled to believe their tales and scolded Churchill for speaking openly about secret activities. She warned them off mercenary activity, but kept quiet on Britain's ongoing efforts in Afghanistan. Thatcher did not want some private operation messing up her own covert action.[27]

At the same time, Julian Amery and Billy McLean, Britain's perennial covert action double act, were on the move. They visited Afghan resistance leaders, toured the local countryside, held meetings with President Zia of

Pakistan, and eagerly reported back to Thatcher in London—much as they had done during many British covert operations since the Second World War. Amery lobbied, on behalf of Pakistan, for Britain to step up its role coordinating military supplies for the rebels. A one-man library of covert action, he drew parallels with British operations in the Yemeni civil war and suggested using 'mercenaries drawn from the SAS reserve' along similar lines. Amery also pressed Thatcher to make better use of Soviet defectors for 'black propaganda or other subversive purposes'.[28]

Unbeknownst to Churchill, Amery, and McLean, SIS was already using special forces teams in Afghanistan. Moreover, SIS had outsourced some of the training to private security firms such as Keenie-Meenie Services, which was staffed by ex-special forces personnel. Back in 1981, Britain had strongly opposed the presence of mercenaries in Afghanistan and even tipped off the Pakistani authorities to arrest two soldiers of fortune as they made their way to the battlefield.[29] By the middle of the decade, however, David Walker, once of the SAS, and Jim Johnson, who had played a leading role in Yemen, were in charge of approved operations.[30] Training apparently took place in secret bases outside of Afghanistan, including in Saudi Arabia and Oman—as well as Scotland and even the Home Counties—and continued until the latter stages of the war. Keenie-Meenie Services remained in conversation with the CIA about training rebels in sabotage and spying as late as 1987.[31]

Supporting the CIA

SIS involvement in Afghanistan gradually decreased. British efforts were dwarfed by those of the CIA and Pakistan's Inter-Services Intelligence. The latter had long sought to monopolize the covert action by insisting that money and weapons went through them. This was a ruse to ensure that Islamabad could support its favoured factions, including Islamist hardliners such as Hekmatyar, rather than Massoud. SIS support of Massoud's men was a fraction of that being received elsewhere.[32] Nonetheless, in 1985, Thatcher told Vice President George Bush that although both of their countries were operating in Afghanistan, 'the UK concealed it better'.[33] In the following year SIS provided Pakistani intelligence with limpet mines to blow up Soviet barges, including on the Soviet side of the border. SIS also allegedly worked with both the Pakistanis and the CIA to launch guerrilla attacks into neighbouring Tajikistan and Uzbekistan, from where the Soviet troops in Afghanistan received supplies.[34] Towards the end of the decade, Mikhail Gorbachev, the new leader in the Kremlin, began withdrawing troops. The last left Afghanistan in 1989.

Britain not only feared Soviet expansionism in Afghanistan, but played close attention to activity in Latin America. In 1986, Iran–Contra, in which America sold weapons to Iran in exchange for the release of hostages but then used the proceeds to illegally fund the Nicaraguan resistance, erupted into the biggest covert action scandal of the decade. This was not a solely American affair: Britain was embroiled in almost every aspect, from turning a blind eye to illegal CIA support for the Nicaraguan Contras to countering the terrorists who took American hostages in Lebanon and even having dealings with shady intermediaries selling arms to Iran.

The Contras included various right-wing military groups formed to oppose the leftist Sandinista government which, in 1979, had established a revolutionary government in Nicaragua. As early as May 1983, British diplomats in Washington speculated whether President Reagan was seeking to overthrow the Nicaraguan regime, despite Congress forbidding this the previous year. They reported back to the Foreign Office that 'a number of US officials are known to be hoping for, if not actually conspiring in, the Sandinistas' demise' and that the 'American policy of "covert" support for the rebels' was causing 'real problems' for the regime. However, they assessed that the Sandinista government would not fall unless US covert action increased dramatically. The Foreign Office also knew that Congress opposed ambitious covert action, but that White House officials were cleverly exploiting both 'the extreme complexity of Congressional procedures' and the lack of coordination amongst Reagan's opponents.[35]

Sitting in the Oval Office two months later, Reagan told Geoffrey Howe, Britain's foreign secretary, that the Contras deserved support. He pointed out that the Soviets and Cubans were supplying the Sandinistas with weapons smuggled from Vietnam and that the West needed to fight back. Howe reassured Reagan that Britain shared his concerns and objectives in the region.[36] Shortly afterwards, Thatcher admitted that America was 'losing the propaganda battle' over Central America in Europe and vowed to do more to help the cause.[37] But by late 1984, Howe and Thatcher, like Congress, had grown wary of American aid to the Contras. They felt that covert action was 'the very thing that is provoking and helping to justify Nicaragua's rearmament'. It was counterproductive, risked escalation, and, according to the Foreign Office, legally 'fuzzy'. They therefore urged Washington to soften its approach but ultimately turned a blind eye to the covert action, so long as there was no visible military intervention.[38] That said, they knew full well that British ability to influence US action, whether covert or overt, was utterly limited.[39] Remarkably, Thatcher's hesitancy caused the Americans to execute covert action against Britain. It is commonly assumed that controversial operations to mine Nicaraguan harbours were designed to aid the Contras in economic sabotage. In reality, this was an influence operation—and Britain was the target. The mines were not powerful enough to inflict much damage; one American involved described them as a 'fart in a bathtub'. Instead, the aim was to compromise the shipping lanes and force underwriters at Lloyd's of London to increase insurance prices. This, in turn, would force Thatcher to adopt a more sympathetic approach to American activity in Nicaragua.[40]

Thatcher and Howe were not the only Brits discussing covert action in Nicaragua. Oliver North, one of the American architects of Iran-Contra, was working with former SAS man David Walker and his Keenie-Meenie Services, the private security company comprised of ex-special forces personnel and already employed in Afghanistan. Walker agreed to recruit pilots to fly aid to the Contras and told North in December 1984 that he would be interested in working with one of the Contra forces to develop expertise in destroying Hind helicopters. North gratefully agreed and put him in touch with the guerrilla leaders.[41] Walker specifically suggested that the Contras buy Blowpipe missiles from Chile to bring down the helicopters. Given that the Blowpipes were British-made and-supplied, the Chileans, in turn, sought approval from London to funnel them secretly into Nicaragua via Guatemala. North hoped that Thatcher would quietly agree, not least because earlier in the year, the British government had indicated willingness to consider sending money to the Contras,[42] perhaps to help Reagan bypass congressional funding restrictions.

Meanwhile in the Middle East, the beginnings of the Iranian aspect of Iran-Contra unfolded. Taking advantage of the ongoing chaotic Lebanese civil war, Hezbollah conducted a brutal kidnapping spree, targeting westerners across Beirut. In 1984, they kidnapped Bill Buckley, the CIA head of station, in such a professional operation that the Americans suspected Iranian support. Beirut was a lawless area throughout much of the decade where terrorist factions and armed gangs ran riot. With the CIA frantically—but ultimately unsuccessfully—trying to find Buckley, SIS used disruptive action to help frustrate the terrorists.

SIS created and sustained a struggle between the rival factions. The idea was to distract them from targeting the UK and allied nationals, including Americans, by making them turn on each other instead.[43] In one case, SIS disruptive action led to a sustained firefight between two terrorist factions. According to Daphne Park, the highly respected intelligence officer who had served in Congo and Vietnam before overseeing western hemisphere operations, SIS excelled at such operations: 'once you get really good inside intelligence about any group, you are able to learn what the levers of power are and what each man fears from another and what each man will credit another of being capable of doing'. SIS set people very discreetly against one another so that they destroyed each other.[44]

Reeling from the death of Bill Buckley, who was murdered in June 1985, and desperate to secure the release of other American hostages, Reagan's team sold weapons to Iran and used the money to fund the Contras. Back in London, British officials wondered where this money was coming from and, over the summer of 1986, MI5 bugged a Heathrow meeting between North, Bud McFarlane, Reagan's national security adviser, and an Iranian arms dealer. They now knew what the White House was up to.[45] Unimpressed, Thatcher despatched Antony Acland, head of the foreign office, and Percy Cradock, her senior intelligence adviser, to Washington to ask questions. They felt upset and betrayed, especially having allowed America to use British bases to bomb Libya in the fight against Middle Eastern terrorism.[46] Perhaps for this reason, Thatcher stalled on allowing the British Blowpipes to reach the Contras via Chile, as suggested by David Walker. On the eve of the scandal, Oliver North and Reagan's National Security Council staff were still seeking British approval.[47] Nonetheless, after Iran-Contra broke, Thatcher privately comforted Reagan. Iran, she said, was now in the past. She wrote 'that there is important work to be done and that YOU are going to do it'.[48]

Thatcher was somewhat hypocritical to feel betrayed by American arms sales to Iran. In 1984, SIS allegedly approached Jamshid Hashemi, an arms dealer implicated in the Iran-Contra affair, and asked him to gather intelligence on Iranian arms procurement. Shortly afterwards SIS tasked him with arranging deals with Iran, including for Chinese Silkworm missiles which threatened Western shipping in the Gulf. SIS wanted intelligence on the weapons, but needed covert action—in the form of instigating arms sales—to gather it. Hashemi also sold them motor boats, armed with machine guns. Both cases, in which Britain covertly aided the arming of Iran, contravened arms embargoes.

Intelligence had long aided British companies in the international arms trade,[49] but occasionally SIS did so even more covertly. The 1980s formed a decade of tangled webs of government, intelligence, and arms dealers, many of whom had an intelligence background themselves. Hashemi demonstrated this, having met Thatcher at Geoffrey Howe's home and donated £55,000 to the Conservative Party.[50] The tangled web was also aptly demonstrated by Walker's involvement in Iran-Contra, Julian Amery and Billy McLean's constant lobbying for arms sales to Africa, and former SIS officer Nicholas Elliott's direct contact with Thatcher about Rhodesia policy whilst on the board of Lonrho, not an arms trader, but a company with extensive business interests in Africa.[51] It is also demonstrated by the case of International Signal and Control, a front company used by the CIA to covertly transfer military technology to South Africa—and which went on to bankrupt a British firm, Ferranti, which bought it in 1987.

Whereas the CIA used front companies to export arms covertly, SIS did so rarely. There was less need given that British arms exporters were already closely associated with the establishment.[52] SIS operations classically involved allowing authentic private businessmen to enter into relationships with hostile countries, before penetrating their networks to gain intelligence.[53] At the same time as facilitating arms sales to Tehran, Britain covertly helped arm Iran's opponent in its war with Iraq. SIS, with the blessing of policymakers, encouraged the export of dual-use technologies to Baghdad (i.e. items that individually were harmless but could become lethal when linked with others), despite likely knowing their ultimate military purpose.[54] The aim was to keep open channels of information on Iraqi arms requirements provided by an SIS source inside the firm supplying the technology, Matrix Churchill.[55]

This may have been the tip of a deep and murky iceberg bringing together arms exporters, government, and intelligence. Disgraced MP Jonathan Aitken, for example, was accused of knowing about arms exports to Iran via Singapore and, although cleared, had to answer prickly questions about his links to the arms trade and relationship with the Saudis. He was variously director of arms exporters BMARC, minister of state for defence procurement, and seemingly a member of Amery's mysterious Cercle. Similarly, Stephan Kock, linked to a host of covert arms deals, had close links to SIS.[56] Like much covert action, the secret aspects complemented broader foreign policy. In this case, Thatcher saw arms exports, including covert deals, as a means of maintaining international influence despite Britain's ongoing decline.[57]

The shadowy world of intelligence, arms, and economics even extended to the Bank of England, with which SIS had long had connections. In the mid-1980s, the bank's governor received an anonymous tip-off that the Bank of Credit and Commerce International (BCCI), which it was supposed to be supervising, engaged in a range of fraudulent and criminal activity, including funding the drugs trade and terrorism. The BCCI was established in the 1970s with Gulf backing to operate as a supranational bank and avoid intrusive regulation. But the Bank of England failed to rein it in, leaving Threadneedle Street vulnerable to legal action from creditors after the BCCI collapsed with $7 billion undeclared debts in 1991. The Bank's Nelsonian eye raised still unanswered questions about why it had been so lax. There is strong suspicion that Western intelligence agencies relied on the BCCI to pay agents abroad, funnel money to the Afghan mujahideen and arrange covert arms deals. There were also strong connections between the BCCI on the one hand and those selling arms to Iran and illegally channelling money to the Contras on the other.[58] It is not beyond the realms of possibility that SIS used the BCCI as its bank of choice for covert—and other intelligence—operations in the mid-1980s. The subsequent British inquiry refused to publish any discussion of intelligence involvement,[59] and Treasury officials later went to great lengths to prevent relevant SIS documents from being handed over to the creditors.[60]

Intriguingly, but perhaps predictably, the scandal dragged a familiar name into the spotlight. Julian Amery, it turned out, was offered—and declined—directorship of the BCCI in 1979, but instead became a paid adviser on an annual salary. When questioned after its collapse, Amery was rather economical with the truth and made out that he had advised on international political developments but had no knowledge of the financial workings of the bank. His letter of appointment made no reference to any such limitations and Amery's biographer has speculated that he may have been involved in organizing finance to the Afghan mujahideen.[61] What is certain is that time and again Julian Amery was never far from the shadier side of British affairs.

Meanwhile, members of the special forces not on loan to SIS also had a busy time helping the Americans. At the start of the decade, the SAS worked closely with the Foreign Office to help secure the release of hostages taken in Gambia.[62] Towards the end, from autumn 1988, special forces teams covertly arrived in Colombia to support Reagan's war on drugs. They began in an advisory capacity but gradually became more directly involved.[63] In between, Britain covertly trained resistance fighters opposing the pro-Soviet puppet regime in Cambodia which had been installed after the Vietnamese invasion in 1978. Fearing the spread of Soviet expansionism by proxy, Thatcher sanctioned special forces teams to train guerrillas to use landmines and explosives at a secret Thai base near the Cambodian border from 1984. SIS was closely involved and its station chief in Bangkok handled the logistics. This was in addition to various British nationals hired by Singapore—in a private capacity—to offer instruction in radio broadcasting to the rebels.[64]

As ever, Britain sought to be as indirect as possible by maximizing deniability. The plan involved training Thai special forces who would, in turn, then train the rebels. This soon proved too long-winded and the SAS ended up training both the Thais and the rebels—although the SAS commander promptly deemed the first batch of resistance fighters 'washouts' and sent them home.[65] In March 1985, forty-eight rebels from the Sihanoukist National Army began a three-month programme in Phitsanulok near the border with Laos. The SAS offered training in map-reading, weapons, and demolition. According to one graduate of the covert course, 'many of the guerrillas could not hit the target at first—they were closing the wrong eye'. But 'very quickly' British special forces 'had everybody zeroed in on their target'. The class of 1985 soon infiltrated back across the border and began sabotaging government ammunition stores.[66] Between 1985 and 1989, SAS biannual programmes created a team of 250 men trained in sabotage, explosives, and launching ambushes. The Americans, constrained from authorizing a similar operation in the aftermath of the Iran-Contra scandal, were once again grateful, and British covert action allowed contribution to an otherwise asymmetric relationship. An official in the Ministry of Defence described it as 'one of those classic Thatcher–Reagan arrangements', necessary given that Congress would have been unimpressed had it found out that the CIA was involved.[67]

It was a messy conflict, though, and some of the resistance factions consisted of Khmer Rouge fighters, complicit in the earlier Cambodian genocide. To circumvent this, Thatcher's government sanctioned the SAS to work only with guerrillas loyal to the liberal democrat former prime minister and—in true British style—to the ousted prince, rather than those loyal to Pol Pot, the leader of the Khmer Rouge. When suspicions about a British role arose, Thatcher, in contrast to Carrington's obfuscation over Afghanistan, explicitly denied SAS training of the Khmer Rouge or those allied to them. However, according to a former Khmer Rouge commander, the SAS training did benefit them greatly as the various resistance groups fought together, with the Khmer Rouge ultimately in charge.[68]

Transition

The 1980s saw a resurrection of British covert action. SIS and special forces were deployed—often in support of the CIA—to contain Soviet expansionism and maximize discomfort for its allies in Afghanistan and Cambodia, to disrupt terrorist groups in Lebanon, and to facilitate the transfer of propaganda to the underground resistance in Poland. The dynamics of the Anglo–American covert action relationship had changed from the early Cold War. Britain was now a junior partner, using its expertise to gain leverage in and contribute to an asymmetric relationship. It was a truly murky decade in which the boundaries between the secret state and private intelligence blurred. Thatcher was consistently lobbied and briefed by individuals with links to shadowy organizations such as the Cercle, whilst companies including Keenie-Meenie Services became embroiled in Afghanistan and Nicaragua. As intelligence mixed with international trade and economics, the 1980s became a conspiracy theorist's dream and it remains difficult to separate fact from fiction.

By the end of the decade, the Cold War was over. Despite this raising fundamental questions about the role and even existence of secret service, and despite deep cuts to SIS itself, covert action continued long after the Berlin Wall fell in November 1989. It became more ad hoc and flexible, more tactical and operational, but remained a key means of executing foreign policies and maintaining Britain's global role in an age of illusions. Perhaps more than ever before, covert action became a force multiplier. In the early 1990s, one of Queen Elizabeth's private secretaries lunched at Century House, SIS's headquarters. He asked: 'What shall I tell her Majesty her Secret Intelligence Service is for?' Gerry Warner, the deputy chief, replied: 'Please tell her it is the last penumbra of her Empire.'[69] For Percy Cradock, chairman of the Joint Intelligence Committee (JIC) and foreign policy adviser to John Major, intelligence was Britain's 'top card' to be played for all its worth.[70]

In the post-Cold War world, the security agenda became more diverse. The former Soviet bloc remained a key area and the SIS controller for Eastern Europe remembered it as being 'an extremely busy time'.[71] But attention also covered humanitarian work, economic well-being, peace support operations, counter-terrorism, combating the illegal drugs trade, and preventing the proliferation of weapons of mass destruction. SIS played an important role in each of these diverse areas, often with the aim of disrupting the operations of others.

One of the first challenges of the new era came in the Gulf, an area to which SIS were no strangers. Percy Cradock and Colin McColl, the SIS chief, met in mid-August 1990 to discuss how Britain's secret services could respond to the Iraqi invasion of Kuwait two weeks earlier. With the approval of William Waldegrave, minister of state in the Foreign Office, and then Margaret Thatcher, they agreed to support the nascent Kuwaiti resistance. Shortly afterwards, SIS sent a Middle Eastern specialist and veteran of covert action in 1970s Oman to run the operation alongside the SAS from a training camp in Saudi Arabia. But the Kuwaiti volunteers were not particularly effective fighters and the covert action soon fizzled out. Its value, like some of the early Cold War operations in Eastern Europe, was more as a political gesture to Kuwait and a means to gather intelligence on Iraq than actual liberation.[72] After the Gulf War in early 1991, when US-led forces successfully expelled Iraq from Kuwait, Saddam Hussein, the Iraqi president, did face a rebellion. This time it came from the Kurds, in part encouraged by Western propaganda. SIS smuggled tapes containing seditious messages into Iraq via Jordan and Turkey whilst also, alongside the CIA, inciting rebellion via Radio Free Iraq from December 1990.[73] Sadly for the Kurds, and again echoing the early Cold War, Britain and America offered little material support. Saddam easily eliminated many of the rebels. When asked about the impact of the earlier appeals to revolt, one British intelligence officer simply responded: 'we hadn't thought it through properly'.[74]

A new agenda

Even before the end of the Cold War, SIS had been moving towards a new agenda of countering narcotics, organized crime, and weapons proliferation. These areas soon became much more important, as SIS fought to justify its cost and existence. Like all SIS work, intelligence-gathering formed the bulk of its activity in these areas, but policymakers also turned to covert action to disrupt criminal activity. Facing a variety of low-intensity threats from transnational actors, SIS's greatest challenge was in operational tempo.[75] Covert action had to be fast and flexible.

To aid this, SIS became more integrated into Whitehall, with intelligence officers increasingly seconded to other departments and, in an effort to demonstrate impact, drawn away from pure intelligence-gathering.[76] In an era of budget cuts, SIS served as a means to deliver political objectives.[77] In December 1993, John Major asked Michael Quinlan, recently retired as the senior official at the Ministry of Defence, to examine intelligence requirements in the post-Cold War world. Quinlan reported that an important part of SIS business related to 'taking action rather than collecting intelligence', and this required separate guidance from ministers.[78] The introduction of the Intelligence Services Act in 1994 did little to stem covert action. It formally allowed SIS to engage in these 'other tasks' and protected officers from prosecution, so long as the foreign secretary had signed off on the operation.[79] John Major's private office drew his attention to a particularly sensitive section of the bill which gave the foreign secretary power to authorize any act overseas. They thought it might be seen as a 'licence to kill'. Major responded by annotating the text with a single word, 'Hitler', perhaps offering the classic Whitehall analogy of when lethal force could be considered.[80] Throughout the decade, the SIS charter, known as the Order Book, maintained the capacity to mount special operations abroad.[81]

Back in 1988, SIS had created a counter-narcotics section. Originally focused on Latin America, it soon expanded to cover Poland, Czechoslovakia, Pakistan, Afghanistan, and Iran. At around the same time, SIS counter-proliferation efforts expanded into a new section called Production and Targeting, Counter-Proliferation, whist the service also created an organized crime operations group.[82] All three sought to disrupt targets, whether through emptying a foreign bank account, working with special forces to raid boats carrying drugs, retarding nuclear programmes, or spraying an abrasive dust inside computers to sabotage floppy disks.[83]

Julian Amery's shadowy Cercle was also adapting to the post-Cold War world. Now sporting a wispy grey beard and increasingly frail, Amery had not lost his anti-communist zeal. In 1992, he addressed delegates with talk of a new world order and the dangers of Islamist extremism, drugs, American retreat, and German hegemony.[84] Still sceptical of official approaches to covert action even in his twilight years, he warned that there were 'crises on the horizon and we cannot be sure that our bureaucrats will be able to deal with them'.[85] The bureaucrats were, however, rising to the challenge. And the chief of SIS, Colin McColl, dismissively referred to 'Julian's unceasing ability completely to fascinate'.[86] In 1993, McColl created a new Global Issues section, which officers nicknamed Funny Money, to consolidate narcotics, proliferation, and serious crime into a single unit.[87] Over the next few years, SIS worked alongside special forces to disrupt drug trafficking in the Eastern Mediterranean;[88] criminal networks running through Prague;[89] and Iranian nuclear ambitions.[90] SIS also saw success in disrupting the flow of arms to the Provisional Irish Republican Army in the early 1990s.[91] Later in the decade, a senior SIS officer visited Number 10 as part of an annual cost justification exercise. He revealed that the nuclear Non-Proliferation Treaty had been re-approved in the United Nations by a massive margin and that SIS had used bribery and blackmail to gain around forty-five of the votes. When asked which countries had been bribed and which blackmailed, he responded that it was difficult to tell. For the difficult targets, SIS had to do both.[92]

Such activity was aided by another new SIS department called Information Operations, or I/Ops. Established around 1993 and seeking to rectify deficiencies exposed during the Gulf War, it resurrected many of the capabilities of the old Special Political Action section which, as we have seen, disbanded in the 1970s. The unit consisted of around twenty officers whose primary role was in media and public relations work. Domestically, this included discreetly briefing the media that SIS had moved away from Cold War-era dirty tricks, especially in the aftermath of the Intelligence Services Act. Internationally, I/Ops tipped off SIS staff serving abroad about friendly journalists in each country. Using pseudonyms, and with ministerial approval, SIS fed material into the foreign press. Themes included the need for continued surveillance on Russia, instability in Iraq, and IRA links to foreign states.[93] In 1998, SIS apparently told a UN weapons inspector that 'we have some outlets in foreign newspapers—some editors and writers who work with us from time to time—where we can spread some material'.[94] Accordingly, in May and June of that year, SIS officers discreetly met UN inspectors twice to discuss how best to make public the discovery of a banned nerve agent found on Iraqi missile warheads. They established Operation Mass Appeal to insert sanitized intelligence into the press in a deniable manner, but it had to be aborted after details of the nerve agent leaked to the press in Washington.[95]

Britain's increasingly varied covert action agenda extended to the Balkans. After Yugoslavia disintegrated at the end of the Cold War, a series of ethnic conflicts between Serbs, Croats, and Albanians broke out across its erstwhile territory spanning much of the decade. In spring 1993, an SIS officer heading the Balkan Target Team, tasked with creatively thinking up new sources of intelligence, devised a plan. He suggested assassinating a radical Serb nationalist—unnamed, but not President Slobodan Milosevic—who looked as if he might sweep to power, destabilize the region, and increase the likelihood of ethnic cleansing. Whilst making the usual comparisons with Hitler, the SIS officer went further than previous advocates of assassination by criticizing his service's ethos. He rather dismissively argued that he had 'been brought up and trained in a service that dealt with peaceful cold war . . . spy games' that were a million miles from this 'bloody civil war in the centre of Europe, where tens of thousands of innocent people are being killed'. So, he continued, perhaps SIS needed to revisit the dictum that assassination was never allowed. His plan included two options: to use either dissidents or British special forces to take out the leader.[96]

The officer took his plan straight to the SIS regional controller, thinking him likely to give a more positive response than his immediate boss.[97] But the controller rejected it outright. 'The whole idea of SIS being involved in targeted assassination', he argued, 'is repugnant to the ethos of the service and certainly repugnant to me personally.'[98] The officer's line manager then harangued him for going behind his back, accused him of causing 'a stir', and told him that 'an order had gone out for the document to be destroyed'.[99]

Assassination may have been ruled out, but Britain later became involved in aggressive snatch operations in the Balkans. By 1997, the Joint Action Committee, which had met less and less, had disbanded.[100] Demonstrating a more ad hoc approach, Whitehall added a new committee for special military operations in the Cabinet Office. Bringing together SIS, special forces, the Ministry of Defence, the Foreign Office, and legal advisers, this new group oversaw attempts to find, track, and catch fugitives wanted for war crimes in western Bosnia. On the ground, Britain ran operations out of an SIS/SAS station in a metal factory in Banja Luka. The first mission, executed in summer 1998, was a failure after the SAS bundled the wrong set of twins into the back of a minivan, but successes soon followed. A year later, the SAS pulled off a classic snatch operation perfected on the streets of Northern Ireland. An unmarked car pulled out in front of the target, Radoslav Brdjanin, whilst a second pulled up behind. Suddenly a Land

Rover emerged from a junction ahead, causing the first car to break sharply and the others to crash, pinning the target between them. SAS soldiers smashed the window and dragged Brdjanin out through shards of broken glass.[101] After a slow start for the International Criminal Tribunal, established in 1993, SAS snatches helped turn the system into an effective force towards the end of the decade. According to journalists on the ground, the SAS had 'developed an unrivalled expertise in "snatching" war criminals'.[102] These skills were not universally appreciated. The Americans were livid and thought that rendition of suspects would put the delicate peace deal at risk. It led to a massive argument in which American NATO personnel accused the British of insubordination and formed the largest rupture in the 'special' intelligence relationship for years. With the Cold War over, some in Washington demanded that the CIA now be allowed to spy on London.[103]

Throughout the 1990s, Britain's approach to covert action involved high-speed operations to disrupt low-intensity threats. Despite this focus on less ambitious operations, Britain apparently did work to instigate at least one coup. The CIA had long been covertly funnelling money to Kurdish rebels in an attempt to destabilize—or even unseat—Saddam Hussein. With little progress made, SIS suggested a new approach in 1996. Despite being vastly superior, financially at least, to their British counterparts, the CIA welcomed SIS plans because London had long become a centre for Iraqi exiles, thereby giving British intelligence useful contacts and insight. In January, SIS officers agreed with the CIA's head of station in London to aid the Iraqi National Accord in removing Saddam. Based in Jordan, a country with which Britain still had much influence, the Iraqi National Accord consisted of former military personnel and Ba'ath Party officials who had defected from Iraq and hoped to launch a coup. In conjunction with the Jordanian and Saudi intelligence services, SIS and the CIA sent money, weapons, and communications equipment to the group. It proved as unsuccessful as many of the similar Cold War operations. Saddam Hussein's security forces were more impressive than many realized and had penetrated the rebel group. This allowed Saddam to intercept the communications gear and execute the conspirators.[104]

Eighteen months later, SIS came under pressure for involvement in another coup, this time in Sierra Leone on the West African coast. In 1998, Sandline International, a private military company, provided logistical support, including arms, to the ousted president Tejan Kabbah, allowing him to launch a counter-coup. Kabbah, a former United Nations official, had won free and fair elections in 1996 but spent much of his time in office dealing with a bitter civil war which led to a coup against him the following year. Sandline claimed that, despite the shipments breaking an embargo, the Foreign Office had approved the sale of 30 tonnes of arms. This left SIS facing accusations that it was at the very least complicit in illegal arms sales to support a coup.[105] David Spedding, the chief of SIS, confirmed that his organization had had contacts with Sandline in the latter half of 1997 but insisted that SIS was not in any way involved in the coup.[106]

This may well be true, although Robin Cook, the foreign secretary, refused to allow SIS to give evidence to the subsequent parliamentary inquiry.[107] Accordingly, the Foreign Affairs Select Committee refused to clear SIS and strongly rebuked diplomats for failing to pass intelligence offering 'very strong evidence' of illegality to their superiors.[108] Either way, the Sierra Leone affair raised important questions about covert action in the era of private military companies, with thin lines existing between state intelligence and mercenaries. Many of the private contractors involved in Sierra Leone had previously worked for special forces or intelligence and maintained contact with their old colleagues. Spedding recognized the difficulties that arose from interaction between SIS and private contractors, and urged his staff not to instigate contact. However, the Intelligence and Security Committee recognized that these individuals could be valuable sources of intelligence and so should not be cut off completely, thereby again raising the issue of allowing events, such as arms deals or coups, to happen in order to gather intelligence. Muddying the field further, companies used informal contacts and their employment of former SIS officers to give a false impression that their actions carried official endorsement.[109]

Acquiring useful intelligence from the private sector whilst not appearing to be in league with mercenaries was a difficult balance. A few years later, in 2004, a similar crisis emerged when Simon Mann, a former British army officer, was arrested trying to launch a coup in Equatorial Guinea, in an operation backed by Margaret Thatcher's son, Mark. According to spy writer Nigel West, SIS, on this occasion, 'exercised a passive neutrality'.[110] As with the rise of private organizations operating in 1960s Yemen, state intelligence might be in touch with mercenaries and mercenaries might be acting in state interests, but that does not mean they are under state control.

★ ★ ★

The Cold War may have ended, but British covert action did not abate. Instead, it diversified to counter a wider range of threats. With intelligence officers keen to demonstrate their worth and escape the Treasury's axe, SIS turned to disruptive operations designed to counter organized crime, the arms trade, terrorism, and weapons of mass destruction proliferation. These were often short-term, high-tempo operations carried out in conjunction with special forces, all the while backed by less tangible influence operations. It was a diverse agenda in which SIS sought to use covert operations as a means of managing risk, multiplying force, and maintaining the illusion of global British influence.

In 2001, Britain's covert action agenda narrowed considerably. Although the fundamental principles of disruption and risk management still applied, terrorism now formed the prime target for both SIS and special forces. Tony Blair, who had been prime minister since 1997, now wasted little time unleashing the power of Britain's hidden hand.

14

counter-terrorism

Disrupting Threats, Managing Risks

I suggest . . . we mount <u>covert operations</u> with people and groups with the ability to topple Saddam.

Tony Blair, 2001[1]

O n 11 September 2001, devastating terrorist attacks in the US using hijacked civilian airliners as weapons brought international terrorism to the apex of the security agenda. Intelligence and special forces communities suddenly found themselves in high demand, their existence and worth firmly guaranteed. Although various residual covert campaigns lingered from the previous decade, Britain's special forces, according to their director Graeme Lamb, were 'absolutely consumed' by 9/11.[2] Meanwhile, Cabinet Secretary Richard Wilson immediately recommended a 5-per cent increase to the intelligence budget.[3] As early as 20 September 2001, Tony Blair and his director of communications, Alastair Campbell, pressed for 'a well-staffed US–UK-led propaganda team' to manage the Western response.[4] Campbell was quick to see the potential in using the spooks, as he called them, in media campaigns. Months before 9/11 he had visited the Secret Intelligence Service (SIS) headquarters to hear about the latest information operations. In return, SIS asked Campbell for advice on when to release intelligence to the press.[5]

Wilson opened the Cabinet Office Briefing Room, the highly secure situation room known in the press as COBRA, indefinitely and on a round-the-clock basis. He ensured that, by seven o'clock every evening, an executive report was issued with 'Special operations' as the first heading.[6] Under Blair, however, the cabinet secretary's traditional role advising on intelligence and covert action diminished—a process begun during the Thatcher administration. With secret issues becoming more mainstream and demanding more attention, Wilson's successor, Andrew Turnbull, transferred the function to a new intelligence and security coordinator from 2002. The first incumbent was David Omand. Although these arrangements lapsed in 2005, David Cameron resurrected the division in 2010 by creating the post of national security adviser.[7]

Since 2001, SIS and special forces have continued to play a force-multiplying role. Policymakers rely on them to fix problems, to disrupt terrorist networks, and to prevent threats from materializing. They offer a means of anticipatory self-defence, using a light footprint to obviate the burdens of 'victory' in places like Afghanistan and Iraq, where state-building proved very difficult indeed.[8] A continual stream of covert action had become a form of risk management.[9]

The War on Terror

Afghanistan had harboured those responsible for 9/11. Accordingly, it was the West's first target in responding to the attacks—and covert action featured high on the agenda. Frustratingly for SIS, its main contact from the 1980s Afghan–Soviet war, Ahmad Shah Massoud, was killed by suicide bombers just two days before the Twin Towers fell. If they were going to track down Osama bin Laden and prevent further atrocities, SIS needed some new friends.[10] Fortunately, during the 1990s British intelligence undertaken counter-narcotics and broader counter-terrorism work in Afghanistan and established a network of contacts. On 28 September 2001, Jack Straw, the foreign secretary, approved the deployment of SIS to Afghanistan 'to support the US-led military and covert action'.[11]

Shortly afterwards, a team of SIS officers, armed with a budget of $7 million and including Paul Bergne, a polymath plucked from retirement, began to seek new alliances, predominantly through bribing, bartering, and intimidation.[12] Backed by SIS and the Central Intelligence Agency (CIA), the Northern Alliance, a military front which had been fighting the Taliban since its creation in the mid-1990s, soon achieved notable victories. Amidst fast-moving developments and much confusion, one Special Boat Service (SBS) team landed before the Foreign Office had informed the Northern Alliance. This caused a diplomatic incident in which local authorities almost evicted the team.[13] The operations were successful, though, and between October and December 2001 air strikes, local troops, and Western special forces deposed the regime. Tony Blair later described SIS as 'unsung heroes' who, demonstrating how covert action should complement broader policy, had made the intervention possible.[14]

Despite removing the Taliban government from Afghanistan, stabilization proved more difficult. SIS and the SBS proved unsuccessful in tracking bin Laden through the caves around Tora Bora and Western forces soon found themselves embroiled in a lengthy counter-insurgency campaign against resistance fighters. As the years passed and the Taliban enjoyed a resurgence in rural southern areas, SIS continued its operations. Covert action now sought to split Taliban rebels into so-called 'reconcilables' and 'irreconcilables', or moderates and extremists. SIS attempted to exploit divisions and bribe commanders to leave the fight and to engage in some discreet diplomacy, although the approach aimed to promote discord as much as dialogue.[15] Director of Special Forces Adrian Bradshaw made a similar point about dealing with insurgents in Iraq, another country soon invaded as part of the War on Terror. He argued that irreconcilables had to be circumvented to create space for political progress. Counter-insurgency, he ominously continued, 'is not a gloves-on activity'.[16] Unfortunately for SIS, and for the Labour government which had quietly endorsed the approach, the Afghan operation collapsed in 2010 when it transpired that SIS had actually been negotiating with a grocer from Quetta, whom they had mistakenly assumed was a Taliban leader.[17]

SIS also deployed deniable diplomacy and disruption elsewhere in the Middle East. In early 2003, officers drew up a secret plan to improve security in Palestine. British intelligence was already working with the Palestinian Authority to target groups which had rejected the peace process. SIS now sought to build on this by launching a wide-ranging security drive against suicide bombers, rockets, those funding terrorism, and tunnels used to smuggle arms. Having done so, SIS then planned to degrade 'the capabilities of the rejectionists—Hamas, Palestinian Islamic Jihad, and the Al Aqsa Brigades—through the disruption of their leaderships' communications and command and control capabilities'. SIS even planned the temporary internment of leading Hamas and Palestinian Islamic Jihad figures. Hiding their involvement behind freelance training missions, they noted that the Palestinian Authority must have 'a sense of ownership' and, ensuring deniability, that the plan would not work unless it was seen to be devised and monitored independently.[18]

Meanwhile, SIS and special forces took on a deniable role in Iraq. By December 2001, as the White House continued to link Saddam Hussein's Iraq to the 9/11 attacks despite a lack of evidence, Tony Blair suggested 'mounting covert operations in support of those "with the ability to topple Saddam"', including the Kurds in the North and the Marsh Arabs in the South. Importantly, he recommended to President Bush that SIS and the CIA should let these groups know that Britain and America would use air power to support any uprising militarily. Blair now advocated a gradual approach, bringing the Iraqi population towards the West, undermining Saddam but without going too far and frightening off potential allies. Covert action offered a middle ground between massive intervention and doing nothing.[19] Blair also suggested using covert operations to eliminate al-Qaeda cells in Somalia.[20]

Planners inside the Cabinet Office's Defence and Overseas Secretariat worked through Blair's ideas. In consultation with SIS and the Ministry of Defence, they considered 'covert support to opposition groups to mount an uprising/coup' in spring 2002. The Secretariat brought together Michael Jay, the new permanent secretary at the Foreign Office, his Ministry of Defence counterpart, as well as John Scarlett, chairman of the Joint Intelligence Committee (JIC), and David Omand, the new intelligence and security coordinator.[21] The plan involved bringing 'down the regime by internal revolt, aided by the defection or at least acquiescence of large sections of the Army'. Kurds would tie down Saddam's forces in the north, the Shia would rise up in southern cities, and Sunni generals would 'depose Saddam if they decided the alternative was defeat'.[22] The JIC added that Turkey, Saudi Arabia, and other regional allies would all have strongly preferred 'covert operations to topple Saddam rather than a full scale attack'.[23]

David Manning, Blair's foreign policy adviser, reported that Bush was receptive to the prime minister's ideas.[24] However, the new head of the CIA's Iraqi Operations Group warned that, having learned from the string of failed attempts to remove Saddam since 1991, covert action alone would not succeed this time either.[25] Cabinet Office planners agreed that it would require air support, but warned that the rebels would not trust the West to back them. Iraqis had long memories and would not forget the failure to support the 1991 Kurdish rebellion. To make things worse, the main external opposition groups lacked domestic credibility and most Iraqis saw them as Western stooges. Likewise, the internal opposition was bitterly divided and more interested in seeking advantage over each other than removing Saddam.[26] As for assassination, the Cabinet Office swiftly dismissed it as illegal,[27] whilst defence intelligence officials thought it unfeasible.[28] Although Whitehall's planners did not rule out covert action as a precursor to military intervention, they knew that only a ground offensive would remove Saddam and so attention turned to media operations to highlight the Iraqi threat and prepare public opinion for a conflict.[29]

In reality, the Americans were calling the shots and President Bush ultimately opted for war. When the military intervention came in March 2003, as was so often the case, those in charge of special forces had to lobby Whitehall for a role. With the regime quickly toppled, many in London naively assumed that the conflict was over by June and Graeme Lamb, the director of special forces, had to make a case for continued involvement.[30] After successful lobbying, the Special Air Service (SAS), and to a lesser extent the SBS (which maintained a larger presence in Afghanistan), soon took on a man-hunting role tracking down Saddam's erstwhile colleagues, before moving on to threats to the coalition more broadly. Whitehall left it late to recognize the value of special forces and Britain's operations were utterly dwarfed by their American counterparts.[31]

By the start of 2004, the Ministry of Defence had created a global counter-terrorist campaign, which included a core special forces dimension.[32] Meanwhile, SIS received a budget increase to support, as the Intelligence and Security Committee put it, 'covert action against terrorist and proliferation targets'.[33] As the insurgency in Iraq continued, Britain's special forces gradually took on a greater counter-terrorism role, working closely with SIS, to find and eliminate key targets. However, they remained semi-detached from Washington's more aggressive approach, amidst fears that the Americans were too trigger-happy and too brutal in their treatment of detainees. Britain's director of special forces was dismayed at the conditions in one detention centre and felt they put the UK in an awkward position.[34] American special forces were undertaking counter-terrorism on an almost industrial scale, rapidly hunting terrorists, sweeping each location for new intelligence, which would then enable another operation somewhere else. It was a cycle which led to numerous raids—up to fourteen—every night, with each only possible owing to intelligence gathered during the previous one. It was fast, aggressive, and violent. It was also highly intensive, and with

British special forces spending much of their time pursuing old Ba'athists rather than terrorists, the Pentagon turned to Whitehall for help. When General Petraeus took charge of the multinational force in 2007, he visited London and specifically stressed the importance of the SAS and SIS in countering terrorism in Iraq.[35]

Those running British special forces faced a choice. They could join the Americans in high-speed operations—and in doing so, as one defence official put it, buy strategic credits—or maintain a more cautious approach.[36] Gradually, Richard Williams, the commanding officer of the SAS, adopted the American style, pressuring his regiment to up the tempo. Closely supported by SIS, special forces did a great deal to disrupt and diminish al-Qaeda in Iraq,[37] before applying this new approach to Afghanistan.[38] SIS also felt the need to increase its own ability to handle material in a high-tempo operational environment, and, in 2009, John Scarlett, now the SIS chief, oversaw a new project to upgrade information systems, giving his staff in Iraq, the UK, and elsewhere timely access to classified information. Benefits, SIS claimed, would include 'strengthening intelligence collection and covert action capability by enabling more secure operations through much wider access to key information'.[39]

Adrian Bradshaw, who headed special forces towards the end of the Iraq campaign, felt that close cooperation with the Americans 'had a transformative effect on UK Special Forces'. It brought Britain into the twenty-first century. This was not without problems, though, as special operations began to move so fast that they outpaced Ministry of Defence policy and Whitehall found itself playing catch-up. According to Bradshaw, the SAS and SBS were 'expanding the envelope' whenever they could and sooner or later came 'up against a policy hump' which had to be 'got through'.[40]

Meanwhile, British personnel took the lead in cultivating Sunni leaders to fight al-Qaeda in the Anbar province in western Iraq. In May 2006, the American-led forces established a working group, known as the Force Strategic Engagement Cell. Headed by the British military, working closely with SIS and the CIA, it aimed to turn key tribes into friendly militias. The CIA even advocated arming them. The Pentagon, by contrast, was nervous and, in an interesting reversal from British thinking in the early Cold War, insisted that the British took charge to protect Washington from blame if it went wrong. First under Robert Fry and then Graeme Lamb, successively the most senior British soldiers in Iraq, the Cell met tribal leaders, in an attempt to exploit existing divisions and tension between the Sunnis and al-Qaeda in Iraq.[41] According to Tim Dowse, chief of the assessments staff in the Cabinet Office, it was an 'initiative to co-opt Sunni tribes in Anbar province'. Lamb, in particular, busily negotiated with the various internal factions, persuading them to unite and fight al-Qaeda in the region, and pioneered a pilot scheme in both Anbar and Baghdad. By May 2007, he reported significant progress.[42] At around the same time, SIS received another increase in its budget to strengthen both intelligence collection and covert action.[43]

By then, terrorism had truly become transnational. Al-Qaeda and its various offshoots flooded the Internet with propaganda, radicalizing Muslims across the Middle East—and in the UK. Whitehall needed to launch some sort of counter-propaganda campaign in response and created the Research, Information and Communications Unit (RICU) in 2007. Demonstrating the blurred boundaries between international and domestic activity, RICU was, and remains, a cross-government agency bringing together the Department for Communities and Local Government, the Foreign Office, the Home Office, and later the Ministry of Defence.[44] Its open-plan office sits on the fifth floor of the Home Office building in Westminster, with a nondescript conference room in the corner overlooking the street below.

RICU's aim was to challenge Islamist propaganda.[45] It operated both in the UK and in priority countries abroad—particularly Pakistan—to challenge extremist activities and communications at a local level through so-called counter-ideological projects.[46] With an initial budget of around £1 million a year, RICU began by examining the language of counter-terrorism and disseminated a rather blunt message: 'Terrorists are criminals and murderers and they attack the values that we all share'.[47] By 2009, RICU was devoting more effort to communicating counter-extremism policies to audiences in Britain and beyond, challenging terrorist propaganda that the West was waging a war on Islam.[48] It consisted of around thirty-five people, including some providing advice from the private sector.[49]

RICU's counter-propaganda activity raises comparisons with the old Information Research Department (IRD). Charles Farr, a former intelligence officer who set up RICU when overseeing the Office for Security and Counter-Terrorism, acknowledged the Cold War flavour of its acronym.[50] Despite this, its staff insisted that RICU was neither modelled on, nor inspired by, the IRD. Whitehall lacked the corporate memory to do so.[51]

Unlike the Information Research Department, RICU maintained that all its material was open-source, that its staff had no access to secret material, and that the revolving door between SIS and the IRD no longer existed. Nonetheless, certain staff had weekly access to the intelligence chiefs and could verify information to ensure that their material was accurate in much the same way the IRD used intelligence for background and research purposes.[52] Moreover, RICU denied that its propaganda was unattributable in any way, although in practice it can be very difficult to trace the source. This is deliberate and the government hand was as low-key as possible in order to maintain authenticity and credibility. As Theresa May, then home secretary, put it: 'Often it is more effective to be working through groups that are recognised as having a voice' than 'it is being seen to be government trying to give a message'.[53]

Some of RICU's earliest programmes targeted audiences overseas. They included sponsoring Arabic-language children's television programming in Jordan to promote tolerance and working through the British Council to provide English-language training to tutors at Al-Azhar University in Cairo.[54] In 2009, RICU and Foreign Office staff told their American counterparts about three counter-propaganda programmes overseas, and pressed for closer coordination with Washington. The first involved sending British Muslim professionals to Pakistan 'to undermine the myth that British Muslims are mistreated in the UK'. The second, which began as a domestic programme but extended to Pakistan, promoted 'mainstream Islamic arguments against extremism' through prominent religious scholars holding open fora to discuss jihad and martyrdom. The third worked with the Quilliam Foundation, a counter-extremism think tank, to send a deradicalized Muslim on a lecture tour of Pakistan to discuss why he had turned his back on terrorism. RICU was keen to point out that, because of close relations between British Muslims and Pakistan, these programmes had a domestic effect too. Indeed, RICU prioritized building links between British and Pakistani civil society.[55]

RICU's early days saw limited success. The Foreign Office worried that RICU would impatiently issue messages before they had conducted enough research about audience and content, potentially doing more harm than good. The Americans noted that RICU's claims of success were anecdotal and that Britain lacked metrics for proper evaluation.[56] In truth, counter-propaganda did not have much of an impact until the Arab Spring and the rise of Islamic State.

The Arab Spring and continued counter-terrorism

Although the so-called War on Terror was winding down by the turn of the decade, events in the Middle East quickly became more unstable. In January 2011, a series of uprisings swept across the region in what became known as the Arab Spring. Like many prime ministers before him, David Cameron turned to covert action and special forces to intervene. With Britain facing deep austerity, swingeing defence cuts, and an increasingly war-weary population, covert action seemed especially appealing.[57] Indeed, successive reviews into British defence and security highlighted the important role of intelligence and special forces, not just as force multipliers used to project power globally, but also to add value to the asymmetric relationship with America.[58]

Military chiefs, echoing their early Cold War predecessors, also pressed for covert action. As the chief of defence staff, Nick Houghton, put it, 'all the instruments of national power' needed constantly to be in play for Britain to compete in the twenty-first-century global environment.[59] Accordingly, Cameron's coalition government highlighted the importance of investing in special forces as well as using proxies.[60] These capabilities consistently escaped the Treasury's axe and, between 2010 and 2015, he authorized operations in Libya, Syria, and Yemen.[61]

Much of this activity came through the new National Security Council (NSC) machinery established shortly after Cameron came to power in 2010. The NSC enjoyed a broad remit, but was certainly conducive to covert action because it brought the heads of SIS and GCHQ around the same table as the prime minister, foreign secretary, and defence secretary every week. Iain Lobban, then head of GCHQ, praised the NSC as a major success insofar as it took the sentiment in the room and then tasked each intelligence organization accordingly.[62] Likewise, John Sawers, chief of SIS, has stated that ministers told his service 'what they want us to achieve' and that SIS took its direction from the NSC.[63] Through the NSC, Cameron asked intelligence and special forces to disrupt, sabotage, or fix certain problems.[64] He was an avid reader of intelligence and greatly appreciative of SIS capabilities, but some of those at the meetings held the opinion that he seriously lacked judgement in assessing risk.[65] The NSC would have to keep him in line.

The civil war in Libya provided the first test for this new machinery. Policymakers and intelligence chiefs soon debated the scope and purpose of covert action around the NSC table. One idea put forward by Cameron involved dropping 200 million unused Libyan banknotes, worth £1 billion, into the country to help the rebels. Dominic Grieve, the attorney general, had to veto it, pointing out that the move would breach a United Nations freeze on all Libyan assets and that Cameron could be sent to jail.[66]

The first attempt that Whitehall sanctioned fared little better. Back in 2007, an elite team, known as E squadron, was established as a composite force of SAS, SBS, and Special Reconnaissance Regiment personnel. It operated at the disposal of SIS and the director of special forces.[67] In March 2011, William Hague, the foreign secretary, approved a team from this unit, dressed in black and led by a young SIS Middle Eastern specialist, to land in the middle of the night in a Libyan farmyard and make contact with the rebels. The impetus for covert action came from SIS and, as ever, was signed off through departmental channels by the foreign secretary. The NSC machinery set the direction of travel and coordinated objectives, but did not conceive of or approve covert action. After all these years, the diplomats still guarded their turf jealously.[68] Unfortunately for Britain and the Foreign Office, the landing aroused suspicion and locals swiftly detained and deported the team; or, as a Cabinet Office report into the incident put it, the team was 'withdrawn after a serious misunderstanding about its role, leading to its temporary detention'.[69]

Exposure of the blunder reignited Whitehall debates about the utility of covert action. Some around the NSC table pushed back against further SIS and special forces operations.[70] As a result, SIS, in conjunction with Foreign Office and Ministry of Defence officials, conducted smaller-scale economic operations, through a Libyan Oil Cell, to increase pressure on Gaddafi. Action included assisting a blockade of Gaddafi-held ports, spotting overland smuggling routes, and helping the rebels secure access to oil.[71]

As the civil war dragged on, the NSC coordinated more ambitious covert operations. SIS and special forces teams operated alongside other subterranean teams from France, Qatar, and the UAE to organize the rebels, train them in weapons handling, and offer tactical advice on plans to take Tripoli.[72] All the while, the Ministry of Defence publicly disavowed sending any ground troops. Members of parliament have since criticized these denials—as well as the broader operations. They bypassed parliamentary scrutiny and supported local militias rather than the transitional government, which did not command its own units.[73] SIS backed the covert action, but its chief,

John Sawers, sagely worried about what would happen afterwards and whether Libya would descend into lawlessness.[74]

Others expressed concern about the impact that recent developments in government real-time communications technology would have on covert action. Cameron, and his more hawkish colleagues such as George Osborne, chancellor of the exchequer, could now become more operationally involved. This risked tactical and short-term operations at the expense of greater strategic thinking.[75] Demonstrating this, Hague blamed SIS's earlier bungled attempt to contact the Libyan rebels on pressure from ministers to do something.[76] As one intelligence official quietly lamented, the 'kids have been put in charge of the toys'.[77]

Sawers was right. After Gaddafi was killed in October 2011, Libya slipped into chaos and became a breeding ground for terrorism and disorder. SIS and special forces maintained a discreet presence and rumours about their activity soon swirled. By spring 2012, Hillary Clinton, the American secretary of state, took seriously false reports that SIS, in conjunction with French intelligence, were helping tribal leaders establish a semi-autonomous zone on the grounds that the provisional government had been slow to organize pro-European business deals.[78] As late as December 2015, Cameron despatched special forces to Libya to tackle terrorism,[79] and numerous reports surfaced the following year about their operations. In May, for example, special forces apparently blew up a truck laden with explosives.[80] Cameron used deniable operations to disrupt terrorist activity in Libya until the dying days of his premiership.

At the same time, a more complex civil war dragged on in Syria. Competing and fractured rebel groups, including Islamist extremists, fought to topple President Assad. Once again, senior policymakers, the chiefs of staff, and John Sawers debated the pros and cons of covertly supporting the rebels. Cameron rejected one particularly ambitious plan to work with the opposition to create an army amongst Syrian exiles, leaving David Richards, chief of the defence staff, frustrated. Richards later vented: 'If they'd had the balls, they would have gone through with it . . . if they'd done what I argued, they wouldn't be where they are with ISIS'.[81] For William Hague, the only chance for success lay in a defection of generals and an assassination.[82]

The civil war turned into a messy quagmire, spawning a refugee crisis and creating a hub for international terrorism. Cameron and Hague approved other covert actions, seeing them as the easy option to protect British interests. A debate broke out amongst the NSC about whether to pursue diplomacy, military intervention, or deniably work with the rebels. Ministers pressed for the latter as an easy compromise. They knew that such operations would not have to receive approval from a war-weary public. Cynically, they also knew that covert action would allow the UK to show its allies, especially the CIA, that it was doing *something*. Intelligence chiefs protested that, whilst covert action was possible, it would have little effect on the outcome of the civil war. Cameron had little sympathy.[83]

In early 2012, SIS helped a CIA operation to move weapons from Gaddafi's stores into Syria, often using front companies established in Libya. As usual, SIS input was useful for the Americans because it allowed the CIA to class the operation as liaison rather than a covert action and therefore avoid reporting it to Congress.[84] Despite losing a vote on military intervention in Syria eighteen months later, Cameron again turned to deniable intervention and sanctioned a new proactive special forces approach to countering the Islamic State in Syria, apparently giving the SAS and SBS 'carte blanche' to launch raids inside the country.[85]

All the while, propaganda and political action underpinned paramilitary operations. In 2013 the Intelligence and Security Committee requested more information operations, especially in the cyber realm.[86] The Ministry of Defence also recognized that success against agile adversaries required a greater emphasis on non-kinetic operations and the chief of defence staff pointed to a 'significant increase in the power of a potent narrative'.[87] Emphasizing the need to win the battle for ideology, Cameron compared the fight against Islamic State to the Cold War, itself a high point for underground battles over ideology, culture, and media.[88]

In Syria, the American National Security Agency looked to SIS and GCHQ for, in its words, 'recommended courses of action to influence the outcome'. This included 'online effects operations': electronic covert action.[89] GCHQ's capabilities now encompassed false flag activity such as writing blog posts and sending emails under a false identity to incriminate a target and changing a target's photos on a social networking site. Staff boasted how this took '"paranoia" to a whole new level'. Other ways GCHQ could manipulate targets included the ability to increase website traffic or page views artificially, and to manipulate the outcome of online polls.[90]

GCHQ targeted terrorists and criminals in the cyber realm. In 2012, the Intelligence and Security Committee explicitly called for an increase in deniable online disruption operations.[91] Techniques included sending viruses and denial of service attacks (known as ROLLING THUNDER and PREDATORS FACE), whilst ANGRY PIRATE was a tool that could permanently disable a target's account on their computer. In Afghanistan, GCHQ disrupted Taliban operations by blitzing mobile phones with text messages and calls every ten seconds. GCHQ officers now talked of 'active covert internet operations', proactive means of accessing data, and using this to make something happen in the real or cyber world.[92] Another operation, known as Cupcake, altered an al-Qaeda bomb-making pamphlet to include cupcake recipes instead. Many of these techniques, especially ones designed to discredit, targeted terrorist recruiters by undermining their authority.[93] Interestingly, one US intelligence official conceded that Britain was 'slightly ahead' of the Americans when it came to such activity.[94]

The Ministry of Defence also engaged in information and media operations.[95] In 2013, officials worked in conjunction with the Foreign Office to bolster the moderate Syrian opposition. They hired contractors, working out of Istanbul, to produce videos, photos, radio material, and websites for the fighters. The aim was to select and train a spokesman to represent and unify the moderate armed opposition groups; to offer media coaching to prominent individuals; and to run a central media office on behalf of the fighters.[96] At around the same time, Philip Hammond, the defence secretary, emphasized the importance of building 'a dedicated capability to counter-attack in cyber space and, if necessary, to strike in cyber space as part of our full-spectrum military capability'.[97]

RICU also played a role in the Syrian civil war, albeit with a domestic target in mind. In 2013, its research showed that British Muslims travelled to Syria either to join the jihad or for humanitarian reasons. To counter this RICU asked a private partner, Breakthrough Media Network, to work through a group called Help for Syria. Targeting Muslim men between 15 and 39 years old, the campaign disseminated adverts on social media, leafleted 760,000 households, broadcast films on YouTube, and visited numerous university campuses. Breakthrough thought the campaign had successfully influenced people to reconsider travelling to Syria, but those working for Help for Syria have said they had no knowledge of government involvement.[98]

By this time, RICU had become a much larger unit. Despite its counter-narrative work being of variable quality and lacking precision in target audiences and messages, RICU had received a boost in 2011 when Theresa May relaunched the government's counter-terrorism strategy, Prevent. Both she and David Cameron had become important backers of RICU's work in Whitehall and, although policymakers still looked for better results,[99] they increased its budget to £2–3 million.[100] RICU could now work, in the words of one insider, 'at an industrial scale and pace' to counter terrorist propaganda.[101]

From 2011 it worked with credible civil society organizations to challenge radical views in their local communities and deliver demonstrable behavioural change.[102] The *modus operandi* of RICU, which did not fund these organizations, was threefold. First, it focused on data about violence levels and the economy rather than engaging in complex ideological or theological debates. Second, RICU opted for a long-term, low-key approach rather than broadcasting easy slogans. According to its director, negative propaganda was quick but counterproductive, as demonstrated in Northern Ireland. Third, despite denying planting stories in the press, RICU put groups in contact with local journalists, whose stories might then have been picked up in the national press. As such, RICU demonstrated a more authentic approach by allowing stories to filter up from the local domain.[103]

By early 2015, RICU had run thirteen national campaigns. Adopting methodologies from advertising and taking advantage of new computer-based tools enabled precise targeting unavailable to the IRD. It produced content accessed by audiences over a million times.[104] One example was a film about the London Olympics featuring athletes from Afghanistan and Pakistan as they trained to compete. It challenged the idea that the Olympic Games were unIslamic due to their coinciding with the holy month of Ramadan. Thirty million Muslims worldwide watched it.[105] In spring 2016, a *Guardian* investigation exposed, and sensationalized, areas of RICU's activity. This left staff deeply frustrated. They were accordingly delighted when Leicester City Football Club improbably won the English Premier League shortly afterwards. The remarkable victory captured the popular imagination and forced RICU off the front pages, preventing the revelations from gathering momentum. One staffer joked that RICU's ability to fix the Premier League to shift the news agenda demonstrated the power of the secret state in all its glory![106]

Counter-terrorism extended to Yemen, Somalia, and Pakistan, where operations sparked renewed debates about drone strikes and targeted killing. British authorization of targeted killings outside of war zones has long been opaque—a position drawing criticism from senior parliamentarians. In 2015, the National Security Council allegedly approved a so-called 'kill list' of twenty-four individuals to be targeted as a last resort to disrupt and prevent terrorist activities. If true, the process about how individuals are identified, and kept under review, is shrouded in secrecy. The government denies having a 'targeted killing' policy, but senior parliamentarians have pointed to a 'policy to use lethal force abroad outside armed conflict for counter-terrorism purposes'.[107]

Despite SIS officers long opposing assassination, they faced a difficult conundrum in Yemen, Somalia, and Pakistan. Intelligence that they, GCHQ, and special forces supplied to America was being used to target drone strikes. GCHQ supplied in-depth surveillance of the Federally Administered Tribal Areas, the area of Pakistan most hit by US drone strikes, including coverage of satellite telephone communications. It also provided tactical intelligence to support military operations there. This, GCHQ noted, was an imminent and high priority.[108] Critics have asked similar questions about British intelligence enabling drone strikes in Somalia too.[109] That said, clear procedures were in place to ensure that British intelligence did not aid unacceptable operations. SIS met with other intelligence agencies, notably the CIA and Mossad, in advance of sharing its intelligence and stipulated that if lethal force were to be used then it had to meet British, rather than looser American or Israeli, criteria. Those within SIS and GCHQ insist that partner countries play by these rules. Without rules, they claim, the entire intelligence liaison and sharing system would break down.[110]

In Yemen, the CIA was, once again, keen to draw on British experience to complement its own activities. According to a CIA officer responsible for Yemeni operations, 'the British have been in the Gulf States for decades. They have a reservoir of knowledge, contacts, and experience that is very important.'[111] SIS believed that President Obama greatly valued British assistance, particularly the interplay between intelligence and special forces which allowed nimble units to work across borders more effectively than the Americans.[112] Demonstrating the blurred lines between intelligence liaison, intelligence-gathering, and covert action, the British were keen to be involved in CIA operations as a means of gathering more intelligence on potential threats to the UK.

In May 2012, SIS intelligence helped the CIA target Fahd al-Quso, an al-Qaeda commander in the Arabian Peninsula who had participated in the bombing of the USS Cole back in 2000. The pattern was similar to other CIA drones strikes: an SIS agent told his handler about the travel plans of a target; SIS then sought corroboration from GCHQ before informing the

CIA.[113] GCHQ has also been at the forefront of this activity and, working with American and Australian signals intelligence, helped develop a programme called Overhead which used a combination of satellite, radio, and phone collection to track individuals. GCHQ also monitored fixed locations and tracked movements in and out of buildings, corroborating identities with other forms of visual intelligence such as clothing or gait. By 2010, and at the request of the National Security Agency (NSA), Overhead turned its attention to Yemen. It appears that intelligence from GCHQ and Overhead was instrumental in tracking and targeting two terrorists, one of whom was a doctor specializing in surgically implanted explosives. A CIA drone strike killed both in March 2012.[114] Later in the same year, the family of a tribal elder killed by a drone strike in Pakistan launched a legal case against the British government accusing GCHQ officers of accessory to murder. Judges refused to rule, fearing that doing so could harm Britain's international relations.[115]

At the same time, special forces from Britain's Special Reconnaissance Regiment trained Yemeni paramilitary forces in counter-terrorism. The head of the Yemeni unit described the British trainers as highly secretive, having prevented their students from taking photos or mentioning names. Other British special forces personnel allegedly flew in and out of Yemen as part of speedy kill or capture missions near the capital Sana'a.[116] To ensure deniability, Whitehall seconded British military personnel to the Foreign Office and away from the Ministry of Defence. That way, defence ministers could deny any British military support for American covert operations in the country. According to a lawyer for Reprieve, the human rights organization, this amounted to Britain outsourcing military activity to the intelligence agencies to hide involvement, exactly as the Americans have long done.[117]

★ ★ ★

Between June 2013 and December 2016, British intelligence, according to SIS chief Alex Younger, disrupted twelve terrorist plots. Many of these emanated from Iraq and Syria. He added that in doing so SIS agents operated 'in the most dangerous and hostile environments on earth'. Both SIS officers and their agents do things for their countries which would not be justifiable in pursuit of private interests but, Younger argued, are 'necessary, proportionate, and legal' in the context of national security.[118]

By now, GCHQ had also become a covert action player, with both intelligence agencies working closely alongside special forces. Indeed, mirroring post-war tension between the Foreign Office and the chiefs of staff, GCHQ fought off the military for control of cyberweapons, arguing that they should be intelligence-led and covert, because transparent capabilities would allow opponents to fix any vulnerabilities in advance.[119] Increasingly the main aim had become disruption. Since the end of the Cold War, intelligence moved closer to action. Threatened by budget cuts and questions about their role, intelligence officers wanted greater relevance and impact. John Sawers, for example, wanted to *do* things and not, as he put it, 'just collect intelligence quietly and build up the files'.[120] The diversification of threats, a fluid international environment, and a fast-paced security agenda all created a climate conducive to covert action.

Nevertheless, much of this had become smaller-scale: less provocative, more short-term, and more tactical. It generally aimed to disrupt rather than make kings. After 9/11, disruption focused on terrorist networks but it extended to other areas too. Sawers has admitted, for example, that SIS ran a series of covert operations to slow down Iranian nuclear development in the late 2000s.[121] And it appears that senior intelligence personnel in SIS and GCHQ contributed to the US–Israeli cyberattack on Iranian nuclear facilities, known as Stuxnet, whilst GCHQ may have been involved in the espionage precursor to the sabotage known as Flame.[122] Facing a gap between capabilities and the desire to play a global role, Britain is still turning to covert action. The past decade has witnessed a growing fusion between intelligence and special forces, as well as SIS and GCHQ working proactively and operationally in their own right. The 2015 defence and security review, signed off by the prime minister himself, recognized the importance of intelligence in 'disrupting threats'.[123] It has allowed SIS to grow by almost a third in size to around 3,500 people, the biggest in its history. Its chief, Alex Younger, realizes that it is not simply a numbers game though: 'intelligence is not an infantry battle' and SIS will continue to punch above its weight.[124] Since the start of the twenty-first century covert action has become increasingly important, with even the signals intelligence agencies transforming themselves from silent sentries in the shadows to interventionist armies of the night.

CONCLUSION
The British Way

This modern technique of doing everything in public makes our life almost intolerable.
Harold Macmillan[1]

Since 1945, British leaders have turned to covert action regularly and with remarkable continuity. Driven by international events and shaped by departmental competition, covert action has consistently risen above party politics. Winston Churchill's incoming Conservative administration continued, almost exactly, Labour's approach in Europe and Iran from 1951. Harold Wilson's Labour governments continued secret wars begun under the Conservatives in Yemen and Indonesia in the 1960s, and, on returning to Downing Street the following decade, in Oman. It is now possible, for the first time, to distil a British way in covert action. The evidence points to a distinctive approach including defensiveness, inherent caution, indirectness or maximum deniability, and close policy integration. In the post-imperial era, covert action strives for influence rather than power. As Julian Amery long believed, Britain needs to play its weak hand carefully and effectively.[2]

Defensive attempts to maintain the status quo

Policymakers in Westminster and Whitehall traditionally used covert action in what they perceived as a defensive manner. They aimed to maintain the status quo, preserve influence, and counter perceived challenges. Successive governments have turned to covert action to prevent, or mask, decline. It was a form of fancy footwork to meet Britain's global responsibilities and try to assert some control in an uncertain environment. Importantly, Britain has not turned to covert action to gain more power or territory.

Covert action is a choice. And policymakers chose to use deniable means to implement policy under certain conditions: when international pressures of non-interventionism, exacerbated by growing anti-imperialism, prevented visible interference in the affairs of others. This reached a tipping point at the start of the 1950s, before being exacerbated by Suez; and Britain cared deeply about its image as an arbiter of fair play and upholder of global norms. Leaders did not want to be seen as aggressors. When Harold Wilson was elected in 1964, for example, he promised to transform Britain into 'a nation of Gentlemen in a world of players'.[3] Policymakers also turned to covert action when visible interference risked escalation into military conflict with the Soviets or, more likely, risked derailing a diplomatic summit. Leaders valued their global statesman personae highly and invested much energy in summitry. At the same time, covert action allowed them to negotiate from a position of strength. Like intelligence more broadly, it gave them an edge. Indeed, it was not always a choice between deniable or open action. Oftentimes, covert means complemented the broader position, such as in the early Cold War when Britain used the Secret Intelligence Service (SIS) to undermine Soviet rule whilst the Foreign Office built up pro-Western positions. Policymakers also chose deniable means to protect relationships with other states, such as during the overthrow of Sultan Sa'id in Oman when visible action would have undermined British military personnel seconded to other governments. British covert action was defensive, designed to preserve influence, and to protect London's international image.

Governments used covert action defensively to counter communist attempts to undermine British allies. Examples include political action and propaganda in Southeast Asia alongside MI5 liaison with regimes in the Middle East.[4] Governments also used covert action preventatively, such as in Congo and former colonies, to forestall Moscow's exploitation of potential power vacuums. Even seemingly offensive covert action, such as undermining Soviet control in Eastern Europe, was perceived in defensive terms. For the British, this was about causing problems in the Soviet backyard in order to impede the Kremlin's foreign adventures. This theme extended to other theatres, such as targeting Indonesia in the 1960s to frustrate its activities against Malaysia, targeting South Yemen in the following decade to hamper its escapades against neighbouring Oman, or targeting Hezbollah in the 1980s to distract terrorists from attacking westerners.

Attempts to overthrow the Albanian regime from 1949 were framed as defending Greece. Operation Boot in Iran defended Britain's regional influence in the face of a nationalist challenge.

This presents a paradox. How can British leaders use covert means to visibly maintain the status quo? There are three answers. First, covert action was an enabler allowing Britain to fulfil its public commitments. Operation Boot again forms a useful example. Its role was deniable but the outcome ensured access to oil and supposedly maintained Britain's status. It allowed negotiation from a position of strength. Similar thinking applied to covert action in Yemen in the 1960s. The operation was deniable, but the outcome—tying Nasser down and protecting the Aden base—allowed, in theory at least, Britain to maintain its colonial position and regional status. By using covert means to underpin a broader conventional position, Britain sought to preserve influence and an illusion of power.

Second, policy elites, who had grown up on the idea of Britain's global role, knew that they were doing *something* to maintain it. As Pierson Dixon, a diplomat who chaired the covert action committee of his day, put it, 'we are still determined to act as a Great Power, which is half the battle of being a Great Power'.[5] Third, similar logic applied to clandestine relations with allies for whom covert action served as a means of demonstrating British potency. In Syria, David Cameron used deniable assets to show his allies, notably the Central Intelligence Agency (CIA) and Gulf States, that Britain was doing *something* despite the lack of conventional military intervention and war-weariness at home. Intriguingly, executing covert action—as opposed to just the outcome—is sometimes designed with an audience in mind.

In fact, there can be multiple audiences. Covert action allows the few in the know—both inside government and amongst allies—to feel that, despite constraints, Britain is doing something to meet its responsibilities. It can also show resolve to adversaries, albeit at a level below open conflict. Certain British covert actions lacked plausible deniability; this was not necessarily a bad thing. In line with defending the status quo, covert action, implausibly deniable and visible to the target, could signal determination that Britain was not relinquishing its position any time soon. Mossadeq was convinced of SIS operations in Iran and expelled British intelligence and diplomatic officials accordingly. Nasser rounded up an SIS spy ring prior to Suez and knew about covert action in Yemen the following decade. Britain assumed that Indonesia was aware of, but could not prove, special forces incursions in the 1960s. Covert action in Afghanistan was visible to the Russians and, as we have seen, Carrington refused to deny SIS involvement so as to keep pressure on the Soviets to find a political solution. Multiple levels of exposure exist and it is simplistic to think only of covert and overt action.[6]

Maintaining the status quo allowed Whitehall to frame covert action as counter-offence. The first wave of covert operations authorized against the Soviets from 1948 was wrapped up as a 'counter-attack' or defensive-offensive. The second wave, from 1955, followed suit as counter-subversion: to defend against the rising challenges of communist and nationalist subversion. This remained the case when countering Yemeni activity in Oman in the 1970s and Soviet expansionism into Afghanistan in the 1980s. Meanwhile, officials described operations against the IRA in Northern Ireland as 'counter-action'.[7] All along, Britain conducted 'counter-propaganda' rather than propaganda. The framework remains relevant in the twenty-first century: when discussing Britain's need for online capabilities in 2013, Philip Hammond, the defence secretary, emphasized the importance of being able to 'counter-attack'.[8]

British governments are rarely proactive. As one official in charge of propaganda once admitted: 'Nobody wants to do anything unless they have to. If you find certain things going on that make you uncomfortable, then you start responding.'[9] Indeed, much covert action was reactionary, characterized by ad hoc improvisation in response to international developments. It sought to maintain Britain's position by containing and frustrating the adversary. Operations prolonged conflicts in Yemen, Indonesia, and Afghanistan, whilst covert action in Eastern Europe prevented expansionism elsewhere. This resonates with a broader British approach to international affairs: eschewing mission statements in favour of muddling through.[10]

At the same time, British leaders perpetuated amongst themselves the idea that the UK only resorts to such underhand tactics when forced to do so by a less gentlemanly adversary. Covert action is a controversial and risky business, raising difficult questions about accountability and transparency in liberal democracies. By constantly framing it as counter-attack, planners implied that Britain did not engage in these measures first. Forming a reluctant 'they started it' approach to international relations, covert action, like nuclear strategy, relied on a second-strike capability. Similarly, it mirrors broader thinking on the use of lethal force, including targeted killing, which, as the attorney general put it in 2017, is only ever used in self-defence.[11]

This defensive framing, when followed through into implementation, created a strategic weakness. Merely reacting to events risked covert action lacking initiative; it was subject to drift and ill-considered improvisation. On more than one occasion, Britain demonstrated a 'whack-a-mole' approach. This was, and still is, a difficult problem to overcome and will remain so long as Britain sees covert action as a reactive tool. Policymakers should not, of course, adopt a purely proactive and offensive approach, yet British covert action traditionally worked most effectively when planners had a framework to execute operations swiftly in a well-considered, coordinated, and consistent manner.

Caution

A proactive approach is unlikely because British covert action is marked by an inherent caution. Constrained by Cabinet Office scrutiny or by reluctant diplomats in the Foreign Office, it has not succumbed to the gung-ho excesses associated with the CIA during the Cold War. Hawks within both the military and SIS may have lobbied for more aggressive operations, but they found themselves checked by the deft bureaucratic manoeuvres of the Foreign Office. Covert action was the outcome of compromise and bargaining.

There was certainly regular talk of more ambitious operations and it can be difficult to distinguish real activity from barroom bluster. SIS sometimes used the language of liberation to recruit émigrés into what were predominantly intelligence-gathering operations. Meanwhile, the likes of Julian Amery and Billy McLean talked a good talk and scurried across the world plotting coups. From the cosy hearths of London's pubs, George Young boasted with his friends about grand operations which would redraw the entire landscape of the Middle East. Much of this existed only in the haze of cigar smoke and brandy fumes. All of this creates a toxic combination for the sober historian trying to distinguish fact from fantasy. Likewise, it is difficult to distinguish those operations officially—if deniably—sanctioned by the British government from those executed in a private capacity on behalf of foreign governments. Harold Macmillan once described Amery as having his own Foreign Office.[12] The rise of mercenary organizations from the 1960s complicated this further.

Britain did engage in some larger-scale covert operations, from Yemen to Indonesia, Oman to Afghanistan. Officials did so, however, within a cautious framework exhibiting limited and well-defined objectives. On each occasion, the bureaucrats in Whitehall successfully tempered more aggressive proposals emanating from the military and, in many cases, from British representatives on the ground. Ambitious attempts to overthrow governments in Egypt and Syria in the 1950s were the exception rather than the rule, although even the latter progressed incrementally. Britain has not overthrown a government since 1970. Instead, SIS relied on pinpricks and pilot schemes. Rather than being ambitious from the start, operations had limited objectives and involved strikes against select targets. Without risking dramatic escalation or political embarrassment, pinpricks gradually chipped away at the target's authority by exploiting weaknesses, undermining the economy, promoting dissension, and spreading distrust. In doing so, they also gently tested the feasibility of more ambitious proposals. Covert action was about nuisance value, supporting existing forces, and exploiting existing cleavages. This was particularly the case when it came to Eastern Europe, where SIS took a long-term and gradualist approach. Even the more ambitious operations, such as the attempted liberation of Albania and the overthrow of Mossadeq, began as pilot schemes to be escalated incrementally. Sometimes, SIS officers argued, the best way to determine capabilities and hone technique was by conducting smaller-scale operations and then expanding them upwards.

Disruption has therefore long characterized British covert action. Such activity is more often associated with post-Cold War operations. Facing complex transnational adversaries and operating in a risk-averse climate, policymakers prefer short-term means of disrupting targets, from terrorists to drug smugglers, to longer-term means of resolving a threat. Disruption has, in fact, been a core theme since the early Cold War. The pinprick approach was essentially disruptive, whether through planting stink bombs in Communist Party meetings or instigating go-slow campaigns in Czechoslovakian factories. In the mid-1950s, Harold Macmillan, as foreign secretary, called for SIS to disrupt anti-British activities at source.[13] Since then, Britain has used covert action to disrupt Egyptian subversive bases in Yemen; Indonesian military activity against Malaysia; supply routes feeding the Omani insurgency; terrorists in Northern Ireland, Uruguay, and Lebanon; and Soviet activity in Afghanistan. Most recently, Alex Younger, chief of SIS, has spoken of his agency as an 'upstream service' seeking to disrupt threats as early as possible and as far away from the UK as possible. He added, 'we want to be playing in their half of the pitch, not ours'.[14]

Caution created another strategic weakness. Covert action can only do so much to disrupt an adversary. Limitations and constraints risked disconnecting means from ends. Covert operations may be tactically successful in discrediting a specific Communist Party official or eliminating a specific terrorist, but they may not have much strategic impact if the aim is liberation or forcing an adversary to withdraw from territory. This was exacerbated by consistent refusal to back operations with conventional military force. At best, therefore, covert action led to attrition, as in Yemen and Indonesia, or created space for successful negotiations, as attempted in Iran. At worst, it was tactically successful yet ultimately futile, as certain special forces operations against Indonesia and, more recently, in Syria demonstrated.[15] Ironically some covert actions, designed as an alternative to military intervention, only succeed if they are backed by the very military intervention they were supposed to obviate. Afghanistan in the 1980s forms a potential exception, but the scale of American covert action was unprecedented and *im*plausible.

Refusal to back covert action with force led to failed uprisings. Tough security forces quashed rebels whilst the West watched from the sidelines. That is not to say that covert action should be followed through with conventional military force; doing so without considering the consequences of escalation would have been reckless. It does, however, raise the question of whether to support dissidents covertly in the first place, and this did vex Britain's planners—albeit for practical rather than ethical reasons. Policymakers had to consider carefully whether covert action could deliver the stated objectives, how it fitted into broader policy, and how to prevent it from escalating into an unending commitment.

Maximizing deniability

Stemming from both Whitehall caution and SIS's lack of paramilitary capability, British planners consistently strove to maximize deniability. They avoided overthrowing a regime themselves, but neither did they always directly arrange for someone else to do it. On the surface this seemed sensible, as it reduced the likelihood of operations being traced back to London. Yet, the quest for deniability involved a bargain in which Whitehall took a more indirect role, sacrificing control for the sake of anonymity. It was often a hands-off approach, which meant that covert action sometimes became more dangerous. The quest to maximize deniability took three interlinking forms: empowering rebels, creating conditions conducive to a particular outcome, and working through allies.

From the days of the Special Operations Executive (SOE), Britain liked to operate at arm's length by empowering rebels and partisans rather than taking offensive action itself.[16] This idea remained in place after the war when SIS continued to lack a paramilitary capability comparable to that of the CIA. SIS-trained Albanian émigrés, discreetly encouraged the Indonesian military's crackdown against communism, and assisted Polish dissident networks. In fact, British covert action was often primarily about facilitation, such as during the early years of the Soviet–Afghan war when Carrington merely lobbied other countries to act.

More indirectly still, SIS often created the conditions conducive to a coup. Officers covertly laid the groundwork for what then appeared to be a spontaneous uprising. As Julian Amery explained in 1956, Britain's anti-Nasser policy amounted to 'creating the very conditions in which he may well be overthrown'.[17] The *modus operandi* from 1951 and Iran onwards involved creating a class with a vested interest in cooperation, finding the right horse to back, and shaping developments by propaganda, bribery, and false flag activity.

In deciding which faction to support, Britain traditionally turned to strong men and exiled royalty. The Foreign Office knew overthrowing Mossadeq would mean an authoritarian regime and that General Zahedi was a ruthless strongman.[18] Similarly, diplomats showed few qualms during secret overtures made towards the Muslim Brotherhood and the former Syrian dictator Adib Shishakli among others. According to the Foreign Office's Evelyn Shuckburgh, British policy to counter Soviet subversion in the Middle East 'relied partly upon the ability of "strong men" like Nuri, General Zahedi and Colonel Nasser to suppress Communist activities'.[19] The other faction of choice was exiled royalty. One diplomat candidly summarized Middle Eastern policy in the 1950s as one of 'supporting feudal and monarchical regimes to serve our ends'.[20] Covert action favoured King Zog during operations in Albania and Egypt, and royalist factions in the Yemeni civil war. From the late 1970s, British officials favoured the exiled Ethiopian prince against newly installed military rulers, the rebel Cambodian faction headed by another ousted prince, and, in Afghanistan, initially sought to work through the former king to aid the mujahideen, before the Americans interjected. It is also worth noting that Britain often preferred to work with external forces, such as exiled royalists or dissidents, to achieve their goal. It was rarer to try to cultivate contacts inside governments in order to effect change from within, an approach for which the Yugoslavs strongly criticized Western operations in Albania.

Britain's indirect, maximum deniability, approach was perhaps most pronounced when it came to assassination. This was—and remains—a taboo subject within Britain's secret state. On the rare occasions it surfaced, such as in Uganda, Thailand, and Yugoslavia, officials objected swiftly and firmly. SIS is not, and has never been, in the business of killing people. This, however, is not necessarily the full story. Time and again, SIS and Foreign Office planners created a climate conducive to assassination, thereby maintaining distance and deniability. There are surprisingly many examples. In April 1953, British propaganda and subversion whipped anti-Mossadeq forces into a fervour which led to the murder of General Mahmoud Afshartus. Two years later, Fergie Dempster, the SIS officer in Saigon, tried to start a row within the Hanoi politburo intended to spark a chain of events leading to the assassination of the North Vietnamese president, Ho Chi Minh.[21] It did not happen: Ho lived to see the backs of the British, French, and Americans. At around the same time, SIS knew that had the opposition successfully taken power in Egypt, Nasser would have been killed.[22] Between 1960 and 1961, a series of covert operations, conducted in conjunction with the CIA, created the climate in which Patrice Lumumba was assassinated. In the 1970s and 1980s, British propaganda and policies in Northern Ireland engendered an atmosphere conducive to collusion, resulting in the deaths of numerous republicans. More recently, evidence has emerged of SIS and GCHQ complicity in American targeted killing operations in Yemen and elsewhere. Taken together, a pattern exists of indirect involvement in killings, without British agents having to pull the trigger—or even give the order—themselves.

Alliances also maximized deniability. Not only did they serve as a practical means of executing and bankrolling covert action, but encouraging other states' involvement lengthened the chain of responsibility between London and the theatre. Intelligence may be a jealously guarded area of state activity, but Whitehall officials were keen to entice external support for certain covert operations. The CIA was a prime target, and the British successfully solicited American assistance to overthrow Mossadeq in 1953. This was obviously useful in terms of drawing on Washington's resources, but, as CIA officers recognized, London had little to lose if the operation went wrong. In the end, it succeeded, but America still endured the bulk of recriminations once the intervention came to light.

Iran was not a one-off. Britain tried to draw America into covert operations against Syria later in the decade. SIS and the Foreign Office then used Iraq as a regional partner to undertake the covert action. When the first operation collapsed in late 1956 it was Baghdad that shouldered the blame, with Syria publicly labelling the operation 'the Iraqi Plot'. When attempting to overthrow the Syrian regime again the following year, both London and Washington recognized the importance of working through Arab states. By the 1980s, Carrington was lobbying regional governments to support the Afghan resistance. Meanwhile, in Southeast Asia, Britain agreed to train Thai special forces who, in turn, trained Cambodian rebels fighting the new Vietnamese-sponsored regime in Phnom Penh. In each case, Britain sought to lengthen the chain of responsibility and ensure the maximum deniability possible.

The most important alliance was, of course, with the US. As with the broader intelligence relationship, British covert action cannot be considered in isolation from CIA activity. A clear shift has taken place since the end of the Second World War, when the nascent CIA hoped to learn from British experience and expertise. In return, SIS looked across the Atlantic for money. Gradually, however, and as early as the Albanian operation, American officials became disillusioned with SIS capabilities, whilst British diplomats saw the CIA as dangerously cavalier. Nonetheless, SIS informed the CIA of nearly every one of its covert operations in the early Cold War.

Despite the Suez debacle and much sniping from both sides, pragmatic cooperation continued throughout the 1950s and 1960s. This time it was Washington which deemed SIS reckless in some of its approaches to the Middle East, whilst Whitehall lambasted American hypocrisy over covert action in the colonies. The interdependent working group system collapsed amongst accusations of a lack of intelligence-sharing in the early 1960s, and American ambivalence towards operations in Yemen and Indonesia frustrated British diplomats shortly afterwards. Nonetheless, Britain tried to work alongside America wherever possible. By the 1980s, it was the Americans who set the agenda and, in part seeking to bypass congressional restrictions, urged SIS involvement in their own schemes. British special forces faced a crossroads in the mid–2000s regarding whether to adopt the more industrial American approach to counter-terrorism. Eventually, they agreed.

Since 1945, both sides have misled the other, manipulated the other, tried to recruit the other, and restrained the other. Nonetheless, four factors ensured Anglo–American cooperation persisted, despite various disagreements (i) British desire to maximize influence by providing unique or complementary functions and compensating for its dwindling military input; (ii) both sides' attempts to gain access to increased flows of intelligence which might not otherwise have been shared; (iii) both sides' attempts to restrain the other if deemed to be going too far; and (iv) to share burdens and outsource dirty work. Britain's flexible and nimble approach to covert action, alongside loose parliamentary oversight and ministerial ability to neither confirm nor deny, are greatly appreciated by allies in America—and across the world. A former director of GCHQ and intelligence and security coordinator, David Omand, caricatured the Anglo–American intelligence relationship nicely in 2013: 'We have the brains. They have the money. It's a collaboration that's worked very well.'[23]

Policy integration

British caution also derives from sensible attempts to integrate covert action into policy. Ever since the friction between SIS and SOE during the Second World War, senior policymakers have made this a fundamental principle in Whitehall's approach. Covert action, as Norman Brook put it, must be a servant of policy: those conducting operations should not be able to go rogue.[24] This is important from a democratic and accountability perspective, but it is also important practically. Given its inherent secrecy, covert action risks operating in its own isolated realm, and disconnection from policy is a common cause of covert action failure. It should be a deniable means of achieving stated policy goals, rather than a secret foreign policy competing with the regular diplomats.

To achieve this, SIS remained closely tied to the Foreign Office and responsible to the foreign secretary. Very few occasions exist when SIS conducted operations without ministerial approval, broadly defined. Problems, however, arose when action cut across multiple policy areas, particularly defence. Officials had to develop separate clearance procedures for special military operations. Even today, military and intelligence aspects of covert action go up separately to the defence and foreign secretaries respectively. When debating these issues from 1945, officials fluctuated between what were known as 'horizontal' and 'vertical' approaches.

The former involved inter-departmental committees to coordinate and scrutinize covert action whilst ensuring it remained harmonious to broader policy, including defence, objectives. On the downside, they proved cumbersome, often ended in gridlock, and, if too large, prevented discussion of the most sensitive matters. The latter was more departmentally orientated and ensured that covert action was fully integrated into the policy process with flexibility and speed. It allowed the Foreign Office to dominate. With the diplomats fighting to maintain control and the military lobbying for a greater voice, covert action machinery seemed to go around in circles. The chiefs of staff continually pressured the diplomats, who then countered with fancy bureaucratic footwork by keeping certain committees secret or even creating front committees designed purely to contain military sniping and allow the chiefs to vent their frustration in a controlled environment. The National Security Council serves as a neat combination of the vertical and horizontal approaches. It coordinates objectives and sets the direction of travel, but covert action is devised and authorized within departmental, mainly Foreign Office, channels.

Within the Whitehall system of bargaining and compromise, the role of individuals is still important. Some ministers have taken different approaches to covert action. Ernest Bevin was initially intransigent about sanctioning operations. More recently, William Hague was a thoughtful judge of proposals when foreign secretary.[25] The history of British covert action is not defined by rogue elephants, but has been shaped by strong, even maverick, participants. For all their bluster, interventions by Amery, McLean, and even Brian Crozier, did encourage ministers to toughen their stance at various points. Some prime ministers themselves, notably Churchill and Thatcher, were more naturally inclined towards covert action than others, although remarkable continuity existed inside Number 10. Likewise, chiefs of SIS also had differing approaches, with Maurice Oldfield being more sceptical than, say, Dick White, who, despite having a reputation for temperance sanctioned—and even normalized—numerous operations. British covert action is a product of personality, departmental rivalries, and bureaucratic processes, as well as a rational response to a rising threat.

Success, failure, and impact

Judging the effectiveness of covert action is incredibly difficult. Operations can be a short-term success but a long-term failure. They can be an operational success, in that they stayed secret and were executed effectively, but a failure if they did not achieve the required impact. Measuring success against stated objectives is equally complicated given that those objectives, a result of compromise and bargaining, seemed to shift on an almost weekly basis. There were times when even those planning covert action did not seem to know the ultimate goals. It is also extremely difficult to judge the outcome covert action had on history and the way in which events would have unfurled had certain operations not taken place. This is an issue of agency and impact, and it is important not to overplay the hidden Western hand at the expense of local forces which may have achieved their goal regardless. Covert action stands more chance of success if it builds on pre-existing forces, and it is difficult to separate the two when assessing impact. To make matters worse, numerous successes may not yet have come to light.

Propaganda has formed the cornerstone of much British covert action, yet measuring its success is especially difficult. In 1970, even the Foreign Office admitted that it was practically impossible to determine whether the Information Research Department (IRD) actually worked.[26] Before then, success was judged simply on whether broadcasts could be heard in a certain area, with little attempt to monitor their impact on behaviour. The best that can be said is that propaganda had some broader and intangible impact in shaping perceptions. The effects of propaganda, even in a totalitarian state, can only ever be partial.[27] With parsimonious ministers demanding demonstrable results to justify investment, this casualness is now changing. The Research, Information and Communications Unit (RICU) is taking advantage of developments in information communications technology to monitor behaviour by examining the Internet activity of individual targets. Others believe that Britain has never been much good at information operations. This is partly because the government has never invested enough in propaganda activity, especially since the heyday of the IRD in the mid-1950s, and partly because it is difficult for liberal democracies to manipulate the press and construct a narrative behind which a pluralist society can rally.[28]

Despite these methodological problems, we can say with confidence that British covert action has had a mixed record since 1945. There have been obvious failures in Albania, Egypt, and Syria, whilst covert action in the colonies amounted to little. But there have also been apparent successes in Iran, Indonesia, and Oman. Other examples are more open to interpretation: from Northern Ireland, where the secret war disrupted and discredited the IRA but often proved counterproductive, to Libya, where, after initial failure, covert action helped overthrow President Gaddafi but created a vacuum for international terrorism. A similar allegation is often made against operations in Afghanistan in the 1980s. Likewise, covert action in 1960s Yemen could be a success, insofar as it prolonged the civil war, helped create 'Egypt's Vietnam', damaged Nasser, and precipitated defeat in the Six Day War with Israel in June 1967.[29] Yet it did little to prevent Britain's ignominious scuttle from Aden in 1967.

Any success, however defined, in covert action has depended on several factors. It had to be integrated into policy and serve a broader strategic purpose. For example, covert action in Afghanistan in the 1980s complemented overt diplomatic and economic pressure on the Soviets. By contrast, early operations in Syria in the late 1940s and some targeting Nasser the following decade ran parallel to official foreign policy and floundered.

Covert action had to be properly coordinated, with limited objectives and clear parameters. This was the case regarding the early pinprick approach in Eastern Europe and under the Joint Action Committee in the mid- to late 1960s. Planners knew what they were allowed to do and, equally importantly, what they were not allowed to do. Without such a framework in place, covert action drifted and was ineffectual, as demonstrated shortly after the Second World War. Likewise, covert action struggled when there were too many variables involved. Managing Iraq, Jordan, and Turkey when planning operations against Syria proved difficult in 1957.

Covert action stood more chance of success when built on existing movements in areas where SIS already had agents and experience. This was the case in Iran, Yemen, and Afghanistan. It was far more difficult to design and deliver operations from scratch, as proved the case in China after the Second World War. Likewise, successful disruption was more likely when exploiting pre-existing tensions amongst targets. This was the case when exploiting Cold War 'contradictions' as well as during counter-terrorism in Latin America, Northern Ireland, and the Middle East. The third parties to be supported proved equally crucial in determining success—but were often problematic. Covert action was likely doomed to failure when Britain relied on émigrés, who proved factional, prone to security leaks, and lacking contacts in their home country. Following on from this, accurate intelligence was crucial for success. Planners needed to understand the ability and strengths of the dissidents, the level of government security, and the nuances of conditions on the ground. Failure in Albania can, in part, be traced back to a misunderstanding of each. Planners also had to understand the nature of the threat, including whether it was externally driven, for example from Moscow, or based on internal disaffection. This was necessary to divide and discredit targets, shaping the propaganda message and determining the scope of operations.

These ideals are not easy to achieve. British covert action is a constant balance between action and caution; between encouraging the spirit of resistance without creating false hope; and between ensuring a speedy and flexible response without sacrificing scrutiny, inter-departmental harmony, and a consensus-based approach. This begs the question, as important as it is difficult to answer, of whether covert action had an impact.

Intelligence was an important factor in Britain's comparatively smooth decolonization process.[30] Yet despite appetite in Whitehall, covert action had little impact in colonial territories. The main area in which it played a role, complementing more visible measures, was in helping to ensure the 'least bad' option took power after independence, in places such as Nigeria and Zambia, and to ensure as much British influence as possible. Covert action helped mask decline in other places such as the Middle East. Yet it could only stem the tide of nationalism for so long. The failure at Suez, Jordan's expulsion of the British commander of the Arab Legion in 1956, the Iraqi coup overthrowing Britain's closest ally in the region two years later, and the fact that Nasser stayed in power until 1970 all attest that covert action and the broader policy it served had little material effect. Meanwhile, plots and subterfuge gave rise to mistrust of the British across the region.[31] At the same time, however, covert action did make life difficult for the likes of Egypt, Syria, and Yemen—and there is no way of knowing what these countries could have achieved if under less pressure from SIS.

Covert action did not win the Cold War. Historians have posited many different explanations for the fall of the Soviet Union, from Gorbachev's reforms and desire to give peace a chance to Reagan's anti-communist policies dragging the Kremlin to the negotiating table. Other important factors include disillusionment in communist ideology, shaped by de-Stalinization in 1956 and repression in Hungary and Czechoslovakia; the faltering Soviet economy; the restrictive political system; overstretch in support of

Cuba, Vietnam, and southern African guerrillas; and the spread of liberal ideas.[32] Indeed, by the mid-1970s, Foreign Office planners thought broader changes in transnational communications had made covert action less useful. They felt that the freer movement of people across Europe, conducted entirely through non-governmental channels, was having a much bigger impact on spreading Western values than any amount of secret radios, smuggled literature, or cultural warfare.[33]

Yet covert action—and the broader policy it supported—played a role in pushing these forces along. Pinpricks and disruption formed the rhythm of Britain's approach. Although rarely making a difference alone, they quietly worked away in the background creating the space in which a broader policy might be successful. Long-term operations against the Soviets helped spark paranoia and purges at home, exploited divisions to foment nationalist unrest, highlighted oppression, and frustrated Soviet adventures. In 1953, one American diplomat distilled Britain's approach as 'pragmatic and cold-blooded'. The British, he wrote, were 'given to seeking gains piecemeal while avoiding anything which might call for a showdown'.[34] This was fair and by the late 1970s British diplomats sought to foster a more questioning attitude inside Eastern Europe, but knew that their role had to be 'so gradual that the Soviet Union finds no easy way of drawing a line between the acceptable and the unacceptable'.[35] Whilst it is impossible to isolate the impact of covert action—and the British hand specifically—from internal factors, it played a part in gradually, intangibly, giving history a helping hand.

At the same time, however, the psychological effect of covert action helped to prolong the Cold War. Fear of Western subversion created paranoia inside Moscow, with leaders assuming that such activity represented a serious attempt to overthrow their regime. Western covert action may have been portrayed internally as defensive, but the Soviets saw it as anything but. In return, some in London adopted similar attitudes about Soviet covert action. They feared that it posed a serious threat to the entire system and so saw subversion everywhere. Others took on broader, less ideological, fears about treachery and spies within. All of this perpetuated Cold War as a hostile and uneasy peace, cementing the idea of the Soviet Union as a great power.[36] It hardened the adversarial image of each side.[37]

SIS now prefer narrow, clearly defined, and tactical objectives against which outcomes can be definitively measured. SIS judge covert action a success if it disrupts a known terrorist attack, if it prevents goods from reaching a particular target, or if it stops a particular person from boarding a plane. It is these specific outcomes which intelligence leaders report back to ministers.[38] They are keen to point to a lack of attacks on British soil and recent setbacks suffered by the Islamic State group as evidence of success, but covert action—alongside the broader military responses—has done little to offer longer-term solutions to problems of political violence across the Middle East. Disruption can only achieve so much.

Covert action has proved useful in other, less obvious or direct, ways. It injected a real contribution into an otherwise asymmetric Anglo–American relationship and served as a force-multiplier for an impecunious nation. British flexibility, skill, and lack of oversight are valued by allies and still seen as an important asset in its ability to operate on the international stage. According to one former chief of SIS, covert operations are the 'last redoubt of our national sovereignty'.[39] Britain successfully punched above its weight during the Cold War—and continues to do so today. The reasons are many: its soft power, reputation as an international power broker, relationship with the US, armaments industry, and its global connections dating back to the days of empire.[40] Importantly, covert action is bound up in many of these. Soft power has long been accentuated by propaganda, both attributable and unattributable; the Anglo–American relationship fostered numerous covert actions; intelligence is intertwined with arms sales; and Britain has long drawn on its global connections both physically and in terms of human networks to launch influence operations.

Covert action is a highly useful tool in the state's foreign and security policy arsenal. It is also an inherently limited one. At best, covert action achieves little on its own. At worst, it is counterproductive and can be highly damaging to a state's long-term security and political interests. Covert action can only be used effectively if it serves the broader policy to multiply existing capabilities, create space for negotiations, or enforce sanctions. Covert action is not a silver bullet, and governments must be careful about how to deploy it in order to achieve maximum benefit and avoid the dangerous side effects.

The present as an interruption to the past

Beware the neologists.[41] Not everything in international relations is new and the past provides an important prism through which to understand the present. In some ways covert action, and intelligence more broadly, are changing, but *plus ça change, plus c'est la même chose.*

One such area is the challenge to government secrecy. Investigative journalists, whistle-blowers, and global civil society can shine a bright light on the darkest corridors of Britain's secret state. Operations are now less likely to remain plausibly deniable for long. This is increasingly the case in a digital, globalized world: more people have access to databases of classified information in the first place; massive files of documents can be shared instantly across borders; and smartphones turn citizens into aspiring photojournalists. Some have termed it 'regulation by revelation'.[42] In 2011, policymakers deployed special forces to Libya, but Al Jazeera soon uploaded photos of them to the Internet.[43] Two years later, Edward Snowden, an American contractor for the National Security Agency, was able to leak data not only on mass surveillance programmes but also on British covert action. When prime ministers and foreign secretaries approve covert action they must now assess whether they can publicly justify the operation if it leaks. Yet, Britain has long been cautious and policymakers worried about exposure as soon as the Second World War ended. The CIA failure at the Bay of Pigs brought the point home to Whitehall and fears reached new heights in the mid-1970s when SIS chiefs panicked about their own secrets spilling out from various congressional inquiries into CIA activities. Delayed disclosure may have become more imminent, but it is not altogether new.

The cyber domain will be important in the future of covert action. In an era of macro data and micro targeting, information communications technology offers intelligence services a discreet means of manipulating reality, both real and online. RICU relies on close targeting, borrowed from the world of advertising, to promote its messages, and GCHQ now possesses capabilities for online covert action. It should be remembered, however, that much of this activity provides a cyber-twist on classic tradecraft. GCHQ can launch false flag operations, discredit terrorists, and disrupt operations. These have all been constants in the British experience. The change is one of means, actor, and ease rather than principle.

Twenty-first-century threats are diffuse. The UK operates in a networked world in which political authority carries less agency than before. Mass communication, social movements, and grass-roots change have all created more variables to control and it is perhaps now far harder for the state to effect manageable change.[44] Covert action will therefore become more small-scale, tactical, and disruptive. Yet as we have seen, pinpricks and disruption operations date back to the early Cold War and form a key tradition in British approaches. That said, developments in technology and big data do leave the door open to more ambitious operations, as allegedly demonstrated by Russian interference in the 2016 American presidential election. Even so, the principle—of influencing an electoral outcome—is, of course, nothing new.

Russia still poses a threat to Western interests, and many think the Kremlin is changing the landscape of covert action. Moscow's so-called 'hybrid warfare' combines propaganda, cyber operations, subversion, disruption, and supporting local militias and insurgents. It is a holistic approach bringing together a wide range of players, from secret intelligence to the fisheries ministry. In 2016, Alex Younger, the chief of SIS, described it as a fundamental threat to British sovereignty and accused Putin of using hybrid warfare to undermine Western democracy.[45] Russian annexation of Crimea in 2014 is the most notorious and successful example of such activity. Elsewhere, American intelligence blames Russia for attempting to influence the 2016 US presidential election. Others have pointed to influence operations in Holland, France, the Czech Republic, Austria, and Hungary designed to undermine the European Union. Russia also stands accused of shipping illegal immigrants into Norway and Sweden, spreading disinformation about migrant sexual offences in Germany, launching cyberattacks against Estonia, despatching agents provocateurs to Latvia to stir up minority Russian groups, inserting friendly officials into the Turkish civil service, and even plotting to assassinate the leader of Montenegro as a means of preventing the country from joining NATO. All of this is deniable—and indeed denied by Moscow. The aim, as one expert on Soviet intelligence put it, is for Russian action to be sufficient to 'keep the wound bleeding' but insufficient to warrant massive retaliation.[46] The Kremlin is operating in a grey space, blurring the lines between internal disorder and external intervention, acceptability and unacceptability: an idea remarkably familiar to those planning British covert action behind the Iron Curtain during the Cold War.

Intelligence officers and policymakers alike are debating how best to counter this threat. Conversations taking place across Whitehall in 2017 echoed those of the early Cold War. The ghosts of Julian Amery, John Slessor, Ivone Kirkpatrick, and George Young stalk the corridors of ministries and think tanks. What is legitimate in peacetime? Should Britain fight fire with fire? How proactive should covert action be? How can covert responses be integrated into the broader promotion of good governance? Russia is prodding and poking until it hits Western resistance, but at what point should resistance begin? The similarities are unsurprising, for hybrid warfare is not as novel as many assume. Russian activities in Crimea and eastern Ukraine mirrored those against Poland as long ago as the 1920s.[47] KGB operations to influence European elections took place in the late 1940s and 1950s. Soviet intelligence spread disinformation accusing American soldiers of sex attacks in Germany to undermine NATO, a scheme remarkably similar to so-called 'fake news' accusing migrants of sex attacks in Germany to undermine the European Union. Even the fear of hybrid warfare, as operating in permanent support of some clearly defined foreign policy goal, is reminiscent of Cold War thinking. It perpetuates an idea of a powerful Kremlin, a scheming and dangerous chess master needing to be countered.[48] Russia may be up to its old tricks, but Britain has been here before. Covert action will remain a constant as long as the UK competes for influence, for a global role. Its politicians will shout loudly about their achievements, but, beneath the surface, if we listen carefully enough, the rhythm of the quiet option can still be heard.

Notes

INTRODUCTION

1. CAB121/305, Selborne, 'The Future of Special Operations', CoS(45)360, 27/5/45.
2. Adams, 'Elizabeth I and the Sovereignty of the Netherlands, 1576–1585', pp.315–16.
3. Zamir, *The Secret Anglo-French War in the Middle East*, pp.83–4, p.17.
4. Satia, *Spies in Arabia*, pp.7, 49.
5. Linderman, *Rediscovering Irregular Warfare*, pp.43–4.
6. See Foot, *SOE*.
7. See Garnett, *The Secret History of PWE*.
8. See Herman, *Intelligence Power in Peace and War*, p.2.
9. ISC, *Annual Report 2004–2005*, (London: Crown, 2005), para.20; ISC, *Annual Report 2007–2008*, (London: Crown, 2008), para.75; ISC, *Annual Report 2008–2009*, (London: Crown, 2009), paras 69, 89.
10. GCHQ, 'Cyber Integration: The Art of the Possible', *SigDev Spy Conference*, (2012), powerpoint slides available via NBC News, *The Snowden Files: British Spies used Sex and 'Dirty Tricks'*, (2014), http://msnbcmedia.msn.com/i/msnbc/sections/news/snowden_cyber_offensive1_nbc_document.pdf.
11. Army Field Manual Volume One, Combined Arms Operations, Part 10, Counter Insurgency Operations (Strategic and Operational Guidelines), Revised and Updated Version, (2007), Annex A, para.17.
12. Private information.
13. Ibid.
14. Doherty, *Public Law*, p.498.
15. SIS website, 'Our Mission'.
16. 1947 National Security Act, quoted in O'Brien, 'Covert Action', p.24.
17. For a discussion on Special Forces see Finlan, *Special Forces*, p.xi.
18. Stanley, *How Propaganda Works*, p.165.
19. Private information.
20. CAB 134/4, AC(O) Minutes, 3AC(O)(50)10th Meeting, 1 March 1950.
21. Louis, 'Britain and the Overthrow of the Mossadeq Government', p.131.
22. On disambiguation see Scott, 'Secret Intelligence, Covert Action, and Clandestine Diplomacy'.
23. Goodman, 'The British Way in Intelligence', p.128.

24. For discussion see Wiant, 'A Guide to the Teaching About Covert Action', p.55.

25. Aldrich, *Intelligence and the War Against Japan*, pp.222–9; CAB163/6, Cavendish Bentinck and Capel Dunn, 'The Intelligence Machine'.

26. FO1093/375, Menzies, 'The Capabilities of Secret Service in Peace in Support of an Overall Political Plan', 20/1/48.

27. See Wiant, 'A Guide to the Teaching About Covert Action', p.56.

28. 'CAB21/2750, Proposed Activity Behind the Iron Curtain' (Third Revise), AC(O)(50)52, November 1950.

29. CAB301/17, Brook, 'The Secret Intelligence and Security Services', March 1951, para.20.

30. CAB176/6, 'Future of SOE—Draft report to the Chiefs of Staff', para.3 attached to minutes of the second meeting of an ad hoc committee on the future of SOE chaired by Cavendish Bentinck. JIC/835/45, 19/6/45.

31. See Lulushi, *Operation Valuable Fiend*; Aldrich, *The Hidden Hand*.

32. Davies, *MI6*, p.224.

33. DEFE28/1, Ward to Elliott, Attached: ' "Deception" Organisation', 20/2/50.

34. This subject is rarely discussed but see Dover, 'For Queen and Company', pp.683–708. See also Phythian, *The Politics of British Arms Sales*.

35. CHIL: Evidence of Director of Special Forces 2003–2005, (2010), p.10.

36. See Hashimoto, *The Twilight of the British Empire*.

37. Berkowitz and Goodman, 'The Logic of Covert Action'.

38. Many important works on British history and foreign policy overlook the role of covert action, despite it being a key tool to implement policy. See, for example, Reynolds, *Britannia Overruled*; Sanders, *Losing an Empire*; Young, *Britain and the World in the Twentieth Century*. Likewise some of the more influential books on twentieth-century history more broadly give little weight to subterranean activity. See, for example, Young and Kent, *International Relations since 1945*. See also Dunbabin, *The Post-Imperial Age*, which offers a brief mention of covert action in relation to countering Iran and maintaining access to oil, p.346. Many works on British decolonization also traditionally neglected the intelligence angle. See, for example, Brendon, *The Decline and Fall of the British Empire*; Hyam, *Britain's Declining Empire*. For discussion of this see Andrew and Walton, 'Still the "Missing Dimension"'. Wm Roger Louis offered an early antidote (see 'Introduction'), whilst Calder Walton has more recently offered a compelling account of MI5's role in decolonization (see *Empire of Secrets*).

39. For an impressive recent example see Callanan, *Covert Action in the Cold War*. See also Knott, *Secret and Sanctioned*; Daugherty, *Executive Secrets*; Long, *The CIA and the Soviet Bloc*. The classic and most influential texts are also from the American perspective. See, for example, Godson *Covert Action*; and Treverton, *Covert Action*.

40. See Jeffery, *MI6*; Davies, *MI6*; Andrew, *Defence of the Realm*; Aldrich, *GCHQ*; Goodman, *The Joint Intelligence Committee*.

41. For an example of this in particularly influential works see Lowenthal, *Intelligence*, p.229; and Andrew, *Defence of the Realm*, p.460.

42. Some of the former is written by sceptics and critics such as Bloch and Fitzgerald, *British Intelligence and Covert Action*. Books written by journalists risk falling into this category too. For an example which treads the fine line effectively see Corera, *The Art of Betrayal*. For examples of scholarly but narrow case study approaches see Jones, 'The Preferred Plan'; Louis, 'Britain and the Overthrow of the Mossadeq Government'; Cormac, 'Coordinating Covert Action'; and Tuck, 'The Limits of Covert Action'. Richard Aldrich offers a more comprehensive overview of intelligence, including covert action, in his seminal *The Hidden Hand*. This, however, only covers the period until the mid-1950s and thousands of documents have been released since its publication in 2001.

43. Callanan uses this categorization effectively when outlining American covert action in the early Cold War. See Callanan, *Covert Action in the Cold War*.

44. See Hennessy, *Muddling Through*.

45. CAB176/6, 'Future of SOE—Draft report to the Chiefs of Staff', memorandum attached to minutes of the second meeting of an ad hoc committee on the future of SOE chaired by Cavendish-Bentinck, JIC/835/45, 19/6/45, para.3; CAB121/305, Selborne, 'The Future of Special Operations', CoS(45)360, 27/5/45, para.4B. For detailed discussions of the wartime relationship between SOE and others in Whitehall see Aldrich, *The Hidden Hand*, pp.43–63; Jeffery, *MI6*, pp.352–60.

46. BOD: MS.Eng.hist.*c.*1001–3, Stephenson to Selborne, 21/6/45.

47. CAB301/53, Selborne, 'The Future of Special Operations', 22/5/45, Annex to: copy of letter dated 22 May 1945 from Minister of Economic Warfare to Secretary, Chiefs of Staff Committee, COS(45)360(O), 27/5/45.

48. Ibid.

49. CAB120/827, Eden to Churchill, PM/44/716, 23/11/44.

50. Wilkinson and Astley, *Gubbins and SOE*, p.232.

51. CAB301/48, Bland Committee, 'Future Organisation of the Secret Intelligence Service (SIS): The Bland Report', 12/10/44, pp.2, 16.

52. Jeffery, *MI6*, p.630.

53. For detailed discussion see Davies, 'From Special Operations to Special Political Action', pp.55–76.

54. CAB301/17, Brook, 'The Secret Intelligence and Security Services', March 1951, para.3.

55. Davies, 'From Special Operations to Special Political Action', p.61.

56. MacKenzie, *Special Force*, pp.20–2, 32, 36; Macintyre, *Rogue Heroes*, pp.308–10.

57. Although the SBS title was adopted by the Royal Marines and the SAS was resurrected as part of the Territorial Army in 1947. See MacKenzie, *Special Force*.

58. Jeffery, *MI6*, p.620.

59. AIR19/816, 'Extract from Conclusion of COS(46)12th Meeting, held on 23rd January 1946'.

60. CAB301/48, Bland Committee, 'Future Organisation of the Secret Intelligence Service (SIS): The Bland Report', 12/10/44, p.16.

61. CAB121/305, 'Directive to Special Operations Executive', CoS(45)64, 10/11/45, para.1.
62. CAB121/305, CoS Minutes, CoS(46)12th Meeting, 23/1/46.
63. See Aldrich, 'Unquiet in Death'.
64. AIR19/816, 'Extract from Conclusion of COS(46)12th Meeting, held on 23rd January 1946'.
65. Jeffery, *MI6*, p.694.
66. See Lewis, *Changing Direction*; Folly, *Churchill, Whitehall and the Soviet Union*.
67. CAB301/17, Brook, 'The Secret Intelligence and Security Services', March 1951, para.15.
68. FOI: 'The SIS Role and the Relationship with Departments of State and the Armed Services in the Conduct of Deniable Operations in Conditions Short of War', JAC(64)3, 2/11/64.

CHAPTER I

1. FO371/66370, Peterson to FO, No.1375, 20/6/47.
2. Haslam, *Russia's Cold War*, pp.87–94. Andrew and Mitrokhin, *The Mitrokhin Archive*, pp.360–2.
3. Larres, 'Britain and the Cold War', p.143.
4. Hennessy, *Secret State*, p.20.
5. See Deighton, 'Britain and the Cold War, 1945–1955', p.188; Young and Kent, *International Relations since 1945*, pp.127–8.
6. KCLMA, SUEZOHP, 7, 'Transcript of Interview with Sir William Hayter Conducted by Anthony Gorst and W. Scott Lucas'.
7. Ibid.
8. The Colonial Office, Commonwealth Relations Office, and BBC all eventually became members as well.
9. DEFE11/275, Slim to Tedder, 22/1/49.
10. FO371/56885, Russia Committee Terms of Reference, 12/4/46.
11. Aldrich, *The Hidden Hand*, p.129.
12. FO371/56885, Sargent, 'Circular to Heads of Political and Functional Departments: Committee on Policy Towards Russia', 13/5/46; see also FO371/56832, Warner, 'The Soviet Campaign against this Country and our Response to it', 2/4/46; Schwartz, *Political Warfare against the Kremlin*, p.37.
13. FO371/56887, Ronald, 'Memorandum', October 1946.
14. See Haslam, *Near and Distant Neighbours*, pp.143–55.
15. Lomas, *Intelligence, Security and the Attlee Governments*, p.85.
16. FO371/56885, Sargent, 'Circular to Heads of Political and Functional Departments: Committee on Policy Towards Russia', 13/5/946; 'Committee on Policy Towards Russia: Anti-Communist Propaganda', 30/4/46; FO 371/56887, Kirkpatrick, 'Russia in the Middle East: Publicity Directive', 11/10/46; KCLMA, SUEZOHP, 7, 'Transcript of Interview with Sir William Hayter Conducted by Anthony Gorst and W. Scott Lucas'.

17. Aldrich, 'Putting Culture into the Cold War', pp.109–33.

18. Aldrich, *The Hidden Hand*, p.151.

19. Selverstone, *Constructing the Monolith*, p.41.

20. Defty, *Britain, America and Anti-Communist Propaganda*, p.44; Footitt, 'A Hideously Difficult Country', p.156.

21. Schwartz, *Political Warfare against the Kremlin*, p.44.

22. Vaughan, 'Cloak without Dagger', p.59.

23. Lane, 'Kirkpatrick, Sir Ivone Augustine (1897–1964)', *ODNB*.

24. Lomas, *Intelligence, Security, and the Attlee Governments*, p.86.

25. Aldrich, *The Hidden Hand*, p.135; Defty, *Brittan, America and Anti-Communist Propaganda*, pp.42–3.

26. Goodman, *Joint Intelligence Committee*, p.242.

27. Ibid., p.243.

28. Ibid.; Aldrich, *The Hidden Hand*, pp.135–6.

29. Goodman, *Joint Intelligence Committee*, p.243.

30. Aldrich, *The Hidden Hand*, pp.135–6; FO371/56887, Warner to Peterson, 29/10/46; Defty, *Britain, America, and Anti-Communist Propaganda*, p.43.

31. For broader discussions of British intelligence, propaganda and the Palestine conflict, see Utting, 'British Propaganda'; Utting, 'Palestine'; and Walton, 'British Intelligence and the Mandate of Palestine'. The most detailed discussion of this particular operation, with access to classified sources, can be found in Jeffery, *MI6*.

32. PREM8/624, Attlee to McNeil, April 1947.

33. Aldrich and Cormac, *The Black Door*, p.153.

34. Jeffery, *MI6*, pp.689–97.

35. Haslam, *Near and Distant Neighbours*, p.166.

36. Selverstone, *Constructing the Monolith*, p.77.

37. BOD: MS Sherfield 523, Gladwyn Jebb, 'The United Nations and the Inevitable War', 9/9/47.

38. Selverstone, *Constructing the Monolith*, p.77.

39. Aldrich, *The Hidden Hand*, pp.130–1.

40. Rob Cameron, 'Police close case on 1948 death of Jan Masaryk—murder, not suicide', Radio Prague, 6/1/04.

41. CAB129/25, 'The Threat to Western Civilisation', C(48)72, 3/3/48.

42. AIR75/116, Slessor to Liddell Hart, 22/1/48.

43. DEFE28/31, 'Special Operations', Joint Planning Staff, JP(47)118(8) Draft, 1012/47; FO 1093/375, Stapleton to Sargent, 23/12/47.

44. PREM8/1365, Bevin to Attlee, PM/49/69, 19/4/49; Aldrich, *The Hidden Hand*, p.145.

45. Lomas, *Intelligence, Security, and the Attlee Governments*, p.92.

46. FO1093/375, 'Anti-Communist propaganda', 12/3/48.

47. CAB195/6, Cabinet Minutes, C.M.19(48), 5/3/48.

48. CAB 134/53, 'Revised Draft Report', C(49)13(Revise), 11/7/49; FO1093/375, Circular telegram from Foreign Office to His Majesty's representatives abroad, 23/1/48.

49. FCO79/182, 'Information Research Department', Appendix A, 'Evolution of IRD', 1970.

50. KCLMA: SUEZOHP17-REDDAWAY, 'Interview with Norman Reddaway conducted by Anthony Gorst and W Scott Lucas', Suez Oral History Project.

51. BDOHP: 'H.H Tucker, commonly known as "Tommy" Tucker, [interviewed] by J. Hutson on 19th April 1996', p.5.

52. Private information.

53. FCO79/182, IRD, 'Information Research Department', Appendix A, 'Evolution of IRD', 1970.

54. Ibid.

55. Jenks, *British Propaganda and News Media in the Cold War*, pp. 104–6.

56. FCO79/182, 'Information Research Department', Appendix A, 'Evolution of IRD', 1970. See also Defty, *Britain, America, and Anti-Communist Propaganda*, p.77.

57. Schwartz, *Political Warfare against the Kremlin*, p.52.

58. Defty, *Britain, America, and Anti-Communist Propaganda*, p.63.

59. FO1093/375, 'Confidential Annex: Meeting of the Chiefs of Staff held on 10 March, 1948'.

60. FO1093/375, Sargent to Stapleton, 9/1/48.

61. FO1093/375, Menzies, 'The Capabilities of Secret Service in Peace in Support of an Overall Political Plan', 20/1/48.

62. Goodman, *Joint Intelligence Committee*, p.231.

63. Lomas, *Intelligence, Security, and the Attlee Governments*, p.120.

64. FO1093/375, Note by Hayter, 17/3/48; McNeil to Bevin, 21/4/48.

65. Gwinnett, 'Attlee, Bevin & Political Warfare', p.9.

66. Lomas, *Intelligence, Security, and the Attlee Governments*, p.105.

67. FO1093/375, Sargent to Bevin, 30/3/48.

68. FO1093/375, Handwritten note by Bevin on Sargent to Bevin, 30/3/48.

69. FO1093/375, McNeil to Bevin, 29/4/48; Hayter to Balfour, April 1948; CAB 134/53, 'Revised Draft Report', C(49)13(Revise), 11/7/49.

70. Corke, *US Covert Operations and Cold War Strategy*, p.51.

71. Daugherty, *Executive Secrets*, p.115.

72. FO1093/375, McNeil to Bevin, 19/4/48.

73. FO1093/375, Hayter to Balfour, April 1948.

74. FO1093/375, Balfour to Hayter, 25/5/48.

75. Corke, *US Covert Operations and Cold War Strategy*, p.58.

76. Selverstone, *Constructing the Monolith*, p.45.

77. FO1093/375, Sargent to Hayter and Warner, 13/548.

78. CAB21/3486, Minutes of an ad hoc Ministerial Meeting (Gen 164/1) chaired by Attlee, 6/1/47.

79. FO371/1687, Russia Committee Minutes, 4/3/48.

80. Ibid., 28/10/48; Defty, *Britain, America and Anti-Communist Propaganda*, pp.106–7.

81. FO 371/1687, Russia Committee Minutes, 28/10/48.

82. Lomas, *Intelligence, Security, and the Attlee Governments*, p.108.

83. Mistry, *The United States, Italy and the Origins of Cold War.*

84. Corke, *US Covert Operations and Cold War Strategy*, p.47; Callanan, *Covert Action in the Cold War*, p.40.

85. FO371/1687, Russia Committee Minutes, 16/12/48.

86. Defty, *Britain, America and Anti-Communist Propaganda*, pp.106–7. See also Callanan, *Covert Action in the Cold War*, pp.24–45, for an overview of the operation.

87. Haslam, *Russia's Cold War*, p.102.

88. Callanan, *Covert Action in the Cold War*, pp.43–4.

89. CREST, Hoyt S. Vandenburg, 'Section 202 of the Proposed National Security Act', 3/1/47.

90. See Brogi, *Confronting America.*

91. FO1093/375, Warner to Sargent, 6/2/48.

92. FO1093/375, Hayter to Balfour, April 1948; 'Clandestine Support for Anti-Communist Propaganda', 13/2/48.

93. FO1093/375, Hayter to Menzies, 2/6/48.

94. FO1093/375, Menzies to Hayter, 15/6/48.

95. Ibid., 24/4/48.

96. FO1093/375, Warner to Kirkpatrick, 31/5/48.

97. FO1093/375, Vienna to Hayter, 4/3/48.

98. FO1093/375, Note by Dean, 2/6/48.

99. Harrington, *Berlin on the Brink*, p.95.

100. FO1093/375, Sargent to Hayter and Warner, 13/5/48.

101. FO1093/447, Menzies to Sargent, 25/6/48; Note by Halford, 12/8/48.

102. FO1093/447, Hayter to Sargent, 15/10/48; Sargent to Bevin, 19/10/48.

103. FO1093/370, Confidential annex to CoS(48)139th Meeting, 29/9/48.

104. CAB134/53, 'Cabinet Committee on Communism: Revised Draft Report', C(49)13, 11/7/49.

105. Aldrich, 'Unquiet in Death', pp.201–2.

106. FO1093/375, Warner to Kirkpatrick, 31/5/48.

107. FO1093/375, Hayter to Menzies, 28/6/48.

108. FO1093/375, Anon., 'The Building up of a Liberal Party in Egypt', 13/2/48.

109. See discussions in FO1093/456, 'Baghdad: Expenditure from Special Funds'.

110. Zamir, *The Secret Anglo-French War*, pp.8, 17, 132.

111. Ibid., p.132.

112. FO1093/370, Confidential annex to CoS(48)139th Meeting, 29/9/48.

113. KCLMA: SUEZOHP, 18, 'Interview with Sir Patrick Reilly Conducted by W Scott Lucas'.

114. Campbell, 'Jebb, (Hubert Miles) Gladwyn, first Baron Gladwyn (1900–1996)', *ODNB.*

115. FO371/70272, 'Report of the sub-committee set up to examine the problem of planning in relation to policy towards the Soviet Union and the Soviet Orbit,' RC(25)48, 14/12/48 [hereafter Report of the sub-committee].

116. FO371/1687, Russia Committee Minutes, 25/11/48.

117. FO1093/563, 'The Cold War' draft aide-memoire for CIA, 24/3/49.
118. Selverstone, *Constructing the Monolith*, p.96; FO371/70272, 'Report of the sub-committee'.
119. FO371/77623, Russia Committee Minutes, 15/2/49.
120. FO371/70272, 'Report of the sub-committee'.
121. FO371/70272, 'Report of the sub-committee'.
122. Aldrich, *The Hidden Hand*, pp.165–6.
123. CREST: Anon, 'Our Relations with the Ukrainian Nationalists and the Crisis over BANDERA', 12/3/54.
124. Callanan, *Covert Action in the Cold War*, p.60.
125. Ibid., p.57.
126. Corera, *Art of Betrayal*, pp.55–6.
127. Haslam, *Near and Distant Neighbours*, p.154.
128. Pearce, *Spymaster*, pp.96–7.
129. Andrew and Gordievsky, *KGB*, p.389.
130. Ibid., p.383.
131. CREST: Anon, 'Our Relations with the Ukrainian Nationalists and the Crisis over BANDERA', 12/3/54.
132. Davies, 'From Special Operations to Special Political Action', p.63.
133. FO371/70272, 'Report of the sub-committee'; Cradock, *Know Your Enemy*, p.84.
134. FO371/1687, Russia Committee Minutes, 11/11/48.
135. FO1093/429, Sargent to Stevenson, 17/11/48.
136. FO1093/429, Stevenson to Sargent, 30/11/48.
137. Jeffery, *MI6*, p.699; Baxter, 'A Closed Book?', p.17.
138. FO1093/429, Stevenson to Sargent, 30/11/48.
139. Ibid.; CAB134/285, Far East (Official) Committee Minutes, FE(O)(48)8th Meeting, 4/12/48; FO371/70272, 'Report of the sub-committee'.
140. CAB134/285, 'The Situation in China', FE(O)(48)34(Revise), 10/12/48.
141. DNSA: US Intelligence and China, CIA, 'Propose Chinese Nationalist Plan to Recover South China', 25 July 1950; Riley Ennis (US Far East Command) to Chief of Staff, US Far East Command, 21/9/51.
142. DNSA: US Intelligence and China, US embassy Taiwan to US Director of Naval Intelligence, 14/11/50.
143. CAB134/285, Far East (Official) Committee Minutes, FE(O)(48)8th Meeting, 4/12/48.

CHAPTER 2

1. CAB301/133, Seymour, 'The Secret Intelligence Service: Report of Enquiry by Sir Horace Seymour', June 1952.
2. See Gwinnett, 'Attlee, Bevin & Political Warfare', p.15.
3. Vickers, *The Labour Party and the World*, p.174; Kent, *British Imperial Strategy and the Origins of the Cold War*, p.77; Smith and Zametica, 'The Cold Warrior', pp.246–8; see also Gwinnett, 'Attlee, Bevin & Political Warfare', p.16.

4. Jones, *Post-war Counterinsurgency and the SAS*, pp.41–77; FO1110/61, Murray, 'Political Warfare in Greece', June 1948; Dimitrakis, *The Hidden Wars in China and Greece*, pp.35–6; FO1110/61, Tedder, 'Greece', 27/5/48.

5. BOD: MS.Eng.c.6920, Patrick Reilly, 'A Second Communist Rebellion', undated, pp.78–9; Patrick Reilly, 'A Deteriorating Situation', undated, p.152.

6. FO1093/452, 'Notes on Counter Guerrilla Action in Albania', 20/12/48.

7. FO1093/452, 'Communist Action in Albania', 3/2/49.

8. FO1093/576, Minutes of PUSC, PUSC(49)14th Meeting, 8/6/49.

9. FO1093/452, Porter, 11/1/49; Sargent to Menzies, 18/2/49; 'Communist Action in Albania', 3/2/49; Jeffery, *MI6*, p.713.

10. FO1093/452, Menzies to Strang, 4/3/49.

11. FO1093/452, Scribbled note by Halford on minute of 25/2/49.

12. Deighton, 'Strang', *ODNB*.

13. FO1093/452, Strang to Bevin, 21/3/49.

14. Ibid., 14/4/49.

15. Ibid., 21/3/49.

16. Jeffery, *MI6*, p.708.

17. FO371/77623, Russia Committee Minutes, 15/2/49.

18. FO371/78308, 'Greece etc.: Office Meeting with the Secretary of State at 5.30p.m. on March 4th'.

19. FO800/437, Strang to Attlee, 26/3/49.

20. Aldrich, *The Hidden Hand*, p.79; Smith and Zametica, 'The Cold Warrior', p.237.

21. FO800/437, Attlee scribbled note on Strang to Attlee, 26/3/49.

22. Ibid.

23. FO800/437, Memorandum from Strang to Attlee, 5/4/49.

24. Bailey, 'Smiley', *ODNB*.

25. Smiley, *Albanian Assignment*, pp.163–4.

26. Ibid., pp.165–6; Macintyre, *Spy Among Friends*, p.124.

27. Corke, *US Covert Operations and Cold War Strategy*, p.84.

28. Lomas, *Intelligence, Security and the Attlee Governments*, p.125.

29. FO1093/452, Makins to Bevin, 'Albania', 30/5/49.

30. CCC: GLAD 1/1/1, Kenneth Younger to Jebb, quoting Dean Acheson, 16/550.

31. CREST: Redacted, 'Review of BG FIEND', 8/2/50.

32. Long, *The CIA and the Soviet Bloc*, p.175.

33. CREST: anon, 'Memorandum for COP: Current Status of Project BGFIEND with Particular Reference for OPC Organization', 16/8/49.

34. Callanan, *Covert Action in the Early Cold War*, p.75; Thomas, *The Very Best Men*, p.38.

35. FO1093/452, Record of a meeting held at the State Department, 14/9/49.

36. Long, *The CIA and the Soviet Bloc*, p.175.

37. FRUS: (1949) vol.5, Memorandum of Conversation, by the Secretary of State, Meeting with Bevin, 14/9/49.

38. CREST: Kermit Roosevelt, 'Revaluation of the Project BGFIEND', 29/11/49.

39. FO1093/452, Hayter to Menzies, undated 1949.

40. Grose, *Operation Rollback*, p.156.
41. CREST: Kermit Roosevelt, 'Revaluation of the Project BGFIEND', 29/11/49; Lulushi, *Operation Valuable Fiend*, p.55.
42. Lulushi, *Operation Valuable Fiend*, pp.93–5.
43. FO1093/563, Note by Hayter, 20/5/49.
44. FO1093/452, 'Notes on Counter Guerrilla Action in Albania', 20/12/48.
45. See Harrison, 'The British Special Operations Executive and Poland', pp.1071–91.
46. Quoted in Onslow, 'Julian Amery and the Suez Operation', p.76.
47. Bailey, 'McLean', *ODNB*.
48. CCC: AMEJ 1/1/65, Julian Amery diary, 1/5/49.
49. Ibid., 4/5/49.
50. Ibid., 21/5/49.
51. Ibid., 14/5/49.
52. Ibid., 21/5/49.
53. Jeffery, *MI6*, p.715; FO1093/452, Bateman to Hayter, 'Albania', 22/6/49; MI6 telegram to Paris, 23/7/49; FO1093/453, 'Valuable' Foreign Office meeting, 29/11/49.
54. Aldrich, *The Hidden Hand*, p.163.
55. CCC: AMEJ 1/1/65, Account of Amery's talks regarding the committee, 2/8/49.
56. Quoted in Bassett, *Last Imperialist*, p.139.
57. Fielding, *One Man in his Time*, p.78.
58. CCC: AMEJ 1/1/65, Account of Amery's talks regarding the committee, 2/8/49.
59. CREST: Kermit Roosevelt, 'Re-evaluation of the Project BGFIEND', 29/11/49.
60. CREST: Redacted IMB, 'Draft', 17/7/52.
61. NARA: RG 49, Box 312, Records of Post CFM meetings, 'Conversations Between Bevin and Acheson on Albania', 14/9/49.
62. FO800/437, 'Policy Towards Albania', 21/3/49.
63. Ibid.
64. FO1093/452, 'Resistance in Albania', sent to Foreign Office Southern Department, 29/7/49.
65. FO1093/452, Street, account of a meeting chaired by Strang, 24/8/49.
66. Smiley, *Albanian Assignment*, p.167; Macintyre, *A Spying Among Friends*, pp.125, 127–9.
67. FO1093/452, Bicknell to Street, 26/10/49; Bicknell to Rumbold, 7/11/49; Jeffery, *MI6*, p.715.
68. FO1093/453, 'Albania', Brief for Bevin by Rumbold, 20/12/49.
69. FO1093/453, 'Valuable' Foreign Office meeting, 29/11/49.
70. CREST: Redacted, 'Review of BG FIEND', 8/2/50.
71. CREST: Kermit Roosevelt, 'Re-evaluation of the Project BGFIEND', 29/11/49.
72. CREST: Redacted, 'Review of BG FIEND', 8/2/50.
73. CREST: Redacted, Project BG FIEND Report, November 1951.

74. FO 093/453, Untitled memorandum, written by the OPC and approved by the State Department, 6/12/49.

75. FO1093/453, 'Albania', Brief for Bevin by Rumbold, 20/12/49; 'Albania: Intelligence Summary', Bicknell to Joy, 9/12/49.

76. Ibid.

77. CAB134/53, Cabinet Committee on Communism Minutes, C(49)3rd Meeting, 7/6/49.This was a small body established in May 1949 charged with examining the existing machinery and policy. See also Davies, 'The Rump SOE'.

78. CAB134/4, AC(O) Minutes, AC(O)(50)4th Meeting, 15/2/50; CAB301/133, Seymour, 'The Secret Intelligence Service: Report of Enquiry by Sir Horace Seymour', June 1952.

79. FO1093/375, McNeil to Bevin, 29/4/48; Hayter to Balfour, April 1948.

80. This is particularly the case amongst early works, such as Bethell, *The Great Betrayal*; Page et al., *Philby*. Other biographies, such as Macintyre, *Spy Among Friends*, also look to Philby's role. More recent accounts see Philby's betrayal as one factor among many and suggest that the operation would have failed regardless. See, for example, Aldrich, *The Hidden Hand*. For discussion see Callanan, *Covert Action in the Cold War*, pp.70, 79, 222–3. See also Philby, *My Silent War*, pp.194–9.

81. Halsam, *Near and Distant Neighbours*, p.155.

82. Jeffery, *MI6*, p.716.

83. CREST: Chief EE-1, 'Project BGFIEND Report', 29/11/51; Jeffery, *MI6*, p.716; CAB134/53, Cabinet Committee on Communism Minutes, C(49)2nd Meeting, 1/6/49; CAB134/4, AC(O) Minutes, AC(O)(50)4th Meeting, 15/2/1950; FO1093/375, Sargent to Hayter and Warner, 13/5/48.

84. Auten, 'Political Diasporas and Exiles as Instruments of Statecraft', p.337.

85. Long, 'Strategic Disorder', p.462; Corke, *US Covert Operations and Cold War Strategy*, p.6.

86. FO1093/452, 'OperationValuable', 26/7/49.

87. Roberts, 'Ernest Bevin as Foreign Secretary', pp.30, 38.

88. CAB134/53, 'Revised Draft Report', C(49)13(Revise), 11/7/49.

89. Goodman, *Spying on the Nuclear Bear*.

90. Davies, *MI6*, p.219; see also Aldrich, 'British Intelligence and the Anglo-American "Special Relationship" During the Cold War', pp.339–40.

91. FO1093/453, Reilly to Hoyer Millar, 2/1/50; CREST: Redacted, Project BG FIEND Report, November 1951; Redacted, 'Status of Operations Against Albania', July 1951.

92. See, for example, Callanan, *Covert Action in the Cold War*, p.81, which argues that British involvements had ceased by the end of 1951.

93. Lulushi, *Operation Valuable Fiend*, pp.93–5.

94. FRUS: (1949) vol.5, 'Memorandum by the Assistant Secretary of State for European Affairs (Perkins) to the Secretary of State', 13/9/49, p.314.

95. CREST: Anon, 'Memorandum for CPP: Re-evaluation of the Project BG FIEND', 7/9/49.
96. CREST: Redacted, Untitled OPC project overview of BG FEIND, 19/11/52.
97. Ibid.
98. CREST: Anon, 'Joint PW Policy Guidance for BGFIEND', 3 August 1950; Anon, 'SE Albanian Program—A Brief Historical Resume', undated [1952].
99. CREST: Redacted, Project BG FIEND Report, November 1951; Redacted, 'Status of Operations Against Albania', July 1951.
100. Ibid., pp.156–7.
101. CREST: Redacted, Project BG FIEND Report, November 1951.
102. Callanan, *Covert Action in the Cold War*, p.78.
103. CREST: Anon, 'CIA/OPC 1952 Albanian Operations', 18/12/51.
104. CREST: Redacted, 'Memorandum for the Record: BG Fiend', 21/10/52.
105. DNSA: Database: The Soviet Estimate: US Analysis of the Soviet Union, 1947–1991: CIA, 'Consequences of an Attempt to Overthrow the Present Regime in Albania', 30/12/52.
106. CREST: Minutes of the 'London March Conference' between SIS and the CIA, March 1952.
107. CREST: Redacted [Gratian Yatsevich, OPC commander of FIEND], Chief EE-1, 'Liaison With the British in Washington on Projects FIEND and VALUABLE', 28/8/51; Lulushi, *Operation Valuable Fiend*, p.129.
108. Thanks to Michael Goodman for pointing this out.
109. Macintyre, *Spy Among Friends*, p.132.
110. For a historiographical discussion on Philby's role, see Callanan, *Covert Action in the Cold War* pp.70, 81–4.
111. CREST: Redacted, Untitled OPC project overview of BG FEIND, 19/11/52.
112. CREST: Chief, SE, 'Memorandum for DD/P [Deputy Director of Plans]: Operation BGFIEND', 28/10/52.
113. Ibid.
114. Ibid., pp.184–204.
115. Lulushi, *Operation Valuable Fiend*, p.157.
116. CREST: OPC, Paramilitary Staff, 'Annex C: Albanian coup instigated militarily by US, UK, and Yugoslavia', 6/2/53.
117. NARA: RG59, Records of the Bureau of Intelligence and Research, Record Sets of National Intelligence Estimates, Special Estimates, and Special National Intelligence Estimates, 1950–1954, CIA, 'Yugoslav Intentions toward Albania', NIE-42/1, 20/10/52.
118. CREST: 'KUBRAK-BPBERM Meeting in Belgrade on 16–17 February 1953'.
119. Dixon, 'Record of a Meeting Between the Secretary of State and Marshal Tito', 18/9/52. Thanks to the Radio 4 'Document' team for sharing this document and to Steve Long for finding it.
120. CREST: 'KUBRAK-BPBERM Meeting in Belgrade on 16–17 February 1953'.
121. Callanan, *Covert Action in the Early Cold War*, pp.75-6.

122. CREST:'KUBRAK–BPBERM Meeting in Belgrade on 16–17 February 1953'.

123. CREST: Anon, 'FY 1953 Program', undated.

124. CREST: Anon, 'Brief Historical Review', undated [1954].

125. CCC: AMEJ 1/2/88, Amery to Selwyn Lloyd, 7/5/54.

126. DDRS: Jackson to Eisenhower, 'Memorandum to the President', 1/3/54, ref: CK3100616286.

127. CCC: AMEJ 1/2/88, Swire to Amery, 14/6/54.

128. CCC: AMEJ 1/2/88, Amery to Eden, 17/3/54.

129. CCC: AMEJ 1/2/88, Eden to Amery, 26/3/54.

130. CREST: Prole Administrative Mailing Staff to Deputy Director, Plans, 'Termination of OBLIVIOUS Project', 14/6/56; DNSA: Database: The Soviet Estimate: US Analysis of the Soviet Union, 1947–1991: CIA. Director of Central Intelligence, 'Anti-Communist Resistance Potential in the Sino-Soviet Bloc—Annex a, Albania', 4/3/58.

131. DNSA: Database: The Soviet Estimate: US Analysis of the Soviet Union, 1947–1991: CIA, Director of Central Intelligence, 'Anti-Communist Resistance Potential in the Sino-Soviet Bloc', 12/4/55.

132. FO371/135615, 'UK Policy Towards the East European Satellites', SC(58)46, 17/10/58.

133. DNSA: Database: The Soviet Estimate: US Analysis of the Soviet Union, 1947–1991: CIA, Director of Central Intelligence, 'Anti-Communist Resistance Potential in the Sino-Soviet Bloc—Annex a, Albania', 4/3/58.

CHAPTER 3

1. Attlee quoted in Aldrich, *The Hidden Hand*, p.295.

2. KCLMA: SUEZOHP, 18, Reilly, 'Interview with Patrick Reilly Conducted by W. Scott Lucas'; FO371/1687, Warner to Jebb, 20/11/48.

3. CAB134/53, 'Ministerial Statements regarding His Majesty's Government's Anti-Communist Policy', C(49)9, 22/6/49.

4. CAB134/53, 'Committee on Communism: Report to the Secretary of State for Foreign Affairs', July 1949.

5. See Davies, *MI6*, p.219; Aldrich, 'British Intelligence and the Anglo-American "Special Relationship" During the Cold War', pp.339–40.

6. FO1093/580, 'British Overseas Obligations', PUSC(79)4th Revise, 31/1/50.

7. Ibid.; FO1093/582, 'Treasury Comments on "British Overseas Obligations" (PUSC 19 Final Revise)', PUSC(50)14, undated.

8. Campbell, 'Jebb, (Hubert Miles) Gladwyn, first Baron Gladwyn (1900–1996)', *ODNB*.

9. CAB134/53, 'Cabinet Committee on Communism: Summary of Report', draft, C(49)13, 11/7/49.

10. CAB134/53, 'Cabinet Committee on Communism: Report to Secretary of State for Foreign Affairs', 12/7/49.

11. For discussion see Selverstone, *Constructing the Monolith*, pp.116–21.

12. FO800/503, 'British Policy towards Soviet Communism', PUSC(31)Final, 28/7/49.
13. Selverstone, *Constructing the Monolith*, pp.154–5.
14. CAB134/3, AC(O) Minutes, AC(O)(50)17th Meeting, 26/5/50; AC(O) Minutes, AC(O)(50)19th Meeting 7/6/50; 'Planning Staff for Cold War Activities', Attached: 'Draft Letter to Heads of Missions', AC(O)(50)35, 19/7/50.
15. FOI: Kirkpatrick, circular to overseas representatives, OPS/1/56, 17/5/56.
16. CAB134/3, 'Planning Staff for Cold War Activities', AC(O)(50)35, 19/7/50.
17. CAB134/3, 'The "Cold War" in South East Asia', AC(O)(50)39, 15/8/50.
18. CAB134/3, 'Planning Staff for Cold War Activities: Attached—Draft Letter to Heads of Missions', AC(O)(50)35, 19/7/50.
19. Ibid.
20. CAB301/17, Brook, 'The Secret Intelligence and Security Services', March 1951.
21. FO1093/375, Menzies, 'The Capabilities of Secret Service in Peace in Support of an Overall Political Plan: Annex B—Special Operations other than Clandestine Propaganda', 20/1/48.
22. BOD: MS Sherfield 524, 'Lecture by Sir Gladwyn Jebb to the Imperial Defence College on 24th February, 1950'.
23. West, *At Her Majesty's Secret Service*, p.55; Jeffery, *MI6*, p.478, Cave Brown, *C*, p.689.
24. Cave Brown, *C*, pp.672, 677.
25. See Dorril, *MI6*, p.5; Jeffery, *MI6*, pp.742, 748; Cave Brown, *C*, p.685.
26. CAB21/2750, 'Proposed Activities Behind the Iron Curtain' (Third Revise), AC(O)(50)52, November 1950; CAB21/5003, Cliffe to Brook, Attached: Brief for Prime Minister ahead of AC(M) meeting, 20/12/50.
27. CAB134/4, AC(O) Minutes, AC(O)(50)4th Meeting, 15/2/50; CAB21/2750, 'Proposed Activities Behind the Iron Curtain' (Third Revise), AC(O)(50)52, November 1950.
28. Attlee quoted in Aldrich, *The Hidden Hand*, p.295.
29. CAB134/4, AC(O) Minutes, AC(O)(50)25th Meeting, 6/9/50; AC(O) Minutes, AC(O)(50)26th Meeting, 27/9/50.
30. CAB134/4, AC(O) Minutes, AC(O)(50)26th Meeting, 27/9/50.
31. CAB134/4, AC(O) Minutes, AC(O)(50)4th Meeting, 15/2/50.
32. Theakston, 'Brook, Norman Craven, Baron Normanbrook (1902–1967)', *ODNB*.
33. PREM8/1365, Alexander to Attlee, 6/6/49; Attlee to Bevin, 8/5/49; Gwinnett, 'Attlee, Bevin & Political Warfare', pp.1–24.
34. PREM8/1365, Brook to Attlee, 20/4/49.
35. This offers a more nuanced understanding of Bevin than the dominating figure portrayed in the orthodox literature. See, for example, Bullock, *Ernest Bevin*. For an excellent recent discussion of this, see Gwinnett, 'Attlee, Bevin & Political Warfare'.
36. CAB134/4, AC(O) Minutes, AC(O)(50)17th Meeting, 26/5/50.

37. Ure, 'Reilly, Sir (D'Arcy) Patrick (1909–1999)', *ODNB*.
38. Cooper, 'Dean, Sir Maurice Joseph (1906–1978)', *ODNB*.
39. PREM8/1365, Brook to Attlee, 30/11/50.
40. DEFE28/1, Ward to Elliott, Attached: ' "Deception" Organisation', 20/2/50.
41. Beesley, *Cabinet Secretaries*, p.63.
42. Lomas, *Intelligence, Security, and the Attlee Governments*, p.132.
43. CAB301/17, Brook, 'The Secret Intelligence and Security Services', March 1951.
44. Beesley, *Cabinet Secretaries*, p.72.
45. PREM8/1365, Brooks to Attlee, 'Meeting of the Ministerial Committee on Communism, 21st December 1950', 20/12/50.
46. CAB132/2, 'Anti-Communist Activities in Europe', AC(M)(50)1, 15/12/50; PREM8/1365, Prime Minister's Office to Cliffe, 21/12/50; CAB134/2, 'Anti-Communist Activities in Europe', AC(M)(50)2, 22/12/50.
47. CAB134/4, AC(O) Minutes, AC(O)(50)27th Meeting, 16/10/50.
48. Lomas, *Intelligence, Security, and the Attlee Governments*, p.135.
49. Quoted in Jeffery, *MI6*, p.668.
50. For discussion of the division of Germany and Britain's role see, Deighton, *The Impossible Peace*; and Hughes, *Britain, Germany and the Cold War*.
51. Blake, *No Other Choice*, p.166.
52. Ibid., p.167.
53. Maddrell, 'British Intelligence through the Eyes of the Stasi', pp.51, 53.
54. CAB21/2750, 'Proposed Activities behind the Iron Curtain', AC(O)(50)52(Third Revise), November 1950.
55. Ibid.
56. Maddrell, 'British Intelligence through the Eyes of the Stasi', pp.65–6.
57. Maddrell, 'What we have Discovered', p.245.
58. Maddrell, 'British Intelligence through the Eyes of the Stasi', pp.65–6.
59. Maddrell, 'What we have Discovered', p.246.
60. Dorril, *MI6*, pp.112–13.
61. CAB 21/2750, 'Proposed Activities behind the Iron Curtain', AC(O)(50)52(Third Revise), November 1950.
62. Maddrell, *Spying on Science*, p.78.
63. Maddrell, 'What we have Discovered', p.250.
64. Maddrell, 'British Intelligence through the Eyes of the Stasi', pp.54–67.
65. Haslam, *Russia's Cold War*, pp.195–6.
66. CAB21/2750, 'Proposed Activities behind the Iron Curtain', AC(O)(50)52(Third Revise), November 1950.
67. FO800/503, 'British Policy towards Soviet Communism', PUSC(31)Final, 28/7/49; FO1093/584, Russia Committee, 'Western Measures to Counter Soviet Expansion, Together with some Indication of their Effect', 20/5/50; Hughes, 'A Coalition of "Compromise and Barter"', pp.73, 71.
68. BOD: MS Sherfield 524, 'Lecture by Sir Gladwyn Jebb to the Imperial Defence College on 24th February, 1950'.

69. Maddrell, 'British Intelligence through the Eyes of the Stasi', p.73.
70. CAB21/2750, 'Proposed Activity Behind the Iron Curtain' (Third Revise), AC(O)(50)52, November 1950.
71. Gray, *Germany's Cold War*, pp.13–16.
72. CAB21/2750, 'Proposed Activity Behind the Iron Curtain' (Third Revise), AC(O)(50)52, November 1950; CAB134/4, AC(O) Minutes, AC(O)(50)6th Meeting, 1/3/50.
73. BOD: MS Sherfield 524, 'Lecture by Sir Gladwyn Jebb to the Imperial Defence College on 24th February, 1950'.
74. FO371/70272, 'Report of the sub-committee set up to examine the problem of planning in relation to policy towards the Soviet Union and the Soviet Orbit', RC(25)48, 14/12/48.
75. NARA: RG59, Box 6, Executive Secretariat, Psychological Strategy Board Working File, 1951–3, US-UK Meeting on Political Warfare, Action Meeting of 1st Meeting, 28 April 1952. Thanks to Thomas Maguire for sharing this file.
76. CAB21/2750, 'Proposed Activity Behind the Iron Curtain' (Third Revise), AC(O)(50)52, November 1950.
77. FO1093/375, 'Special Operations', JP(47)118, 17/12/47.
78. DEFE28/1, Ward to Elliott, Attached: '"Deception" Organisation', 20/2/50; CAB134/53, 'Revised Draft Report', C(49)13(Revise), 11/7/49.
79. CAB134/53, C(49)4th Meeting, Cabinet Committee on Communism Minutes, 9/6/49.
80. Dylan, 'Super-Weapons and Subversion', p.719.
81. Ibid., pp.717–19.
82. FO1093/375, Cheetham to Hayter, 4/3/48.
83. CAB134/4, AC(O) Minutes, AC(O)(50)7th Meeting, 9/3/50.
84. Ure, 'Reilly, Sir (D'Arcy) Patrick (1909–1999)', *ODNB*.
85. CAB134/4, AC(O) Minutes, AC(O)(50)6th Meeting, 1/3/50.
86. PDP: Dixon to McNeil, 5/1/50; private information.
87. PDP: Dixon to McNeil, 10/1/50.
88. FO371/70272, 'Report of the sub-committee set up to examine the problem of planning in relation to policy towards the Soviet Union and the Soviet Orbit: Appendix B—Satellite Contradictions', RC(25)48, 14/12/48.
89. CAB134/4, AC(O) Minutes, AC(O)(50)6th Meeting, 1/3/50; AC(O) Minutes, AC(O)(50)10th Meeting, 31/3/50.
90. CAB134/2, 'The Work of the Official Committee on Communism (Overseas)', AC(M)(51)4, 23/6/51.
91. CAB134/4, AC(O) Minutes, AC(O)(50)6th Meeting, 1/3/50; CAB134/4, AC(O) Minutes, AC(O)(50)8th Meeting, 15/3/50.
92. Weinberg, *A World at Arms*, p.396.
93. Dylan, *JIB*, p.69.
94. CAB21/2750, 'Selective Buying', Draft Memorandum by the Overseas Planning Section, Undated but likely to be January 1951.

95. See Dylan, *JIB*, p.82. The shadowy group was known, rather verbosely, as the Clandestine Trade Sub-Committee of the Security Export Controls Working Party.

96. CAB21/2750, 'Selective Buying', Draft Memorandum by the Overseas Planning Section, Undated but likely to be January 1951.

97. Dylan, *JIB*, pp.69, 74.

98. Aldrich, *The Hidden Hand*, pp.174–6; Haslam, *Russia's Cold War*, pp.102–4.

99. Quoted in Correra, *Art of Betrayal*, p.29.

100. CAB134/53, 'Foreign Office Information activities with Special Reference to Anti-Communist Propaganda', C(49)3, 31/5/49.

101. See Maguire, *British and American Intelligence*, pp.79–87.

102. CAB134/4, AC(O) Minutes, AC(O)(50)19th Meeting, 7/6/50.

103. CAB134/3, 'The "Cold War" in the Far East', Foreign Office Memorandum, AC(O)(50)31, 19/7/50; CAB134/4, AC(O) Minutes, AC(O)(50)19th Meeting, 7/6/50; for more information see Goodman, *Joint Intelligence Committee*, pp.301–19.

104. CAB134/3, 'The "Cold War" in the Far East', Foreign Office Memorandum, AC(O)(50)31, 19/7/50; CAB 134/4, AC(O) Minutes, AC(O)(50)19th Meeting, 7/6/50.

105. See Aldrich, 'Legacies of Secret Service', pp.130–48.

106. CAB134/4, AC(O) Minutes, AC(O)(50)11th Meeting, 6/4/50; Jeffery, *MI6*, p.705.

107. CAB134/3, 'The "Cold War" in the Far East', AC(O)(50)31, 19/7/50.

108. Ibid.

109. CAB134/4, AC(O) Minutes, AC(O)(50)31st Meeting, 16/11/50.

110. Aldrich, *The Hidden Hand*, pp.288–9.

111. CAB134/4, AC(O) Minutes, AC(O)(50)19th Meeting, 7/6/50.

112. CAB134/3, 'Anti-Communist Measures in the Far East', AC(O)(50)37, 15/8/50.

113. CAB134/4, AC(O) Minutes, AC(O)(50)19th Meeting, 7/6/50.

114. Ibid.

115. Baxter, 'A Closed Book?', p.19.

116. CAB134/3, 'The "Cold War" in the Far East', Foreign Office Memorandum, AC(O)(50)31, 19/7/50.

117. CAB 134/3, 'Anti-Communist Measures in the Far East', Memorandum by the Overseas Planning Section, AC(O)(50)37, 15/8/50.

118. Goodman, *Joint Intelligence Committee*, pp.301–19.

CHAPTER 4

1. FO371/135615, 'UK Policy Towards the East European Satellites', SC(58)46, 17/10/58.

2. Jenkins, 'The Churchill Government', p.492; See also Hennessy, *The Prime Minister*, pp.183–5. For a discussion on Churchill and intelligence more broadly see Aldrich and Cormac, *The Black Door*, pp.161–81.

3. Young, *Winston Churchill's Last Campaign*, pp.12–52; see also Larres, *Churchill's Cold War*.

4. NARA: RG59, Box 6, Executive Secretariat, Psychological Strategy Board Working File, 1951–53, Robert Joyce, 'Final Meeting in London with British Foreign Office and SIS Representatives', 20/12/51. Thanks to Thomas Maguire for sharing this file.

5. CREST: Chief EE-1, 'Memorandum for the Record: Conversation between [Redacted] and [Redacted]', 18/12/51.

6. NARA: RG59, Box 6, Executive Secretariat, Psychological Strategy Board Working File, 1951–53, Robert Joyce, 'Final Meeting in London with British Foreign Office and SIS Representatives', 20/12/51.

7. FO371/25002, 'Future Policy Towards Soviet Russia', PUSC(15)16, 17/1/52.

8. Ibid.

9. CAB21/3217, Strang, 'Soviet Reactions to Western Pressures on "Sore Spots"', 8/9/52.

10. NARA: RG59, Box 6, Executive Secretariat, Psychological Strategy Board Working File, 1951–53, 'US–UK Meeting on Policy Relating to Covert Activity vs. USSR and Soviet Orbit in Europe', 30/4/52.

11. Maddrell, 'What we have Discovered', pp.250–1; Bower, *Perfect English Spy*, p.262.

12. FO371/25002, 'Future Policy towards Soviet Russia, PUSC(15)16, 17/1/52.

13. Deighton, *Britain and the Cold War*, pp.129–30.

14. CAB21/3217, Dean, 'Talks with Russia—What Next?', PUSC2(55), 31/3/55; PUSC 'Permanent Under-Secretary's Committee', PUSC3(55), 19/4/55.

15. Tang, *Britain's Encounter with Revolutionary China*, pp.97–8.

16. FO371/25002, 'Future Policy Towards China', PUSC(52)6, 31/3/52.

17. NARA: RG59, Box 6, Executive Secretariat, Psychological Strategy Board Working File, 1951–53, Robert Joyce, 'Final Meeting in London with British Foreign Office and SIS Representatives', 20/12/51.

18. CCC: AMEJ 1/1/51, Anon., 'Note on Cold War', May 1952.

19. Quoted in Bassett, *Last Imperialist*, p.147.

20. DDEL: Jackson Papers, Box 47, Dodds-Parker to Jackson, 17/2/53.

21. NARA: RG59, Box 6, Executive Secretariat, Psychological Strategy Board Working File, 1951–53, Robert Joyce, 'Final Meeting in London with British Foreign Office and SIS Representatives', 20/12/51.

22. CAD: MS 191/1/2/2, Shuckburgh Diary, 27/8/53; Aldrich and Cormac, *The Black Door*.

23. CAD: Avon Papers, FO 800/820, Eden to Churchill, 16/4/52.

24. FO371/100825, Hohler, 'minutes of a meeting held in William Strang's office to discuss the "sore spots" paper on 22nd February 1952', 1/3/52.

25. Beesley, *Cabinet Secretaries*, p.62.

26. CAB301/133, Sinclair to Winnifrith, 30/10/52.

27. CAB301/133, Seymour, 'The Secret Intelligence Service: Report of Enquiry by Sir Horace Seymour', June 1952.

28. CAB301/133, Sinclair to Reilly, 29 December 1952.

29. CAB301/133, 'Record of a Meeting with C about Matters Arising from the Seymour Report', May 1953.

30. CAB301/133, Seymour, 'The Secret Intelligence Service: Report of Enquiry by Sir Horace Seymour', June 1952. For an excellent overview of SIS bureaucracy see Davies, *MI6*.

31. CAB301/133, Menzies, 'Comments by C on the Report by Sir Horace Seymour on his Enquiry into the Secret Intelligence Service', 9/7/52.

32. CAB21/5003, Young to Brook, 'AC(O) and AC(M)', 31/1/55.

33. PREM11/1582, Brook to Eden, 21/10/55.

34. CCC: AMEJ 1/1/51, 'Note on Cold War', May 1952; Beesley, *Cabinet Secretaries*, p.113.

35. Aldrich and Cormac, *The Black Door*; Dorril, *MI6*, p.489; Young, *Winston Churchill's Last Campaign*, pp.37, 70, 85; Young, 'The British Foreign Office and Cold War Fighting', pp.1–8.

36. Grose, *Spymaster*, p.338.

37. Young, *Winston Churchill's Last Campaign*, p.37; Corke, *US Covert Operations*, pp.153–5: Larres, *Churchill's Cold War*, pp.163–7.

38. CAD: MS 191/1/2/1, Shuckburgh Diary, 5/1/52.

39. PREM8/1365, Brooks to Attlee, 'Meeting of the Ministerial Committee on Communism, 21st December 1950', 20/12/50.

40. NARA: RG59, Box 6, Executive Secretariat, Psychological Strategy Board Working File, 1951–53, 'US–UK Meeting on Policy Relating to Covert Activity vs. USSR and Soviet Orbit in Europe, 29/4/52.

41. FO371/100825, Gascoigne to Hohler, 3/1/52. The letter is actually dated 1951 but this is most likely a typo.

42. FO371/25002, 'Future Policy Towards Soviet Russia', PUSC(15)16, 17/1/52. For more detail see Aldrich, *The Hidden Hand*, pp.323–34.

43. Aldrich, *The Hidden Hand*, p.326.

44. NARA: RG59, Box 6, Executive Secretariat, Psychological Strategy Board Working File, 1951–53, 'Comments on "Future Policy Towards Russia"', US Psychological Strategy Board, undated but early 1952. Thanks to Thomas Maguire for sharing this file.

45. NARA: RG59, Box 6, Executive Secretariat, Psychological Strategy Board Working File, 1951–53, Robert Joyce, 'Final Meeting in London with British Foreign Office and SIS Representatives', 20/12/51.

46. NARA: RG59, 611.41/8-1253, US embassy London, 'British Attitudes toward US Policy', 12/8/53.

47. Grose, *Operation Rollback*, pp.171–2, 177.

48. Quoted in Corera, *Art of Betrayal*, p.59.

49. Grose, *Operation Rollback*, pp.171–2, 177.

50. Quoted in Beesley, *Cabinet Secretaries*, p.112.

51. NARA: RG59, Box 6, Executive Secretariat, Psychological Strategy Board Working File, 1951–53, Robert Joyce, 'Final Meeting in London with British Foreign Office and SIS Representatives', 20/12/51.

52. BOD: MS Sherfield 959, Strang to Makins, 9/5/53; CAD: MS 191/1/2/1, Shuckburgh Diary, 5/1/52.

53. NARA: RG59, Box 6, Executive Secretariat, Psychological Strategy Board Working File, 1951–53, Ad Hoc Meeting on Preparation for US–UK Talks on Political warfare, 23/4/52. Thanks to Thomas Maguire for sharing this file.

54. DDEL: NSC Staff Papers, PSB Central File Series, Box 15, PSB091.4, Eastern Europe (3), Irwin to Debevoise, 'Probable British Outlook on Eastern European Problems', 7/7/53.

55. DDEL: NSC Staff Papers, PSB Central File Series, Box 15, PSB091.4 Eastern Europe (1), PSB, 'Interim US Psychological Strategy Plan for Exploitation of Unrest in Satellite Europe', PSB D-45, 22/7/53; DDEL: Office of the Special Assistant for National Security Affairs, NSC Series, Policy Papers Subseries, Box 10, NSC5412/2—Covert Operations,' National Security Council Directive on Covert Operations', March 1954; DDEL: NSC Staff Papers, PSB Central File Series, Box 15, PSB091.4, Eastern Europe (3), Irwin to Debevoise, 'Probable British Outlook on Eastern European Problems', 7/7/53.

56. DDEL: NSC Staff Papers, PSB Central File Series, Box 15, PSB091.4, Eastern Europe (3), Irwin to Debevoise, 'Probable British Outlook on Eastern European Problems', 7/7/53.

57. For detailed discussion of this in a series of essays see Larres and Osgood (eds.), *The Cold War after Stalin's Death*.

58. Goodman, *Joint Intelligence Committee*, pp.265–8; see also Haslam, *Russia's Cold War*, pp.133–64.

59. Beesley, *Cabinet Secretaries*, p.90.

60. See Ovendale, *British Defence Policy Since 1945*, pp.97–8.

61. PREM11/1582, Macmillan to Eden, 19/10/55.

62. FOI: Dodds-Parker to Lloyd, OPS/72/56, 28/3/56. Thanks to Chikara Hashimoto for sharing this document.

63. West, *Her Majesty's Secret Service*, p.72; Lucas, *Deception*, p.234.

64. Andrew and Gordievsky, *KGB*, p.387.

65. Gaddis, *We Now Know*, p.208.

66. CIA Office of the Historian, 'Khrushchev and the Twentieth Congress of the Communist Party, 1956', available at https://history.state.gov/milestones/1953-1960/khrushchev-20th-congress.

67. Loewenstein, 'Re-emergence of Public Opinion in the Soviet Union', pp.141–2.

68. Haslam, *Russia's Cold War*, pp.167–8; Goodman, *Joint Intelligence Committee*, pp.268–9.

69. Tucker, 'US–Soviet Cooperation', p.306.

70. FOI: Kirkpatrick to Foreign Secretary, 'Summary of Recommendations on Prime Minister's Memorandum on Counter-Subversion', OPS/1/56, undated but likely January 1956.

71. FOI: Kirkpatrick, circular to overseas representatives, OPS/1/56, 17/5/56.

72. FOI: Dean to Macmillan, 'Counter-Subversion', OPS/1/56, 19/3/56; Kirkpatrick to Overseas Posts, OPS/1/56, 17/5/56. Thanks to Chikara Hashimoto for sharing this document.

73. Haslam, *Russia's Cold War*, p.264.

74. FOI: Dean to Foreign Secretary, 'Counter-Subversion: Annex, Continental Europe, 19/3/56.

75. FOI: Kirkpatrick to Overseas Posts, OPS/1/56, 17/5/56.

76. FOI: Dean to Foreign Secretary, 'Counter-Subversion: Annex, Iceland', 19/3/56.

77. FO371/122493, Henderson to Lloyd, 4/7/56.

78. Ingimundarson, 'Buttressing the West in the North', pp.80–103.

79. FO371/122493, Henderson to Lloyd, 4/7/56; FOI: Dean to Foreign Secretary, 'Counter-Subversion: Annex, Iceland', 19/3/56.

80. Aldrich, *The Hidden Hand*, p.140.

81. See Kemp-Welch, 'Dethroning Stalin', pp.73–96.

82. DNSA: Database: The Soviet Estimate: US Analysis of the Soviet Union, 1947–1991: CIA, Director of Central Intelligence, 'Anti-Communist Resistance Potential in the Sino-Soviet Bloc – Annex E, Hungary', 12/4/55.

83. Webb, 'Cold War Radio and the Hungarian Uprising', p.222; Grose, *Operation Rollback*, p.217.

84. Haslam, *Russia's Cold War*, p.170. See also Gati, *Failed Illusions*, p.2, which argues that America kept the Hungarians' hopes alive without making any preparations to help them diplomatically or militarily. A similar argument is made in Sebestyen, *Twelve Days*.

85. Byrne (ed.) *The 1956 Hungarian Revolution.*

86. Goodman, *Joint Intelligence Committee*, p.270.

87. Corera, *Art of Betrayal*, p.83.

88. Blake, *No Other Choice*, p.168.

89. Aldrich, *The Hidden Hand*, p.338; Dorril, *MI6*, p.516.

90. NSA: Kai Bird Donation, Box 17, Luce, 'Feelings about Suez', 1/11/56.

91. CCC: AMEJ 1/2/128, Pomian to Macmillan, 31/12/56.

92. DNSA: Database: The Soviet Estimate: US Analysis of the Soviet Union, 1947–1991: CIA, Director of Central Intelligence, 'Anti-Communist Resistance Potential in the Sino-Soviet Bloc – Annex F, Hungary,' 4/3/58.

93. Lindermann, *Rediscovering Irregular Warfare*, p.9.

94. Goodman, *The Joint Intelligence Committee*, p.381.

95. FO371/135615, 'UK Policy Towards the East European Satellites', SC(58)46, 17/10/58.

96. Ibid.

97. Reynolds, 'The European Dimension of the Cold War', p.167.

98. FO371/135615, 'UK Policy Towards the East European Satellites', SC(58)46, 17/10/58.

99. Ibid.

100. Aldrich and Cormac, *The Black Door*, pp.193–4.

101. CCC: AMEJ 1/1/51, Anon., 'Note on Cold War', May 1952.
102. FOI: Kirkpatrick to Overseas Posts, OPS/1/56, 17/5/56.
103. Much existing literature on British policy towards Eastern Europe focuses on trade and economics. See Jackson, *The Economic Cold War*, pp.128–59.
104. FO371/143689, 'UK Policy towards the East European Satellites: Present Policy', SC(58)46, undated, 1958.
105. Maddrell, 'British Intelligence through the Eyes of the Stasi', p.55.
106. FO371/135615, 'UK Policy Towards the East European Satellites', SC(58)46, 17/10/58.
107. Ibid.
108. Ibid.
109. Quoted in Haslam, *Near and Distant Neighbours*, p.178.
110. Bittman, *The Deception Game*, pp.91–2.
111. Maddrell, 'What we have Discovered', p.251.
112. Maddrell, 'British Intelligence through the Eyes of the Stasi', pp.70–1.
113. Prazmowska, 'Polish Communism, the Hungarian Revolution, and the Soviet Union', p.45.

CHAPTER 5

1. Quoted in Goodman, *Joint Intelligence Committee*, p.362.
2. Ibid., p.357.
3. Ibid., pp.357, 360.
4. Everly, 'The Top Secret Cold War Plan to Keep Soviet Hands of Middle Eastern Oil', *Politico*, 23 June 2016. See also HTL: President's Secretary's Files, Box 117, National Security Council, NSC 26 report, 'Removal and Demolition of Oil Facilities, Equipment and Supplies in the Middle East', 19 August 1948; POWE33/1899, anon. Foreign Office, 'Summary of Minutes Returned to Mr Reilly', May 1951; POWE33/1899, Foreign Office to Ministry of Fuel and Power, 7 June 7 1951; Joint Planning Staff, 'Oil Denial in the Middle East', JP(56)59, 16 May 16 1956.
5. LHCMA: Woodhouse 8/1, Woodhouse, 'Iran 1950–3', 16 August 1976, p.9.; see also DDEL: CD Jackson Papers, Box 52, Jackson to Keating (AIOC), 6 August 1951; DNSA: CIA History Staff, 'Battle for Iran', c.mid-1970s, http://nsarchive.gwu.edu/NSAEBB/NSAEBB476/docs/Doc%201%20(b)%20-%20Battle%20for%20Iran%20-%202014%20release%20-%20pages%2026-80.pdf pp.27–8; Kinzer, *All the Shah's Men*, p.201.
6. DNSA: Berthoud, 'Persia,' 15/6/51. http://nsarchive.gwu.edu/NSAEBB/NSAEBB477/docs/Doc%205%20--%201951-06-15%20Lambton%20on%20Persia%20propaganda.pdf.
7. DNSA: Berthoud, 'Persia', 15/6/51.
8. FO248/1528, Furlonge to Shepherd, 21/7/51.
9. Louis, 'Britain and the Overthrow of the Mossadeq Government', p.131.
10. DNSA: Berthoud, 'Persia', 15/6/51.

11. Smiley, *Albanian Assignment*, p.165.
12. Louis 'Musaddiq and the Dilemmas of British Imperialism', p.236.
13. Louis, 'Britain and the Overthrow of the Mossadeq Government', p.132; Dorril, *MI6*, p.564.
14. Goodman, *The Joint Intelligence Committee*, p.358.
15. DNSA: Berthoud, 'Persia', 15/6/51.
16. LHCMA: Woodhouse 8/1, Woodhouse, 'Iran 1950–3', 16/876, p.3.
17. FO800/653, Makins to Attlee, 'Approach to a new Persian Government', 26/9/51.
18. Louis, 'Britain and the Overthrow of the Mossadeq Government', p.132; Kramer, 'Miss Lambton's Advice'.
19. FO371/125003, 'The Problem of Nationalism', PUSC Final, 21/11/52.
20. FO371/91472, Tehran to Furlonge, 19/11/51.
21. Abrahamian, *The Coup*, p.152.
22. LHCMA: Woodhouse 8/1, Woodhouse, 'Iran 1950–3', 16/8/76, p.4; Louis, 'Britain and the Overthrow of the Mossadeq Government', p.146.
23. Wilber, *Regime Change in Iran*, p.81; Gasiorowski, 'Conclusion', p.264.
24. FO248/2529, Shepherd to Strong, 4/9/51; see also Louis, 'Britain and the Overthrow of the Mossadeq Government', p.140.
25. Abrahamian, *The Coup*, p.152.
26. LHCMA: Woodhouse 8/1, Woodhouse, 'Iran 1950–3', 168/76, p.4; Louis, 'Britain and the Overthrow of the Mossadeq Government', p.138; Wilber, *Regime Change in Iran*, p.83.
27. Louis, 'Britain and the Overthrow of the Mossadeq Government', p.138; Wilber, *Regime Change in Iran*, p.83.
28. FRUS: Iran, 1951–54, doc.56, Henderson, Telegram from the Embassy in Iran to the Department of State, 28/11/51.
29. Goodman, *The Joint Intelligence Committee*, p.358.
30. CCC: AMEJ 1/2/93, Amery to Woodhouse, 71/52; Woodhouse to Amery, 13/2/52; Amery to Lloyd, 25/3/52.
31. FO248/1531, handwritten note by Zaehner, 13/7/52.
32. NARA: RG59, 250/49/18/7, 'Memorandum of Conversation: The Iranian Situation', 30/4/52.
33. Goodman, *The Joint Intelligence Committee*, p.358; FO248/1531, Zaehner, 15/5/52.
34. Kinzer, *All the Shah's Men*, p.136.
35. CAD: Avon Papers, FO800/808, Eden to Churchill, 20/7/52.
36. DNSA: Berthoud, 'Persia', 15/6/51; Goodman, *The Joint Intelligence Committee*, p.359.
37. Abrahamian, *The Coup*, p.136.
38. CCC: AMEJ 1/2/93, Amery to Qavam, 14/3/52; Lloyd to Amery, 16/4/52; Amery to Lloyd, 25/3/52; AMEJ 1/2/93, Lloyd to Amery, 16/4/52; Amery to Lloyd, 25/3/52.
39. FO248/1531, handwritten note by Falle, 22.4/52; handwritten note by Zaehner, 23/4/52; Zaehner, 'Qavam-us-Saltaneh', 24/4/52.

40. CCC: AMEJ 1/2/69, Amery, 'The Middle East', undated.
41. FRUS: Iran, 1951–54, doc.95, Holmes, Telegram from the Embassy in the United Kingdom to the Department of State, 21/7/52.
42. Kinzer, *All the Shah's Men*, p.141.
43. FO248/1531, Franks to Foreign Office, 'The Mob in Iran', 26/7/52.
44. PREM11/236, Middleton to Foreign Office, 28/7/52; Kinzer, *All the Shah's Men*, p.142; Abrahamian, *The Coup*, p.147.
45. PREM 1/236, American embassy in London to Foreign Office, 'Persia', August 1952.
46. FO371/98691, Note by Ross, 28/7/52.
47. FO800/813, Eden to Franks, 'Situation in Persia', 6/8/52; see also Rahnema, *Behind the 1953 Coup in Iran*, p.21.
48. CAD: Avon Papers, FO800/808, Tehran to Foreign Office, 28/8/52.
49. Cavendish, *Inside Intelligence*, p.140; Gasiorowski, 'Conclusion', pp.262, 266; Mokhtari, 'Iran's 1953 Coup Revisited', pp.477, 485.
50. Wilber, *Regime Change in Iran*, p.23.
51. FRUS: Iran, 1951–54, doc. 53 [classified CIA], Memorandum for the Record, 9/11/51.
52. KV4/473, Diary of Guy Liddell, 15/11/51, p.178.
53. DNSA: Scott Koch, CIA History Staff, *'Zendebad, Shah!': The Central Intelligence Agency and the Fall of Iranian Prime Minister Mohammed Mossadeq, August 1953*, June 1998, http://www2.gwu.edu/~nsarchiv/NSAEBB/NSAEBB435/docs/Doc%204%20-%20CIA%20-%20Zendebad%20Shah%20-%202000%20release.PDF pp.9–10.
54. FRUS: Iran, 1951–54, doc. 99, Acheson, Telegram From the Department of State to the Embassy in the United Kingdom, 26/7/52.
55. FRUS: Iran, 1951–54, doc. 122, Memorandum From the Chief of the Iran Branch, Near East and Africa Division (Leavitt) to the Chief of the Near East and Africa Division, Directorate of Plans, Central Intelligence Agency (Roosevelt), 22/9/52; 133, Memorandum From the Assistant Secretary of State for Near Eastern, South Asian, and African Affairs (Byroade) to the Deputy Under Secretary of State (Matthews), 15/10/52.
56. NARA: RG 59, General Records of the Department of State, 1950-54 Central Decimal File, 788.00/11-2652: Byroade to Matthews, 'Proposal to Organize a Coup d'état in Iran', 26/11/52; 788.00/12-352: Jernegan, 'Memorandum of Conversation: British Proposal to Organize a Coup d'état in Iran', 3/12/52. Thanks to Clive Jones for sharing these documents.
57. LHCMA: Woodhouse 8/1, confidential account of conversation with Eden and Macmillan, 2/12/54.
58. FO371/91609, Berthoud, 'Persia', 2/11/51.
59. FRUS: Iran, 1951–54, Doc.30, Acheson, Telegram From the Department of State to the Embassy in Iran, 29/5/51; 32, Grady, Telegram From the Embassy in Iran to the Department of State, 3/6/51; 133, Memorandum From the Assistant Secretary of State for Near Eastern, South Asian, and African Affairs

(Byroade) to the Deputy Under Secretary of State (Matthews), 15/10/52; 169, Dulles, Memorandum From Director of Central Intelligence Dulles to President Eisenhower, 1/3/53.

60. FRUS: Iran, 1951–54, doc.133, Memorandum From the Assistant Secretary of State for Near Eastern, South Asian, and African Affairs (Byroade) to the Deputy Under Secretary of State (Matthews), 15/10/52; 134, Memorandum From the Deputy Assistant Secretary of State for Near Eastern, South Asian, and African Affairs (Jernegan) to the Deputy Under Secretary of State (Matthews), 23/10/52.

61. Abrahamian, *The Coup*, p.174; Woodhouse, *Something Ventured*, p.117; LHCMA: Woodhouse 8/1, Woodhouse, 'Iran 1950–3', 16/8/76, p.4, 5b.

62. FO248/1531, Falle, 'The American Proposals', 4/8/52.

63. Israeli, 'The Circuitous Nature of Operation Ajax', p.253.

64. CCC: AMEJ3 1/2/69, Amery, 'The Middle East', undated; NARA: RG59, Records relating to State Department Participation in the Operations Coordinating Board and the National Security Council, 1947–63, Lot 63D351, NSC, Box 68, 'NSC 136: U.S. and Policy regarding the Present Situation in Iran', 20 November 1952; NARA: RG59, 250/49/18/7, Eden to Acheson, 9/8/52; Kinzer, *All the Shah's Men*, pp.144–7.

65. CREST: National Intelligence Estimate, 'Probable Developments in Iran Through 1953', 13/11/52.

66. Kinzer, *All the Shah's Men*, p.151.

67. DNSA: CIA History Staff, 'Battle for Iran', *c.*mid-1970s, pp.39–40; Eisenhower to Churchill, 5 May 1953, in Boyle (ed.), *Churchill-Eisenhower Correspondence*, p.52; Aldrich and Cormac, *Behind the Black Door*; NARA: RG59 250/49/18/7, Department of State Memorandum of Conversation, 'Interest in Iranian Oil', 19/1/53.

68. FO371/104257, Colville to Strang, 22/5/53.

69. PREM11/514, Dixon to Churchill, 22/8/53; Churchill to Dixon, 24/8/53; FO371/104257, Colville to Strang, 22/5/53.

70. LHCMA: Woodhouse 8/1, confidential account of conversation with Eden and Macmillan, 2/12/54.

71. LHCMA: Woodhouse 8/1, Woodhouse, 'Iran 1950–3', 16/8/76, pp.5, 5a, 7, 8.

72. Dorril, *MI6*, p.581.

73. Louis, 'Britain and the Overthrow of the Mossadeq Government', pp.166–7.

74. FO371/104562, Ross, 'Persia', 26/2/53.

75. NARA: RG59 888.2553/7-3053, US embassy, London, to Secretary of State, 30/7/53.

76. Eden, *Full Circle*, p.209.

77. Ibid., p.211; see also CAD: MS 191/1/2/2, Shuckburgh Diary, 16/1/53.

78. CAD: Avon Papers, FO800/814, Washington to Strang and Eden, 27/2/53.

79. FRUS: Iran, 1951–54, doc.179, State Dept., Memorandum for the Record, 18/3/53.

80. LHCMA: Woodhouse 8/1, Woodhouse, 'Iran 1950–3', 16/8/76, pp.9, 11a.

81. FRUS: Iran, 1951–54, doc.159, Briefing Notes Prepared in the Central Intelligence Agency for Director of Central Intelligence Dulles, undated [Feb.1953]; 162, Telegram From the Embassy in Iran to the Department of State, 26/2/53.

82. DNSA: CIA History Staff, 'Battle for Iran', c.mid-1970s, p.30; CAD: Avon Papers, FO800/814, Washington to Foreign Office, 9/3/53.

83. Wilber, *Regime Change in Iran*, p.21.

84. PDP: Dixon pocket diary, 23/2/53.

85. BOD: MS Sherfield 959, Strang to Makins, 15/4/53; Strang to Makins, 8/5/53.

86. PDP: Dixon diary 1953, 3/5/53.

87. LHCMA: Woodhouse 8/1, Woodhouse, 'Iran 1950-3', 16/8/76, pp.12, 16.

88. CAB301/117, Trend to Bligh, 'S.I.S. Reserves', 18/6/53; Trend to Bridges, 20/5/54.

89. Louis, 'Britain and the Overthrow of the Mossadeq Government', p.168.

90. Louis, *Ends of British Imperialism*, p.768; West, *At Her Majesty's Secret Service*, pp.39–53. Dorril, *MI6*, p.494.

91. DNSA: CIA History Staff, 'Battle for Iran', c.mid-1970s, p.32; Abrahamian, *The Coup*, p.151; Dorril, *MI6*, p.574.

92. Wilber, *Regime Change in Iran*, pp.14, 33, 69–70; Abrahamian, *The Coup*, p.178.

93. Wilber, *Regime Change in Iran*, pp.22, 63.

94. Ibid., pp.14, 26.

95. DNSA: CIA History Staff, 'Battle for Iran', c.mid-1970s, p.36.

96. Wilber, *Regime Change in Iran*, p.82.

97. Ibid., pp.82–3; Curtis, *Secret Affairs*, p.50; Dorril, *MI6*, pp.560–1; Gasiorowski, 'Conclusion', p.266; Mokhteri, 'Iran's 1953 Coup Revisited', p.488.

98. Bale, 'The May 1973 Terrorist Attack at Milan Police HQ', p.135.

99. Wilber, *Regime Change in Iran*, pp.37, 85.

100. FCO371/104581, Ross, Untitled Memorandum, 5/5/53.

101. Abrahamian, *The Coup*, pp.178–9.

102. LAB13/1069, Thomas to Greenhough, 28/7/52.

103. DNSA: CIA History Staff, 'Battle for Iran', c.mid-1970s, pp.37, 54.

104. Wilber, *Regime Change in Iran*, p.27. Churchill had since suffered a stroke so it was likely that Norman Brook, the cabinet secretary, approved the plan in accordance with Churchill's known wishes.

105. Callanan, *Covert Action in the Cold War*, p.189.

106. CAD: Avon Papers, FO800/814, Salisbury to Churchill, 8/7/53.

107. LHCMA: Woodhouse 8/1, Woodhouse, 'Iran 1950-3', 16/8/76, p.2.

108. DNSA: CIA History Staff, 'Battle for Iran', c.mid-1970s, p.47.

109. FO371/104565, Ross, 'Persia', 15/4/53.

110. FRUS: Iran, 1951–64, doc.210, State Dept, Memorandum for the Record, 21/5/53.

111. LHCMA: Woodhouse 8/1, Woodhouse, 'Iran 1950–3', 16/8/76, pp.12, 16.

112. Dorril, *MI6*, p.588.

113. Wilber, *Regime Change in Iran*, p.31.

114. Ibid., p.33; Dorril, *MI6*, p.589.

115. Wilber, *Regime Change in Iran*, pp.23, 82.

116. DNSA: CIA History Staff, 'Battle for Iran', c.mid-1970s, p.54.

117. Abrahamian, *The Coup*, p.184.

118. Ibid., Bedell Smith to Eisenhower, 'Memorandum for the President', 18/8/53.

119. FRUS: Iran 1951–54, doc.307, Record of Meeting in the Central Intelligence Agency, 28/8/53.

120. DNSA: Baghdad to Secretary of State, 17/8/53, http://nsarchive.gwu.edu/ NSAEBB/NSAEBB477/docs/Doc%206%20--%201953-08-17%20Baghdad%20 cable%2092%20re%20Shah%20meeting%20with%20Berry.pdf.

121. DDEL: Eisenhower Papers as President, International Series, Box 32, Iran 1953–59 (8), Baghdad to Secretary of State, telegram number 92, 17/8/53.

122. DNSA: Eisenhower Diaries, 8/10/53, http://nsarchive.gwu.edu/NSAEBB/ NSAEBB477/docs/Doc%201%20--%201953-10-08%20Eisenhower%20 diary%20covering%20Iran%20Aug%2019.pdf.

123. Goodman, *The Joint Intelligence Committee*, p.360.

124. Wilber, *Regime Change in Iran*, p.51.

125. DNSA: CIA History Staff, 'Battle for Iran', c.mid-1970s, pp.62, 66; Wilber, *Regime Change in Iran*, pp.17, 44, 47.

126. Wilber, *Regime Change in Iran*, p.48.

127. Abrahamian, *The Coup*, pp.188–9.

128. Wilber, *Regime Change in Iran*, p.52.

129. West, *Secret Service*, p.69.

130. Wilber, *Regime Change in Iran*, pp.49–50.

131. DNSA: CIA History Staff, 'Battle for Iran', c.mid-1970s, p.66; Abrahamian, *The Coup*, p.192.

132. DNSA: Scott Koch, CIA History Staff, *'Zendebad, Shah!': The Central Intelligence Agency and the Fall of Iranian Prime Minister Mohammed Mossadeq, August 1953*, June 1998, p.63.

133. LHCMA: Woodhouse 8/1, Woodhouse, 'Iran 1950–3', 16/8/76, p.5.

134. Wilber, *Regime Change in Iran*, p.84.

135. Abrahamian, *The Coup*, p.194.

136. LHCMA: Woodhouse 8/1, Woodhouse, 'Iran 1950–3', 16/8/76, pp.13, 16.

137. PDP: Dixon pocket diary, 19/8/53.

138. Goodman, *The Joint Intelligence Committee*, p.362.

139. Wilber, *Regime Change in Iran*, p.58.

140. DNSA: Eisenhower Diaries, 8/10/53.

141. Roosevelt, *Countercoup*, p.207; Mokhtari, 'Iran's 1953 Coup Revisited', p.477.

142. Eden, *Full Circle*, p.214.

143. NARA: RG59, 788.00/8-2453, US embassy, London, to State Department, 24/8/53.

144. FO371/104577, Dixon, untitled memorandum, 21/8/53.
145. CAD: Avon Papers, FO800/814, Salisbury, 'Record of Conversation', 26/8/53.
146. DDEL: Eisenhower Papers as President, International Series, Box 32, Iran 1953–59 (7), State Department, 'Visit of the Shah of Iran', December 1954.
147. DDEL: Eisenhower Papers as President, International Series, Box 32, Iran 1953–59 (8), Redacted author (but likely Roosevelt), 'Memorandum for the President', undated.
148. FO371/104577, Gandy, 'Note for Lord Salisbury's Meeting with the Press', 28/8/53.
149. Wilber, *Regime Change in Iran*, p.59.
150. Louis, *Ends of British Imperialism*, p.768.
151. Wilber, *Regime Change in Iran*, pp.59, 62.
152. CAD: Avon Papers, FO800/808, Priestman to Shuckburgh, 19/1/54.
153. DDEL: Eisenhower Papers as President, International Series, Box 32, Iran 1953–59 (8), Redacted author (but likely Roosevelt), 'Memorandum for the President', undated.
154. Wilber, *Regime Change in Iran*, p.67.
155. Louis, 'Britain and the Overthrow of the Mossadeq Government', p.141.
156. Takeh, 'What Really Happened in Iran'.
157. CAB128/26, Cabinet Conclusions, CC(53)50th Conclusions, 25/8/53; DNSA: CIA History Staff, 'Battle for Iran', c.mid-1970s, p.28.
158. FO800/814, Salisbury, 'Record of Conversation', 26/8/53.
159. Quoted in Goodman, *Joint Intelligence Committee*, p.362.

CHAPTER 6

1. FOI: Eden, 'Memorandum by the Prime Minister, S 50/96/4, 14 December 1955.
2. FO 371/135610, Foreign Office Steering Committee, 'Overseas Planning Committee and Political Intelligence Group', SC(58)6, undated, 1956.
3. LHCMA: Woodhouse 8/1, Note by Woodhouse, 2 December 1954; Note by Woodhouse, 10 December 1954.
4. PREM 11/1582, Macmillan to Eden, 19 October 1955.
5. CAD: Shuckburgh diary, 20 February 1956.
6. Beesley, *Cabinet Secretaries*, p.133.
7. FOI: Eden, 'Memorandum by the Prime Minister, S 50/96/4, 14 December 1955.
8. Pearce, *Spymaster*, p.149; Maguire, *British and American Intelligence*, p.217.
9. FOI: Kirkpatrick circular to representatives abroad, OPS/1/56, 17 May 1956; see also PREM 11/1582, Brook to Eden, 28 November 1955.
10. PREM 11/1582, Brook to Eden, 21 October 1955.
11. FO 371/125003, 'The Problem of Nationalism', 21 November 1952.

12. PREM 11/1582, Macmillan to Eden, 19 October 1955; CO 1035/116, 'Cold War – Countering Covert Aggression', CoS(55)262, 12 October 1955; CAB 301/126, 'Meeting at Number 10 Downing Street to Discuss Intelligence and Intelligence Targets', December 1959; FOI: Dean to Kirkpatrick, OPS/1/56, 3 January 1956; Dean, 'Record of Meeting' held by Kirkpatrick to discuss countering subversion, 19 January 1956; Dean to Foreign Secretary, 'Counter-Subversion', 19 March 1956. Thanks to Chikara Hashimoto for sharing the latter.

13. Haslam, *Russia's Cold War*, pp.154, 156.

14. FO 371/125003, 'The Problem of Nationalism', 21 November 1952.

15. FO 371/135615, 'Steering Committee: Points for a Middle East Policy: Part II', SC(58)40(Final), Summer 1958.

16. Mawby, 'The Clandestine Defence of Empire', p.105.

17. John Bruce Lockhart, 'Young, George Kennedy (1911–1990)', *ODNB*.

18. Young, *Who Is My Liege?* p.80.

19. CAB 301/148, Foreign Secretary, 'Annex A: Possible Reaction of the Soviet Union to the United States Policy on Syria in Areas other than the Middle East' and 'Annex B: Possible Reactions of the Soviet Union in the Middle East Area to United States Policy on Syria', undated, 1957.

20. CAB 21/5003, Brook, 'Note for Record', 28 February 1955; CAB 21/2992, Dean to Harold Parker (PUS MoD), 9 March 1956; CAB 21/5003, Young to Brook, 'AC(O) and AC(M)', 31 January 1955.

21. PREM 11/1582, Brook to Eden, 21 October 1955; Brook to Eden, 28 November 1955.

22. PREM 11/1582, Brook to Eden, 21 October 1955.

23. PREM 11/1582, Brook, 'Counter-Subversion', Undated, (November–December 1955).

24. Goodman, *The Joint Intelligence Committee*, p.381; FO 371/135610, 'Minutes of the 6th Meeting of the Steering Committee', 21 January 1958.

25. FO 371/135610, 'Overseas Planning Committee and Political Intelligence Group', SC(58)6, January 1958; Dean to Lloyd, 'Counter-Subversion' and country-specific annexes, 19 March 1956; Dean to Lloyd, 19 March 1956; Minutes, Cabinet: Counter-Subversion, S.50/96/4/1st Meeting, 24 Feb 1956; Kirkpatrick circular to representatives abroad, OPS/1/56, 17 May 1956; 'The Russia Committee and the Overseas Planning Committee', 18 July 1957; FO 371/135610 'Overseas Planning Committee and Political Intelligence Group', Foreign Office Steering Committee, SC(58)6, undated. The OPC absorbed the Russia Committee in 1957—and was subsequently renamed the Political Intelligence Committee.

26. FO 371/135610, 'Minutes of the 6th Meeting of the Steering Committee', 21 January 1958; 'Overseas Planning Committee and Political Intelligence Group', SC(58)6, January 1958; see also LHCMA: SUEZOHP6:DP, 'Interview with Sir Douglas Dodds-Parker conducted by Anthony Gorst and W Scott Lucas'.

27. CAB 301/118, Compton, 'Secret Vote: Reserves', 17 January 1957.

28. CAB 301/118, Compton to Brook, 'Secret Service Reserve Funds', 21 May 1958.
29. CAB 301/117, Kirkpatrick to Bridges, 9 August 1956; Trend to Constant, 5 January 1954; Trend to Compton, 20 May 1954.
30. Zamir, 'The Missing Dimension', pp.791–899.
31. CAB 301/118, Compton to Brook, 'Secret Service Reserve Funds', 21 May 1958.
32. CAB 301/117, Trend to Bligh, 'S.I.S. Reserves', 18 June 1953; Trend to Bridges, 20 May 1954.
33. CAB 301/117, Trend to Bridges, 20 May 1954.
34. CAB 301/117, Kirkpatrick to Bridges, 9 August 1956.
35. FOI: Dean to Lloyd, 'Counter-Subversion' and country-specific annexes, 19 March 1956; FOI: Patrick Dean, 'Counter-Subversion', OPS/10/56, 29 March 1956.
36. Ibid.
37. Hashimoto, *The Twilight of the British Empire*.
38. Quoted in Thomas, *The Very Best Men*, p.181.
39. Mawby, 'The Clandestine defence of Empire', pp.105–17.
40. CAB 301/118, Wade-Gery to Compton, 1 August 1957.
41. CAD: MS 191/1/2/4, Shuckburgh Diary, 6 October 1955.
42. FOI: Kirkpatrick, circular note, OPS/1/56, 17 May 1956.
43. CAD: MS 191/1/2/4, Shuckburgh Diary, 28 January 1955.
44. Rathmell, *Secret War in the Middle East*, pp.113, 114, 118.
45. CAD: MS 191/1/2/4, Shuckburgh Diary, 6 October 1955.
46. Wilford, *America's Great Game*, p.224.
47. FO 371/121273, 'Report by Chairman, Chiefs of Staff, on Visit to Washington 3rd–5th April, 1956'.
48. CAB 128/30, Cabinet Minutes, CM24(56), 21 March 1956.
49. Quoted in Rathmell, *Secret War in the Middle East*, p.118.
50. FO 371/121858, Baghdad to Foreign Office, 19 March 1956.
51. FO 371/121858, Lloyd to Eden, Syria', 15 March 1956.
52. FO 371/121871, 'Record of Conversation between the Secretary of State and the Pakistani Foreign Ministers', undated 1956.
53. CAB 301/118, Dean to Compton, 18 July 1957.
54. FO 371/115954, 'Middle East: Record of Conversation in State Department on October 27, 1955'.
55. DDEL: National Security Council Staff Papers, OCB Central Series, Box 55, OCB91 Syria (2), OCB, 'Preparation of Courses of Action against Communism in Syria, Annex: Individual Recommendations Re Courses of Action Against Communism in Syria', 9 January 1956; OCB91 Syria (3), Gustin to Staats, 'Courses of Action in Syria', 18 July 1956.
56. Wilford, *America's Great Game*, p.247.
57. Hashimoto, *The Twilight of the British Empire*, p.132.
58. Lucas, *Divided We Stand*, p.117.

59. Rathmell, *Secret War in the Middle East*, p.121.
60. FO 371/128220, British Embassy, Beirut, to Foreign Office, 18 January 1957.
61. Lucas, *Divided we Stand*, p.218.
62. Wilford, *America's Great Game*, p.254.
63. Dorril, *MI6*, p.637.
64. FO 371/115954, G. Arthur, 'Iraq and Syria: The Fertile Crescent', 10 October 1955.
65. CAD: MS 191/1/2/4, Shuckburgh Diary, 6 October 1955.
66. Hashimoto, *The Twilight of the British Empire*, p.132.
67. Wilford, *America's Great Game*, p.256.
68. DDEL: John Foster Dulles Papers, Box 4, Meetings with the President Aug. thru Dec. 1956 (3), Memorandum of Conversation between the President, Secretary of State, and Under-Secretary of State, 7 November 1956. See Wilford, *America's Great Game*, p.260.
69. Jones, 'The Preferred Plan', p.403; Rathmell, *Secret War in the Middle East*, p.122; Kyle, *Suez*, p.367.
70. FOI: Dean to Lloyd, 'Counter-Subversion' and country-specific annexes, 19 March 1956; FOI: Patrick Dean, 'Counter-Subversion', OPS/10/56, 29 March 1956.
71. DDEL: Dulles Papers, Subject Series, Box 11, Eden–Macmillan–Lloyd Correspondence 1955–56 (2), Eden to Eisenhower, January 1956.
72. CCC: AMEJ 1/2/137, Handwritten Diary, 22 February 1956; FO 800/723, British Embassy, Cairo, 'Egypt', 2 May 1956; FOI: Dean to Lloyd, 'Counter-Subversion' and country-specific annexes, 19 March 1956; FOI: Patrick Dean, 'Counter-Subversion', OPS/10/56, 29 March 1956.
73. DEFE 32/3, Chiefs of Staff Committee, 'Confidential Annex to COS(53)114th Meeting Held on Thursday, 8th October, 1953'; Ministry of Defence to GHQ Middle East Land Forces, COS(ME)28, 30 October 1953; GHQ Middle East Land Forces to Ministry of Defence, 11 November 1953.
74. DEFE 32/3, Chiefs of Staff Committee, 'Confidential Annex to COS(53)128th Meeting Held on Monday, 16th November 1953.'
75. CAD: MS 191/1/2/4, Shuckburgh Diary, 6 October 1955.
76. PREM 11/1122, Jedda to Foreign Office, 2 October 1956.
77. Lucas, *Divided We Stand*, p.117.
78. Eveland, *Ropes of Sand*, p.170.
79. FO 371/121273, 'Report by Chairman, Chiefs of Staff, on Visit to Washington 3rd–5th April, 1956'.
80. Eveland, *Ropes of Sand*, p.170.
81. Wilford, *America's Great Game*, p.221.
82. DDEL: National Security Council Staff Papers, PSB Central Files Series, Box 13, PSB091 Iran, H. MacLean, 'Memorandum for the Record', 10 September 1953.
83. Eveland, *Ropes of Sand*, p.170.
84. Wilford, *America's Great Game*, pp.221, 222.

85. NSA: Kai Bird Donation, Box 17, US Embassy, London, to Secretary of State, 9 October 1956.

86. Rathmell, *Secret War in the Middle East*, p.137.

87. Niblock, *Saudi Arabia*, p.41.

88. Ashton, *King Hussein of Jordan*, pp.42–3.

89. Shlaim, *Lion of Jordan*, p.61.

90. CAD: MS 191/1/2/4, Shuckburgh Diary, 7 July 1955.

91. Goodman, *The Joint Intelligence Committee*, p.377.

92. Owen, *In Sickness and in Power*, pp.117–21.

93. Beesley, *Cabinet Secretaries*, p.135.

94. CCC: AMEJ 1/2/137, Amery to Lloyd, 16 May 1956.

95. CCC: AMEJ 1/2/137, Amery, 'The Next Stage in the Middle East', 14 May 1956.

96. CAB 301/118, Wade-Gery to Compton, 25 October 1957; Dean to Compton, 18 July 1957.

97. CAB 301/118, Dean to Compton, 18 July 1957.

98. Goodman, *The Joint Intelligence Committee*, p.387.

99. Quoted in Hashimoto, *The Twilight of the British Empire*, p.85.

100. Onslow, 'Julian Amery and the Suez Operation', p.77.

101. Lucas, 'Divided We Stand', p.101.

102. Pearson, *Albania as Dictatorship and Democracy*, p.594.

103. CCC: AMEJ 1/2/137, Julian Amery, 'Note of a Meeting to Visit King Zog, 29/30 Jan. 1956'.

104. Ibid.

105. CCC: AMEJ 1/2/137, Amery, 'The Next Stage in the Middle East', 14 May 1956; see also Onslow, 'Julian Amery and the Suez Operation', pp.77–8.

106. Young, *Who is My Liege?*, p.79.

107. Aldrich, *The Hidden Hand*, pp.481–2; Bower, *Perfect English Spy*, p.200; Lucas, *Divided we Stand*, p.101; Lucas, 'Suez—The Missing Dimension'; Gerolymatos, *Castles Made of Sand*, pp.13–14; LHCMA: SUEZOHP1:AMERY, 'Interview with Julian Amery conducted by Anthony Gorst and W Scott Lucas 12 June 1989'.

108. Lucas, *Divided We Stand*, pp.193–4.

109. Onslow, 'Julian Amery and the Suez Operation', pp.78, 79.

110. *The Daily Telegraph*, 'John Farmer', 29 November 2012, http://www.telegraph.co.uk/news/obituaries/9712479/John-Farmer.html.

111. Deacon, '*C*', p.111.

112. Bower, *Perfect English Spy*, pp.191, 200.

113. Onslow, 'Julian Amery and the Suez Operation', pp.79, 81.

114. Goodman, *Joint Intelligence Committee*, pp.378, 408.

115. Beesley, *Cabinet Secretaries*, p.143.

116. LHCMA: SUEZOHP6: DP, 'Interview with Sir Douglas Dodds-Parker conducted by Anthony Gorst and W Scott Lucas'.

117. Quoted in Aldrich, *The Hidden Hand*, p.479.

118. Bower, *Perfect English Spy*, pp.185–6.

119. Corera, *The Art of Betrayal*, pp.79–80.

120. Simon Usborne, 'Top Secret: A Century of British Espionage', *The Independent*, 6 October 2009; Aldrich, *The Hidden Hand*, p.480; Bower, *Perfect English Spy*, p.192; Dorril, *MI6*, pp.633–4; Gerolymatos, *Castles Made of Sand*, p.10.

121. Dorril, *MI6*, pp.633, 639; Curtis, *Secret Affairs*, pp.62–3; Kyle, *Suez*, p.555; Bower, *Perfect English Spy*, p.192.

122. CAD: Avon Papers, FO 800/775, Churchill to Cairo, 27 October 1954.

123. YUL: Buckley Papers, Box 544, Folder 117, Copeland to Avon, 25 June 1975; Aldrich and Cormac, *The Black Door*, p.202.

124. Hennessy, *The Prime Minister*, p.216; Bower, *Perfect English Spy*, p.186.

125. Kyle, *Suez*, p.555.

126. Corera, *The Art of Betrayal*, p.80; Lucas, *Divided we Stand*, p.193.

127. Richelson, 'When Kindness Fails', p.251.

128. Pearce, *Spymaster*, p.158.

129. McDermott, *The New Diplomacy*, p.142.

130. CCC: AMEJ 1/2/137, Amery, 'Notes on Propaganda to the Middle East'; Rawnsley, 'The Voice of Britain and Black Radio Broadcasting in the Suez Crisis', p.497.

131. Beesely, *Cabinet Secretaries*, p.136.

132. FO 1110/880, Dodds-Parker to Foreign Secretary, 'Propaganda and Political Warfare in the Middle East', 18 October 1956.

133. Dodds-Parker's advisory committee served the ministerial Egypt committee. It included John Rennie, head of the IRD and also chair of the Information Co-ordination Executive; John Drew, a former MI5 officer then in charge of deception; Dick White, head of SIS; Patrick Dean, the diplomat overseeing intelligence and security in the Foreign Office; Charles Hambro, formerly of the SOE; and Hugh Carleton-Greene from the BBC. In the chairman's words they were 'all people who knew what clandestine activities were'. Dodds-Parker's committee was disbanded in February 1957, but the Executive continued to run. See CAB 21/3406, Lloyd to Brook, 27 February 1957; FO 1110/880, Dean to Rennie, 'Organisation of Political Warfare for Suez', 3 August 1956; Rennie, 'Organisation for Political Warfare', 8 August 1956; Kirkpatrick, 'Information Coordination Executive', 21 August 1956; 'Record of Meeting of Mr Dodds-Parker's Advisory Committee at 10.30am, August 24, 1956'; LHCMA: SUEZOHP6:DP, 'Interview with Sir Douglas Dodds-Parker conducted by Anthony Gorst and W Scott Lucas'.

134. Kyle, Suez, pp.554–5; Dodds-Parker, *Political Eunuch*, p.110.

135. FO 1110/880, Dodds-Parker to Foreign Secretary, 'Propaganda and Political Warfare in the Middle East', 18 October 1956.

136. For a more detailed discussion see Vaughan, *Unconquerable Minds*.

137. DEFE 28/11, 'Confidential Annex to DCC(57) 6th Meeting of 15th March, 1957'; 'Joint Psychological Warfare Committee Middle East: Brief on Psychological Warfare for Chairman, for BDCC(ME) Meeting with the

Minister of Defence on 25th April 1957', Annex to PWC/3516/ME, 24 April 1957.

138. DO 35/6227, Top Secret Submission to the Dodds-Parker Committee by the Information Executive Coordination Executive, 15 November 1956; FO 1110/880, Dodds-Parker to Foreign Secretary, 'Propaganda and Political Warfare in the Middle East', 18 October 1956.

139. Beesley, *Cabinet Secretaries*, p.141.

140. DO 35/6227, 'ICE Progress Report', undated but presumably October 1956; DEFE 28/11, 'Brief on Psychological Warfare for Chairman, for BDCC(ME) meeting with the Minister of Defence on 25th April 1957'.

141. CREST: CIA Information Report, 'Second Unidentified Anti-Nasir Station', 4 October 1956.

142. Wilford, *America's Great Game*, p.259.

143. Bower, *Perfect English Spy*, p.185.

144. Hashimoto, *The Twilight of the British Empire*.

CHAPTER 7

1. Quoted in Jones, 'Preferred Plan', p.408.

2. CAD: MS 191/1/2/5, Shuckburgh Diary, 5/12/56.

3. FO371/135623, 'Future Policy', PUSD Planning Section, 15/1/58.

4. PREM11/2401, NFC to Moreton, 30/12/56.

5. Mawby, 'The Clandestine defence of Empire' pp.105–17.

6. PREM11/2401, 'Aden Protectorate: Proposed Special Operations against the Yemen in Dhala Area', PM(56)79, October 1956.

7. FOI: Dean to Lloyd, 'Counter-Subversion' and country-specific annexes, 19/3/56; Dean, 'Counter-Subversion', OPS/10/56, 29/3/56; CAB301/118, Dean to Compton, 18/7/57.

8. CAB301/118, Dean to Compton, 18/7/57.

9. Wilford, *America's Great Game*, p.268.

10. Hashimoto, *The Twilight of the British Empire*. One other mysterious covert action was codenamed Operation Lidget and authorized at the same time, but it is unclear where it targeted. See CAB301/118, Dean to Compton, 18/7/57.

11. Corera, *The Art of Betrayal*, pp.79–80.

12. CAD: MS 191/1/2/5, Shuckburgh Diary, 7/5/57.

13. Callanan, *Covert Action in the Cold War*, p.103; Eveland, *Ropes of Sand*, pp.244–7.

14. FO371/125423, Brenchley, 'Egypt: Wafdist Plot', 26/7/57.

15. FO371/135642, Ramsbotham, 'Middle East Policy', 28/8/58, attached: 'Points for a Middle East Policy', PUSD, 27/8/58; Aldrich, *The Hidden Hand*, p.483; Rawnsley, 'The Voice of Britain and Black Radio Broadcasting in the Suez Crisis', pp.511–12; Kyle, *Suez*, p.151.

16. Khrushchev, *Khrushchev Remembers*, pp.438–9.

17. Hashimoto, *The Twilight of the British Empire,* pp.128–9

18. FO1110/1220, Barclay to Wright, 24/10/59.

19. FO1110/1220, Foreign Office minute, 10/12/59.

20. Hashimoto, *The Twilight of the British Empire*. See also Boyd, 'Sharq Al-Adna/ The Voice of Britain', pp.443–55.

21. Bittman, *The Deception Game*, pp.19–20, 29.

22. CAB301/118, Compton to Lloyd, 'Secret Vote: Special Operations', 29/4/57.

23. FOI: Brook, 'Special Political Action', 31/7/58.

24. CAB301/118, Trend, 'Reserves', 25/3/58.

25. CAB301/118, Compton to Brook, 'Secret Service Reserve Funds', 21/5/58.

26. Ibid.

27. FOI: Brook, 'Special Political Action', 31/7/58.

28. DDEL: Oral History Interview, Winthrop Aldrich, 16/10/72, pp.11–12; DDEL: John Foster Dulles Papers, Box 4, Meetings with the President, Aug. thru Dec. 1956 (3), Memorandum of conversation between the President and Secretary of State, 17/11/56; NSA: Kai Bird Donation, Box 17, CD Jackson to Luce, 26/11/56.

29. Thomas, *The Very Best Men*, p.143.

30. Larres, 'Britain and the Cold War', pp.147–8.

31. Quoted in Thomas, *The Very Best Men*, p.173.

32. BDOHP: 'Interview with Lord Greenhill of Harrow on 14 February 1996', p.5; NARA: RG59, Bureau of Near Eastern and South Asian Affairs, Records of the United Arab Republic Affairs Desk, 1956–62, Department of State: Biographic Information Division, 'Harold Macmillan', 20/3/61.

33. DDEL: CD Jackson Papers, Box 48, Dulles, Allen (1), Jackson to Dulles, 25/3/59.

34. USDDO: State Dept, 'Bermuda Meeting, March 21–23, 1957, Syria, (Expected to be raised by the British)', 21/3/57.

35. CREST: CIA, 'Possible Soviet Satellitization of Syria: Targets, Techniques and Indicators', 10 December 1957; CIA, 'NSC Briefing: Repercussions of Developments in Syria', 20/8/57.

36. CAD: MS 191/1/2/5, Shuckburgh Diary, 7/5/57.

37. CAB301/118, Wade-Gery to Compton, 25/10/57.

38. Jones, 'The Preferred Plan', pp.403–10; Rathmell, *Secret War in the Middle East*, p.120; Gerolymatos, *Castles Made of Sand*, pp.151–2.

39. USDDO: Dulles to Lloyd, 21/8/57.

40. For details on Turkey's role see Bezci, *Turkey and Western Intelligence Cooperation*, p.210.

41. CREST: Special National Intelligence Estimate, 36-7-57, 'Developments in the Syrian Situation', 3 September 1957; USDDO: JF Dulles to Macmillan, 27/8/57.

42. CREST: Special National Intelligence Estimate, 30-3-56, 'Nasser and the Middle East Situation', 31/7/56; Special National Intelligence Estimate, 30-4-56, 'Probably Repercussions of British–French Military Action in the Suez Crisis', 5/9/56.

43. USDDO: Burdett, 'Joint US–UK Working Group Report on Syria', 21/9/57.

44. Ibid.
45. Wilford, *America's Great Game*, p.275.
46. DDEL: Eisenhower Papers as President, International Series, Box 48, Syria (2), Goodpaster, 'Memorandum for the Record', 23/8/57.
47. USDDO: Dulles to Lloyd, 21/8/57.
48. USDDO: Rountree), Memorandum of Conversation between Caccia and JF Dulles, 'Syria', 10/9/57; USDDO: Burdett, 'Joint US–UK Working Group Report on Syria', 21/9/57.
49. USDDO: Burdett, 'Joint US–UK Working Group Report on Syria', 21/9/57.
50. USDDO: Rountree, Memorandum of Conversation between Caccia and JF Dulles, 'The Syrian Crisis', 13/9/57.
51. USDDO: Burdett, 'Joint US–UK Working Group Report on Syria', 21/9/57.
52. Ibid.
53. Jones, 'The Preferred Plan', p.407.
54. USDDO: Burdett, 'Joint US–UK Working Group Report on Syria', 21/9/57.
55. Ibid.
56. Jones, 'The Preferred Plan', pp.406–7.
57. USDDO: Burdett, 'Joint US–UK Working Group Report on Syria', 21/9/57.
58. Quoted in Jones, 'Preferred Plan', p.408.
59. Ibid.
60. Ibid.
61. DNSA: The Soviet Estimate: US Analysis of the Soviet Union, 1947–91, 'Probable Soviet Action in Various Contingencies Affecting Syria', Special National Intelligence Estimate 11-9-57, 24/9/57.
62. DDEL: Oral History Interview, Charles Yost, 13/9/78, pp.25–6.
63. Wilford, *America's Great Game*, p.275.
64. FO371/121859, Kirkpatrick, untitled memorandum, 1/12/56.
65. See Ashton, *Eisenhower, Macmillan and the Problem of Nasser*; Blackwell, 'Britain, the United States and the Syrian Crisis', p.153.
66. Jones, 'Anglo–American Relations After Suez', p.51.
67. NARA: RG59, Bureau of Near Eastern and South Asian Affairs, Records of the United Arab Republic Affairs Desk, 1956–62, Burdett, 'Macmillan Visit: Background Paper: The Anglo–American Alliance', 21/3/61.
68. CAB130/14, Foreign Office, 'Interdependence', briefing for the Prime Minister, 4/6/58.
69. Dumbrell, *A Special Relationship*, pp.160–87.
70. CAB130/14, Foreign Office, 'Interdependence', briefing for the Prime Minister, 4/6/58.
71. USDDO: John Foster Dulles, 'Memorandum of Conversation with Prime Minister Macmillan', 24/10/57.
72. DDEL: Eisenhower Papers as President, International Series, Box 48, Syria (2), Untitled note to John Foster Dulles, presumably by Macmillan, undated; DDEL: Eisenhower Papers as President, International Series, Box 48, Syria (2),

handwritten notes by General Cutler made during conference with the President, 7/9/57.

73. USDDO: Macmillan and Eisenhower, Memorandum of Understanding, 25/10/57.

74. Ashton, 'Harold Macmillan and the "Golden Days" of Anglo–American Relations Revisited', p.700; Ashton, *Macmillan and the Problem of Nasser*, p.137; CAB130/137, 'Anglo–American Cooperation', Minutes of meeting chaired by Brook, GEN 617/1st Meeting, 30/10/57; PREM11/2324, 'Propaganda / Counter-Subversion: Note for the Prime Minister', Undated; FO371/135610, 'Minutes of the 7th Meeting of the Steering Committee', 26/2/58.

75. FOI: Brook, 'Special Political Action', 31/7/58.

76. USDDO: State, 'Macmillan Talks: Memorandum of Conversation: Countering Soviet Subversion', 11 June 1958.

77. Ibid.

78. Daugherty, *Executive Action*, p.140.

79. USDDO: State, 'Macmillan Talks: Memorandum of Conversation: Countering Soviet Subversion', 11 June 1958.

80. USDDO: Burdett, 'Joint US–UK Working Group Report on Syria', 21/9/57.

81. Jones, 'The Preferred Plan', pp.405, 411–12.

82. PREM11/2401, Brook to Macmillan, 'Aden', 7/5/58; CAB130/14, Foreign Office, 'Interdependence: Annex B—Progress of Working Groups', briefing for the Prime Minister, 4/6/58.

83. Jones, *Blowtorch*, p.52.

84. USDDO: State, 'Briefing for Macmillan talks: Yemen Situation', 9/6/58.

85. Jones, *Blowtorch*, p.58. See also Mawby, *British Policy in Aden*; Day, *Regionalism and Rebellion in Yemen*, p.38.

86. USDDO: State, 'Briefing for Macmillan talks: Yemen Situation', 9/6/58.

87. USDDO: Dale, Memorandum of conversation between JF Dulles and Macmillan, 10/6/58.

88. PREM11/2401, Brook to Macmillan, 'Aden', 7/5/58; CAB130/14, Foreign Office, 'Interdependence: Annex B—Progress of Working Groups', briefing for the Prime Minister, 4/6/58.

89. NARA: RG 59, Bureau of Near Eastern and South Asian Affairs, Records of the Arabia Peninsula Affairs Desk, 1958–63, Box 3, anon note to Jones and Thacher, 'Exchange of Information with UK on Yemen', 19/5/60.

90. Newsinger, *British Counterinsurgency*, p.140.

91. Ibid., p.142; Grob-Fitzgibbon, 'Those who Dared', p.547. It should be noted, however, that the UK had used air power against the rebels for some months prior to this.

92. Grob-Fitzgibbon, 'Those who Dared', p.548.

93. MacKenzie, *Special Force,* pp.77–93.

94. FO371/135643, Falle, 'Middle East Policy', 27/11/58.

95. See Pipes, *The Hidden Hand*.

96. Maguire, *British and American Intelligence*, p.218.

97. CAB130/14, Foreign Office, 'Interdependence: Annex B—Progress of Working Groups', briefing for the Prime Minister, 4/6/58.

98. Aldrich, *The Hidden Hand*, p.587.

99. Callanan, *Covert Action in the Cold War*, p.133; Thomas, *The Very Best Men*, p.158.

100. Smith, *Portrait of a Cold Warrior*, p.228.

101. Grose, *Allen Dulles*, p.452.

102. Kahin and Kahin, *Subversion as Foreign Policy*, p.126; NARA: RG 59, Department of State, Central Files, 611.56D/1-258, Robertson (State) to Secretary of State, 'United States Policy towards Indonesia', 2/1/58.

103. NARA: RG 59, Department of State, Central Files, 756D.00/1-658, Memorandum of a conversation on Indonesia, participants included the Secretary of State, Director of the CIA, and Frank Wisner, 2/1/58.

104. FO 371/129531, Scott to Macmillan, 12 December 1957; Aldrich, *The Hidden Hand*, p.586.

105. FO 371/135878, Chiefs of Staff Minutes, Confidential Annex to CoS(58)34th Meeting, 15/4/58.

106. Kahin and Kahin, *Subversion as Foreign Policy*, p.121; FO 371/135847, Notes for discussion of Indonesia in Cabinet, SEA Department, 5/2/56. The document is dated 1956, but seems to relate to discussions from February 1958.

107. Curtis, *Unpeople*, p.193; Kahin and Kahin, *Subversion as Foreign Policy*, pp.121, 124, 126, 156; Jones, 'Maximum Disavowable Aid', p.1994.

108. Quoted in Kahin and Kahin, *Subversion as Foreign Policy*, p.133.

109. PREM11/2324, 'Propaganda/Counter-Subversion: Note for the Prime Minister', Undated.

110. FO371/135610, 'Minutes of the 7th Meeting of the Steering Committee', 26/2/58.

111. DDEL: Dulles Papers, Subject Series, Box 11, Macmillan-Lloyd Correspondence, 1957 (2), Macmillan to Eisenhower, 29/3/57.

112. FO371/143671, Brook to Laithwaite, 25/3/59; CAB130/137, Foreign Office, 'Working Group on Anglo–American Cooperation: Progress of Anglo–American Interdependence: Annex A—Security of Working Group Procedure', GEN 617/4, 10/3/59; see also Jones, 'The Preferred Plan', pp.411–12; Jones, 'Anglo–American Relations After Suez', pp.60–1; Ashton, 'Harold Macmillan and the "Golden Days" of Anglo–American Relations Revisited', p.705.

113. CAB130/137, Foreign Office, 'Working Group on Anglo–American Cooperation: Progress of Anglo–American Interdependence', GEN 617/4, 10/3/59.

114. CAB130/14, Foreign Office, 'Interdependence: Annex B—Progress of Working Groups', briefing for the Prime Minister, 4/6/58.

115. Jones, 'Maximum Disavowable Aid', p.1201.

116. FO371/135878, CoS Minutes, Confidential Annex to CoS(58)34th Meeting, 15/4/58; DEFE4/106, Chiefs of Staff Minutes, CoS(58)33rd Meeting, 10/4/58; Jones, 'Maximum Disavowable Aid', p.1202.

117. PREM11/2324, 'Note for the Prime Minister: Propaganda / Counter-Subversion', Undated.

118. Quoted in Grose, *Allen Dulles*, p.454.

119. Talbot, *The Devil's Chessboard*, p.367.

120. Macmillan quoted in Aldrich, *The Hidden Hand*, p.587.

121. CAB130/14, Foreign Office, 'Indonesia', briefing for the Prime Minister, 4/6/58.

122. NARA: RG59, Office of Southwest Pacific Affairs; subject files relating to Indonesia, 1953–59, Box 21, Underhill 'Indonesian Foreign Policy Reappraisal', 11/6/59.

123. FRUS: vol. XVII, document 57, Memorandum of conversation between J. F. Dulles and Caccia, 13/4/58.

124. NARA: RG59, Office of Southwest Pacific Affairs; subject files relating to Indonesia, 1953–59, Box 21, Robertson (State) to Secretary of State, 'US Policy on Indonesia, NSC 5901', 27/1/59.

125. CAB130/14, Foreign Office, 'Indonesia', briefing for the Prime Minister, 4/6/58.

CHAPTER 8

1. PREM11/1582, Lennox-Boyd to Eden, PM(55)82, 15/11/55.

2. Thomas, *Empires of Intelligence*. See also Bayly, *Empire and Information*.

3. Davey, 'Conflicting Worldviews, Mutual Incomprehension', pp.541, 543.

4. For discussions on the interplay between nationalism and communism see Westad, *The Global Cold War*; Connelly, *A Diplomatic Revolution*.

5. For an overview see French, *The British Way*; and Mumford, *The Counter-Insurgency Myth*.

6. DEFE28/10, DDFP(ME) to DFP, 'psychological support', 26/9/58; FCO141/6227, Henderson, 'Project No.17', 14/11/55.

7. Zubok, 'Cold War Strategies', pp.309–10; Bittman, *The Deception Game*, p.94.

8. Walton, *Empire of Secrets*; Andrew, *Defence of the Realm*.

9. PREM11/1582, Brook to Eden, 21/10/55.

10. PREM11/1582, Lennox-Boyd to Eden, PM(55)82, 15/11/55.

11. FOI: Kirkpatrick to Dean, 10/1/56; Dean and Kirkpatrick to Foreign Secretary, 16/12/55. MI5 had long insisted 'on the right of veto by Governors, if they thought any measures proposed were likely to be a source of grave embarrassment'. KV4/474, The Diary of Guy Liddell, 15/7/50.

12. Andrew, *Defence of the Realm*, pp.442–3; Jeffery, *MI6*, pp.638–9, 688; Murphy, 'Creating a Commonwealth Intelligence Culture', pp.143–4.

13. NARA: RG59, Bureau of Near Eastern and South Asian Affairs, Records of the United Arab Republic Affairs Desk, 1956–62, Department of State: Biographic Information Division, 'Brook, Sir Norman', 20/3/61; Theakston, 'Brook, Norman Craven, Baron Normanbrook (1902–1967)', *ODNB*.

14. CO1035/116, Watson to Carstairs, 14/3/56.

15. CO1035/125, 'Draft: Official committee on counter-subversion in the colonial territories—the Caribbean', Undated, May 1956.

16. CO1035/125, Rogers to British Guiana, 30/7/56; 'British Guiana: Memorandum by the Colonial Office', Undated draft, July 1956.

17. CO1035/116, Carstairs to Brook, 20/3/56; Dean to Trend, 23/3/56; CAB130/114, Committee on Counter-Subversion in the Colonial Territories minutes, GEN. 520/1st Meeting, 16/3/56.

18. Andrew, *Defence of the Realm*, p.479; CO1035/125, Renison to Colonial Office, 26/9/56; CO1035/120, Piper to Barton and Cox, 3/4/56.

19. Andrew, *Defence of the Realm*, p.479; Maguire, *British and American Intelligence*, p.234.

20. CO1035/117, Barton, handwritten note, 13/4/56; Cox, handwritten note, 12/4/56; FCO141/4942, Gold Coast to Colonial Secretary, 'Communism in Africa', 12/6/50.

21. FOI: Dean and Kirkpatrick to Foreign Secretary, 16/12/55; Kirkpatrick to Foreign Secretary, 'Summary of Recommendations on Prime Minister's Memorandum on Counter-Subversion', OPS/1/56, undated but likely January 1956.

22. Bower, *Perfect English Spy*, p.220.

23. Andrew, *Defence of the Realm*, p.460.

24. FO1110/1102, Note by Dean, 15/5/58.

25. Ibid.; FOI: Brook to Laithwaite, 3/10/58.

26. FOI: Brook, 'Special Political Action', 31/7/58.

27. Ibid.; Beasley, *Cabinet Secretaries*, p.173.

28. FOI: [Redacted], CRO, to Brook, 26/1/59; Macpherson to Brook, 23/1/59; FO1110/1103, Murray to Harvey, 'The Cold War', 27/5/58; FO 1110/1102, Note by Dean, 15/5/58.

29. FOI: Hoyer Millar to Brook, 23/1/59.

30. BBC, 'Rigging Nigeria', *Document* (Radio 4: 20 July 2007).

31. Thomas et al., *Crises of Empire,* p.16; Thomas, *Empires of Intelligence*, p.293.

32. White, *Decolonisation*, p.105.

33. FOI: 'Cabinet: Counter Subversion' minutes, GEN.645/1st Meeting, 25/4/58.

34. Walton, *Empire of Secrets*, p.226; Higham, *Britain's Declining Empire*, p.185.

35. See Biney, 'The Development of Kwame Nkrumah's Political Thought in Exile', p.84; Montgomery, *The Eyes of the World Were Watching*, p.209.

36. Smith, *Portrait of a Cold Warrior*, p.199.

37. CAB301/118, Dean to Compton, 18/7/57.

38. CO822/1449, Turnbull to Colonial Secretary, 10/5/59; Higham, *Britain's Declining Empire*, p.276.

39. BBC, 'Rigging Nigeria', *Document* (Radio 4: 20 July 2007); Smith, *Blue Collar Lawman* (unpublished autobiography). The accuracy of Smith's account has, however, been questioned. See Brendon, *Decline and Fall*, p.538.

40. Hayes, *Queen of Spies*, p.198.

41. Andrew, *Defence of the Realm*, p.477.

42. Maguire, *British and American Intelligence*, p.236.

43. CO1035/123, Carstairs to Dean, February 1956; KV4/427, Minute by Hollis, 20/12/55. See also Maguire, *British and American Intelligence*, pp.245–53.

44. Smith, *Portrait of a Cold Warrior*, pp.136–7.
45. Ibid., p.139.
46. Maguire, *British and American Intelligence*, p.237.
47. DDEL: Office of the Special Assistant for National Security Affairs, NSC Series, Policy Papers Subseries, Box 10, NSC5412/2—Covert Operations, Gray, 'Notes on Allen Dulles' Briefing on January 15 after the President Departed the Special Meeting', 19/1/59.
48. Andrew, *Defence of the Realm*, p.477.
49. Curtis, *Unpeople*, p.281; PREM11/3666, Record of meeting in State Department, 6/4/61.
50. NARA: RG59, Policy Planning Staff/Council Country Files, 1947–61, Box 28, State, 'Action Program for British Guiana', 29/8/61.
51. Andrew, *Defence of the Realm*, p.478.
52. NYPL: 321.3, Schlesinger Diary, March 1962.
53. PREM11/366, Douglas-Home to Rusk, 26/2/62.
54. PREM11/366, Record of conversation between Secretary of State and Rusk in Geneva, 12/3/62.
55. See PREM11/3666, Macmillan to Brook, 'British Guiana', 3/5/62; Curtis, *Unpeople*, p.279.
56. Macmillan quoted in Walton, *Empire of Secrets*, pp. 160, 161.
57. CO1035/118, Carstairs to Macpherson, 14/2/58.
58. CO1035/139, Note by Watson, 25/4/48.
59. Andrew, *Defence of the Realm*, p.478.
60. Walton, *Empire of Secrets*, p.160; Curtis, *Web of Deceit*, p.353.
61. USDDO: State Dept, 'NATO Ministerial Meeting, Position Paper: United Kingdom', 10/12/63.
62. Callanan, *Covert Action in the Cold War*, pp.179–81; Andrew, *Defence of the Realm*, pp.477–80.
63. CAB301/158, Eisenhower to Macmillan, 11/7/60.
64. CAB301/158, British embassy, Havana, to Foreign Office, 20/7/60.
65. Pearce, *Spymaster*, p.192.
66. CAB301/158, Brook to Macmillan, 13/7/60.
67. CAB301/158, Eisenhower to Macmillan, 8/8/60; Macmillan to Eisenhower, 25/7/60.
68. JFK: Lord Harlech (William David Ormsby-Gore) Oral History Interview—JFK#1, 3/12/65, p.29; Macmillan, diary entry, 18 & 19/3/58, Catterall (ed.), *Macmillan Diaries*, pp.374–5.
69. DEFE28/151, Drew to Watkinson, 26/7/61.
70. See papers in DDEL: US National Security Council Presidential Records, Intelligence Files: 1953–61, Box 1–2.
71. Zeilig, *Lumumba*, p.100.
72. Gerard and Kuklick, *Death in the Congo*, p.60.
73. Haslam, *Russia's Cold War*, pp.183–7.
74. Macmillan, *The Macmillan Diaries II*, 1/12/60, p.339.

75. FO371/46645, Scott to Douglas-Home, 14/9/60.
76. CAB128/34, Cabinet Conclusions, CC(60)50th Conclusions, 15/9/60; Corera, *Art of Betrayal*, p.121; Davies, *MI6*, p.227.
77. Hayes, *Queen of Spies*, p.164.
78. CREST: CIA, 'Central Intelligence Bulletin', 20/7/60; CIA, 'Central Intelligence Bulletin', 21/7/60.
79. Devlin, *Chief of Station*, pp.63, 70.
80. Ibid., p.66; Hayes, *Queen of Spies*, p.164.
81. Devlin, *Chief of Station*, p.67.
82. Hayes, *Queen of Spies*, pp.164–8.
83. Private information.
84. Hayes, *Queen of Spies*, pp.164–8.
85. CREST: CIA, 'Current Intelligence Weekly Summary,' 11/8/60.
86. Hayes, *Queen of Spies*, pp.164–8.
87. Quoted in ibid., p.168.
88. Corera, *Art of Betrayal*, p.125.
89. See FO371/146646, Scott to Foreign Office, 27/9/60.
90. FO371/146650, Smith, 'The Congo', 28/9/60.
91. FO371/146650, Ross, 28/9/60; Corera, *The Art of Betrayal*, p.125.
92. Burleigh, *Small Wars, Far Away Places*, p.402.
93. Corera, 'MI6 and the Death of Patrice Lumumba', *BBC News* (2/4/13), http://www.bbc.co.uk/news/world-africa-22006446.
94. Macmillan, *The Macmillan Diaries II*, 3/12/60, p.340.
95. Hayes, *Queen of Spies*, p.168; Devlin, *Chief of Station*, pp.95, 132. For detailed discussion of the CIA's assassination plans see DDEL: Richard Bissell papers, Box 6, 'Alleged Assassination Plots Involving Foreign Leaders, An Interim Report of the Select Committee to Study Governmental Operations with Respect to Intelligence Activities', Nov 1975, pp.19–30.
96. FO371/146646, Scott to Foreign Office, 10/10/60.
97. Corera, 'MI6 and the Death of Patrice Lumumba'.
98. Fielding, *One Man in his Time*, p.120.
99. Hayes, *Queen of Spies*, pp.178, 181.
100. DEFE28/151, 'Counter-Subversion: Introduction', Annex to JP(62)94(D) (Flimsy), Undated but likely late 1962.
101. DEFE28/151, Counter Subversion Committee, 'The Counter Subversion Questionnaire', CSC/Q/15/62, 19/10/62.
102. FOI: 'Cabinet: Counter Subversion' minutes, GEN.645/1st Meeting, 25/4/58.
103. DEFE 28/146, Directorate for Forward Plans, 'Counter-Subversion Structure: Annex D—Interdepartmental Review Committee', 27 July 1966. By the mid-1960s an Interdepartmental Review Committee had been established to address this by advising the PSIS how the Secret Vote should be spent.
104. FO1110/1102, Drew to McLeod, 9/5/58.
105. FO1110/1102, Note by Dean, 15/5/58.

106. DEFE28/145, 'Review of the Activities of the Counter Subversion Committee, 1961–1964', Undated but likely March 1964; DEFE11/371, Shattock, 'Memorandum for the Chiefs of Staff', 11/2/64; CAB134/2543, 'Functions of the Committee—Note by the Secretaries, Annex: 'Memorandum for the Chiefs of Staff, the Counter Subversion Committee', SV(64)3, 14/2/64.

107. DEFE28/151, Glass, 'Counter Subversion Committee (Draft)', 11/12/62; CAB21/5379, McIndoe to Trend, 2/12/63.

108. See Ferris, *Nasser's Gamble*.

109. Walton, *Empire of Secrets*, p.319.

110. CAB 134/2543, 'Counter Subversion Committee Minutes', SV(64)1st Meeting, 10/1/64; SV(64) 2nd Meeting, 5/2/64; DEFE 28/147, Counter Subversion Committee: Working Group on Aden', 23/3/64; Cormac, 'Coordinating Covert Action', p.700; DEFE28/144, Drew to CDS, attached, 'The Counter Subversion Committee: Note by Chief of Defence Staff', draft, 24/2/64.

111. Mawby, 'The Clandestine Defence of Empire', pp.109–14, 117–18; Mawby, *British Policy*, p.140.

112. Mawby, 'Clandestine Defence of Empire', p.113; PREM11/2401, Lennox-Boyd to Eden, Aden Protectorate: Proposed Special Operations Against the Yemen in Dhala Area, PM(56)79, October 1956.

113. See, for example, CCC: AMEJ 1/7/3, McLean, 'Report on Visit to the Yemen and Middle East', April 1963.

114. Cooper, *One of the Originals*, pp.159, 160.

115. Hart-Davies, *The War That Never Was*, p.17.

116. Cormac, 'Coordinating Covert Action', p.699; Mawby, 'The Clandestine Defence of Empire', p.119; CO1035/210, Trevaskis, 'Counter-Subversion in the Aden State', 24/10/63; FO371/174511, McCarthy, untitled minute, 19/2/64.

117. CO1035/213, Trevaskis, 'A Note on Countering Subversion in the Aden State', October 1963.

118. Jones, *Blowtorch*, p.58.

119. NARA, RG59, Office of Near Eastern Affairs, Records of the South Arabian Desk, 1958–63, Box 5, Memorandum of Conversation between Wright and Davies, 'British Assessments of the Military Situation in Yemen', 31/10/63.

120. NARA: RG59, Office of Near Eastern Affairs, Records of the South Arabian Desk, 1958–63, Box 5, Brown to Russell, 'The Respective Military Positions of the Royalist and Republican Forces in Yemen', 29/4/63.

121. NARA: RG 59, Bureau of Near Eastern and South Asian Affairs, Records of the Arabia Peninsula Affairs Desk, 1958–63, Box 3, Memorandum of Conversation, 'Yemen Situation', 12/10/62; NARA: RG59 Bureau of Near Eastern and South Asian Affairs, Records of the Arabian Peninsula Affairs Desk, 1958–63, Box 4, Talcott Seelye, 'The Aden Folly', 26/12/63.

122. USDDO: Kennedy to Macmillan, 8/3/63.

123. LBJ: NSI country files, Box 213, Meeting between Butler and Rusk, 'Countering UAR Pressure against the British Position in Aden', 27/4/64.

124. NSA: Kai Bird Donation, Box 17, US embassy, Cairo, to Secretary of State, 9 December 1964; LBJ: NSI country files, Box 213, Komer to Bundy, 28/4/64.

125. LBJ: NSI country files, Box 213, Komer to Bundy, 21/4/64.

126. Ibid., 28 April 1964; FRUS: vol.XXI, document 333, Komer to Bundy, 28/4/64.

127. Mawby, *British Policy*, p.110; Mawby, 'The Clandestine Defence of Empire,' pp.118–22. See also Cormac, 'Coordinating Covert Action', pp.692–717.

128. Hart-Davis, *The War That Never Was*, pp.34–5.

129. CREST: CIA, 'The Zanzibar Revolt of 12 January 1964 in Retrospect,' 26/10/64.

130. DEFE28/151, 'Counter Subversion in Zanzibar', Colonial Office to Zanzibar (Draft for CSC Comments), 23/8/62.

131. DEFE11/371, Drew to CDS, COS1350/12/2/64, 14/2/64.

132. DDEL: NSC Presidential Records, Intelligence Files, Box 1, NSC5412 Special Group Minutes and Agendas 1960 (4), Parrott, 'Memorandum for the Record', 23/3/60.

133. Thomas, *The Very Best Men*, p.213.

134. CIA report, 1962, quoted in 'Times Diary: Liquidating Sukarno', *The Times* (8/8/86), issue 62530.

135. Easter, 'British and Malaysian Covert Support', p.195.

136. PREM11/4346, de Zulueta to Macmillan, 27/12/62; Easter, 'British and Malaysian Covert Support', 1963–66, p.196.

137. Tuck, *Confrontation*, p.16.

138. Ibid., p.163. See also Wilson, *The Labour Government,* p.42.

139. PREM11/4905, 'Extract from Record of Conversation at HM Embassy Washington', 26/11/63; Easter, 'British and Malaysian Covert Support', p.198.

140. Easter, 'British and Malaysian Covert Support', pp.198–200.

141. DEFE25/158, Thorneycroft to PM, 'Indonesia (Draft)', 30/9/63.

142. Easter, 'British and Malaysian Covert Support', p.197.

143. DEFE13/387, Hockaday to CDS, 'Other Defence Measures Against Indonesian Confrontation', 4/12/63.

144. Tuck, 'Cut the Bonds Which Bind our Hands', p.607; Tuck, 'Borneo, 1963–1966', pp. 97, 105.

145. DEFE11/371, Shattock, 'Memorandum for the Chiefs of Staff', 11/12/64; Easter, 'Intelligence and Propaganda', pp.91, 93.

146. CAB148/42, 'Progress Report by the Chairman of the Counter-Subversion Committee to the Defence and Oversea Policy (Official) Committee', attached to 'Counter Subversion Committee—Progress Report: Note by the Secretaries', OPD(O)(65)14, 11/3/65; Defence officials agreed. See DEFE28/1, 'Directorate of Forward Plans: Counter Subversion Committee', 10/5/66.

147. Easter, 'British and Malaysian Covert Support', p.200; DEFE28/144, High Commission, Malaysia, to Commonwealth Relations Office, 19/12/63.

148. Tuck, 'Cut the Bonds which Bind our Hands', pp.605–6, 608, 609.

149. Tuck, *Confrontation, Strategy and War Termination*, p.7.

150. Ibid., chapter 1.

151. DEFE28/1, 'Directorate of Forward Plans': A, Counter Subversion Committee', 10/5/66.
152. DEFE28/151, Glass to Wild, 11/12/62.
153. DEFE28/151, Glass, 'Counter Subversion Committee (Draft)', 11/12/62.
154. CAB134/2544, 'Summary of recent activities by working groups', SV(65)3, 8/2/65.
155. DEFE28/145, 'Review of the Activities of the Counter Subversion Committee, 1961–1964', Undated but likely March 1964.
156. Ibid.; DEFE11/371, Shattock, 'Memorandum for the Chiefs of Staff', 11/2/64; FO1110/1614, Barclay, 'Lord Strang's report on IRD', 4/9/63.
157. CAB21/5379, Plowden to Trend, 'Counter Subversion Committee', 22/7/64; Drew to Nicholls, attached: 'The Counter Subversion Committee': Note by CDS, 19/2/64; DEFE28/144, 'Counter Subversion Committee', anonymous but presumably Halliday, undated (presumably April 1964).
158. CAB165/408, Rogers, 'Note for the record: Counter Subversion Committee', 10/10/66.

CHAPTER 9

1. FOI: JAC, 'The MI6 Role and Relationships with Departments of State and the Armed Services in the Conduct of Deniable Operations in Conditions Short of War', JA(64)3, 2/11/64.
2. See FCO7/1864 and CAB134/3329; FO371/190462, Counter Subversion Committee, 'Ad Hoc Meeting on the Sudan', 13/9/66; CAB134/3329, CSC Minutes, SV(70)1st Meeting, 21/1/70.
3. CAB165/408, Rogers to Moriarty, 'Counter Subversion Committee', 26/4/67.
4. Private information.
5. Curtis, *Web of Deceit*, p.105.
6. Aldrich and Cormac, *The Black Door*, pp.272–3.
7. DEFE28/54, MoD Director of Equipment Policy to Directorate of Forward Plans, August 1962.
8. DEFE13/570, Note from Douglas-Home to Butler, 20/7/64; Jones, *Britain and the Yemen Civil War*, p.111.
9. Goodman, *Joint Intelligence Committee*, Vol. 2 (forthcoming).
10. CAB163/130, 'Brief for Chairman JIC—29th October', 28/10/64.
11. Cormac, *Confronting the Colonies*, p.109.
12. CAB163/50, Halliday, 'JIC Secretariat Establishment' 20/4/66; Anon., Untitled note on recommendations for the organisation of the JIC secretariat, 20/8/64; FOI: Trend to Burrows, WSZ2/7, 13/8/64.
13. Goodman, *Joint Intelligence Committee*, Vol. 2.
14. Heath, 'Trend, Burke Frederick St John, Baron Trend (1914–1987)', *ODNB*; Beesley, *Cabinet Secretaries*, p.211; Seldon and Meakin, *The Cabinet Office*, pp.150, 155.
15. 'Sir Leslie Glass: Obituary', *The Times*, 21 December 1988.

16. FOI: 'Composition and Terms of Reference: Joint Action Committee', JA(64)1, 13/8/64; See also DEFE11/525, Gribbon to Vice Chief of the Defence Staff, 4/1/67; DEFE13/710, McIndoe to Burrows, 'RANCOUR II', 26/3/65; CAB164/130, Burrows to Rogers, 18/8/66; DEFE11/710, Poynton to Trend, 15/10/65.

17. FOI: JAC Minutes, JA(64)1st Meeting, 8/9/64.

18. FOI: Burrows to Trend, WSZ2/3, 12/8/64; 'Composition and Terms of Reference: Joint Action Committee', JA(64)1, 13/8/64; DEFE28/146, Directorate for Forward Plans, 'Counter-Subversion Structure: Annex [? Counter-subversion committee structure diagram]', 27/7/66.

19. Scott and Rosati, '"Such Other Functions and Duties"', p.101.

20. FOI: JAC, 'The MI6 Role and Relationships with Departments of State and the Armed Services in the Conduct of Deniable Operations in Conditions Short of War', JA(64)3, 2/11/64.

21. FOI: JAC, 'The Conduct of Deniable Operations in Conditions Short of War', JAC(64)7, 2/11/64.

22. FOI: JAC Minutes, JAC(64)3rd Meeting, 21/10/64.

23. FOI: JAC, 'The MI6 Role and Relationships with Departments of State and the Armed Services in the Conduct of Deniable Operations in Conditions Short of War', JA(64)3, 2/11/64.

24. PREM11/47, 'Draft letter from the Minister of Defence to Fitzroy McLean MP: Irregular Warfare', undated, 1952.

25. ADM185/114, Groves, 'Roles, Manning and Training of SBS in the 1970s', 6/11967.

26. FOI: JAC, 'The MI6 Role and Relationships with Departments of State and the Armed Services in the Conduct of Deniable Operations in Conditions Short of War', JA(64)3, 2/11/64.

27. Ibid.

28. CAB165/408, McIndoe to Rogers and Plowden, 16/10/64.

29. FOI: JAC Minutes, JA(64)1st Meeting, 8/9/64; DEFE13/404, 'Aden and the Federation: Ministerial Meeting held at No.10 Downing Street at 11.30 am on Wednesday, November 25, 1964'.

30. DEFE13/404, 'Aden and the Federation: Ministerial Meeting held at No.10 Downing Street at 11.30 am on Wednesday, November 25, 1964: Annex A—Memorandum by the Joint Action Committee'.

31. Jones, *Britain and the Yemen Civil War*, pp.87, 102, 106–7; Mawby, 'The Clandestine Defence of Empire' p.123.

32. CAB13/570, Butler to Douglas-Home, 'Supply of Arms to a Dissident Group in Taiz', 11/9/64; Jones, *Britain and the Yemen Civil War*, p.98.

33. Connor, *Ghost Force*, p.192.

34. MacKenzie, *Special Force*, pp.101–2; Connor, *Ghost Force*, p.197.

35. Hoe, *David Stirling*, p.358; Connor, *Ghost Force*, p.194.

36. Hart-Davies, *The War That Never Was*, p.19; Fielding, *One Man in his Time*, p.145.

37. Hart-Davies, *The War that Never Was*, pp.86, 173, 239.

38. DEFE13/570, 'Note from Foreign Secretary to Prime Minister', 11/9/64; DEFE13/404, 'Aden and the Federation: Ministerial Meeting held at No.10 Downing Street at 11.30 am on Wednesday, November 25, 1964: Annex A— Memorandum by the Joint Action Committee'; Jones, *Britain and the Yemen Civil War*, pp.111, 171.

39. Bassett, *Last Imperialist*, p.182.

40. MacKenzie, *Special Force*, pp.101–2; Cooper, *One of the Originals*, pp.174–5; Connor, *Ghost Force*, pp.180–4.

41. CO1035/213, Colonial Office, 'South Arabia: Propaganda', February 1965.

42. DEFE13/404, 'Aden and the Federation: Ministerial Meeting held at No.10 Downing Street at 11.30 am on Wednesday, November 25, 1964: Annex A— Memorandum by the Joint Action Committee'.

43. Treverton, 'Covert Action', pp.15, 193.

44. Jones, *Britain and the Yemen Civil War*, pp.87, 94–5; Mawby, 'The Clandestine Defence of Empire', pp.122–4.

45. DEFE13/404, 'Aden and the Federation: Ministerial Meeting held at No.10 Downing Street at 11.30 am on Wednesday, November 25, 1964: Annex A— Memorandum by the Joint Action Committee'.

46. Ibid.

47. DEFE13/404, 'Aden and the Federation: Ministerial Meeting held at No.10 Downing Street at 11.30 am on Wednesday, November 25, 1964'.

48. DEFE13/710, Number 10 to McIndoe, 26/3/65.

49. See various notes of confirmation in DEFE13/498.

50. FO371/185195, Foreign Office to Bonn, 30/3/66.

51. CREST: CIA Office of National Estimates, 'Nasser's Prospects and Problems in Yemen', pp.9–65, 18/2/65.

52. DEFE25/158, Extract of note of meeting, 'Indonesian Confrontation of Malaya', 14/7/64.

53. Tuck, 'The Limits of Covert Action', p.1004.

54. DEFE25/158, Extract of note of meeting, 'Indonesian Confrontation of Malaya', 14 July 1964.

55. Connor, *Ghost Force*, pp. 118–23, 134; De La Billière, *Looking For Trouble*, p.242.

56. MacKenzie, *Special Force*, pp.120–8.

57. Connor, *Ghost Force*, p.137.

58. See Parker, *SBS*, pp.197–8, 206–7.

59. FOI: JAC, 'The MI6 Role and Relationships with Departments of State and the Armed Services in the Conduct of Deniable Operations in Conditions Short of War', JA(64)3, 2/11/64.

60. Easter, 'British and Malaysian', p.201.

61. PREM13/430, Trend to Wilson, 'Malaysia', 23/2/65; FO371/181503, JAC 'British Policy Towards Indonesia', JAC(65)9, February 1965.

62. FO371/181503, JAC, 'British Policy Towards Indonesia', JAC(65)9, February 1965.

63. Ibid.; DEFE11/593, VCDS to Mountbatten, 2/7/65; DEFE13/475, Mountbatten to Healey, 12/7/65; Easter, 'British and Malaysian', pp.203–4, 206.

64. Connor, *Ghost Force*, p.140.

65. MacKenzie, *Special Force*, pp.120–8; De La Billière, *Looking For Trouble*, pp.241, 246.

66. CREST: CIA National Intelligence Estimate, 'Prospects for Indonesia and Malaysia', 54/55-65, 1/7/65.

67. Tuck, 'The Limits of Covert Action', p.998.

68. Mackenzie, *Special Force*, p.128.

69. Tuck, 'The Limits of Covert Action', pp. 1003, 1006.

70. Ibid., pp.1001–3.

71. Ibid., p.1014.

72. Tuck, '"Cuts the Bonds which Bind our Hands"'.

73. Private information.

74. Easter, *Britain and the Confrontation with Indonesia*, p.83.

75. Private information.

76. Thomas, *The Very Best Men*, pp.158–9.

77. FO1110/1102, 'Psychological Warfare in War—Composition, Organisation, and Functions of SPA: Attached, copy of Minute from Mr J.A. Drew, Ministry of Defence, to Major General R.W. Macleod, Dated 9th May 1958', 12/5/58; DEFE28/1, DFP, 'Deception', 10/5/66.

78. PREM13/430, Trend to Wilson, 'Malaysia', 23/2/65.

79. Private information.

80. DEFE11/371, 'Intensification of the War of Nerves Against Indonesia: Summary of Action by DFP', 1/4/65.

81. Bittman, *The Deception Game*, p.117.

82. USDDO: US embassy, Indonesia, to State Dept, 12/10/65.

83. FO371/180317, Office of the Political Advisor to the Commander-In-Chief (Far East) to Foreign Office, 5/10/65.

84. Ibid.

85. Challis, *Shadow of a Revolution*, pp.95, 97.

86. Easter, 'British Intelligence and Propaganda', p.95.

87. Foreign Office Joint Malaysia–Indonesia Department, November 1965, quoted in Easter, 'British Intelligence and Propaganda', p.96.

88. FRUS: vol.XXVI, document 151, US embassy, Indonesia, to State Department, 10/10/65.

89. Easter, 'Pot Boiling', pp.64, 67.

90. NSA: East Timor Indonesia, Box 1, CIA, 'Indonesian Army Attitudes toward Communism', 22/11/65.

91. Foreign Office Joint Malaysia–Indonesia Department, November 1965, quoted in Easter, 'British Intelligence and Propaganda', p.97.

92. Easter, 'British Intelligence and Propaganda', pp.98–9.

93. Easter, 'Pot Boiling', p.68.

94. NSA: East Timor Indonesia, Box 1, CIA, 'The Changed Political Scene in Indonesia', 3/1/66.

95. Tuck, 'Borneo 1963–66', p.108.

96. MacKenzie, *Special Force*, pp.115, 128.

97. Mawby, *British Policy*, p.141.

98. CCC: AMEJ 1/7/8, 'A proposal from Watchguard International for the Formation and Deployment of a Task Force in the Yemen', attached to note from Stirling to Amery, 7/7/67.

CHAPTER 10

1. Crawford, quoted in Thomson, 'Document'; DEFE24/1856, 'Chiefs of Staff Meeting, Wednesday 15th July 1970: Meeting with Major General R C Gibbs OBE DSO MC Commander British Forces Gulf', 14/7/70.

2. O'Halpin, 'White, Sir Dick Goldsmith (1906–1993)', *ODNB*.

3. Deacon, *'C'*, p.150; CREST: 'Obituary: Sir John Rennie', *London Times*, 2 October 1981; Clive, 'Rennie, Sir John Ogilvy (1914–1981)', *ODNB*.

4. Pearce, *Spymaster*, p.254.

5. Beesley, *Cabinet Secretaries*, p.272.

6. West, *At Her Majesty's Secret Service*, pp.145–6.

7. Deacon, *'C'*, pp.167, 179.

8. Haines, *Glimmers of Twilight*, pp.84–5; see also Aldrich and Cormac, *The Black Door*, p.314.

9. Pearce, *Spymaster*, p.289.

10. Beesley, *Cabinet Secretaries*, pp.315–16, 337.

11. Bassett, *Last Imperialist*, pp.203, 223, 226.

12. Beesley, *Cabinet Secretaries*, p.320.

13. Ibid., p.253.

14. CAB21/5516, Note of a Meeting Held in Sir Burke Trend's Room, 15/11/65.

15. Beesley, *Cabinet Secretaries*, p.254.

16. Wood, *A Matter of Weeks Rather Than Months*, p.67; Aldrich and Cormac, *The Black Door*, p.266.

17. See Curtis, *Unpeople*, pp.169–83.

18. Cobain, *The History Thieves*, p.45.

19. Connor, *Ghost Force*, p.231; Fielding, *One Man in his Time*, p.176.

20. Hoe, *David Stirling*, pp.405–10; Deacon, *'C'*, pp.156–7.

21. Aldrich and Cormac, *The Black Door*, p.319.

22. See Connor and Hebditch, *How to Stage a Military Coup*, pp.125–9.

23. Richard Dowden, 'Revealed: How Israel Helped Amin to Take Power', *The Independent*, 16 October 2003.

24. See Elder Bauman, *The Diplomatic Kidnappings*, pp.96–103.

25. FCO37/876, Empson to Holmer, 'East Pakistan Internal Situation', 2/3/71.

26. See for example files relating to SAS training in Jordan, Qatar, and Brunei respectively in FCO93/2411, FCO8/3672, FCO24/437.

27. FCO7/1880, FCO to Buenos Aires, 27/5/71. Thanks to Richard Aldrich and Lewis Herrington for sharing this document.

28. FCO7/2078, Hunter to Brimelow, 27/5/72. Thanks to Richard Aldrich and Lewis Herrington for sharing this document.
29. FCO7/2080, Hunter to Hankey, 'Kidnapping—Suggested use of ESP', 16/8/71.
30. FCO7/1880, FCO to Buenos Aires, 27/5/71.
31. Haslam, *Russia's Cold War*, p.278.
32. FCO7/1880, FCO to Buenos Aires, 27/5/71.
33. Connor, *Ghost Force*, p.234.
34. Geraghty, *Who Dares Wins*, p.181.
35. CAB186/5, 'Sultanate of Muscat and Oman: The Military and Political Situation in Dhofar in the Shorter Term', JIC(A)(70)6, 17/4/70.
36. Private information.
37. Von Bismarck, 'A Watershed in our Relations with the Trucial States', pp.15–18; von Bismarck, *British Policy in the Persian Gulf*, pp.148–53; Sato, *Britain and the Formation of the Gul States*, pp.36–9. See also Zahlan, *The Making of the Modern Gulf States*, p.117.
38. Von Bismarck, 'A Watershed in our Relations with the Trucial States', pp.15–18.
39. Ibid., pp.171–2.
40. Smith, *Britain's Revival and Fall in the Gulf*, p.20.
41. Ibid., p.65. See also Sato, *Britain and the Formation of the Gul States*, pp.36–9; Zahlan, *The Making of the Modern Gulf States*, p.117; Rabi, 'Britain's Special Position in the Gulf', p.358; von Bismarck, *British Policy in the Persian Gulf*, pp.168, 170–85.
42. DEFE24/1867, 'The Sultanate of Muscat and Oman, HMG's Policy', 25/2/70; Takriti, 'The 1970 Coup in Oman Reconsidered', pp.158–9.
43. CAB186/5, 'Sultanate of Muscat and Oman: The Military and Political Situation in Dhofar in the Shorter Term', JIC(A)(70)6, 17/4/70.
44. Acland quoted in Thomson, 'Document'; see also DEFE24/1856, Acland to Hayman, 'The Sultanate of Muscat and Oman: Possibility of a Coup', 8/7/70.
45. DEFE24/1867, 'The Sultanate of Muscat and Oman, HMG's Policy' 25/2/70; On the role of the Joint Intelligence Committee, see Cormac, *Confronting the Colonies*, pp.186–91.
46. DEFE24/1855, Stewart to Healey, 15/4/70.
47. DEFE24/1867, 'The Sultanate of Muscat and Oman, HMG's Policy' 25/2/70; Takriti, 'The 1970 Coup in Oman Reconsidered', pp.158–61; see also Owtram, *A Modern History of Oman*, p.127; Takriti, *Monsoon Revolution*, p.164.
48. DEFE24/1856, Acland to Hayman, 'The Sultanate of Muscat and Oman: Possibility of a Coup', 8/7/70.
49. Takriti, *Monsoon Revolution*, p.173.
50. DEFE24/1856, 'Chiefs of Staff Meeting, Wednesday 15th July 1970: Meeting with Major General R C Gibbs OBE DSO MC Commander British Forces Gulf', 14/7/70; Acting Chief of the Defence Staff, 'Muscat and Oman', 16/7/70; see also Takriti, 'The 1970 Coup in Oman Reconsidered', pp.165–6.
51. Takriti, *Monsoon Revolution*, p.181.

52. Weir quoted in ibid., pp.178, 180.

53. DEFE24/1856, Ministry of Defence, Army Department, 'Qabus' Imminent Bid for Power in Muscat and Oman', 15/7/70; 'Chiefs of Staff Meeting, Wednesday 15th July 1970: Meeting with Major General R C Gibbs OBE DSO MC Commander British Forces Gulf', 14/7/70.

54. Takriti, 'The 1970 Coup in Oman Reconsidered', pp.166–7; Crawford, quoted in Thomson, 'Document'; DEFE24/1856, 'Chiefs of Staff Meeting, Wednesday 15th July 1970: Meeting with Major General R C Gibbs OBE DSO MC Commander British Forces Gulf', 14/7/70.

55. Bassett, *Last Imperialist*, p.218.

56. Takriti, *Monsoon Revolution*, p.188.

57. Gardiner, *In the Service of the Sultan*, pp.23–4. See also Allen and Rigsbee, *Oman under Qaboos*, p.29; Takriti, 'The 1970 Coup in Oman Reconsidered', p.172.

58. Acland quoted in Thomson, 'Document'.

59. DEFE24/1856, MoD to APS/Secretary of State, 'Former Sultan of Muscat and Oman', 25/8/70.

60. DEFE24/1856, Douglas-Home to Maudling, 20/8/70.

61. DEFE24/1856, Maudling to Douglas-Home, 26/8/70.

62. MacKenzie, *Special Force*, p.137.

63. SAS solider, quoted in Cobain, *The History Thieves*, p.87.

64. MacKenzie, *Special Force*, p.138; Geraghty, *Who Dares Wins*, p.184.

65. Geraghty, *Who Dares Wins*, p.186.

66. DEFE11/736, Defence Operational Planning Staff, 'Future United Kingdom Defence Activity in Oman, 31/10/72.

67. MacKenzie, *Special Force*, p.141; De La Billière, *Looking For Trouble*, p.270; Connor, *Ghost Force*, pp.222, 243.

68. DEFE24/1855, Name redacted (SAS), 'An Outline Plan to Restore the Situation in Dhofar Using Special Air Service Regiment Troops', 6/4/70.

69. MacKenzie, *Special Force*, p.151.

70. Ibid., pp.142–3.

71. DEFE11/736, Defence Operational Planning Staff, 'Future United Kingdom Defence Activity in Oman', 31/10/72; see also Cole and Belfield, *SAS Operation Storm*.

72. DNSA: Presidential Directives on National Security, Part II, NSC Interdepartmental Group for the Near East and South Asia to Kissinger, 'Evolution of our Policy Toward Oman', 29/1/75.

73. DEFE11/736, Defence Policy Staff, 'United Kingdom Defence Activity in Oman During 1973', October 1972.

74. DEFE11/736, Wright, 'Subversive Activity Against the PDRY: Annex, The Proposed Mahra Operation', 26/10/72; Hughes, 'A Proxy War in Arabia', p.97.

75. Quoted in Hughes, 'A Proxy War in Arabia', p.97.

76. DEFE11/736, Ramsbotham, 'CGS Visit to Muscat—17 October 1972', 23/10/72; Hughes, 'A Proxy War in Arabia', p.97.

77. DEFE11/736, Defence Planning Staff, 'Request from Oman for British Military Aid for the Support of Guerrilla Bands on Special Operations', DOP Note 726/72, 19/10/72; Wright, 'Subversive Activity Against the PDRY', 26/10/72.

78. DEFE11/736, Hawley to Foreign Office, 10/10/72.

79. Ibid., 18/10/72.

80. DEFE11/736, Wright, 'Subversive Activity against the PDRY', 25/10/72; Hughes, 'A Proxy War in Arabia', pp.97–8.

81. Hughes, 'A Proxy War in Arabia', pp.97–8.

82. DEFE11/736, Director of Defence Operational Plans, 'The Mahra Project: Cover Story', 20/10/72.

83. DEFE11/761, Carver, 'Increasing the Scope of Operation Dhib', 15/5/73.

84. DEFE11/761, Hawley to Foreign Office, 22/5/73.

85. DEFE32/22, CSAF to Defence Attache, Muscat, 'Trans Border Operations', 18/10/74.

86. DEFE32/22, Carver to Defence Secretary, 'Operation Dhib', 9/1/74; Bridges to Mumford, 'Oman', 17/1/74.

87. DEFE32/22, CSAF to Defence Attache, Muscat, 'Trans Border Operations', 18/10/74; Omand to Gilmour, 'Operation Dhib', 11/1/74; DEFE11/761, Defence Secretary, 'Draft Minute to the Prime Minister', 31/5/73; see also Hughes, 'A Proxy War in Arabia', pp.100–1.

88. DEFE32/22, Carver to Minister of State, 'Operation Dhib', 6/1/75.

89. DEFE32/22, Defence Attache to Chiefs of Staff secretary, 21/10/74.

90. DEFE32/22, CSAF to Defence Attache, Muscat, 'Trans Border Operations', 18/10/74; Hughes, 'A Proxy War in Arabia', p.101.

91. DEFE5/197/5, Chiefs of Staff Committee, 'The Higher Direction and Employment of Special Forces', COS37/73, 19/9/1973.

92. Private information.

93. PREM19/238, FCO Planning Staff, 'Planning Paper on Détente and the Future Management of East/West Relations', 15/12/76.

94. Lipsey, *In the Corridors of Power*, p.93.

95. Lashmar and Oliver, *Britain's Secret Propaganda War*, p.171.

96. Owen, *Time to Declare*, p.348.

97. Dorril, *MI6*, p.742.

CHAPTER 11

1. Cursey, *MRF*, p.231.

2. WO279/649, Ministry of Defence, 'Land Operations Volume III Counter-Revolutionary Operations Part I Principles and General Aspects', 29/8/69.

3. BSI: Colonel INQ 1873, 'Oral Testimony to the Bloody Sunday Inquiry', 2/10/02, p.8.

4. BSI: Mooney, Statement to Bloody Sunday Inquiry, 20/7/99, para.5.

5. See Lord Saville et al., *Report of the Bloody Sunday Inquiry*, vol. IX, chapter 178.

6. BSI: Colonel INQ 1873, 'Oral Testimony to the Bloody Sunday Inquiry', 2/10/02, p.4.
7. BSI: Mooney, Supplementary Statement, 11/9/02, para.66.
8. For a much more detailed discussion of IRD propaganda in Northern Ireland see Cormac, 'The Information Research Department', pp.1074–1104.
9. FCO79/241, Aspin, 'Transfer of IRD to Open Vote', 4/10/71; BSI: Mooney, Supplementary Statement to Bloody Sunday Inquiry, 11/11/02, para.15; FCO79/240, Wright to Morrison, 1/1/71; FCO95/1007, Greenhill to Heads of Mission, 'IRD Mark II,' 28/7/71.
10. BSI: Heath, Evidence to the Bloody Sunday Inquiry, 15/1/03, pp.72–3; Maitland to Heath, 4/11/71; Trend to Heath, 'Northern Ireland', 29/10/71; Maitland to McDowell, 15/10/71.
11. BSI: Crawford to Woodfield, 15/7/71.
12. CJ4/261, Armstrong to Cairncross, 7/8/72; Mike Thomson, 'Britain's Propaganda War During the Troubles', *BBC News*, 22/3/10.
13. BSI: Mooney, Supplementary Statement, 11/9/02, para.18.
14. Ibid., para.15.
15. Beesley, *Cabinet Secretaries*, p.110.
16. Maguire, 'Counter-Subversion in Early Cold War Britain', p.642.
17. See Wilford, *The CIA, The British Left, and the Cold War: Calling the Tune?*
18. Gliddon, 'The British Foreign Office and Domestic Propaganda on the European Community', pp. 159, 164–5.
19. BSI: Henn to Tugwell, 10/11/71. Emphasis added.
20. BSI: Mooney, Statement to the Bloody Sunday Inquiry, 20/7/99, paras.3–4.
21. FCO26/1570, Turner to Metcalfe, 'Northern Ireland: Information Policy Coordination Committee', 18/12/74.
22. BSI: Rayner, 'IRD Type Work for Northern Ireland', 3/11/70.
23. BSI: Mooney, Supplementary Statement, 11/9/02, paras.28–32.
24. BSI: Henn, Ministry of Defence, 'Organisation of Information Activity for Northern Ireland', 30/11/71; Henn to Tugwell, 10/11/71.
25. BSI: Mooney to Welser, quoted in Colonel INQ 1873, 'Oral Testimony to the Bloody Sunday Inquiry', 2/10/02, p.14.
26. See Dillon, *The Dirty War*, pp.66–8; Jenkins, *Black Magic and Bogeymen*; Kennedy-Pipe, *The Origins of the Present Troubles in Northern Ireland*, p.90; Thomson, 'Document'.
27. Myers, *Watching the Door*, p.136.
28. BSI: Mooney to Welser, undated.
29. Lashmar and Oliver, *Britain's Secret Propaganda War*, p.160.
30. FCO95/588, Simpson to Flack, 'Inspection of the Irish Republic: Brief from IRD', 15/8/69.
31. BSI: Mooney to Welser, undated.
32. Ibid.
33. CJ4/645, Oatley, 'Note of a Meeting to Discuss Policy on Releasing Information about the Recent Discovery of IRA Plans', 13/5/74. Thanks to Tony Craig for sharing this file.

34. Hamill, *Pig in the Middle*, pp.173–4.
35. Maguire, 'The Intelligence War in Northern Ireland', pp.154–5.
36. Saville et al., *Report of the Bloody Sunday Inquiry*, vol IX, chapter 178.
37. Murphy, *The Poison Chalice*, p.82; Dixon, 'Hearts and Minds', p.461.
38. Kennedy-Pipe, *The Origins of the Present Troubles in Northern Ireland*, p.91.
39. Mike Thomson, 'Britain's Propaganda War During the Troubles', *BBC News*, 22/3/10.
40. Miller, *Don't Mention the War*, p.91.
41. De Silva, *The Report of the Patrick Finucane Review*, chapter 15, para.12.
42. Ibid., paras.20, 22–3.
43. Ibid., paras.28–9.
44. See FCO26/1570, Information Policy Coordinating Committee, 'Information Policy: Its Use in Northern Ireland', November 1974; de Silva, *The Report of the Patrick Finucane Review*, chapter 15, paras.10–14, 20, 22–3, 28–9; King quoted in Miller, *Don't Mention the War*.
45. BSI: Mooney, IRD in Northern Ireland—Preliminary Report, June–September 1971.
46. Private information.
47. BSI: Crawford to Reddaway, 'Northern Ireland', 8/7/71.
48. Private information.
49. Ibid.
50. CJ4/2995, Woodfield, handwritten on note by Stewart, untitled, 19/4/71.
51. Private information.
52. Ibid.
53. Ibid.
54. Ibid
55. Hughes and Tripodi, 'Anatomy of a Surrogate', p.5; Mumford, *The Counter-Insurgency Myth*, pp.8–9.
56. Cesarani, *Major Farran's Hat*, p.63.
57. Comber, *Malaya's Secret Police*, pp.165, 292; Aldrich, *Hidden Hand*, pp.511–12, 574; Mumford, *The Counter-insurgency Myth*, p.40; Kitson, *Gangs and Counter-Gangs*, p.76; Hughes and Tripodi, 'Anatomy of a surrogate', pp.16–17; Dimitrakis, 'British Intelligence and the Cyprus Insurgency', p.388; Andrew, *Defence of the Realm*, p.463; Blaxland, *The Regiments Depart*, p.312; Robbins, 'The British Counter-Insurgency in Cyprus', p.729.
58. Mumford, *The Counter-Insurgency Myth*, p.80.
59. Kemp, *The SAS*, p.78.
60. DEFE25/282, 'Northern Ireland—Special Reconnaissance Unit' attached to Carver to Heath, 28/11/72.
61. WO32/21954, Carver, 'Northern Ireland—Appreciation of the Security Situation as at 4th October 1971', 4/10/71.
62. DEFE25/282, 'Northern Ireland—Special Reconnaissance Unit' attached to Carver to Heath, 28/11/72.

63. DEFE24/544, VCGS to Carrington, 'Northern Ireland—Military Reaction Force', 11/5/72.

64. BBC, *Panorama*.

65. Cursey, *MRF*, pp.65–6; BBC, *Panorama*.

66. DEFE25/282, 'Northern Ireland—Special Reconnaissance Unit' attached to Carver to Heath, 28/11/72.

67. DEFE25/282, Carver to Carrington, 'Special Reconnaissance Squadron—Northern Ireland', 17/11/72.

68. DEFE24/544, VCGS to Carrington, 'Northern Ireland—Military Reaction Force', 11/5/72; see also Cursey, *MRF*, p.78.

69. Cursey, *MRF*, p.173.

70. Siegriste, *SAS Warlord*, p.18.

71. BBC, *Panorama*; Bowcott, 'Pat Finucane Report', *The Guardian*, 12/12/12.

72. Cursey, *MRF*, pp.106–7.

73. Bowcott, 'Pat Finucane Report', *The Guardian*, 12/12/12; Cursey, *MRF*, pp.67, 160.

74. BBC, *Panorama*; Cursey, *MRF*, p.66; Dillon, *The Dirty War*, pp.56–7; Punch, *State Violence*, p.88.

75. Cursey, *MRF*, pp.169–70, 143, 218.

76. DEFE24/544, VCGS to Carrington, 'Northern Ireland—Military Reaction Force', 11 May 1972.

77. Ibid.

78. Cursey, *MRF*, p.176; BBC, *Panorama*.

79. Taylor, *Brits*, p.130.

80. BBC, *Panorama*.

81. Documents quoted in BBC, *Panorama*.

82. BBC, 'Military Reaction Force: Breakthrough in PSNI Investigation', *BBC News Website*, 2/12/15.

83. Cursey, *MRF*, p.126; Siegriste, *SAS Warlord*, pp.61–3, 163.

84. DEFE25/282, Carver to Carrington, 'Special Reconnaissance Squadron—Northern Ireland', 17/11/72.

85. Connor, *Ghost Force*, p.268; see also Geraghty, *Who Dares Wins*, p.219.

86. CAB130/561, Whitelaw, 'Security Policy in Northern Ireland', 19/9/72.

87. DEFE24/544, VCGS to Carrington, 'Northern Ireland—Military Reaction Force', 11/5/72.

88. DEFE25/282, 'Northern Ireland—Special Reconnaissance Unit' attached to Carver to Heath, 28/11/72.

89. DEFE24/544, VCGS to Carrington, 'Northern Ireland—Military Reaction Force', 11/5/72.

90. WO32/21954, Glover, 'Northern Ireland Visit', 10/2/72.

91. DEFE25/282, 'Northern Ireland—Special Reconnaissance Unit' attached to Carver to Heath, 28/11/72.

92. Urban, *Big Boys' Rules*, pp.35–7; Dillon, *The Dirty War*, pp.35–7; Punch, *State Violence*, p.88.

93. Kitson, *Low Intensity Operations*, p.130; Kitson, *Bunch of Five*, p.289.
94. BBC, *Panorama*.
95. DEFE25/282, Carver to Heath, 28/11/72; CJ4/1304, Watson to Smith, 5/12/73.
96. PREM16/154, Northern Ireland Office, 'Defensive Brief D—Meeting Between the Prime Minister and the Taoiseach, 5 April 1974: Army Plain Clothes Patrols in Northern Ireland', 2/4/74.
97. DEFE25/282, Carver to Heath, 28/11/72.
98. DEFE25/282, Curtis to CGS office, 20/11/72.
99. CJ4/1304, Watson to Smith, 5/12/73; FCO87/583, Cragg to Meadway, 'The SAS and the Special Reconnaissance Unit (SRU) in Northern Ireland', 20/9/76.
100. FCO87/583, Mason, 'The SAS and the Special Reconnaissance Unit in Northern Ireland', 8/9/76; Wright to Cragg, 'The SAS and the Special Reconnaissance Unit in Northern Ireland', 24/9/76; DEFE25/262, Nicholls, 'Robert Fisk's Article on the SAS', 20/3/74.
101. CJ4/1304, Watson to Smith, 5/12/73.
102. CJ4/1304, Nicholls to Roberts, 12/9/73.
103. DEFE25/282, Carver to Carrington, 'Special Reconnaissance Squadron—Northern Ireland', 17/11/72.
104. Finegan, 'Intelligence and Counter-terrorism in Northern Ireland', p.503; Cursey, *MRF*, pp.xiii, 79–80, 203.
105. Geraghty, *Who Dares Wins*, p.222; Connor, *Ghost Force*, p.269.
106. Camsell, *Black Water*, p.75.
107. Finegan, 'Intelligence and Counter-terrorism in Northern Ireland', p.503.
108. Parker, *SBS*, p.280; Camsell, *Black Water*, p.52.
109. CJ4/1304, Railton, GOC, 'Op Contravene: PR Instruction Covering Special Air Service Operations in South Armagh', 16/4/76.
110. DEFE13/1403, Mason to Mulley, 18/5/77.
111. MacKenzie, *Special Force*, pp.204, 201.
112. Geraghty, *Who Dares Wins*, p.235; Kemp, *The SAS*, p.127.
113. Connor, *Ghost Force*, p.272.
114. MacKenzie, *Special Force*, p.204; de la Billière, *Looking for Trouble*, pp.315–16; Connor, *Ghost Force*, p.281.
115. Kemp, *The SAS*, p.129.
116. Geraghty, *Who Dares Wins*, p.261.
117. Finegan, 'Intelligence and Counter-terrorism in Northern Ireland', pp.503, 505, 506–8.
118. MacKenzie, *Special Force*, pp.205–6.
119. De Silva quoted in BBC, 'Has Collusion been Defined?', *BBC News*, 3/12/13.
120. Stevens quoted in O'Brien, *Killing Finucane*, p.4.
121. See Cadwallader, *Lethal Allies*, pp.15–16.
122. Finegan, 'Intelligence and Counter-terrorism in Northern Ireland', p.504.
123. McGovern, 'The Dilemma of Democracy', pp.224–5.

124. Stevens quoted in O'Brien, *Killing Finucane*, p.4.
125. De Silva quoted in Cadwallader, *Lethal Allies*, p.359.
126. De Silva, *The Report of the Patrick Finucane Review*, chapter 7, paras.294, 29, 80; chapter 11, paras.111, 75.
127. Cochrane, 'Security Force Collusion in Northern Ireland', p.85.
128. Police Ombudsman, *Investigative Report*, para.9.
129. Davies, *Ten-Thirty-Three*, pp.22, 164.
130. De Silva, *The Report of the Patrick Finucane Review*, chapter 25, para.4.
131. Ibid., para.18, 30; chapter 11, para.113.
132. McGovern, 'The Dilemma of Democracy', p.224.
133. Cochrane, 'Security Force Collusion in Northern Ireland', p.78.
134. BSI: Gen.47(71)5th Meeting, chaired by Heath, 6/10/71.
135. CJ4/838, Northern Ireland Office, 'UDA and other Protestant Paramilitary Organisations', 23/11/72.
136. CJ4/4198, Northern Ireland Office, 'The Ulster Defence Association', 22/6/82.
137. Green and Ward, *State Crime*, pp.108, 119; Cadwallader, *Lethal Allies*, p.354.
138. Cochrane, 'Security Force Collusion in Northern Ireland', p.79.
139. De Silva, *The Report of the Patrick Finucane Review*, chapter 13, para.1.
140. Cobain, *The History Thieves*, pp.196–7.
141. De Silva, *The Report of the Patrick Finucane Review*, chapter 11, para.86.
142. Cadwallader, *Lethal Allies*, pp.16, 348, 358; see also Punch, *State Violence*, p.191.
143. Punch, *State Violence*, p.183; see also McGovern, 'The Dilemma of Democracy', pp.225–7.
144. Punch, *State Violence*, p.183.
145. De Silva, *The Report of the Patrick Finucane Review*, chapter 3, para.47.
146. Ibid., chapter 8, para.176.
147. Ibid., chapter 8, para.223.
148. Ibid., chapter 25, para.5.
149. Ibid., chapter 8, para.169.
150. Ibid., chapter 25, paras.31–2.
151. Urban, *Big Boys' Rules*, p.168; Punch, *State Violence*, p.189.
152. Punch, *State Violence*, p.191; De Silva, *The Report of the Patrick Finucane Review*, chapter 7, para.55; chapter 16, paras. 21,85–6,; chapter 25, para.25.
153. Cobain, *The History Thieves,* p.199; De Silva, *The Report of the Patrick Finucane Review*, chapter 24, paras.165–70.
154. De Silva, *The Report of the Patrick Finucane Review*, chapter 15, paras.30–8, 46.
155. Ibid., para.51.

CHAPTER 12

1. THA: Thatcher to Carter, 26/1/80.
2. Davies, *Intelligence and Government*, p.228.
3. Owen quoted in Dorril, *MI6*, p.743.
4. FCO49/798, Luard to Owen, 'Coup in Afghanistan', 4/5/78.

5. Aldrich and Cormac, *The Black Door*, pp.340–1.
6. Grob-Fitzgibbon, 'Those who Dared', pp.557–8; FCO8/3470 Tatham, 'Future Use of SAS Anti-Terrorist Squads', 9/5/80; FCO8/3500, Dennis, 'Counter-Terrorist Training', 14/7/80.
7. Pearce, *Spymaster*, pp.283–4.
8. Aldrich and Cormac, *The Black Door*, p.346.
9. Bassett, *Last Imperialist*, pp.237–8.
10. PREM16/1873, 'Somalia: Extract from Meeting Record of PM/Hussein', 22/2/87.
11. FCO31/1834, MacKechnie to Khartoum, 3/4/75; Mackenzie, 'Ethiopia', 24/3/75; PREM16/1873, Owen to Mogadishu, 22/2/78; CCC: AMEJ1/10/44, 'Record of a Conversation with President Mohamed Ziad Barre', 25/2/79.
12. Lawson, *The View from Number 11*, p.314; See also Aldrich and Cormac, *The Black Door*, p.353.
13. FCO49/894, FCO Planning Staff, 'The Prevention of Soviet Expansion in the Developing World', April 1980.
14. FCO49/894, Walden to Alexander, 1/4/80.
15. FCO49/894, FCO Planning Staff, 'The Prevention of Soviet Expansion in the Developing World', April 1980.
16. FCO49/894, Mallaby to Fergusson, 'Soviet Activity in the Third World Post-Afghanistan', 1/2/80; FCO Planning Staff, 'The Prevention of Soviet Expansion in the Developing World', April 1980.
17. FCO49/894, Mallaby to Fergusson, 'Soviet Activity in the Third World Post-Afghanistan', 1/2/80.
18. FCO49/894, FCO Planning Staff, 'The Prevention of Soviet Expansion in the Developing World', April 1980.
19. FCO49/894, Duncan, 'East–West Relations', 6/3/80.
20. FCO49/894, FCO Planning Staff, 'The Prevention of Soviet Expansion in the Developing World', April 1980.
21. FCO28/3981, Wood to Mallaby, 20/2/80.
22. FCO28/3981, Farquharson to Mallaby, 6/2/80.
23. FCO28/3981, Cloake to Mallaby, 11/1/80.
24. FCO28/3981, Pridham to Mallaby, 9/1/80.
25. FCO28/4745, East European and Soviet Department, 'Policy Towards Eastern Europe', 17/9/82.
26. Urban, *Diplomacy and Disillusion*, pp.15, 26.
27. Seldon and Meakin, *The Cabinet Office*, p.199.
28. Norton-Taylor, 'Brian Crozier Obituary', *The Guardian*, 9/8/12.
29. Bloom, *Thatcher's Secret War*, p.69.
30. Crozier, *Free Agent*, p.142.
31. Ibid., p.143.
32. Michaels, 'Brian Crozier and the Institute for the Study of Conflict', pp.155–6.
33. PREM19/137, Centre for Policy Studies, 'Western Strategy in the Wake of Afghanistan: A Report to the Prime Minister', March 1980.

34. PREM19/238, Thatcher to Thomas, 19/5/80.

35. Hanni, 'The Cercle in the Second Cold War', p.163. See invite and acceptance lists in the following files: CCC: AMEJ1/10/45, AMEJ1/10/46, AMEJ1/10/49.

36. CCC: AMEJ1/10/50, Churchill to Amery, 7/7/90.

37. Hanni, 'The Cercle in the Second Cold War', pp.161–3.

38. CCC: AMEJ1/10/45, 'Meeting of the Cercle', undated 1982; CCC: AMEJ1/10/44, Amery, handwritten notes for Cercle address, undated (1977?); Hanni, 'The Cercle in the Second Cold War', p.167.

39. CCC: AMEJ1/10/53, Amery, 'The Group', 13/11/91.

40. PREM19/1437, Lever to Alexander, 16/4/80.

41. CCC: AMEJ2/1/99, Pym to Amery, 5/2/80.

42. PREM19/1437, Thatcher to Amery, 17/4/80.

43. Bassett, *Last Imperialist*, pp.231 234.

44. PREM19/1437, Amery to Thatcher, 29/2/84.

45. PREM19/1437, Coles to Foreign Office, 'Special Operations: Mr Julian Amery MP', 21/2/84.

46. PREM19/1437, Amery to Thatcher, 23/7/85; PREM19/1437, Amery to Thatcher, 31/1/84; Fall to Coles, 20/2/84; Thatcher to Amery, 7/8/85.

47. Hanni, 'The Cercle in the Second Cold War', p.167.

48. Ibid., pp.167–70. Thanks to Daniela Richterova for information on the relationship between Soviet bloc intelligence and Carlos the Jackal.

49. BDOHP: Interview with Sir Antony Acland, 23/4/01, p.37.

50. Urban, *Diplomacy and Disillusion*, pp.27–33.

51. FCO49/894, FCO Planning Staff, 'The Prevention of Soviet Expansion in the Developing World', April 1980.

52. See FCO49/895, Braithwaite, 'The Management of East–West Relations', undated 1980. The eventual outcome of this remains classified.

53. FCO49/895, FCO Planning Staff, 'The Management of East–West Relations', June 1980; Cary, 'OD Paper', 5/6/80.

54. PREM19/238, Foreign Office Planning Staff, 'The Management of East–West Relations', 2/5/80.

55. Lashmar and Oliver, *Britain's Secret Propaganda War*, p.173; Crozier, *Free Agent*, p.189.

56. PREM19/238, Foreign Office Planning Staff, 'The Management of East-West Relations', 2/5/80.

57. Urban, *Diplomacy and Disillusion*, pp.38–9.

58. Private information.

59. Haslam, *Russia's Cold War*, pp.324–5, 326; Haslam, *Near and Distant Neighbours*, pp.245–9; Braithwaite, *Afgansty*, p.114.

60. THA: Special Coordination Committee Meeting on Afghanistan, 17/12/79.

61. THA: Director of Central Intelligence, 'Western Europe: Response to US–Soviet Tension in Wake of the Afghanistan Crisis', 7/1/80.

62. Crile, *Charlie Wilson's War*, pp.196–7.

63. Curtis, *Secret Affairs*, p.141; Crile, *Charlie Wilson's War*, pp.196–7.

64. Corera, *Art of Betrayal*, pp.295–6.
65. Quoted in Braithwaite, *Afgansty*, p.112.
66. FCO37/2387, Bailes to Lavers, 7/1/81.
67. Corera, *Art of Betrayal*, p.293.
68. Crile, *Charlie Wilson's War*, pp.200–1.
69. CAB128/67/1, Cabinet Conclusions, C(80)1st Conclusions, 10/1/80.
70. THA:Thatcher to Carter, 26/1/80.
71. FCO37/2215, Carrington to Vance, 'Afghanistan: Supporting the Resistance', (Draft), undated (January 1980).
72. PREM19/136, Brzezinski to Cabinet Office, 4/2/80.
73. CAB128/67/3, Cabinet Conclusions, C(80)3rd Conclusions, 24/1/80; PREM19/136, Record of conversation between the Prime Minister and the Prime Minister of Australia, 4/2/80; FCO37/2248, 'Call by Economics Minister Bohman on Secretary of State', 6/2/80.
74. PREM 9/135, Carrington to Thatcher, 19/1/80.
75. Woodward, *Veil*, p.78.
76. PREM19/136, Carrington to Thatcher, 'Afghanistan: The Next Steps', 1/2/80; PREM19/387, Carrington to Thatcher, 20/5/81.
77. Corera, *Art of Betrayal*, p.293.
78. PREM19/387, Lyne to Alexander, undated 1980.
79. PREM19/387, Whitmore to Lever, 23/9/80; Braithwaite, *Afgansty*, p.112.
80. PREM19/387, Walden to Alexander, 19/9/80.
81. Curtis, *Secret Affairs*, pp.147–50.
82. PREM19/387, Alexander to Walden, 24/7/80.
83. PREM19/387, Carrington, 'Help for the Afghan Resistance', 19/8/80.
84. CREST: CIA, National Foreign Assessment Center, 'The Supply of Weapons to the Afghan Nationalist Forces'. Memo prepared for DCI', 2/4/80.
85. FCO37/2216, Archer to Wateron, 3/7/80.
86. PREM19/136, Brzezinski to Cabinet Office, 4/2/80.
87. PREM19/135, Carrington to Thatcher, 19/1/80.
88. THA: Carter to Thatcher, 15/10/80.
89. THA:Thatcher to Carter, undated reply to letter sent 15/10/80.
90. FCO49/895, Carrington, 'UK Policy in East–West Relations', 8/9/80.
91. FCO37/2216, Fenn to Acland, 30/6/80.
92. PREM19/387, Carrington, 'Help for the Afghan Resistance', 19/8/80.
93. FCO37/2216, Carrington, 'Guidance Telegram Number 65', 3/7/80.
94. FCO37/2217, note for Foreign Office press officers, 'Afghanistan', 12/11/80.
95. West, *The Third Secret*, pp.196–7.
96. RRL: Executive Secretariat, Country Files, Box 18, box 38, Schweitzer to Allen, 'Action List for Poland', 3/4/81.
97. CREST: CIA, 'Political action', 30/7/82, attached to 'Agenda for Meeting on Political Action', 5/8/82.
98. Andrew, *Mitrokhin Archive*, p.677; West, *The Third Secret*, pp.195–6.
99. FCO28/4512, Wood, 'Poland—Abnormal Surveillance of Attache / Diplomatic Activity', 2/9/81.

100. Andrew, *Mitrokhin Archive*, pp.669–70; Haslam, *Near and Distant Neighbours*, pp.259–60.
101. CREST: James Nance, acting assist to the Pres for Nat Sec affairs, 'National Security Council Meeting', 9/12/81; RRL: Executive Secretariat, NSC Country Files, Box 16–17, box 35, Haig to Reagan, 'The United States and Poland', 12/11/81.
102. CREST: Chief of Soviet/East European Division to Director of Central Intelligence, 5 January 1981; RRL: Executive Secretariat, NSC, Country Files, Box 17, Box 36, US Embassy Warsaw to State Department, 30/12/81.
103. Moore, *Thatcher*, pp.574–5.
104. Maddrell, *Through the Eyes of the Stasi*, pp.71–2.
105. PREM19/871, Record of conversation between Thatcher and Carrington, 20/12/81; Record of conversation between Thatcher and Carrington, 27/12/81.
106. FCO28/4038, Fergusson to Bullard, 'What Attitude Should we take to Soviet Intervention in Poland?', 20/11/80.
107. PREM19/871, Record of conversation between Thatcher and Carrington, 20/12/81; Moore, *Thatcher*, p.576.
108. Bethell, *Spies and Other Secrets*, p.255.
109. THA: UK Embassy Warsaw to FCO, 28/9/81.
110. Crozier, *Free Agent*, pp.198–9.
111. Bernstein, 'The Holy Alliance'.
112. FCO28/4371, Gladstone to Heath, 'Vatican Assessment on Eastern Europe', 21/4/81; Heath to Gladstone, 8/4/81.
113. Bernstein, 'The Holy Alliance'; Andrew, *Mitrokhin Archive*, p.671; West, *The Third Secret*, p.164.
114. RRL: Dobriansky files, Country File, RAC box 45, Box 12, Anon (Dobriansky?), 'Solidarity's Underground Plans', 24/8/82.
115. FCO28/5002, 'Voice of Solidarity', 24/11/82; West, *The Third Secret*, pp.212–13.
116. FCO28/5002, Foreign Office to UK embassy Warsaw, 6/12/82.
117. West, *The Third Secret*, pp.212–13.
118. Bethell, *Spies and Other Secrets*, p.265.
119. RRL: Pipes files, Subject files, Box 3, Pipes, 'A Reagan Soviet Policy' (Working Draft), October 1981.
120. FCO28/5002, Foreign Office to UK embassy Warsaw, 6/12/82; FCO28/4905, Melhuish to Carrington, 'The Rise and Fall of Solidarity', 29/1/82.

CHAPTER 13

1. CCC: AMEJ1/10/45, Amery to Thatcher, 7 November 1983.
2. FCO37/2234, White to Maitland, 7/1981; FCO37/2216, Archer, 'OD Background Brief on Afghan Opposition Groups', undated.
3. FCO37/2216, Lavers to Hurd, 'Afghanistan: Resistance Groups', 23/7/80.

4. FCO37/2387, Coles to Graham, 'Policy towards the Afghan Resistance Groups', 17/2/81.
5. FCO37/3016, 'Meeting between Gailani and FCO', 31/8/83.
6. FCO37/2217, Hiscock to Lavers, 13/12/80.
7. Corera, *Art of Betrayal*, p.296.
8. Ibid., p.298; Davies, *MI6*, p.291; Connor, *Ghost Force*, pp.418–19.
9. Private information.
10. Corera, *Art of Betrayal*, pp.229, 302.
11. Crile, *Charlie Wilson's War*, p.199.
12. Corera, *Art of Betrayal*, p.299; Davies, *MI6*, p.291.
13. Braithwaite, *Afgantsy*, p.134.
14. Private information.
15. RRL: Exec Sec, NSC, Afghanistan, Box 65, Fortier, 'Note for Bud McFarlane', 21/11/83; CREST: CIA, Directorate of Intelligence, 'Afghanistan: The Cease-fire and the Future of the Insurgency in the Panjshar Valley', 1/9/83.
16. Braithwaite, *Afgantsy*, p.185.
17. Corera, *Art of Betrayal*, p.300.
18. Crile, *Charlie Wilson's War*, pp.195–6.
19. Ibid., pp.200–2.
20. Braithwaite, *Afgantsy*, pp.215–16.
21. RRL: Exec Sec, NSC, Afghanistan, Box 65, Pipes to Clark, 'Afghanistan', 29/7/82; Exec Sec, NSC, Afghanistan, Box 65, Eagleburger, 'Pakistan and the Afghan Refugees and Freedom Fighters', 24/11/82.
22. They proved temperamental, and the CIA soon replaced them with Stinger missiles. Nonetheless, as late as 1986 the CIA, through the Pentagon, bought some 300 Blowpipe missiles from Shorts of Belfast for use in Afghanistan. Braithwaite, *Afgantsy*, p.203, Corera, *Art of Betrayal*, pp.304–6; Urban, p.35.
23. FCO106/633, Harrison, 'Official Contacts with Armed Opposition Movements', 17/2/82.
24. FCO37/3446, Blackhouse, 'KHAD Surveillance', 12/9/84.
25. FCO37/3446, Newell to Bevan, 'Afghanistan: KHAD', 30/1/84.
26. FCO37/3089, Coles to Holmes, 'Afghanistan', 29/3/83.
27. Ibid.; FCO37/3089, Burton to Moss, 'Afghanistan', 30/3/83; Holmes to Coles, 31/3/83.
28. CCC: AMEJ1/10/45, Amery to Thatcher, 7/11/83.
29. FCO37/2436, Foreign Office to Islamabad, 27/3/81.
30. Cooley, *Unholy Wars*, p.76.
31. Curtis, *Secret Affairs*, p.143; Curtis, *Web of Deceit*, p.62; Connor, *Ghost Force*, pp.420–1; Corera, *Art of Betrayal*, p.299; West, *The Third Secret*, p.150.
32. Braithwaite, *Afgantsy*, p.201.
33. PREM19/1646, Powell, 'Prime Minister's Meeting with Vice-President Bush', 14/3/85.
34. Corera, *Art of Betrayal*, p.308; Curtis, *Secret Affairs*, p.147.
35. FCO99/1633, Thomas to Ure, 26/5/83.

36. RRL: European and Soviet Affairs Directorate Records, RAC Box 6, box 3, 'Summary of the President's Meeting with British Foreign Secretary, Sir Geoffrey Howe', 14/7/83.

37. Ibid., 'Summary of Conversation between the President and British Prime Minister Margaret Thatcher', 29/9/83.

38. FCO99/1910, Ricketts, 'US/Nicaragua', 3/12/84.

39. FCO99/1910, Joy, 'US/Nicaragua', 27/11/84.

40. Private information.

41. Byrne, *Iran-Contra*, p.55; Aldrich and Cormac, *The Black Door*, p.383.

42. Byrne, *Iran-Contra*, pp.55–6.

43. Davies, *MI6*, p.298.

44. BFI: Park quoted in BBC, *On Her Majesty's Secret Service* (BBC *Panorama*, 22 November 1993).

45. Aldrich and Cormac, *The Black Door*, p.381.

46. FAOHP: Robert Oakley, interviewed 7/7/92, p.121.

47. RRL: European and Soviet Affairs Directorate, RAC Box 15, 16, 17, Burghardt to Poindexter, 'British Concurrence for Use of Blowpipe Missiles in Nicaragua', 14/11/86.

48. THA: Thatcher to Reagan, 4/12/86.

49. Dover, 'For Queen and Company', p.703.

50. Richard Norton-Taylor, 'Jailed "Go-Between" on UK-Iran Arms Deals is Freed to keep MI6 Secrets out of Court', *The Guardian*, 6/2/99; Curtis, *Web of Deceit*, p.187.

51. THA: 'Note of a telephone conversation between the Prime Minister and Mr Nicholas Elliott', 13/8/79.

52. Dover, 'A Silent Debate', p.114.

53. Bergman, *The Secret War with Iran*, p.309.

54. Dover, 'A Silent Debate', p.114; see also Barker, 'Practising to Deceive', pp.41–9.

55. Norton-Taylor, *Truth is a Difficult Concept*, p.51.

56. Blackhurst, 'MPs to Question Aitken over BMARC Arms allegations', *The Independent*, 28/6/95. On Aitken links to the Cercle see CCC: AMEJ1/10/49, '"Cercle" - U.K. Group' (undated 1987–8) which lists Aitken alongside other MPs.

57. Phythian, *The Politics of British Arms Sales*, p.21.

58. Kerry and Brown, 'The BCCI Affair', chapter 11; Willan, *The Vatican at War*, pp.149–51; Beatty and Gwynne, *The Outlaw Bank*, p.xxv.

59. Bingham, *Inquiry into the Supervision of the Bank of Credit and Commerce International*, p.163.

60. Walsh, 'Treasury Seeks New BCCI Gag', *The Observer*, 6/10/02.

61. Bassett, *Last Imperialist*, pp.248–9.

62. RRL: Executive Secretariat, NSC, Country file, Box 20, box 41, US Embassy London to Secretary of State, 11/8/81.

63. Connor, *Ghost Wars*, pp.453–4.

64. Conboy, *The Cambodian Wars*, p.198.

65. Ibid.

66. Ibid., p.212.
67. Pilger, 'How Thatcher Gave Pol Pot a Hand', *New Statesman*, 17/4/00. See also Curtis, *Ambiguities of Power*, p.212; Connor, *Ghost Force*, p.426; Geraghty, *Who Dares Wins*, p.464; Jason Burke, 'Butcher of Cambodia set to expose Thatcher's role', *The Guardian*, 9/1/00.
68. Pilger, 'How Thatcher Gave Pol Pot a Hand'; Burke, 'Butcher of Cambodia set to expose Thatcher's role'.
69. Quoted in Hennessy, *Establishment and Meritocracy*, pp.17–18.
70. Quoted on BFI: BBC, *On Her Majesty's Secret Service*.
71. SBI: Evidence of Witness E (SIS Controller for Eastern Europe), 29/2/08, para.2.
72. Urban, *UK Eyes Alpha*, p.157; Dorril, *MI6*, p.753.
73. Urban, *UK Eyes Alpha*, p.163.
74. Ibid. p.179.
75. Davies, *MI6*, pp.293–5, 297.
76. Corera, *Art of Betrayal*, pp.326–7.
77. Grey, *The New Spymasters*, p.230.
78. FOI: Quinlan, 'Review of Intelligence Requirements and Resources, Part 1: Processes for Handling', 31 March 1994. Thanks to Peter Hennessy for sharing this.
79. HMG, 'Intelligence Services Act 1994', section 1b; section 7. See also Cormac, 'Disruption and Deniable Interventionism'.
80. Beesley, *Cabinet Secretaries*, p.555.
81. SBI: Evidence of Witness E (SIS Controller for Eastern Europe), 29/2/08, paras.20–1.
82. Davies, *MI6*, pp.294–5.
83. BFI: BBC, *On Her Majesty's Secret Service*; Grey, *The New Spymasters*, p.89.
84. CCC: AMEJ1/10/53, Amery, handwritten notes for address to Cercle meeting, May 1992.
85. CCC: AMEJ1/10/55, Amery to Cavendish and Bach, 4/4/95.
86. Quoted in Bassett, *Last Imperialist*, p.17.
87. BFI: BBC, *On Her Majesty's Secret Service*; Davies, *MI6*, p.297; Urban, *UK Eyes Alpha*, p.229. Urban refers to this as the Global Tasks section.
88. Dorril, *MI6*, p.773; Landale and Evans, 'Cook Praises Spy Agencies for Curbing Summer', *The Times*, 24/4/98.
89. BFI: BBC, *On Her Majesty's Secret Service*.
90. Bennetto and Abrams, 'MI6 Thwarts Iranian Plot to get Nuclear Technology', *The Independent*, 20/4/98.
91. Beesley, *Cabinet Secretaries*, p.552.
92. Private information.
93. Dorril, *MI6*, pp.297–8, 787; Urban, *UK Eyes Alpha*, pp.266–7.
94. Ritter, *Iraq Confidential*, p.281.
95. Butler, *Review of Intelligence on Weapons of Mass Destruction*, para.489.
96. SBI: Evidence of witness A, 26 February 2008, paras.174–84.

97. Ibid., paras.180–2.
98. SBI: Evidence of Witness E (SIS Controller for Eastern Europe), 29/2/08, para.7; Evidence of Richard Dearlove, 20/2/08, para.61.
99. SBI: Evidence of witness A, 26/2/08, para.185.
100. Private information.
101. Borger, *The Butcher's Trail*, pp.62–5.
102. Smith, 'France Puts Block on SAS Karadic Snatch', *The Telegraph*, 14/8/00.
103. Private information.
104. Bone, 'MI6 "Proposed Iraqi Coup" To Topple Saddam', *The Times*, 8/3/99; Colvin, 'Targeting Iraq's Elusive Dictator', *Sunday Times*, 22/2/98; Cockburn, 'Iraqi Officers Pay Dear for West's Coup Fiasco', *The Independent*, 17/2/98.
105. Foreign Affairs Select Committee, 'Second Report', 3/2/99, para.102.
106. Intelligence and Security Committee, 'Sierra Leone', April 1999, paras.3, 6.
107. Foreign Affairs Select Committee, 'Second Report', 3/2/99, para.105.
108. Ibid., paras.63, 70, 73, 107.
109. Intelligence and Security Committee, 'Sierra Leone', April 1999, para.4.
110. West, *Secret Service*, p.271.

CHAPTER 14

1. CHIL: Bush to Blair, 'The War Against Terrorism: The Second Phase', 4/12/01.
2. CHIL: Evidence of Director of Special Forces 2001–2003 (2010), p.3.
3. Beesley, *Cabinet Secretaries*, p.668.
4. Campbell, *The Blair Years*, 20/9/01, p.572.
5. Campbell, *Power and Responsibility*, 5/6/99, 26/7/99, and 14/9/99, pp.42, 91, 109–11; Campbell, *The Blair Years*, 14/11/01, p.587.
6. Beesley, *Cabinet Secretaries*, p.674.
7. Seldon and Meakin, *The Cabinet Office*, pp.257, 291.
8. See Coker's precautionary principle in Coker, *War in an Age of Risk*, pp.99–100.
9. For a full discussion see Cormac, 'Disruption and Deniable Interventionism'.
10. West, *Secret Service*, p.247.
11. Intelligence and Security Committee, 'The Handling of Detainees by UK Intelligence Personnel in Afghanistan, Guantanamo Bay and Iraq', 2005, para.35.
12. Corera, *Art of Betrayal*, p.335.
13. Campbell, *The Blair Years*, 16/11/01, p.588.
14. West, *Secret Service*, p.247; Corera, *Art of Betrayal*, p.336.
15. Grey, *The New Spymasters*, p,226.
16. CHIL: Evidence of Director of Special Forces 2005–2009 (2010), p.29.
17. Corera, *Art of Betrayal*, p.399.
18. PAL: SIS, 'Palestinian Security Plan', 1/3/03; see also Grey, *The New Spymasters*, pp.235–6.
19. Chilcot Inquiry, Report of the Iraq Inquiry, Executive Summary, para.59; Section 3.1, para.342; CHIL: Bush to Blair, 'The War Against Terrorism: The Second Phase', 4/12/01.

20. CHIL: Bush to Blair, 'The War Against Terrorism: The Second Phase', 4/12/01.
21. Davies, *Intelligence and Government*, p.50.
22. CHIL: Cabinet Office, 'Iraq: Options Paper', 8/3/02.
23. CHIL: JIC, 'Iraq: Regional Attitudes', 19/4/02.
24. Chilcot Inquiry, Report of the Iraq Inquiry, Section 3.1, Development of UK Strategy and Options, 9/11 to Early January 2002, para.349.
25. Ibid. Section 3.2, Development of UK Strategy and Options, January to April 2002—'Axis of Evil' to Crawford, para.143.
26. CHIL: Cabinet Office, 'Iraq: Options Paper', 8/3/02.
27. Ibid.
28. CHIL: DIS, 'Removing Saddam', 5/3/02.
29. CHIL: Cabinet Office, 'Iraq: Options Paper', 8/3/02.
30. Urban, *Task Force Black*, p.12.
31. CHIL: Evidence of Director of Special Forces 2003–2005 (2010), pp.6–7; Chilcot Inquiry, Section 9.5, June 2006–27 June 2007, para.448; Urban, *Task Force Black*, pp.17–21, 31–2; CHIL: Evidence of Director of Special Forces 2001–2003 (2010), p.11.
32. CHIL: Evidence of Director of Special Forces 2003–2005 (2010), p.5.
33. Intelligence and Security Committee, *Annual Report 2004–2005*, para.20.
34. CHIL: Evidence of Director of Special Forces 2003–2005 (2010), p.20.
35. Urban, *Task Force Black*, pp.48, 68–9, 82–3, 86; Linda Robinson, 'The Future of Special Operations: Beyond Kill and Capture', p.110.
36. CHIL: Evidence of Martin Howard, DG Operational Policy, MoD, 18/6/10, p.36.
37. Urban, *Task Force Black*, pp. 116–17, 218–19, 265–6.
38. CHIL: Evidence of Director of Special Forces 2005–2009 (2010), pp.12, 13.
39. Intelligence and Security Committee, *Annual Report 2008–2009*, para.69.
40. CHIL: Evidence of Director of Special Forces 2005–2009 (2010), p.32.
41. Urban, *Task Force Black*, pp.180–1, 185.
42. Chilcot Inquiry, Section 9.5, June 2006–27 June 2007, paras.771, 595, 829, 911, 909.
43. Intelligence and Security Committee, *Annual Report 2007–2008*, para.75.
44. Charles Farr, witness testimony to Project CONTEST: The Government's Counter—Terrorism Strategy—Home Affairs Committee, 26/2/09.
45. Ibid.
46. Intelligence and Security Committee, *Annual Report 2011–2012*, para.94.
47. FOI: RICU, 'Counter Terrorism Communications Guidance', 4/9/07.
48. HMG, 'Prevent Strategy', 2011, para.8.31.
49. Charles Farr, witness testimony to Project CONTEST: The Government's Counter—Terrorism Strategy—Home Affairs Committee, 26/2/09.
50. Ibid.
51. Private information.
52. Private information.
53. Intelligence and Security Committee, *Annual Report 2011–2012*, para.96

54. WIKI: US Embassy London to Secretary of State, 'EUR Senior Advisor Pandith and S/P Advisor Cohen's Visit to the UK, October 9–14, 2007', 25/10/07.

55. WIKI: Susman, American Embassy, London, to Secretary of State, 'UK Government Seeks Greater Counter-Radicalisation Coordination', 21/8/09.

56. Ibid.

57. See Cormac, 'Disruption and Deniable Interventionism'.

58. See HMG, 'A Secure and Prosperous United Kingdom', paras.1.1, 1.3.

59. Houghton, 'Building a British Military Fit for Future Challenges rather than Past Conflicts'.

60. Ministry of Defence, 'Risk: The Implications of Current Attitudes to Risk for the Joint Operational Concept', (November 2012), para.21; see also Gray, *Another Bloody Century*, p.208.

61. See Cormac, 'Disruption and Deniable Interventionism.'

62. Charles Moore, 'GCHQ: "This is not Blitz Britain. We sure as hell can't lick terrorism on our own"', *The Telegraph*, 11/10/14.

63. John Sawers, 'Sir John Sawers Speech—Full Text', *The Guardian*, 28/10/10.

64. Private information.

65. Private information.

66. D'Ancona, *In it Together*, p.172.

67. Mark Urban, 'Inside Story of the UK's Secret Mission to Beat Gaddafi', *BBC News*, 19/1/12.

68. Private information.

69. National Security Adviser, 'Libya Crisis: National Security Adviser's Review of Central Co-Ordination and Lessons Learned,' p.9; Patrick Wintour, 'William Hague Approved Botched Libya Mission, PM's Office Says', *The Guardian*, 7/3/11.

70. Mark Urban, 'Inside Story of the UK's Secret Mission to Beat Gaddafi', *BBC News*, 19/1/12.

71. Sam Coates, 'How the UK Waged a Secret Oil War in Libya', *The Times*, 1/9/11; James Landale, 'How UK Unite Starved Gaddafi of Fuel', *BBC News*, 31/8/11; Supplementary Written evidence from Rt Hon William Hague MP, Secretary of State for Foreign and Commonwealth Affairs, 26/9/11.

72. Sean Rayment, 'How SAS Brought a New Dawn to the Mermaid of the Med', *The Sunday Telegraph*, 28/8/11, p.5; Mark Urban, 'Inside Story of the UK's Secret Mission to Beat Gaddafi', *BBC News*, 19/1/12.

73. Foreign Affairs Select Committee, *Libya: Examination of Intervention and Collapse of the UK's Future Policy Options*, paras.123–4.

74. Lionel Barber, 'Lunch with the FT: Sir John Sawers', *The Financial Times*, 19/9/14; D'Ancona, *In it Together*, p.178.

75. Seldon and Snowden, *Cameron at 10*, p.111; Kiras, *Special Operations and Strategy*, p.67.

76. Intelligence and Security Committee, *Annual Review 2011–2012*, para.51.

77. Private information.

78. WIKI: Clinton to State Department, 'France and UK behind Libya Breakup. SID', 9/3/12.

79. Bel Trew, 'ISIS Builds New Stronghold on the Mediterranean Coast', *The Times*, 2/12/15; Randeep Ramesh, 'SAS Deployed in Libya since Start of Year, Says Leaked Memo,' *The Guardian*, 25/3/16.

80. Anon, 'British Special Forces "Blew Up ISIS Suicide Truck" in Libya', *The Guardian*, 26/5/16.

81. Quoted in Seldon and Snowden, *Cameron at 10*, p.327.

82. Carr, *Diary of a Foreign Minister*, p.277.

83. Private information.

84. Seymour Hersh, 'The Red Line and the Rat Line', *London Review of Books*, 36/8, 17/4/14.

85. Mark Hookham, 'SAS gets "carte blanche" on ISIS', *The Sunday Times*, 5/7/15, p.13.

86. Intelligence and Security Committee, *Annual Report, 2012–2013*, p.20.

87. General Sir Nicholas Houghton, 'Building a British Military Fit for Future Challenges rather than Past Conflicts', speech at Chatham House, 15/9/15. See also Ministry of Defence, Development, Concept and Doctrine Centre, 'Strategic Trend Programme: Global Strategic Trends—out to 2040', (2010), p.17.

88. David Cameron, 'The Today Programme', *Radio 4*, 29/6/15.

89. Quoted in Aldrich and Cormac, *The Black Door*, p.477.

90. GCHQ, 'JTRIG Tools and Techniques' (2012) available via Glen Greenwald, 'HACKING ONLINE POLLS AND OTHER WAYS BRITISH SPIES SEEK TO CONTROL THE INTERNET', *The Intercept*, 7/7/14; GCHQ, 'JTRIG Tools and Techniques'; GCHQ, 'Cyber Integration: The Art of the Possible', *SigDev Spy Conference* (2012), powerpoint slides available via NBC News, *The Snowden Files: British Spies used Sex and 'Dirty Tricks'* (2014).

91. Intelligence and Security Committee, *Annual Review 2011–2012*.

92. GCHQ, 'JTRIG Tools and Techniques'; GCHQ, 'Cyber Integration: The Art of the Possible'.

93. Corera, *Intercept*, pp.370–1.

94. Mathew Cole et al., 'Snowden Docs: British Spies Used Sex and Dirty Tricks', *NBC News*, 7/2/14.

95. WIKI: Director, Communication Planning, 'Joint Doctrine Publication 3-45.1 Media Operation', 2007.

96. Cobain et al., 'How Britain Funds the "Propaganda War" Against Isis in Syria', *The Guardian*, 3/5/16.

97. Richard Norton-Taylor and Ewen Macaskill, 'Britain plans cyber-strike force—with help from GCHQ', *The Guardian Online*, 30/9/13.

98. Ian Cobain et al., 'Help for Syria: the "Aid Campaign" Secretly Run by the UK Government', *The Guardian*, 3/5/16.

99. HMG, 'Prevent Strategy', paras.8.48, 8.61.

100. Private information.

101. Ian Cobain et al., 'Inside RICU, the Shadowy Propaganda Unit Inspired by the Cold War', *The Guardian*, 2/5/16.

102. Ibid.; Intelligence and Security Committee, *Annual Report 2011–2012*, para.96.

103. Private information.

104. Ian Cobain et al., 'Inside RICU, the Shadowy Propaganda Unit Inspired by the Cold War', *The Guardian*, 2/5/16.

105. Ian Cobain et al., 'Government hid fact it paid for 2012 Olympics film aimed at Muslims', *The Guardian*, 3/5/16.

106. Private information.

107. Joint Committee on Human Rights, 'The Government's Police on the Use of Drones for Targeted Killing', paras. 1.59, 2.38–9, 4.26; 'Government Memorandum to the JCHR', online; Peter Dominiczak, 'SAS "Beefed up" to Take Fight to ISIL', *The Daily Telegraph*, 4/10/15.

108. David Leppard, 'GCHQ Finds Al-Qaeda for American Strikes,' *The Sunday Times*, 25/7/10; Alice Ross and James Ball, 'GCHQ Documents Raise Fresh Questions over UK Complicity in US Drone Strikes,' *The Guardian*, 24/6/15.

109. See, for example, JL Mombasa, 'A Very British Execution?,' *The Economist*, 25/6/12.

110. Private information.

111. Quoted in Richard Norton-Taylor, 'UK Special Forces and MI6 Involved in Yemen Bombing, Report Reveals', *The Guardian*, 11/4/16.

112. Private information.

113. Namir Shabibi and Jack Watling, 'Britain's Covert War in Yemen: A Vice News Investigation', *Vice News*, 7/4/16.

114. Alice Ross and James Ball, 'GCHQ Documents Raise Fresh Questions over UK Complicity in US Drone Strikes', *The Guardian*, 24/4/15; Scahill, *The Assassination Complex*, pp.118–19.

115. Alice Ross and James Ball, 'GCHQ Documents Raise Fresh Questions over UK Complicity in US Drone Strikes', *The Guardian*, 24/4/15.

116. Namir Shabibi and Jack Watling, 'Britain's Covert War in Yemen: A Vice News Investigation', *Vice News*, 7/4/16.

117. Ibid.

118. BBC, 'Terrorism Most Immediate Threat to UK, says MI6', *BBC News*, 8/12/16.

119. Corera, *Intercept*, p.298.

120. Corera, *Art of Betrayal*, pp.397–8.

121. Christopher Hope, 'MI6 Chief Sir John Sawers: We Foiled Iran's Nuclear Weapons Bid', *The Daily Telegraph*, 12/7/12.

122. Corera, *Intercept*, pp.276, 278.

123. HMG, 'National Security Strategy and Strategic Defence and Security Review 2015: A Secure and Prosperous United Kingdom', for example, para.4.39, and Cameron's foreword, p.6.

124. Nick Hopkins, 'MI6 Returns to "Tapping Up" in Effort to Recruit Black and Asian Officers', *The Guardian*, 2/3/17.

CONCLUSION

1. DDEL: Dulles Papers, Subject Series, Box 11, Macmillan–Lloyd Correspondence, 1957 (2), Macmillan to Eisenhower, 29/3/57.
2. Bassett, *Last Imperialist*, p.156.
3. Quoted in Cobain, *The History Thieves*, p.43.
4. James Callanan outlines these three types of CIA covert action (defensive, preventative, and offensive). As we have seen, the idea applies to SIS too. See Callanan, *Covert Action in the Cold War*, pp.3–5; Hashimoto, *The Twilight of the British Empire*.
5. PDP: Dixon, 'Notes for Lecture to Naval Attaches', undated.
6. For discussion see Carson and Yarhi-Milo, 'Covert Communication', pp.124-156.
7. de Silva, *The Report of the Patrick Finucane Review*, para.15.9.
8. Richard Norton-Taylor, 'Britain Plans Cyber-Strike Force', *The Guardian*, 30/9/13.
9. LCHMA: SUEZOHP17-REDDAWAY, 'Interview with Norman Reddaway conducted by Anthony Gorst and W Scott Lucas'.
10. See Hennessy, *Muddling Through*.
11. Jeremy Wright, 'Attorney General's Speech at the International Institute for Strategic Studies', 11/1/17.
12. Bassett, *Last Imperialist*, p.1.
13. PREM11/1582, Macmillan to Eden, 19/10/55.
14. Nick Hopkins, 'MI6 Returns to "Tapping Up" in Effort to Recruit Black and Asian Officers', *The Guardian*, 2/3/17.
15. See Cline, *Secrets, Spies and Scholars*, pp.181–3; and Tuck, 'The Limits of Covert Action'.
16. Linderman, *Rediscovering Irregular Warfare*, p.11.
17. CCC: AMEJ 1/2/137, Amery, 'The Next Stage in the Middle East', 14/5/56.
18. DNSA: CIA, 'Memo from Kermit Roosevelt to [Excised],' 24/9/1953; Curtis, *Web of Deceit*, pp.308–9; Dorril, *MI6*, p.574.
19. CAD: Shuckburgh diary 1955, Shuckburgh, 'Policy in the Middle East', 14/10/55.
20. FO371/135610, Ramsbotham, 'Possible Planning Papers', 5/2/58.
21. Bower, *Perfect English Spy*, p.227.
22. Kyle, *Suez*, pp.150–1.
23. BBC, 'UK Intelligence Work Defends Freedom, Say Spy Chiefs', *BBC News Website*, 7/11/13.
24. PREM11/1582, Brook to Eden, 28/11/55.
25. Ibid.
26. FCO79/182, Anon, 'Information Research Department', 1970.
27. Auerbach and Castronovo, 'Introduction', p.8.
28. Private information.
29. Ferris, *Nasser's Gamble*.
30. Walton, *Empire of Secrets*.

31. Pipes, *The Hidden Hand*.

32. Service, *The End of the Cold War*, pp.3–4.

33. PREM19/238, FCO Planning Staff, 'Planning Paper on Détente and the Future Management of East/West Relations', 15/12/76.

34. DDEL: PSB Central Files Series box 15, PSB, 091.4, Eastern Europe (3), Irwin to Debevoise, 'Possible British Outlook on Eastern European Problems', 7/7/53.

35. PREM19/238, FCO Planning Staff, 'Planning Paper on Détente and the Future Management of East/West Relations', 15/12/76.

36. Herman, 'Intelligence as Threats and Reassurance', pp.791–817 p.801, 817; see also Bisley, *End of the Cold War*, p.136; Service, *The End of the Cold War*, p.81.

37. Herman, 'What Difference did it Make?', p.900.

38. Private information.

39. Quoted in Hennessy, *Establishment and Meritocracy*, p.18.

40. Larres, 'Britain and the Cold War,' p.141.

41. Andrew Mumford coined this phrase regarding British counter-insurgency. It applies to covert action too. See Mumford, *The Counter-Insurgency Myth*, p.2.

42. Aldrich and Cormac, *The Black Door*, pp.486–91.

43. Julian Borger and Martin Chulov, 'Al-Jazeera Footage Captures "Western Troops on the Ground" in Libya,' *The Guardian*, 30/5/11.

44. Cormac, 'Disruption and Deniable Interventionism', p.12.

45. Ben Farmer, 'Head of MI6: Britain faces "fundamental threat to sovereignty from Russian meddling"', *The Telegraph*, 12/8/16.

46. Haslam, *Near and Distant Enemies*, p.279.

47. Ibid., p.276.

48. Renz, 'Russia and "Hybrid Warfare"', p.294.

Bibliography

ARCHIVES AND PRIMARY SOURCE DATABASES CONSULTED
(AND THEIR ABBREVIATIONS USED IN TEXT)

BFI — British Film Institute
BOD — Bodleian Library, University of Oxford
BSI — Bloody Sunday Inquiry
CAD — Cadbury Research Library, University of Birmingham
CCC — Churchill College Archives, University of Cambridge
CHIL — The Iraq Inquiry, chaired by Sir John Chilcot
CREST — CIA Records Search Tool
DDEL — President Eisenhower Library and Archives
DDRS — Declassified Documents Reference System
DNSA — Digital National Security Archive
FAOHP — Association for Diplomatic Studies and Training Foreign Affairs Oral History Project
FOI — Freedom of Information Act
FRUS — Foreign Relations of the United States
HTL — President Truman Library and Archives
JFK — President Kennedy Library and Archives
LBJ — President Johnson Library and Archi
LCHMA — King's College London Liddell Hart Centre for Military Archives
NARA — National Archives and Records Administration, United States
NSA — National Security Archive, George Washington University
NYPL — New York Public Library
PAL — Palestine Papers, leaked to Al Jazeera
PDP — Pierson Dixon Papers
SBI — Inquests into the deaths of Diana, Princess of Wales and Emad El-Din Mohamed Abdel Moneim Fayed (Mr Dodi Al Fayed). Led by Justice Scott-Baker Inquiry
TNA — The National Archives, UK
USDDO — US Declassified Documents Online
WIKI — Wikileaks
YUL — Yale University Library

GOVERNMENT DOCUMENTS AND REPORTS

Lord Justice Bingham, *Inquiry into the Supervision of the Bank of Credit and Commerce International* (London: HMSO, 1992).

Lord Butler et al., *Review of Intelligence on Weapons of Mass Destruction* (London: The Stationery Office, 2004).

John Chilcot et al., *Report of the Iraq Inquiry* (6 July 2016), available at http://www.iraqinquiry.org.uk/the-report/

Desmond de Silva, *The Report of the Patrick Finucane Review* (London: The Stationery Office, 2012).

Foreign Affairs Select Committee, 'Second Report' (London: HMSO, 3 February 1999).

Foreign Affairs Select Committee, *Libya: Examination of Intervention and Collapse of the UK's Future Policy Options* (London: Crown, 2016).

HMG, 'Prevent Strategy' (London: Crown, 2011).

HMG, 'National Security Strategy and Strategic Defence and Security Review 2015: A Secure and Prosperous United Kingdom' (London: Crown, 2015).

HMG, 'Intelligence Service Act 1994', available at http://www.legislation.gov.uk/ukpga/1994/13/pdfs/ukpga_19940013_en.pdf

Intelligence and Security Committee, 'Sierra Leone' (London: Crown, 1999).

Intelligence and Security Committee, *Annual Report 1998–1999* (London: Crown, 1999).

Intelligence and Security Committee, *Annual Report 2002–2003* (London: Crown, 2003).

Intelligence and Security Committee, *Annual Report 2004–2005* (London: Crown, 2005).

Intelligence and Security Committee, *The Handling of Detainees by UK Intelligence Personnel in Afghanistan, Guantanamo Bay and Iraq* (London: Crown, 2005).

Intelligence and Security Committee, *Annual Report 2007–2008* (London: Crown, 2008).

Intelligence and Security Committee, *Annual Report 2008–2009* (London: Crown, 2009).

Intelligence and Security Committee, *Annual Report 2011–2012* (London: Crown, 2012).

Joint Committee on the National Security Strategy, *The Next National Security: First Report of Session 2014–2015* (London: The Stationery Office, 2015).

John Kerry and Hank Brown, 'The BCCI Affair: A Report to the Committee on Foreign Relations United States Senate', December 1992.

Ministry of Defence, Development, Concept and Doctrine Centre, 'Strategic Trend Programme: Global Strategic Trends – out to 2040' (2010) available at https://www.gov.uk/government/uploads/system/uploads/attachment_data/file/33717/GST4_v9_Feb10.pdf.

National Security Adviser, 'Libya Crisis: National Security Adviser's Review of Central Co-Ordination and Lessons Learned,' (2013), available at https://www.gov.uk/government/uploads/system/uploads/attachment_data/file/193145/Lessons-Learned-30-Nov.pdf.

Police Ombudsman for Northern Ireland, *Investigative Report: Statement by the Police Ombudsman for Northern Ireland on her Investigation into the Circumstances Surrounding the Death of Raymond McCord Junior and Related Matters* (Online, 2007). http://cain.ulst.ac.uk/issues/police/ombudsman/poni220107mccord.pdf.

Lord Saville et al., *Report of the Bloody Sunday Inquiry* (London: Crown, 2010).

MEMOIRS AND FIRST-HAND ACCOUNTS

Bethell, N., *Spies and Other Secrets: Memoirs from the Second Cold War* (London and New York: Viking, 1994).

Bittman, L., *The Deception Game* (New York: Ballantine Books, 1972).

Blake, G., *No Other Choice* (London: Jonathan Cape, 1990).

Cadogan, A., and Dilks, D. (ed.), *The Diaries of Alexander Cagogan, 1938–1945* (London: Cassell, 1972).

Campbell, A., *The Blair Years: Extracts from the Alastair Campbell Diaries* (London: Arrow, 2008).

Campbell, A., *Power and Responsibility: The Alastair Campbell Dairies, Vol. 3, 1999–2001* (London: Hutchinson, 2011).

Camsell, D., *Black Water: By Strength and by Guile* (London: Virgin, 2000).

Carr, B., *Diary of a Foreign Minister* (Sydney: NewSouth, 2014).

Cooper, J., *One of the Originals: The Story of a Founder Member of the SAS* (London: Pan, 1991).

Crozier, B., *Free Agent: The Unseen War, 1941–91* (London: HarperCollins, 1993).

Cursey, S., *MRF: Shadow Troop, The Untold True Story of Top Secret British Military Intelligence Undercover Operations in Belfast, Northern Ireland, 1972–1974* (London: Thistle, 2013).

de la Billière, P., *Looking for Trouble: SAS to Gulf Command* (London: HarperCollins, 1994).

Devlin, L., *Chief of Station, Congo: Fighting the Cold War in a Hot Zone* (New York: PublicAffairs, 2008).

Dodds-Parker, D., *Political Eunuch* (London: Springwood, 1986).

Eden, A., *Full Circle* (London: Cassell, 1960).

Elliott, N., *With My Little Eye: Observations along the Way* (Norwich: Michael Russell, 1993).

Eveland, W., *Ropes of Sand: American's Failure in the Middle East* (London: W.W. Norton and Co., 1980).

Gardiner, I., *In the Service of the Sultan: A First Hand Account of the Dhofar Insurgency* (Barnsley: Pen and Sword, 2006).

Garthoff, R., *A Journey through the Cold War: A Memoir of Containment and Coexistence* (Washington DC: Brookings Institution, 2001).

Gates, R., *From the Shadows: The Ultimate Insider's Story of Five Presidents and How They Won the Cold War* (New York: Simon and Schuster, 1996).

Haines, J., *Glimmers of Twilight: Harold Wilson in Decline* (London: Politicos, 2003).

Khrushchev, N., *Khrushchev Remembers* (London: Book Club Associates, 1971).

Lawson, N., *The View from Number 11: Memoirs of a Tory Radical* (London: Bantam, 1992).

Lipsey, D., *In the Corridors of Power: An Autobiography* (London: Biteback, 2012).

Macmillan, H., *The Macmillan Diaries II: 1959–1966*, ed. Peter Catterall (London: Pan, 2012).

Montague Browne, A., *Long Sunset: Memoirs of Winston Churchill's Last Private Secretary* (London: Cassell, 1995).

Myers, K., *Watching the Door: Cheating Death in 1970s Belfast* (London: Atlantic, 2008).

Owen, D., *Time to Declare* (London: Michael Joseph, 1991).

Roosevelt, K., *Countercoup: The Struggle for Control of Iran* (New York: McGraw-Hill, 1980).

Shuckburgh, E., ed. Charmley J., *Descent to Suez: Diaries, 1951–56* (New York: Norton, 1987).

Smiley, D., *Albanian Assignment* (London: Sphere Books, 1984).

Smith, J.B., *Portrait of a Cold Warrior: Second Thoughts of a Top CIA Agent* (New York: Ballantine Books, 1976).

Urban, G., *Diplomacy and Disillusion: At the Court of Margaret Thatcher: An Insider's View* (I.B. Tauris, 1996).

Wilber, D., *Regime Change in Iran* (Nottingham: Spokesman, 2006).

Wilson, H., *The Labour Government, 1964–1970: A Personal Record* (London: Michael Joseph, 1971).

Wolf, M., *Man without a Face: The Autobiography of Communism's Greatest Spymaster,* (New York: Public Affairs, 1997).

Woodhouse, CM., *Something Ventured: An Autobiography* (London: HarperCollins, 1982).

SECONDARY LITERATURE

Abrahamian, E., *The Coup: 1953, the CIA, and the Roots of Modern US–Iranian Relations* (London: The New Press, 2013).

Adams, S., 'Elizabeth I and the Sovereignty of the Netherlands, 1576–1585', *Transactions of the Royal Historical Society*, 6th Series, 14 (2004): 309–19.

Aldrich, R.J., 'Unquiet in Death: The Post-War Survival of the SOE, 1945–51', in A. Gorst, L. Johnman and W.S. Lucas (eds.), *Contemporary British History: Politics and the Limits of Policy* (London: Pinter, 1991): 193–217.

Aldrich, R.J., 'British Intelligence and the Anglo-American "Special Relationship" During the Cold War', *Review of International Studies*, 24/3 (1998): 331–51.

Aldrich, R.J., 'Legacies of Secret Service: Renegade SOE and the Karen Struggle in Burma, 1948–50', *Intelligence and National Security*, 14/4 (1999): 130–48.

Aldrich, R.J., *Intelligence and the War Against Japan: Britain, America, and the Politics of Secret Service* (Cambridge: Cambridge University Press, 2000).

Aldrich, R.J., *The Hidden Hand: Britain, America and Cold War Secret Intelligence* (New York: The Overlook Press, 2002).

Aldrich, R.J., 'Putting Culture into the Cold War: The Cultural Relations Department (CRD) and British Covert Information Warfare', *Intelligence and National Security*, 18/2 (2003): 109–33.

Aldrich, R.J., *GCHQ: The Uncensored Story of Britain's Most Secret Intelligence Agency* (London: HarperCollins, 2011).

Aldrich, R.J. and Cormac, R., *The Black Door: Spies, Secret Intelligence and British Prime Ministers* (London: William Collins, 2016).

Aldrich, R.J., Cormac, R., and Goodman, M.S., *Spying on the World: The Declassified Documents of the Joint Intelligence Committee, 1936–2013* (Edinburgh: Edinburgh University Press, 2014).

Allen, C. and Rigsbee, W.L., *Oman under Qaboos: From Coup to Constitution, 1970–1996* (London: Frank Cass, 2000).

Andrew, C., *Defence of the Realm: The Official History of the Security Service* (London: Allen Lane, 2009).

Andrew, C. and Dilks, D. (eds.), *The Missing Dimension: Governments and Intelligence Communities in the 20th Century* (London: Palgrave Macmillan, 1984).

Andrew, C. and Gordievsky, O., *KGB: The Inside Story of its Foreign Operations from Lenin to Gorbachev* (London: HarperCollins, 1990).

Andrew, C. and Mitrokhin, V., *The Sword and the Shield: The Mitrokhin Archive and the Secret History of the KGB* (New York: Basic, 1999).

Andrew, C. and Walton, C., 'Still the "Missing Dimension": British Intelligence and the Historiography of British Decolonisation', in C. Moran and P. Major (eds.), *Spooked: Britain, Empire and Intelligence since 1945* (Newcastle upon Tyne: Cambridge Scholars, 2009): 73–96.

Anglim, S., 'Orde Wingate and the Special Night Squads: A Feasible Policy for Counter- terrorism?', *Contemporary Security Policy*, 28/1 (2007): 28–41.

Ashton, N., *Eisenhower, Macmillan and the Problem of Nasser: Anglo–American Relations and Arab Nationalism, 1955–59* (London: Macmillan, 1996).

Ashton, N., 'Harold Macmillan and the "Golden Days" of Anglo-American Relations Revisited', *Diplomatic History*, 9/4 (2005): 691–723.

Ashton, N., *King Hussein of Jordan: A Political Life* (New Haven: Yale University Press, 2008).

Auerbach, J. and Castronovo, R., 'Introduction: Thirteen Propositions about Propaganda', in J. Auerbach and R. Castronovo (eds.), *The Oxford Handbook of Propaganda Studies* (Oxford: Oxford University Press, 2013): 1–18.

Auten, B., 'Political Diasporas and Exiles as Instruments of Statecraft', *Comparative Strategy*, 25/4 (2006): 329–41.

Bailey, R., *Target Italy: The Secret War Against Mussolini: The Official History of SOE Operations in Fascist Italy* (London: Faber and Faber, 2014).

Bale, J., 'The May 1973 Terrorist Attack at Milan Police HQ: Anarchist "Propaganda of the Deed" or "False Flag" Provocation?', *Terrorism and Political Violence*, 9/1 (1996): 132–66.

Barker, A., 'Practising to Deceive: Whitehall, Arms Exports and the Scott Inquiry,' *Political Quarterly*, 68/1 (1997): 41–9.

Bassett, R., *Last Imperialist: A Portrait of Julian Amery* (York: Stone Trough, 2015).

Bauman, C.E., *The Diplomatic Kidnappings: A Revolutionary Tactic of Urban Terrorism* (The Hague: Martinus Nijhoff, 1973).

Baxter, C., 'A Closed Book? British Intelligence and East Asia, 1945–1950', *Diplomacy & Statecraft*, 22/1 (2011): 4–27.

Bayly, C.A., *Empire and Information: Intelligence Gathering and Social Communication in India, 1780–1870* (New York, Cambridge University Press, 1996).

BBC, 'On Her Majesty's Secret Service', *Panorama* (22 November 1993).

BBC, 'Britain's Secret Terror Force', *Panorama* (21 November 2013).

Beatty, J. and Gwynne, S.C., *The Outlaw Bank* (New York: Random House: 1993).

Beesley, I., *The Official History of the Cabinet Secretaries* (Abingdon: Routledge, 2016).

Bennett, H., 'From Direct Rule to Motorman: Adjusting British Military Strategy for Northern Ireland in 1972', *Studies in Conflict and Terrorism*, 33/6 (2010): 511–32.

Bennett, H., '"Smoke Without Fire"? Allegations Against the British Army in Northern Ireland 1972–75', *Twentieth Century British History*, 24/2 (2013): 275–304.

Bergman, R., *The Secret War with Iran: The 30 Year Covert Struggle for Control of a 'Rogue' State* (London: Oneworld, 2008).

Berkowitz, B. and Goodman, A., 'The Logic of Covert Action', *The National Interest* (Spring 1998).

Bernstein, C., 'The Holy Alliance', *Time Magazine* (24 February 1992).

Bethell, N., *The Great Betrayal: The Untold Story of Kim Philby's Biggest Coup* (London: Hodder and Stoughton, 1984).

Bezci, E., *Turkey and Western Intelligence Cooperation, 1945–1960* (PhD thesis: University of Nottingham, 2017).

Biney, A., 'The Development of Kwame Nkrumah's Political Thought in Exile, 1966–1972', *Journal of African History*, 50 (2009): 81–100.

Bisely, N. *The End of the Cold War and the Causes of Soviet Collapse* (Basingstoke: Palgrave, 2004).

von Bismarck, H., 'A Watershed in our Relations with the Trucial States: Great Britain's Policy to Prevent the Opening of an Arab League Office in the Persian Gulf in 1965', *Middle Eastern Studies*, 47/1 (2011): 1–24.

von Bismarck, H., *British Policy in the Persian Gulf, 1961–68: Conceptions of Informal Empire* (Basingstoke: Palgrave, 2013).

Blackwell, S., 'Britain, the United States and the Syrian Crisis, 1957', *Diplomacy & Statecraft*, 11/3 (2000): 139–58.

Blaxland, G., *The Regiments Depart* (London: Kimber, 1971).

Bloom, C., *Thatcher's Secret War: Subversion, Coercion, Secrecy and Government, 1974–90* (Stroud: The History Press, 2015).

Blum, W., *Killing Hope: US Military and CIA Interventions Since WWII* (London: Zed Books, 2004).

Borger, J., *The Butcher's Trail: How the Search For Balkan War Criminals Became the World's Most Successful Manhunt* (London: Other Press, 2016).

Bower, T., *The Perfect English Spy* (London: William Heinemann, 1995).

Boyce, F. and Everett, D., *SOE: The Scientific Secrets* (Stroud: Sutton Publishing, 2004).

Boyd, D., 'Sharq Al-Adna/The Voice of Britain: The UK's 'Secret' Arabic Radio Station and Suez War Propaganda Disaster', *Gazette: The International Journal for Communication Studies*, 65/6 (2003): 443–55.

Boyle. P. (ed.), *The Churchill-Eisenhower Correspondence, 1953–56* (Chapel Hill: University of North Carolina Press, 1990).

Braithwaite, R., *Afgansty: The Russians in Afghanistan 1979–89* (London: Profile, 2014).

Brandon, P., *The Decline and Fall of the British Empire, 1781–1997* (London: Vintage, 2008).

Braun, L.F., 'Suez Reconsidered: Anthony Eden's Orientalism and the Suez Crisis', *Historian*, 65/3 (2003): 535–61.

Brendon, P., *The Decline and Fall of the British Empire 1781–1997* (London: Vintage, 2008).

Brogi, A., *Confronting America: The Cold War between the United States and the Communists in France and Italy* (Chapel Hill: University of North Carolina Press, 2011).

Budiansky, S., *Her Majesty's Spymaster: Elizabeth I, Sir Francis Walsingham, and the Birth of Modern Espionage* (London: Viking, 2005).

Bullock, A., *Ernest Bevin, Foreign Secretary, 1945–1951* (London: Norton and Norton, 1984).

Byrne, M., *Iran-Contra: Reagan's Scandal and the Unchecked Abuse of Presidential Power* (Kansas: University Press of Kansas, 2014).

Cadwallader, A., *Lethal Allies: British Collusion in Ireland* (Cork: Mercier, 2013).

Callanan, J., *Covert Action in the Cold War: US policy, Intelligence, and CIA Operations* (London: I. B. Tauris 2010).

Carruthers, S., *Winning Hearts and Minds: British Governments, the Media and Colonial Counter-Insurgency, 1944–1960* (Leicester: Leicester University Press, 1999).

Carson, A. and Yahri-Milo, K., 'Covert Communication: The Intelligibility and Credibility of Signaling in Secret', *Security Studies*, 26/1 (2017): 124–56.

Cave Brown, A., *'C': The Secret Life of Sir Stewart Menzies, Spymaster to Winston Churchill* (New York: Macmillan, 1987).

Cavendish, A., *Inside Intelligence* (London: Collins, 1990).

Cesarani, D., *Major Farran's Hat: Murder, Scandal and Britain's War against Jewish Terrorism, 1945–1948* (London: Heinneman, 2009).

Challis, R., *Shadow of a Revolution: Indonesia and the Generals* (Stroud: Sutton, 2001).

Chi-kwan, M., *Hong Kong and the Cold War: Anglo–American Relations 1949–1957* (Oxford: Clarendon Press, 2004).

Cline, R., *Secrets, Spies, and Scholars: Blueprint of the Essential CIA* (Washington DC: Acropolis, 1978).

Cochrane, M., 'Security Force Collusion in Northern Ireland, 1969–1999': Substance or Symbolism?', *Studies in Conflict and Terrorism*, 36/1 (2013): 77–97.

Coker, C., *War in an Age of Risk* (Cambridge: Polity, 2009).

Cole, R. and Belfield, R., *SAS Operation Storm: Nine Men against Four Hundred* (London: Hodder, 2012).

Collier, S., *Countering Communist and Nasserite Propaganda: The Foreign Office Information Research Department in the Middle East and North Africa, 1954–63* (PhD thesis: University of Hertfordshire, 2013).

Comber, L., *Malayan Secret Police 1945–60: The Role of the Special Branch in the Malayan Emergency* (Clayton: Inst. of South East Asian Studies, 2008).

Conboy, K., *The Cambodian Wars: Clashing Armies and CIA Covert Operations* (Kansas: University Press of Kansas, 2013).

Connelly, M., *A Diplomatic Revolution: Algeria's Fight for Independence and the Origins of the Post-Cold War Era* (Oxford: Oxford University Press, 2002).

Connor, K., *Ghost Force: The Secret History of the SAS* (London: Weidenfeld and Nicolson, 1998).

Cooley, J., *Unholy Wars: Afghanistan, America and International Terrorism* (Sterling, VA: Pluto, 2002).

Corera, G., *The Art of Betrayal: The Secret History of MI6* (London: Pegasus Books, 2013).

Corera, G., *Intercept: The Secret History of Computers and Spies* (London: Weidenfeld and Nicolson, 2016).

Corke, S. J., *US Covert Operations and Cold War Strategy: Truman, Secret Warfare and the CIA, 1945–53* (Abingdon: Routledge, 2008).

Cormac, R., 'Organizing Intelligence: An Introduction to the 1955 Report on Colonial Security, Intelligence and National Security', 25/6 (2010): 800–22.

Cormac, R., 'A Whitehall "Showdown"?: Colonial Office – Joint Intelligence Committee Relations in the mid-1950s', *Journal of Imperial and Commonwealth History*, 39/2 (June 2011): 249–68.

Cormac, R., 'Coordinating Covert Action: The Case of the Yemen Civil War and the South Arabian Insurgency', *Journal of Strategic Studies*, 36/5 (2012): 692–717.

Cormac, R., *Confronting the Colonies: British Intelligence and Counterinsurgency* (London: Hurst, 2013).

Cormac, R., 'Disruption and Deniable Interventionism: Explaining the Appeal of Covert Action and Special Forces in Contemporary British Policy', *International Relations* (iFirst, 2016): 1–23.

Cormac, R., 'The Information Research Department, Unattributable Propaganda, and Northern Ireland, 1971–1973: Promising Salvation but Ending in Failure', *English Historical Review*, CXXXI/552 (2016): 1074–1104.

Cradock, P., *Know Your Enemy: How the Joint Intelligence Committee Saw the World* (London: John Murray, 2002).

Crile, G., *Charlie Wilson's War: The Extraordinary Story of How the Wildest Man in Congress and a Rogue CIA Agent Changed the History of Our Time* (New York: Atlantic, 2007).

Croft, S., et al., *Britain and Defence, 1945–2000: A Policy Re-evaluation* (Abingdon: Routledge, 2013).

Curtis, M., *Secret Affairs: Britain's Collusion with Radical Islam* (London: Serpent's Tail, 2010).

Curtis, M., *Web of Deceit: Britain's Real Role in the World* (London: Vintage, 2003).

Curtis, M., *Unpeople: Britain's Secret Human Rights Abuses* (London:Vintage, 2004).

Daddow, O., 'Constructing a "Great" Role for Britain in an Age of Austerity: Interpreting Coalition Foreign Policy, 2010–2015', *International Relations*, 29/3 (2015): 303–18.

D'Ancona, M., *In it Together: The Inside Story of the Coalition Government* (London: Penguin, 2014).

Daugherty,W., *Executive Secrets: Covert Action and the Presidency* (Kentucky:University Press of Kentucky, 2009).

Davey, G., 'Conflicting Worldviews, Mutual Incomprehension:The Production of Intelligence across Whitehall and the Management of Subversion during Decolonisation, 1944–1966', *Small Wars and Insurgencies*, 25/3 (2014): 539–59.

Davies, N., *Ten Thirty-Three: the Inside Story of Britain's Secret Killing Machine in Northern Ireland* (Edinburgh: Mainstream, 2000).

Davies, N., *Dead Men Talking: Collusion, Cover-Up and Murder in Northern Ireland's Dirty War* (Edinburgh: Mainstream, 2005).

Davies, P., 'From Special Operations to Special Political Action:The "Rump SOE" and SIS Post-War Covert Action capability 1945–1977', *Intelligence and National Security*, 15/3 (2000): 55–76.

Davies, P., *MI6 and the Machinery of Spying* (Abingdon: Frank Cass, 2004).

Davies, P., 'Intelligence Culture and Intelligence Failure in Britain and the United States', *Cambridge Review of International Affairs*, 17/3 (2004): 495–520.

Davies, P., *Intelligence and Government in Britain and the United States, Vol 2: Evolution of the UK Intelligence Community* (Santa Barbara, CA: Preager, 2012).

Day, S., *Regionalism and Rebellion in Yemen: A Troubled National Union* (Cambridge: Cambridge University Press, 2012).

Deacon, R., *'C': A Biography of Sir Maurice Oldfield, Head of MI6* (London: Futura, 1984).

Defty, A., '"Close and Continuous Liaison" British Anti-Communist Propaganda and Cooperation with the United States, 1950–51, *Intelligence and National Security*, 17/4 (2002): 100–30.

Defty, A., *Britain, America, and Anti-Communist Propaganda 1945–1953* (Abingdon: Routledge, 2004).

Deighton, A., *The Impossible Peace: Britain, the Division of Germany, and the Origins of the Cold War, 1945–1947* (Oxford: Clarendon Press, 1993).

Deighton, A., 'Britain and the Cold War, 1945–55', in M. Leffler and O.A. Westad (eds.) *The Cold War, Volume One: Origins* (Cambridge: Cambridge University Press, 2010): 112–32.

Dillon, M., *The Dirty War* (London: Arrow, 1990).

Dimitrakis, P., 'British Intelligence and the Cyprus Insurgency, 1955–1959', *International Journal of Intelligence and CounterIntelligence*, 21/2 (2008): 375–94.

Dimitrakis, P., *The Hidden Wars in China and Greece:The CIA, MI6 and the Civil Wars* (Self-published: 2014).

Dixon, P., 'Hearts and Minds? British Counter-Insurgency from Malaya to Iraq', *Journal of Strategic Studies*, 32/3 (2009): 353–81.

Dockrill, S., 'Review of *British Policy in Aden and the Protectorates, 1955–67: Last Outpost of a Middle East Empire* by Spencer Mawby', *English Historical Review* CXXIII/502, 2008.

Doherty, M., *Public Law* (Abingdon: Routledge, 2016).

Doran, S., *Elizabeth I and Foreign Relations* (Kentucky, KY: Routledge, 2000).

Dorril, S., *MI6: Fifty Years of Special Operations* (London: Fourth Estate, 2000).

Dover, R., 'A Silent Debate: The Role of Intelligence in the UK Arms Trade', *International Journal of Intelligence and CounterIntelligence*, 19/1 (2006): 110–19.

Dover, R., 'For Queen and Company: The Role of Intelligence in the UK Arms Trade', *Political Studies*, 55/4 (2007): 683–708.

Dumbrell, J., *A Special Relationship: From the Cold War to Iraq* (London: Palgrave, 2006).

Dunbabin, J.P.D., *The Post-Imperial Age: The Great Powers and the Wider World* (New York: Routledge, 1994).

Dylan, H., *Defence Intelligence and the Cold War* (Oxford: Oxford University Press, 2014).

Dylan, H., 'Super-Weapons and Subversion: British Deterrence by Deception Operations in the Early Cold War', *Journal of Strategic Studies*, 38/5 (2015): 704–28.

Dyson, T., 'British Policy Towards Axis Reprisals in Occupied Greece: Whitehall vs SOE', *Contemporary British History*, 16/1 (2002): 11–28.

Easter, D., 'British and Malaysian Covert Support for the Rebel Movements in Indonesia during the "Confrontation", 1963–66', *Intelligence and National Security*, 14/4 (1999): 195–208.

Easter, D., 'British Intelligence and Propaganda during the "Confrontation", 1963–1966', *Intelligence and National Security*, 16/2 (2001): 83–102.

Easter, D., '"Keep the Indonesian Pot Boiling": Western Covert Intervention in Indonesia, October 1965–March 1966', *Cold War History*, 5/1 (2005): 55–73.

Elwell-Sutton, L.P., *Persian Oil: A Study in Power Politics* (London: Lawrence and Wishart Ltd, 1955).

Fielding, X., *One Man in his Time: The Life of Lieutenant-Colonel NLD ('Billy') McLean, DSO* (London: Macmillan, 1990).

Finegan, R., 'Shadowboxing in the Dark: Intelligence and Counter-Terrorism in Northern Ireland', *Terrorism and Political Violence*, 28/3 (2016): 497–519.

Finlan, A., *Special Forces, Strategy, and the War on Terror* (Abingdon: Routledge, 2008).

Folly, M.H., *Churchill, Whitehall and the Soviet Union, 1940–45* (London: Palgrave, 2000).

Foot, M.R.D., *SOE: The Special Operations Executive, 1940–1946* (London: Pimlico, 1999).

Foot, P., *Who Framed Colin Wallace?* (London: Macmillan, 1989).

Footitt, H., '"A Hideously Difficult Country": British Propaganda to France in the Early Cold War', *Cold War History*, 13/2 (2013): 153–69.

French, D., *The British Way in Counter-insurgency, 1945–76* (Oxford: Oxford University Press, 2011).

Fry, R., 'Smart Power and the Strategic Deficit', *RUSI Journal,* 159/6 (2014): 28–32.

Gaddis, J.L., *We Now Know: Rethinking Cold War History* (New York: Oxford University Press, 1997).

Ganser, D., *NATO's Secret Armies: Operation Gladio and Terrorism in Western Europe* (London: Frank Cass, 2005).

Garnett, D., *The Secret History of PWE: The Political Warfare Executive, 1939–1945* (London: St Ermin's, 2002).

Gasiorowski, M., 'Conclusion', in M. Gasiorowski and M. Byrne (eds.), *Mohammad Mossadeq and the 1953 Coup in Iran* (New York: Syracuse University Press, 2004): 261–80.

Gaskarth, J., *British Foreign Policy* (Cambridge: Polity, 2013).

Gati, C., *Failed Illusions: Moscow, Washington, Budapest and the 1956 Hungarian Revolt* (Stanford CA: Stanford University Press, 2006).

Geraghty, T., *Who Dares Win: The Special Air Service—1950 to the Gulf War* (London: Little Brown, 1992).

Gerard, E. and Kuklick, B., *Death in the Congo: Murdering Patrice Lumumba* (Cambridge, MA: Harvard University Press, 2015).

Gerolymatos, A., *Castles Made of Sand: A Century of Anglo–American Espionage and Intervention in the Middle East* (New York: Thomas Dunne Books, 2010).

Glenn Gray, W., *Germany's Cold War: The Global Campaign to Isolate East Germany, 1949–1969* (North Carolina: University of North Carolina Press, 2003).

Gliddon, P., 'The British Foreign Office and Domestic Propaganda on the European Community, 1960–72', *Contemporary British History,* 23/2 (2009): 155–80.

Godson, R. (ed.), *Intelligence Requirements for the 1980s: Covert Action* (Washington DC: National Strategy Information Center, 1981).

Godson, R., *Dirty Tricks or Trump Cards: US Covert Action and Counterintelligence* (Washington DC: Transaction, 1995).

Goodman, M.S., *Spying on the Nuclear Bear: Anglo–American Intelligence and the Soviet Bomb* (Stanford: Stanford University Press, 2007).

Goodman, M.S., 'The British Way in Intelligence', in Matthew Grant (ed.), *The British Way in Cold Warfare: Intelligence, Diplomacy and the Bomb, 1945–1975* (London: Continuum, 2011): 127–40.

Goodman, M.S., *The Official History of the Joint Intelligence Committee, Volume 1: From the Approach of the Second World War to the Suez Crisis* (Abingdon: Routledge, 2014).

Gray, C., *Explorations in Strategy* (Greenwood Press, CT: Praeger 1996).

Gray, C., *Another Bloody Century: Future Warfare* (London: Phoenix, 2005).

Green, P. and Ward, T., *State Crime: Governments, Violence and Corruption* (London: Pluto Press, 2004).

Grey, S., *The New Spymasters: Inside Espionage from the Cold War to Global Terror* (London: Viking, 2015).

Grob-Fitzgibbon, B., 'Those Who Dared: A Reappraisal of Britain's Special Air Service, 1950-80', *The International History Review,* 37/3 (2015): 550–64.

Grose, P., *Operation Rollback: America's Secret War behind the Iron Curtain* (New York: Houghton Mifflin, 2000).

Grose, P., *Allen Dulles: Spymaster, the Life and Times of the First Civilian Director of the CIA* (London: Andre Deutsch, 2006).

Hamill, D., *Pig in the Middle: The Army in Northern Ireland, 1969–1984* (York: Methuen, 1986).

Hammer, P., *Elizabeth's Wars* (Basingstoke: Palgrave, 2000).

Hanni, A., 'A Global Crusade Against Communism: The Cercle in the "Second Cold War"', in L. Van Dongen et al. (eds.), *Transnational Anti-Communism and the Cold War* (Basingstoke: Palgrave, 2014): 161-176.

Harrington, D., *Berlin on the Brink: The Blockade, the Airlift, and the Early Cold War* (Lexington: University Press of Kentucky, 2012).

Harrison, E.D.R., 'The British Special Operations Executive and Poland', *The Historical Journal*, 43/4 (2000): 1071–91.

Hart-Davies, D., *The War that Never was: The True Story of the Men who Fought Britain's Most Secret Battle* (London: Century: 2011).

Hashimoto, C., 'Fighting the Cold War or Post-Colonialism? Britain in the Middle East from 1945 to 1958: Looking through the Records of the British Security Service', *The International History Review*, 36/1 (2014): 19–44.

Hashimoto, C., *The Twilight of the British Empire: British Intelligence and Counter-Subversion in the Middle East, 1948–63* (Edinburgh: Edinburgh University Press, 2017).

Haslam, J., *Russia's Cold War: From the October Revolution to the Fall of the Wall* (New Haven: Yale University Press, 2011).

Haslam, J., *Near and Distant Neighbours: A New History of Soviet Intelligence* (Oxford: Oxford University Press, 2015).

Hayes, P., *Queen of Spies: Daphne Park, Britain's Cold War Spy Master* (London and New York: Duckworth Overlook, 2015).

Heiss, M.A., '"Real Men Don't Wear Pajamas": Anglo–American Cultural Perceptions of Mohammad Mussadeq and the Iranian Oil Nationalization Dispute', in P. Hahn and M. Ann Heiss (eds.), *Empire and Revolution: The United States and the Third World Since 1945* (Columbus: Ohio State University Press, 2001): 178–94.

Hennessy, P., *Muddling Through: Politics, Power, and the Quality of Government in Post-War Britain* (London: Phoenix, 1997).

Hennessy, P., *The Prime Minister: The Office and its Holders Since 1945* (London: Allen Lane, 2000).

Hennessy, P., *The Secret State: Whitehall and the Cold War* (London: Allen Lane, 2002).

Hennessy, P., *Establishment and Meritocracy* (London: Haus Curiosities, 2014).

Herman, M., *Intelligence Power in Peace and War* (Cambridge: Cambridge University Press, 1996).

Herman, M., 'Intelligence as Threats and Reassurance', *Intelligence and National Security*, 26/6 (2011): 791–81.

Herman, M., 'The Postwar Organization of Intelligence: The January 1945 Report to the Joint Intelligence Committee on 'The Intelligence Machine', in R. Dover and M.S. Goodman (eds.), *Learning from the Secret Past: Cases in British Intelligence History* (Georgetown: Georgetown University Press, 2011): 11–42.

Herman, M., 'What Difference did it Make?', *Intelligence and National Security*, 26/6 (2011): 886–901.

Hermiston, R., *The Greatest Traitor: The Secret Lives of Agent George Blake* (London: Aurum, 2013).

Hoe, A., *David Stirling: The Authorised Biography of the Creator of the SAS* (London: Little Brown, 1992).

Hopkrik, P., *The Great Game: On Secret Service in High Asia* (London: John Murray, 2006).

Hughes, G., 'The Use of Undercover Military Units in Counter-terrorist Operations: A Historical Analysis with Reference to Contemporary Anti-terrorism', *Small Wars and Insurgencies*, 21/4 (2010): 561–90.

Hughes, G., 'A Proxy War in Arabia: The Dhofar Insurgency and Cross-Border Raids into South Yemen', *The Middle East Journal*, 69/1 (2015): 91–104.

Hughes, G. and Tripodi, C., 'Anatomy of a Surrogate: Historical Precedents and Implications for Contemporary Counter-Insurgency and Counter-Terrorism', *Small Wars and Insurgencies*, 20/1 (2009): 1–35.

Hughes, R.G., *Britain, Germany and Cold War: The Search for a European Détente* (Abingdon: Routledge, 2007).

Hughes, R.G., 'A Coalition of "Compromise and Barter": Britain and West Germany in the Cold War, 1945–1975', in M. Grant (ed.), *The British Way in Cold Warfare: Intelligence, Diplomacy and the Bomb 1945–1975* (London: Continuum, 2009).

Hulnick, A., 'What's Wrong with the Intelligence Cycle', *Intelligence and National Security*, 21/6 (2006): 959–79.

Hyam, R., *Britain's Declining Empire: The Road to Decolonisation, 1918–1968* (Cambridge: Cambridge University Press, 2006).

Ingimundarson, V., 'Buttressing the West in the North: The Atlantic Alliance, Economic Warfare, and the Soviet Challenge in Iceland, 1956–1959', *The International History Review*, 21/1 (1999): 80–103.

Israeli, O., 'The Circuitous Nature of Operation Ajax', *Middle Eastern Studies*, 49/2 (2013): 246–62.

Jackson, I., *The Economic Cold War: America, Britain and East–West Trade, 1948–63* (Basingstoke: Palgrave Macmillan, 2001).

Jeffery, K., *MI6: The History of the Secret Intelligence Service* (London: Bloomsbury, 2010).

Jenkins, R., 'The Churchill Government, 1951–3', in Robert Blake and Wm. Roger Louis (eds.), *Churchill* (Oxford: Clarendon Press, 1993): 491–501.

Jenkins, R., *Black Magic and Bogeymen: Fear, Rumour and Popular Belief in the North of Ireland 1972–74* (Cork: Cork University Press, 2014).

Jenks, J., *British Propaganda and News Media in the Cold War* (Edinburgh: Edinburgh University Press, 2006).

Johansen, I., 'Special Operations Forces – A Weapon of Choice for Future Operations?', in P. Norheim-Martinsen and T. Nyhamar (eds.), *International Military Operations in the 21st Century: Global Trends and the Future of Intervention* (Abingdon: Routledge, 2015): 97–115.

Jones, C., *Britain and the Yemen Civil War, 1962–1965* (Sussex: Sussex University Press, 2004).

Jones, F., *Blowtorch: Robert Komer, Vietnam, and American Cold War Strategy* (Annapolis, MD: Naval Institute Press, 2013).

Jones, M., 'Anglo-American Relations After Suez, the Rise and Decline of the Working Group Experiment, and the French Challenge to NATO, 1957–59', *Diplomacy and Statecraft*, 14/1 (2003): 49–79.

Jones, M., 'The "Preferred Plan": The Anglo–American Working Group Report on Covert Action in Syria, 1957', *Intelligence and National Security*, 19/3 (2004): 401–15.

Jones, M., '"Kipling and All That": American Perceptions of SOE and British Imperial Intrigue in the Balkans, 1943–1945', in N. Wyllie (ed.), *The Politics and Strategy of Clandestine War: Special Operations Executive, 1940–1946* (Abingdon: Routledge, 2007).

Jones, T., *Post-war Counterinsurgency and the SAS, 1945–1952: A Special Type of Warfare* (London: Routledge, 2001).

Kahin, A. and Kahin, G., *Subversion as Foreign Policy: Secret Eisenhower and Dulles Debacle in Indonesia* (New York: The New Press, 1995).

Kemp, A., *The SAS: Savage Wars of Peace, 1947 to the Present* (London: Penguin, 2001).

Kemp-Welsh, T., 'Dethroning Stalin: Poland, 1956 and its Legacy', in T. Cox (ed.), *Challenging Communism in Eastern Europe: 1956 and its Legacy* (Abingdon: Routledge, 2008): 73–96.

Kennedy-Pipe, C., *The Origins of the Present Troubles in Northern Ireland* (Abingdon: Routledge, 1997).

Kent, J., *British Imperial Strategy and the Origins of the Cold War, 1944–49* (Leicester: Leicester University Press, 1993).

Kinzer, S., *All the Shah's Men: An American Coup and the Roots of Middle East Terror* (New Jersey: John Wiley, 2008).

Kiras, J., *Special Operations and Strategy: From World War Two to the War on Terror* (Abingdon: Routledge, 2006).

Kitson, F., *Gangs and Counter-Gangs* (London: Barrie and Rockliff, 1960).

Kitson, F., *Low Intensity Operations: Subversion, Insurgency and Peacekeeping* (London: Faber and Faber, 1971).

Kitson, F., *Bunch of Five* (London, Faber and Faber, 1977).

Knott, S., *Secret and Sanctioned: Covert Operations and the American Presidency* (New York: Oxford University Press, 1996).

Kramer, M., 'Miss Lambton's Advice', Harvard Blog, 2008.

Kyle, K., *Suez: Britain's End of Empire in the Middle East* (London: Weidenfeld & Nicolson, 1991).

Larres, K., *Churchill's Cold War: The Politics of Personal Diplomacy* (New Haven: Yale University Press, 2002).

Larres, K., 'Britain and the Cold War, 1945–1990', in *The Oxford Handbook of the Cold War* (Oxford: Oxford University Press, 2013): 141–59.

Larres, K. and Osgood, K., *The Cold War After Stalin's Death: A Missed Opportunity for Peace?* (London: Rowman and Littlefield, 2006).

Lashmar, P. and Oliver, J., *Britain's Secret Propaganda War* (Gloucestershire: Sutton Mill, 1998).

Lewis, J., *Changing Direction: British Military Planning for Post-war Strategic Defence, 1942–47* (London: Frank Cass, 2003).

Linderman, A.R.B., *Rediscovering Irregular Warfare: Colin Gubbins and the Origins of Britain's Special Operations Executive* (Oklahoma: University of Oklahoma Press, 2016).

Lockhart, J.B., 'Intelligence: A British View', in K.Robertson (ed.), *British and American Approaches to Intelligence* (Basingstoke: Macmillan/RUSI, 1987): 37–52.

Loewenstein, K., 'Re-emergence of Public Opinion in the Soviet Union: Khrushchev and the Secret Speech', in T. Cox (ed.), *Challenging Communism in Eastern Europe: 1956 and its Legacy* (Abingdon: Routledge, 2008): 141–58.

Lomas, D., *Intelligence, Security and the Attlee Governments, 1945–1951: An Uneasy Relationship* (Manchester: Manchester University Press, 2017).

Long, S., 'Strategic Disorder, the Office of Policy Coordination and the Inauguration of US Political Warfare against the Soviet Bloc, 1948–50, *Intelligence and National Security*, 27/4 (2012): 459–87.

Long, S., *The CIA and the Soviet Bloc: Political Warfare, the Origins of the CIA and Countering Communism in Europe* (London: I. B. Tauris, 2014).

Louis, W.R., 'Musaddiq and the Dilemmas of British Imperialism', in J. Bill and W.R. Louis (eds.), *Musaddiq, Iranian Nationalism and Oil* (London: I. B. Tauris, 1988): 228–60.

Louis, W.R., 'Introduction', in W. R. Louis and J. Brown (eds.), *The Oxford History of the British Empire: Vol IV, The Twentieth Century* (Oxford: Oxford University Press, 1999): 1–46.

Louis, W.R., 'Britain and the Overthrow of the Mossadeq Government', in M. Gasiorowski and M. Byrne (eds.), *Mohammad Mossadeq and the 1953 Coup in Iran* (New York: Syracuse University Press, 2004): 126–77.

Louis, W.R., *Ends of British Imperialism: The Scramble for Empire, Suez and Decolonisation* (London: I. B. Tauris, 2006).

Lowenthal, M., *Intelligence: From Secrets to Policy* (Los Angeles: Sage, 2015).

Lownie, A., *Stalin's Englishman: Guy Burgess* (Hodder and Stoughton, 2015).

Lucas, E., *Deception: Spies, Lies, and how Russia Dupes the West* (London: Bloomsbury, 2012).

Lucas, W.S., *Divided We Stand: Britain, the US and the Suez Crisis* (London: Hodder & Stoughton, 1991).

Lucas, W.S., 'Suez – The Missing Dimension', *BBC Radio 4*, 28 October 2006.

Lucas, W.S. and Morris, C.J., 'A Very British Crusade: The Information Research Department and the Origins of the Cold War', in R. Aldrich (ed.), *British Intelligence, Strategy and the Cold War* (London: Routledge, 1992): 85–110.

Lulushi, A., *Operation Valuable Fiend: The CIA's First Paramilitary Strike against the Iron Curtain* (New York: Arcade, 2014).

McCourt, D., 'Has Britain Found its Role?', *Survival*, 56/2 (2014): 159–78.

McDermott, G., *The New Diplomacy and its Apparatus* (London: Plume, 1973).

McGovern, M., 'The Dilemma of Democracy: Collusion and the State of Exception', *Studies in Social Justice*, 5/2 (2011): 213–30.

Macintyre, B., *A Spy Among Friends: Philby* (London: Bloomsbury, 2015).

Macintyre, B., *SAS: Rogue Heroes: The Authorised Wartime History* (London: Penguin, 2016).

MacKenzie, A., *Special Force: The Untold Story of 22nd Special Air Service Regiment (SAS)* (London: I. B. Tauris, 2011).

Maddrell, P., 'What we have Discovered about the Cold War is what we Already Knew: Julius Mader and the Western Secret Services During the Cold War', *Cold War History*, 5/2 (2005): 235–58.

Maddrell, P., *Spying on Science: Western Intelligence in Divided Germany, 1945–61* (Oxford: Oxford University Press, 2006).

Maddrell, P., 'British Intelligence through the Eyes of the Stasi: What the Stasi's Records Show About the Operations of British Intelligence in Cold War Germany', *Intelligence and National Security*, 27/1 (2012): 46–74.

Maguire, K., 'The Intelligence War in Northern Ireland', *International Journal of Intelligence and Counterintelligence*, 4/1 (1990): 145–65.

Maguire, T., *British and American Intelligence and Anti-Communist Propaganda in Early Cold War Southeast Asia, 1948–1961* (PhD thesis: University of Cambridge, 2015).

Maguire, T., 'Counter-Subversion in Early Cold War Britain: The Official Committee on Communism (Home), the Information Research Department, and "State Private Networks"', *Intelligence and National Security*, 30/5 (2015): 637–66.

Mawby, S., 'The Clandestine Defence of Empire: British Special Operations in Yemen, 1951–64', *Intelligence and National Security*, 17/3 (2002): 105–30.

Mawby, S., *British Policy in Aden and the Protectorates, 1955–67: Last Outpost of a Middle East Empire* (Abingdon: Routledge, 2005).

Mawby, S., 'Mr. Smith Goes to Vienna: Britain's Cold War in the Caribbean 1951–1954', *Cold War History*, 13/4 (2013): 541–61.

Merrick, R., 'The Russia Committee and the British Foreign Office of the Cold War, 1946–47', *Journal of Contemporary History*, 2/3 (1985): 453–68.

Michaels, J., 'The Heyday of Britain's Cold War Think Tank: Brian Crozier and the Institute for the Study of Conflict, 1970–79', in L. Van Dongen et al. (eds.), *Transnational Anti-Communism and the Cold War* (Basingstoke: Palgrave, 2014).

Miller, D., *Don't Mention the War: Northern Ireland, Propaganda and the Media* (London: Pluto, 1994).

Mistry, K., *The United States, Italy and the Origins of Cold War: Waging Political Warfare, 1945–50* (Cambridge: Cambridge University Press, 2014).

Mokhtari, F., 'Iran's 1953 Coup Revisited: Internal Dynamics versus External Intrigue', *The Middle East Journal*, 62/3 (2008): 457–448.

Montgomery, M., *The Eyes of the World Were Watching: Ghana, Great Britain, and the United States, 1957–1966* (PhD thesis: University of Maryland, 2004).

Moore, C., *Margaret Thatcher: The Authorized Biography, Vol 1: Not for Turning* (London: Allen Lane, 2013).

Morris, J., 'How Great is Britain? Power, Responsibility, and Britain's Future Global Role', *The British Journal of Politics and International Relations*, 13/3 (2011): 326–47.

Mumford, A., *The Counter-Insurgency Myth: The British Experience of Irregular Warfare* (Abingdon: Routledge, 2012).

Murphy, D., *The Poison Chalice: The Relationship Between Culture, Language, Politics and Conflict* (Belfast: Lapwing, 2008).

Murphy, P., *Alan Lennox Boyd: A Biography* (London: I. B. Tauris, 1999).

Murphy, P., 'Creating a Commonwealth Intelligence Culture: The View from Central Africa 1945–1965', *Intelligence and National Security*, 17/3 (2002): 131–62.

Newsinger, J., *British Counterinsurgency* (Basingstoke: Palgrave, 2015).

Niblock, T., *Saudi Arabia: Power, Legitimacy and Survival* (Abingdon: Routledge, 2014).

Norton-Taylor, R., *Truth is a Difficult Concept: Inside the Scott Inquiry* (London: Fourth Estate, 1995).

O'Brien, J., *Killing Finucane: Murder in Defence of the Realm* (Dublin: Gill and MacMillan, 2005).

O'Brien, K., 'Covert Action: The Quiet Option in International Statecraft', in L. Johnson (ed.), *Strategic Intelligence Volume 3: Covert Action, Behind the Veils of Secret Foreign Policy* (Westport CT: Praeger Security International, 2007): 23–60.

Omissi, D., *Air Power and Colonial Control: The Royal Air Force, 1919–1939* (Manchester: Manchester University Press, 1990).

Onslow, S., 'Julian Amery and the Suez Operation', in S. Smith (ed.), *Reassessing Suez 1956: New Perspectives on the Crisis and its Aftermath* (Abingdon: Routledge, 2008): 67–78.

Ovendale, R., *British Defence Policy since 1945* (Manchester: Manchester University Press, 1994).

Owen, D., *In Sickness and in Power: Illness in Heads of Government during the last 100 Years* (London: Praeger, 2008).

Owtram, F., *A Modern History of Oman: Formation of the State since 1920* (London: I. B. Tauris, 2004).

Page, B., Leith, D., and Knightley, P., *Philby: The Spy who Betrayed a Generation* (London: Penguin, 1977).

Parker, P., *SBS: The Inside Story of the Special Boat Service* (London: Headline, 1997).

Pattinson, J., *Behind Enemy Lines: Gender, Passing, and the Special Operations Executive in the Second World War* (Manchester: Manchester University Press, 2007).

Pearce, P., *Spymaster* (London: Bantam, 2016).

Pearson, O., *Albania as Dictatorship and Democracy: From Isolation to the Kosovo War, 1946–1998* (New York: I. B. Tauris, 2006).

Phythian, M., *The Politics of British Arms Sales since 1964* (Manchester: Manchester University Press, 2000).

Phythian, M., *The Labour Party, War, and International Relations, 1945–2006* (Abingdon: Routledge, 2007).

Pipes, D., *The Hidden Hand: Middle East Fears of Conspiracy* (New York: St Martin's Press, 1996).

Prazmowska, J., 'Polish Communism, the Hungarian Revolution, and the Soviet Union', in A. Kalinovsky and C. Daigle (eds.), *The Routledge Handbook of the Cold War* (Abindgon: Routledge, 2014): 45–55.

Punch, M., *State Violence, Collusion and the Troubles: Counter-Insurgency, Government Deviance and Northern Ireland* (New York: Pluto Press, 2012).

Rabi, U., 'Britain's Special Position in the Gulf: Its Origins, Dynamics and Legacy', *Middle Eastern Studies*, 42/3 (2006): 351–64.

Rahnema, A., *Behind the 1953 Coup in Iran: Thugs, Turncoats, Soldiers and Spooks* (Cambridge: Cambridge University Press, 2014).

Rathmell, A., *Secret War in the Middle East: The Covert Struggle for Syria, 1949–1961* (London: I. B. Tauris, 2013).

Rawnsley, G., 'Overt and Covert: The Voice of Britain and Black Radio Broadcasting in the Suez Crisis, 1956', *Intelligence and National Security*, 11/3 (1996): 407–522.

Renz, B., 'Russia and "Hybrid Warfare"', *Contemporary Politics*, 22/3 (2016): 283–300.

Reynolds, D., *Britannia Overruled: British Policy and World Power in the 20th Century* (London: Longman, 1991).

Reynolds, D., 'The European Dimension of the Cold War', in M. Leffler and D. Painer (eds.), *The Origins of the Cold War: An International History*, 2nd edn (New York: Routledge, 1994): 167–77.

Richards, B., *Secret Flotillas: Clandestine Sea Operations in the Mediterranean, North Africa, and the Adriatic, 1940–1944* (Abingdon: Routledge, 2004).

Richelson, J., 'When Kindness Fails: Assassination as a National Security Option', *International Journal of Intelligence and Counterintelligence*, 15/2 (2010): 243–79.

Riste, O., '"Stay Behind": A Clandestine Cold War Phenomenon', *Journal of Cold War Studies*, 16/4 (2014): 35–59.

Ritter, S., *Iraq Confidential: The Untold Story of America's Intelligence Conspiracy* (London: I.B. Tauris, 2005).

Robbins, S., 'The British Counter-insurgency in Cyprus', *Small Wars and Insurgencies*, 23/4 (2012): 720–43.

Roberts, F., 'Ernest Bevin as Foreign Secretary', in R. Ovendale (ed.), *The Foreign Policy of the British Labour Governments, 1945–1951* (Leicester: Leicester University Press, 1984).

Robinson, L., 'The Future of Special Operations: Beyond Kill and Capture', *Foreign Affairs*, 91/6 (2012): online at https://www.foreignaffairs.com/articles/united-states/2012-11-01/future-special-operations.

Said, E., *Orientalism* (London: Vintage Books, 1979).

Sanders, D., *Losing an Empire, Finding a Role: British Foreign Policy since 1945* (Basingstoke: Macmillan, 1990).

Satia, P., *Spies in Arabia: The Great War and the Cultural Foundations of Britani's Covert Empire in the Middle East* (Oxford: Oxford University Press, 2008).

Sato, S., *Britain and the Formation of the Gulf States: Embers of Empire* (Manchester: Manchester University Press, 2016).

Schwartz, L., *Political Warfare against the Kremlin: US and British Propaganda Policy at the Beginning of the Cold War* (Basingstoke: Palgrave, 2009).

Scott J. and Rosati, J., '"Such Other Functions and Duties": Covert Action and American Intelligence Policy', in Loch Johnson (ed.), *Strategic Intelligence Volume 3: Covert Action, Behind the Veils of Secret Foreign Policy* (Westport CT: Praeger Security International, 2007): 83–106.

Scott, L., 'Secret Intelligence, Covert Action, and Clandestine Diplomacy', *Intelligence and National Security*, 19/2 (2004): 322–41.

Seaman, M., '"A New Instrument of War": The Origins of the Special Operations Executive', in M. Seaman (ed.), *Special Operations Executive: A New Instrument of War*' (Abingdon: Routledge, 2006): 7–21.

Sebestyen, V., *Twelve Days: The Story of the 1956 Hungarian Revolution* (New York: Pantheon, 2006).

Seldon, A., and Snowden, P., *Cameron and 10: The Inside Story* (London: William Collins, 2015).

Seldon, A., with Meakin, J., *The Cabinet Office 1916–2016: The Birth of Modern Government* (London: Biteback, 2016).

Selverstone, M., *Constructing the Monolith: The United States, Great Britain, and International Communism, 1945–1950* (Cambridge, MA: Harvard University Press, 2009).

Service, R., *The End of the Cold War: 1985–1991* (New York: Public Affairs, 2015).

Shlaim, A., *Lion of Jordan: The Life of King Hussein in War and Peace* (London: Penguin, 2007).

Siegriste, T., *SAS Warlord: Shoot to Kill* (Glasgow: Frontline Noir, 2010).

Smith, L., 'Covert British Propaganda: The Information Research Department: 1947–77', *Millennium*, 9/1 (1980): 67–83.

Smith, M., 'Peaceful Coexistence at all Costs: Cold War Exchanges between Britain and the Soviet Union in 1956', *Cold War History*, 12/3 (2012): 537–8.

Smith, R., 'Ernest Bevin, British Officials, and British Soviet Policy', in A. Deighton (ed.), *Britain and the First Cold War* (New York: St Martin's Press, 1990): 32–52.

Smith, R. and Zametica, J., 'The Cold Warrior: Clement Attlee Reconsidered, 1945–7', *International Affairs*, 61 (1986): 237–52.

Smith, S., 'General Templer and Counter-insurgency in Malaya: Hearts and Minds, Intelligence, and Propaganda', *Intelligence and National Security*, 16/3 (2001): 60–78.

Stafford, D., 'Churchill and SOE', in M. Seaman (ed.), *Special Operations Executive: A New Instrument of War*' (Abingdon: Routledge, 2006): 47–60.

Stafford, D., *Mission Accomplished: SOE and Italy, 1943–5* (London: Vintage, 2012).

Stanley, J., *How Propaganda Works* (Princeton: Princeton University Press, 2015).

Takeh, R., 'What Really Happened in Iran: The CIA, the Ouster of Mosaddeq, and the Restoration of the Shah', *Foreign Affairs*, July/August 2014.

Takriti, A.R., 'The 1970 Coup in Oman Reconsidered', *Journal of Arabian Studies*, 3/2 (2013): 155–73.

Takriti, A.R., *Monsoon Revolution: Republics, Sultans, and Empires in Oman, 1965–1976* (Oxford: Oxford University Press, 2013).

Talbot, D., *The Devil's Chessboard: Allen Dulles, the CIA, and the Rise of American's Secret Government* (London: William Collins, 2015).

Tang, J.T-H., *Britain's Encounter with Revolutionary China, 1949–1954* (New York: St Martin's Press, 1992).

Taylor, P., *British Propaganda in the Twentieth Century: Selling Democracy* (Edinburgh: Edinburgh University Press, 1999).

Taylor, P., *Brits: The War against the IRA* (London: Bloomsbury, 2001).

Taylor, T., 'The Limited Capacity of Management to Rescue UK Defence Policy', *International Affairs*, 88/2 (2012): 223–42.

Thomas, E., *The Very Best Men: The Daring Early Years of the CIA* (New York: Touchstone, 1995).

Thomas, M., *Empires of Intelligence* (Berkeley: University of California Press, 2008).

Thomas, M., Moore, B., and Butler, L., *Crises of Empire: Decolonization and Europe's Imperial States* (London: Bloomsbury: 2015).

Treverton, G., *Covert Action: The Limits of Intervention in the Postwar World* (New York: Basic Books, 1987).

Treverton, G., 'Covert Action: Forward to the Past?', in L. Johnson (ed.), *Strategic Intelligence, Vol.3: Covert Action: Behind the Veils of Secret Foreign Policy* (Westport: Praeger Security International, 2007): 1–22.

Trim, D., *Fighting 'Jacob's Wars': The Employment of English and Welsh Mercenaries in the European Wars of Religion: France and the Netherlands, 1562–1610* (PhD thesis: King's College London, 2002).

Tuck, C., 'Borneo 1963–66: Counter-insurgency Operations and War Termination', *Small Wars & Insurgencies*, 15/3 (2004): 89–111.

Tuck, C., '"Cut the Bonds which Bind our Hands": Deniable Operations During the Confrontation with Indonesia', *British Journal of Military History*, 77/2 (2013): 599–623.

Tuck, C., *Confrontation, Strategy and War Termination: Britain's Conflict with Indonesia* (Abingdon: Routledge, 2013).

Tuck, C., 'The Limits of Covert Action: SAS Operations During "Confrontation", 1964–66', *Small Wars and Insurgencies*, 27/6 (2016): 996–1018.

Tucker, R., 'US–Soviet Cooperation: Incentives and Obstacles', in E. Hoffmann and F. Fleron (eds.), *The Conduct of Soviet Foreign Policy* (New York: Aldine de Gruyter, 1980): 301–14.

Urban, M., *UK Eyes Alpha: The Inside Story of British Intelligence* (London: Faber and Faber, 1996).

Urban, M., *Big Boys' Rules: The SAS and the Secret Struggle against the IRA* (London: Faber and Faber, 1996).

Urban, M., *Task Force Black: The Explosive True Story of the SAS and the Secret War in Iraq* (London: Abacus, 2011).

Utting, K., 'British Propaganda and Illegal Immigration into Palestine: The President Warfield or Exodus 1947', in J. Young, E. Pedaliu, and M. Kandiah (eds.), *Britain in Global Politics: From Churchill to Blair, volume 2* (Basingstoke: Palgrave Macmillan, 2013): 42–61.

Utting, K., 'Palestine 1945–48: Policy, Propaganda and the Limits of Influence', in G. Kennedy and C. Tuck (eds.), *British Propaganda and Wars of Empire: Influencing Friend and Foe 1900–2010* (London: Ashgate, 2014): 71–95.

Vaughan, J., '"Cloak Without Dagger": How the Information Research Department Fought Britain's Cold War in the Middle East, 1948–1956', *Cold War History*, 4/3 (2004): 56–84.

Vaughan, J., *Unconquerable Minds: The Failure of American and British Propaganda in the Arab Middle East, 1945–1957* (London: Palgrave, 2005).

Vickers, R., *The Labour Party and the World: The Evolution of Labour's Foreign Policy, 1900–1951* (Manchester: Manchester University Press, 2003).

Wagner, S., 'Whispers from Below: Zionist Secret Diplomacy, Terrorism, and British Security Inside and Outside of Palestine, 1944–47', *Journal of Imperial and Commonwealth History*, 42/3 (2014): 440–63.

Wall, A., 'Demystifying the Title 10–Title 50 Debate: Distinguishing Military Operations, Intelligence Activities and Covert Action', *Harvard Law School National Security Journal*, 3/85 (2011): 85–142.

Walton, C., 'British Intelligence and the Mandate of Palestine: Threats to British National Security Immediately after the Second World War', *Intelligence and National Security*, 23/4 (2008): 435–62.

Walton, C., *Empire of Secrets: British Intelligence, the Cold War and the Twilight of Empire* (London: HarperPress, 2013).

Wark, W.K., 'Coming in from the Cold: British Propaganda and Red Army Defectors, 1945–1952', *The International History Review*, 9/1 (1987): 48–72.

Warner, M., 'Wanted: A Definition of "Intelligence"', *Studies in Intelligence*, 46 (2002): 15–22.

Weale, A., *Secret Warfare: Special Operations Forces from the Great Game to the SAS* (London: Hodder and Stoughton, 1997).

Webb, A., 'Cold War Radio and the Hungarian Uprising, 1956', *Cold War History*, 13/2 (2013): 221–38.

Weinberg, G., *A World at Arms: A Global History of World War Two* (Cambridge: Cambridge University Press, 2005).

West, N., *The Third Secret: The CIA, Solidarity and the KGB's Plot to Kill the Pope* (London: HarperCollins, 2000).

West, N., *At Her Majesty's Secret Service: The Chiefs of Britain's Intelligence Agency, M16* (London: Greenhill, 2006).

Westad, O.A., *The Global Cold War: Third World Interventions and the Making of our Times* (Cambridge: Cambridge University Press, 2011).

White, N., *Decolonisation: The British Experience since 1945* (Abingdon: Routledge, 2014).

Wiant, J., 'A Guide to the Teaching about Covert Action', *The Intelligencer Journal of US Intelligence Studies*, 19/2 (2012): 55–62.

Wilford, H., *The CIA, The British Left, and the Cold War: Calling the Tune?* (Abingdon: Routledge, 2003).

Wilford, H., *America's Great Game: The CIA's Secret Arabists and the Shaping of the Modern Middle East* (New York: Basic Books, 2013).

Wilkinson, P. and Astley, J. B., *Gubbins and SOE* (Barnsley: Pen & Sword Military, 2010).

Willan, P., *The Vatican at War: From Blackfriars Bridge to Buenos Aires* (Bloomington, Indiana: iUniverse, 2013).

Wood, J.R.T., *A Matter of Weeks Rather than Months: The Impasse between Harold Wilson and Ian Smith* (Bloomington, IN: Trafford, 2012).

Woodward, B., *Veil: The Secret Wars of the CIA 1981–1987* (New York: Simon and Schuster, 1987).

Wylie, N., 'SOE and the Neutrals', in Mark Seaman (ed.), *Special Operations Executive: A New Instrument of War* (Abingdon: Routledge, 2006): 157–78.

Wylie, N., *Politics of Strategic and Clandestine War: Special Operations Executive, 1940–46* (Abingdon: Routledge, 2007).

Young, G., *Who is My Liege? A Study of Loyalty and Betrayal in our Time* (London: Gentry, 1972).

Young, J., 'The British Foreign Office and Cold War Fighting in the Early 1950s: PUSC(51)16 and the 1952 Sore Spots Memorandum', *University of Leicester Discussion Papers in Politics*, no. P95/2 (University of Leicester, 1995).

Young, J., *Winston Churchill's Last Campaign Britain and the Cold War 1951–1955* (Oxford: Oxford University Press, 1996).

Young, J., *Britain and the World in the Twentieth Century* (London: Bloomsbury, 1997).

Young, J. and Kent, J., *International Relations since 1945: Global History* (Oxford: Oxford University Press, 2013).

Zahlan, R., *The Making of the Modern Gulf States* (Reading: Ithaca Press, 1998).

Zamir, M., *The Secret Anglo–French War in the Middle East: Intelligence and Decolonisation, 1940–1948* (Abingdon: Routledge, 2015).

Zeilig, L., *Lumumba: Africa's Lost Leader* (London: Haus, 2008).

Zubok, V., 'Cold War Strategies/Power and Culture: Sources of Soviet Conduct Reconsidered', in R. Immerman and P. Goedde (eds.), *The Oxford Handbook of the Cold War* (Oxford: Oxford University Press, 2013): 305–22.

Index